Major:
RMIT Architecture Graduating Projects 2019–2022

Edited by Vivian Mitsogianni, Tom Muratore,
John Doyle, Amy Muir, Mietta Mullaly and Liam Oxlade

ACTAR + RMIT University School of Architecture
and Urban Design

CONTENTS

Introduction
by Professor Vivian Mitsogianni

Architecture schools should be concerned with experimentation that challenges the orthodoxies of the discipline, as well as our underlying assumptions about what architecture is and what it should do next. Architecture schools should be supportive environments for students in which we can collectively strive to point towards possible futures not yet evident within existing understandings of the discipline or the profession.[1] The significant challenges of our time are wicked problems, which require new ideas and transdisciplinary approaches. Architects need to find ways to contribute, be effective and have agency in situations in which architecture — in its expanded definition — is often considered to be a peripheral contributor.

The projects in this book are representative of a school and a culture that constantly strives to make an impact in the discipline and wider societal and cultural spheres — and to do this through design and by designing. Importantly, we seek to develop new design processes and design approaches in order to make this impact. We bend, re-shape and rework existing constraints and potential barriers, aspiring to turn them into opportunities for new, effective design tactics.

This publication contains a curated selection of RMIT Master of Architecture graduating projects from seven semesters between 2019 and 2022. It seeks to capture the ideas, pre-occupations, motivations and propositions of this expanded cohort of architectural designers.

RMIT Architecture students formulate their own independent graduating design project — the Major Project — under the supervision of their chosen supervisor and within a wider cohort of their peers.[2] These design-practice research projects offer students an opportunity to speculate through design and develop ideas that will serve as catalysts for future investigations (perhaps for the next decade) in practice.[3]

RMIT is unique in Australia in offering this type of graduating project format. The challenge posed is for students to step outside the design studio[4] world of ideas — the agendas, approach and scope of which is framed by design tutors, often with decades of experience — in order to shape the scope of the project themselves and, through its design, to assert their architectural position.

What we expect from these projects is exploration, experimentation and a striving through architectural design to offer new ideas, concepts and propositions. We don't consider the Major Project to be a demonstration of skills acquired in the course — we assume students have these skills prior to entry into the Major Project. The Major Project is therefore an opportunity to speculate through projects and develop ideas and a design toolkit that will serve to guide future practice.

1 This framing statement by Vivian Mitsogianni has been used in the online Major Project catalogues (available via architecture.rmit.edu.au/major-catalogue/) and an earlier version was originally part of: Vivian Mitsogianni, 'Failure can be cathartic! The design studio — speculating on three themes' in *Studio Futures: Changing Trajectories in Architectural Education* (Melbourne: Uro Publications, 2015), pp. 25-31.

2 The academic semester is 12 weeks long with a final public presentation in the 15th week and two interim public presentations in weeks five and 10.

3 Many practicing and well-regarded Melbourne architects have observed that the seeds for their current practice design approaches and interests were seeded in their RMIT Master of Architecture Major Project.

4 RMIT Architecture in the Bachelor of Architectural Design and the Master of Architecture does not have a year structure, but instead runs a vertically integrated model in which the student's ability to choose their own path is a driving principle. Students select their design studios each semester from a selection curated by the design studio coordinators, with input from the wider team, around different design approaches and design-practice research interests.

The most successful and interesting projects will often explore multiple ideas in depth. They will develop and capture design-practice research explorations. And they will deploy the agency of the architect and architecture itself in order to offer propositions for the discipline, as well as for issues facing the built environment and society more broadly.

We are committed to the idea that the Major Project is the student's independent project and the place where each student's voice can be heard and concerns explored. The projects are, of course, part of a specific culture and students have benefitted from exposure to staff who have highly developed and long-standing design agendas. The projects are not detached from this culture and the independence of students is not about the 'cult of the individual'. Rather, it aims to empower students to question, to build on this culture and to look for new directions based on their experiences and interests. It aims to empower students to take leadership of their projects and use specific and diverse viewpoints to assert what is important to them and, by extension, their generation. It aims to empower students to advance the school's culture and suggest new directions, not just mirror what already exists.

RMIT Architecture Associate Lecturer Thomas Muratore writes: 'Past Major Project catalogues observed the importance and value of diversity within an architecture school in contrast with models centred around a single voice or design approach, which lead to a static culture.[5] This point is now so often made at RMIT Architecture that its significance is taken for granted by current staff, students and graduates. The graduate projects contained in this publication reaffirm this idea, providing us with new insights into the richness of past and current positions within the school. Like previous RMIT Architecture catalogues, this publication is a benchmark for future students and a contribution to the school's and the profession's body of knowledge. Many challenge us to broaden how we see architecture and its agency, starting their enquiries further back from the designed object and instead looking for alternatives in the policies and the programs that surround it.'[6]

The Master of Architecture Major Project runs twice a year at RMIT. An exhibition of all the graduating projects is held at the end of each semester and is currently accompanied by an online catalogue[7] that includes a small sample of the projects, documented through their 3 x A0 exhibition project panels.[8] Prior to this there had been various iterations of student- and staff-led Major Project publications since 1987.[9]

5 See Emeritus Professor Leon van Schaik's, 'Forward' in *Design 90(2)1(0): An Exhibition of 1991/1992 Major Projects by Design*, edited by Peter Brew and Callum Fraser (Melbourne: RMIT University Press, Department of Architecture, 1993).

6 Thomas Muratore, RMIT Architecture Associate Lecturer, correspondence with Professor Vivian Mitsogianni, 10 March 2023.

7 The online catalogue commenced in Semester 1, 2017 and continues as a document of record produced in time for each end-of-semester exhibition by the graduating cohort, edited by Ian Nazareth (RMIT Architecture Lecturer). These catalogues include every student who completed the semester irrespective of the grade they were awarded. Catalogues are available via architecture.rmit.edu.au/major-catalogue/.

8 This standardised panel format was intended to mimic standard architectural competition submission requirements – and to ensure parity across projects. It came about in response to increased competition amongst students and to provide certainty for students. Over time this has been amended to include artefacts such as books as well as videos and digital presentation content and is currently (2023) under review.

9 Stephen O'Connor and George Yiontis, eds., *Form. Fact. Function – Architecture Direct from the RMIT* (Melbourne, RMIT Department of Architecture & Bates, Smart and McCutcheon, 1987).

To assist in the reimagining of the Major Project catalogue into a book, I invited Amy Muir (architect and Master of Architecture Major Project Coordinator), Dr John Doyle (architect and then Master of Architecture Program Manager) and Thomas Muratore (architect and Architecture staff member) to form the initial editorial group. At this early stage we were joined by publication designers Stuart Geddes, Žiga Testen and Kim Mumm Hansen, who developed a design to account for the many disparate contributions and a model that could be adapted to future graduate-led publications.

This newly formed editorial group then called for contributions from current and past Major Project supervisors and recent graduates via a survey. Participants in the survey were asked to select three projects and themes that have become formative for students and the Major Project in recent years, as well as major projects that had the potential to shape the future of the architectural discipline or profession.[10] Through the survey we also asked recent graduates for expressions of interest to join the editorial panel. Liam Oxlade and Mietta Mullaly were selected as co-editors, and we commenced the challenging task of editing the initial shortlist of projects to 52 for publication. In our selection, we chose projects that were representative of the breadth of the projects in the school. The editorial team and all supervisors were then invited to contribute framing pieces, which form the majority of the textual contributions to this book.

Following from the RMIT Architecture Discourse Series,[11] a public discourse event was held over two evenings in RMIT's Media Portal, curated by Mietta Mullaly and Liam Oxlade with Vivian Mitsogianni. Ten graduates were invited to present their major projects followed by a discussion led by Mietta and Liam. The event was both a reflection and a chance to speculate on the projects and the profession. Extracts from these two evenings are included in this publication with a brief introduction from the graduate editors.

The publication is intended to be read in any order. It starts with an overview text by Vivian Mitsogianni that discusses a culture of experimentation and the gradient of loose thematics and positions across the projects. Amy Muir contributes a text on past Major Project publications. Dr Michael Spooner reflects on the emerging Major Project presentation material and a number of supervisors provided framing pieces around their Major Project students in the publication, with some drawing connections and including past influential projects.

The impact of the global pandemic on education during this period is well documented. However, we must still recognise and applaud the resilience of this cohort of students (2020–2022) who worked through lengthy lockdowns in Melbourne and border closures in Australia, in a time of extreme disruption and uncertainty. This publication captures the activities of the RMIT Architecture community during this period and provides future students with material to position

10 The questions asked were: (a) If you could publish only three RMIT Architecture major projects which would you select and why? (b) Name three major projects that have been formative for other students or have changed the nature of Major Project during this period (2019–2022) and the reasons for your selection. (c) Which major projects have the potential to shape the future of the discipline or the profession? Why? (d) Name three emerging concerns and preoccupations from this Major Project cohort that you have observed (description welcome).

11 The RMIT Architecture Discourse Series was initiated and led by Vivian Mitsogianni shortly after she was appointed to the role of Associate Dean and Architecture Discipline Leader in 2013. It ran in 2015 and 2017 with input from most continuing and many industry staff. It can be accessed via vimeo.com/rmitarchitecture.

themselves around. It presents back to the school our preoccupations but also provides a moment to reflect on what we might need to further consider.

This publication is a backlog of projects, and the aim is that it sets the template for future, more frequent, student and graduate-led publications, continuing a tradition established over 30 years ago in the school.

The overall themes are a reflection of the intellectual design concentrations of the school, and the intellectual projects and ideas that individual tutors and groups of tutors teach in the design studios. At the same time, students are expected, encouraged and have — as demonstrated in this publication — used these as springboards for new directions.

This publication seeks to add to the lineage of curated RMIT Major Project publications as both books of record and reflection of a particular moment in time in the school. RMIT Architecture is an idea defined through the students, staff, our partners and collaborators, who engage with, shape and define what we stand for at any given moment in time. At this moment in time, we are most proud that students and staff have worked hard to create a supportive community of practice in which ideas can thrive and student voices can be heard.

Panels illustrating *The Climactic Image* by Dr Michael Spooner on p. 90

STUDENT Leon Koutoulas
PROJECT The Rub
SUPERVISOR Michael Spooner
YEAR 2019

STUDENT Jack Murray
PROJECT Given, Even
SUPERVISOR Michael Spooner
YEAR 2021

Panels illustrating *The Climactic Image* by Dr Michael Spooner on p. 90

STUDENT Nicola Cortese
PROJECT Work, Work, Work
SUPERVISOR Peter Brew
YEAR 2019

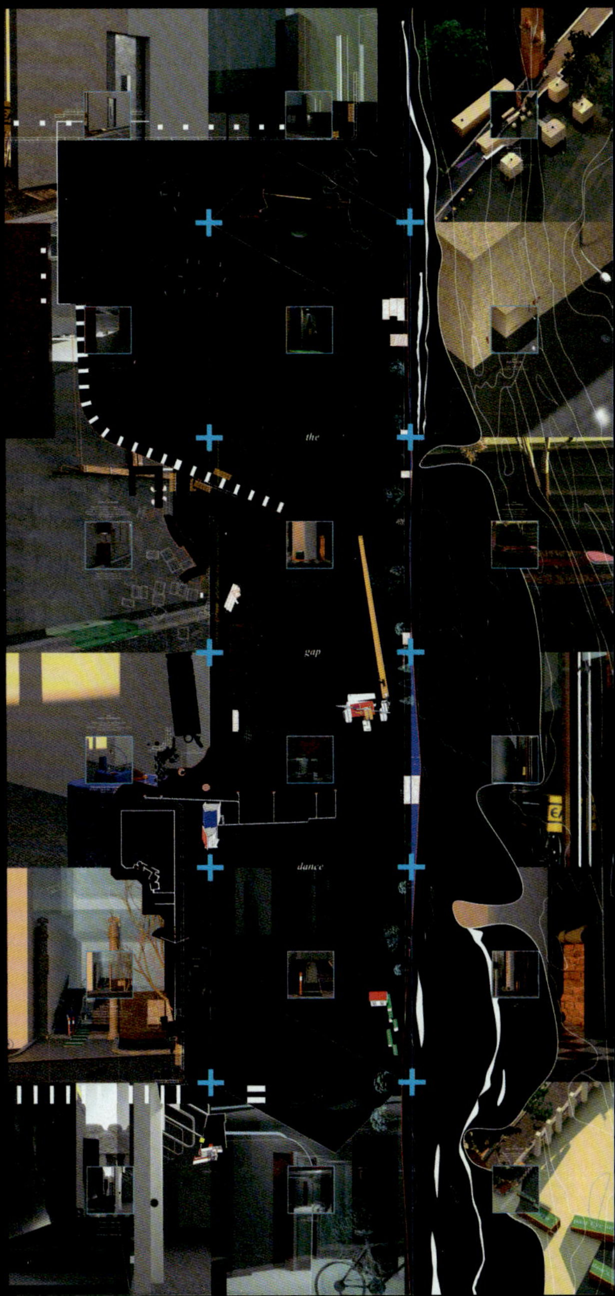

STUDENT Hannah Zhu
PROJECT The Gap Dance
SUPERVISOR Peter Brew
YEAR 2021

Panels illustrating *The Climactic Image* by Dr Michael Spooner on p. 90

STUDENT Julius Egan
PROJECT Collide-a-Scope
SUPERVISOR Emma Jackson
YEAR 2018

STUDENT Alexandra Kemp
PROJECT A Camel is a Horse Designed by Committee
SUPERVISOR Michael Spooner
YEAR 2019

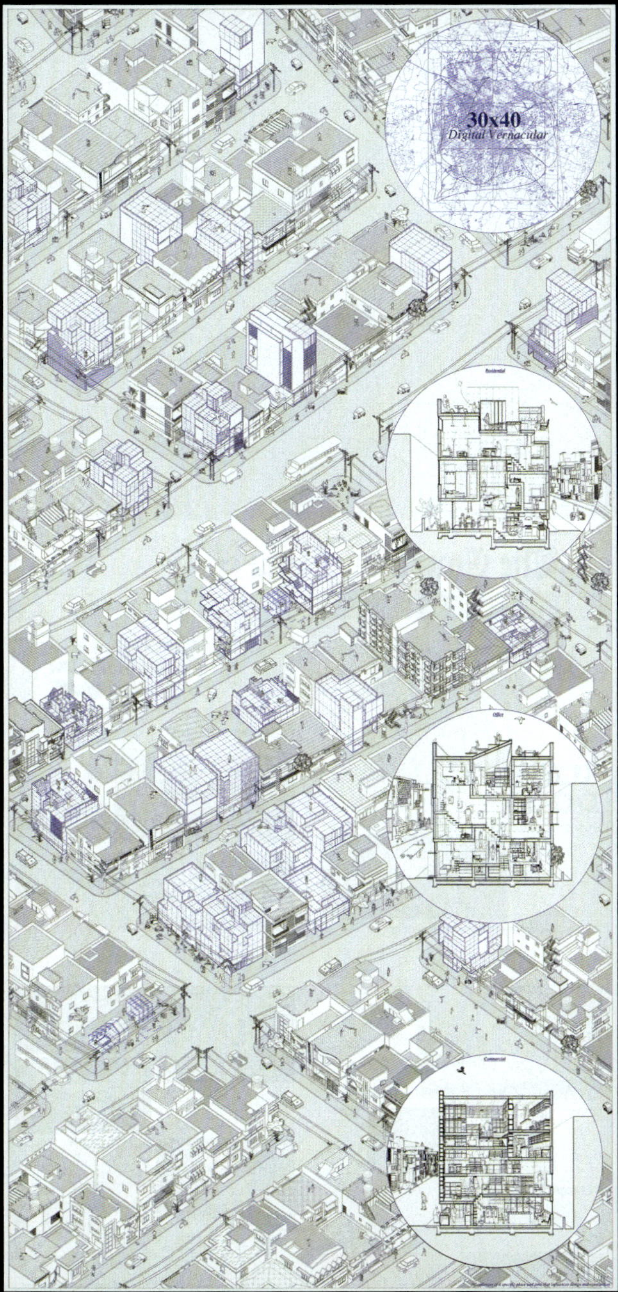

STUDENT David Mundattuchundayil Thomas
PROJECT 30 x 40 Digital Vernacular
SUPERVISOR John Doyle
YEAR 2019

STUDENT Eilidh Ross
PROJECT Here
SUPERVISOR Emma Jackson
YEAR 2020

Panels illustrating *The Climactic Image* by Dr Michael Spooner on p. 90

STUDENT Louis Nuccitelli
PROJECT Beyond the Selfie
SUPERVISOR Christine Phillips
YEAR 2018

STUDENT Nicole Kirby
PROJECT Sliding Doors
SUPERVISOR Dean Boothroyd and Mark Jacques
YEAR 2019

Danolo illustrating *The Climactic Image* by Dr Michael Spooner on p. 90

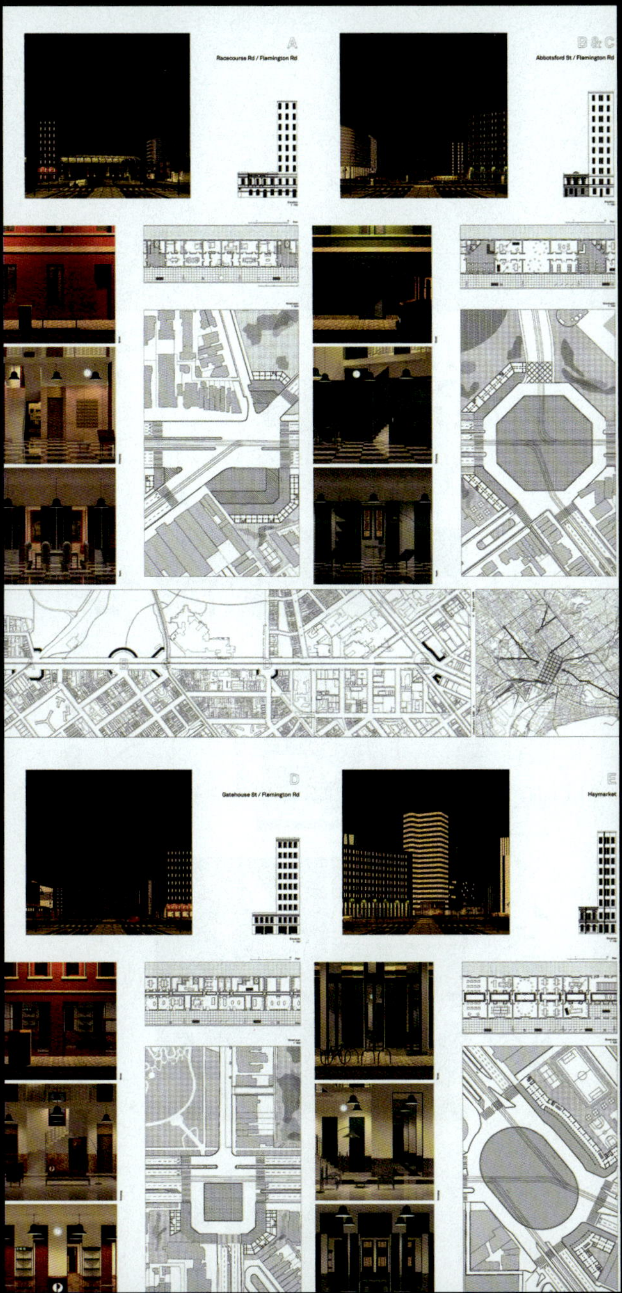

STUDENT Matthew Lochert
PROJECT A Project for Melbourne's Boulevards
SUPERVISOR Simone Koch
YEAR 2019

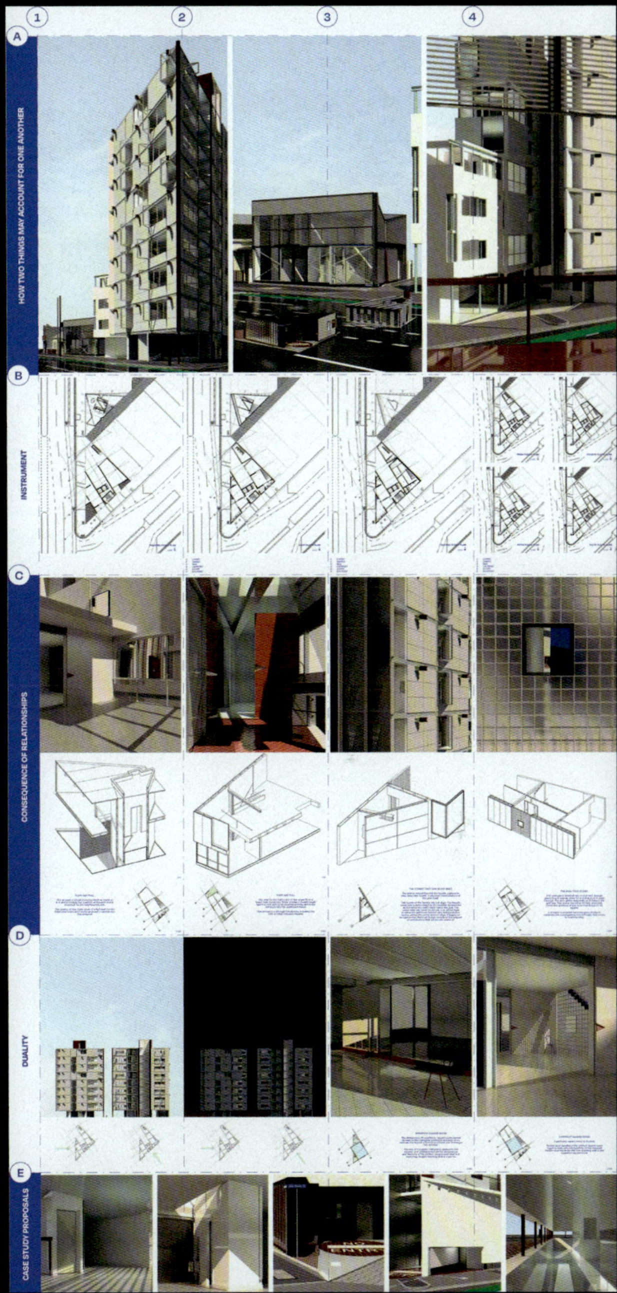

STUDENT Jennifer Chen
PROJECT Double Dutch, Dutch Double
SUPERVISOR Michael Spooner
YEAR 2022

Panels illustrating *The Climactic Image* by Dr Michael Spooner on p. 90

STUDENT Efflorescence and Liturgy of Suburban Irritation
PROJECT Bradley Mitchell
SUPERVISOR Simon Drysdale
YEAR 2017

Panels illustrating *The Climactic Image* by Dr Michael Spooner on p. 90

STUDENT Mietta Mullaly
PROJECT Oversight
SUPERVISOR Peter Brew
YEAR 2021

STUDENT Emma Ka Wing Li
PROJECT In the Blood
SUPERVISOR Michael Spooner
YEAR 2019

Panels illustrating *The Climactic Image* by Dr Michael Spooner on p. 90

STUDENT Andrea Milovanovic
PROJECT Slice, Dust, Polish
SUPERVISOR Peter Brew
YEAR 2020

STUDENT Laura Bailey
PROJECT The Ambassadors
SUPERVISOR Peter Brew
YEAR 2018

Panels illustrating *The Climactic Image* by Dr Michael Spooner on p. 90

STUDENT Liam Oxlade
PROJECT Puzzling Evidence
SUPERVISOR Dean Boothroyd and Mark Jacques
YEAR 2020

Panels illustrating *The Climactic Image* by Dr Michael Spooner on p. 90

STUDENT	Aimee Howard
PROJECT	Deadly Dull
SUPERVISOR	Loren Adams and Peter Brew
YEAR	2021

STUDENT	Emily Davies
PROJECT	The Fourth Wall, or the Library for the Library
SUPERVISOR	Peter Brew
YEAR	2018

Panels illustrating *The Climactic Image* by Dr Michael Spooner on p. 90

STUDENT David Veidt
PROJECT A Careful Occupation of 12 Holland Court - Flemington Library and Heritage Centre
SUPERVISOR Michael Spooner
YEAR 2020

STUDENT Henry Russell
PROJECT Safe as Houses
SUPERVISOR Simone Koch
YEAR 2017

Panels illustrating *The Climactic Image* by Dr Michael Spooner on p. 90

STUDENT Christopher Buchhorn
PROJECT See you in the in between
SUPERVISOR Emma Jackson
YEAR 2021

STUDENT Michael Strack
PROJECT Without
SUPERVISOR Peter Brew
YEAR 2018

Panels illustrating *The Climactic Image* by Dr Michael Spooner on p. 90

STUDENT Yuchen Gao
PROJECT Tricksters Make the World
SUPERVISOR Loren Adams
YEAR 2022

STUDENT Yuchen Gao
PROJECT Tricksters Make the World
SUPERVISOR Loren Adams
YEAR 2022

Panels illustrating *The Climactic Image* by Dr Michael Spooner on p. 90

STUDENT Laura Szyman
PROJECT project/project
SUPERVISOR Peter Brew
YEAR 2019

Panels illustrating *The Climactic Image* by Dr Michael Spooner on p. 90

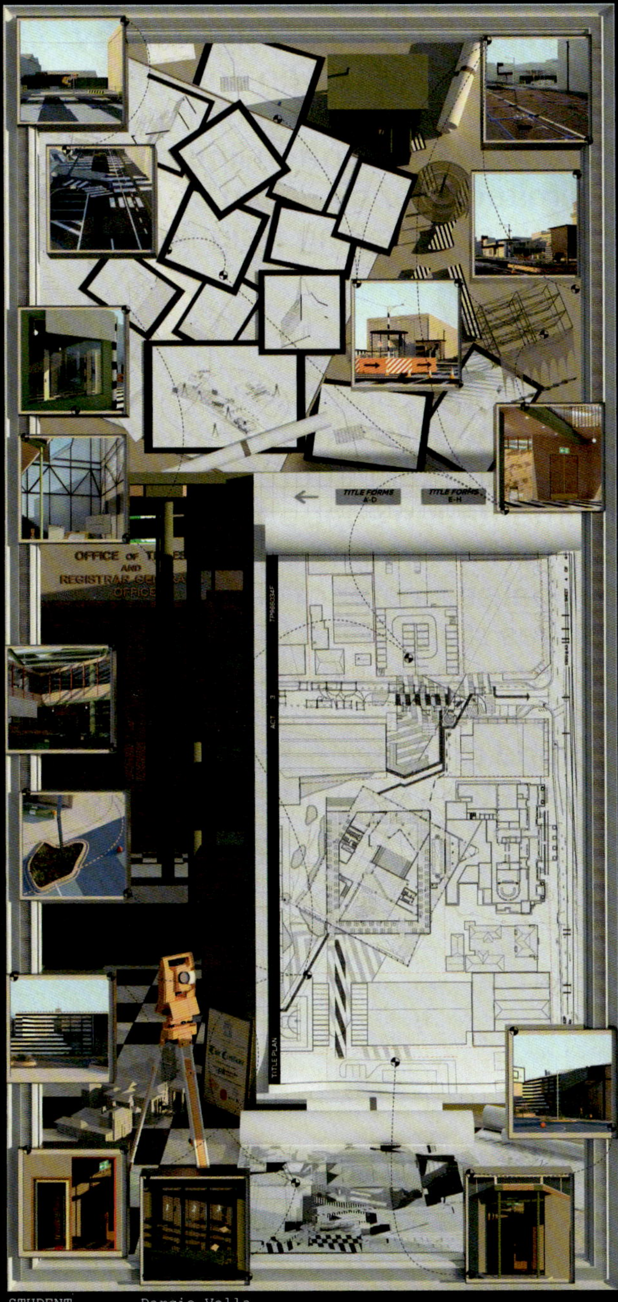

STUDENT Darcie Vella
PROJECT Three Constituent Parts
SUPERVISOR Andre Bonnice and Jean-Marie Spencer
YEAR 2021

STUDENT Senesios Frangos
PROJECT Manual of Monsters
SUPERVISOR Neil Masterton and Ian McDougall
YEAR 2019

Ideas-led and Venturous: Major Propositions by Professor Vivian Mitsogianni

RMIT Architecture values ideas-led, venturous design exploration that aspires to contribute to the future of the architecture discipline and an increasingly complex world. To be venturous is to be brave and take risks. We are interested in experimentation but also the attempt at the realisation of that experimentation, its deep ties to the world around us and its contribution to contemporary questions and concerns.[1]

The projects in this publication are the product of a school culture[2] and environment which is — at all levels — deliberately developed and curated to support experimentation via design-practice research.[3] Architectural design is a specific skillset, and the choreographing of experiments in order to develop new design processes and techniques is also a specific skillset. Experimentation — the development of ideas and propositions — is undertaken through design and by designing. As a collection, the projects here are characterised by an engagement with new and emerging technologies, strong cultural engagement and social mission. Overall, there is a faith that the discipline of architecture — the often limited tools at the architect's disposal and the architect's often limited agency — can be deployed, through design strategies, to punch well above its weight, making a significant contribution to our cities, culture and the realm of ideas.

A culture of experimentation

RMIT Architecture has long-standing processes to support and reward experimentation, including through assessment and moderation. We have developed a pedagogical model curated around the concept of 'differentiation',[4] meaning there is more than one design position or type of experimentation supported within the school. Our ambitions for a collective culture of experimentation, one that strives to find what is not already known, culminates in the final semester of study in the Master of Architecture with the Major Project, which requires students to formulate and undertake their own independent design project under the supervision of their nominated supervisor and within a wider cohort of their peers.[5] The challenge posed is for students to step outside the design studio world of ideas[6] — the agendas, approach and scope of which is framed by a design tutor's often decades-long experience — in order to shape the scope of the project themselves, and in doing so assert their own architectural position.

1 This is the most recent version of the RMIT Architecture mission statement developed by Professor Vivian Mitsogianni (Associate Dean and RMIT Architecture Discipline Leader, 2013-2022) and used most recently in the 2022 RMIT Architecture Accreditation submission.

2 In this context the culture is understood to be developed by students, continuing and industry staff, alumni, our local and global partners and collaborators at any moment in time.

3 The concept of design-practice research and its associated reflective practice methodologies have been adopted from the decades long research pioneered at RMIT Architecture around the reflective practice PhD, which commenced in the late 1980s and was preceded by what Leon van Schaik refers to as 'an ambition to conduct research in the medium of architectural design practice.' See Leon van Schaik and Anna Johnson, eds., *By Practice, By Invitation: Design Practice Research in Architecture and Design at RMIT, 1986-2011* (Barcelona: Actar Publishers, 2019), 14.

4 For more on the concept of differentiation refer to RMIT Emeritus Professor Leon van Schaik, 'Differentiation in Vital Practice: An Analysis Using RMIT University of Technology and Design Interfaces With Architects,' *AD: Architectural Design*, vol. 83 (2013): 106-13.

5 The 10th semester of study refers to the final semester of the Master of Architecture program — the completion of the three year Bachelor of Architectural Design and the two year Master of Architecture. The Master of Architecture is the accredited degree required as a step in the accreditation process. The Major Project semester is 12 weeks long with presentations in the 15th week. Major Project students meet once a week with their nominated supervisor and present at two work-in-progress public reviews to a panel comprised of other Major Project supervisors.

6 RMIT Architecture runs vertically integrated studios that students are able to ballot for both in the Bachelor and Master programs. The studios are curated and taught by continuing and industry staff as well as invited international guests.

What the phrases 'shaping the project' and 'world of ideas' mean is that students develop their own central design exploration, defining what they will explore and what ideas, agendas, design processes and techniques they will work with and towards developing. These explorations can be at the level of design process, or new techniques and propositions for urban, typological, site or other explorations (which can often occur simultaneously).

Ultimately, the projects are expected to be ideas rich, and the students are expected to engage with difficult and topical questions. We ask for projects that are ambitious, brave and contain propositions relevant to their time — in whatever form this might take. We hope that the students' experiments contribute not merely to areas that are well explored, but also to what is yet to come. Importantly, the conditions of our time call for speculation — for new ideas, processes and techniques — because precedents may simply not exist for many contemporary situations or project types. In addition, working out how architectural design strategies can contribute more broadly is an area requiring exploration in and of itself.

When we experiment, we expect flaws and false starts. We do not expect perfect projects. When we venture into unexplored territory, the outcomes can often be raw. When we operate in domains where few specific precedents exist and that have, and should have, their own impossibility built in, we can't just work towards a well-resolved, competent design, because it often takes a lot of effort just to get off the starting block.[7]

What it means to experiment in the school changes over time with the concerns of staff, students and our wider community of practice. These changes are also influenced by cultural and societal shifts outside architecture. What remains consistent is the focus on experimentation, design process and developing new techniques. Included with these methods is a focus on the local — wherever that local happens to be within an international context — and a desire for the student to shape their own directions. In this way, the student is cast as a future design leader and innovator in whatever direction they choose to pursue.

Ideas and propositions

At RMIT Architecture, there have been numerous attempts to curate our activities along strong thematic concentrations. To me, this is useful when speaking outside the school to describe what we do, but internally it can be limiting (particularly in design studio curation). Thematic categorisations can provide clarity but also false certainty; drawing firm lines around approaches can create silos and limit possible new directions.[8]

I prefer to discuss 'vague areas of concentration' in terms of the ideas in the school and to focus on design directions, processes and strategies (the approach), which are routinely re-cast as they develop and change. This strategy aims to avoid silos and give the ideas and architectural positions room to grow, morph and hybridise

7 This last statement was initially published in Vivian Mitsogianni, 'Failure can be cathartic! The Design Studio speculating on three themes' in *Studio Futures: Changing Trajectories in Architectural Education*, edited by D. Bates, V. Mitsogianni and D. Ramirez (Melbourne: Uro Publications), 25-31.

8 Leon van Schaik describes this in relation to his analysis of the tri-polar curatorial system that was once used to curate research concentrations at RMIT Architecture. See Leon van Schaik, 'Differentiation in Vital Practice: An Analysis Using RMIT University of Technology and Design Interfaces With Architects,' *AD: Architectural Design*, vol. 83 (2013): 106-13.

or mutate in new directions.[9] RMIT Architecture is now the kind of place that can cross-fertilise ideas and research approaches among staff and student cohorts, breaking down the artificial barriers and siloed ideologies that often exist in architecture schools and which hinder the formation of new ideas and directions.

In considering the structuring of this overview text, projects were loosely ordered on a gradient that illustrates a series of overlapping and granular concentrations of ideas and influences within the school. The thematics can be recast in numerous different ways but I have chosen to focus on what I consider to be RMIT Architecture's strengths — experimentation and developing new design processes and techniques — as well as the motivations and drivers behind them.

The following projects identify common concerns and approaches within the graduate projects. Around each of these titles, we can cluster a series of projects across a gradient of different perspectives and design processes. This ordering approach is just one of many that was identified in compiling the publication, and we hope the reader can use these titles as markers.

1. Transforming constraints and codes to make civic wonder and re-envision Melbourne's suburbs

RMIT Architecture has a long tradition of exploring and developing new propositions for Melbourne's outer suburbs. More than sites of exploration, these areas are deployed as critical acts and design generators for many studio leaders and Major Project students in the school.

Flynn Eady-Jennings (supervised by Dean Boothroyd and Liam Oxlade) and Caleb Lee (supervised by Dean Boothroyd and Mark Jacques) completed individual but conjoined projects for Riverdale, a new suburb over 30 kms from Melbourne's CBD. Titled *Collision* and *Collusion*, the projects start with the provocation that 'the Australian suburban fringe continues to fall captive to formulaic planning products that, under private hands, fail to prepare our cities for a sustainable future. Energy spent stopping growth, we think, could be better spent reimagining the suburbs as self-sustainable collectives on the frontier of the current climactic emergency.'[10] Both projects draw on themes established in the *Suburban Realism* design studios led by Dean Boothroyd (M@ STUDIO) and a large team of invited collaborators,[11] which assert that the suburbs are 'neglected in the profession's consciousness' and that we need to do better. The studios explore the production of urban form in Melbourne's outer suburbs and greenfield development land parcels. The ambition is for students to understand the formulas that produce urban form 'well enough that they might warp its possible outcomes, and the re-introduction of an idea of the civic, identity, character and place.'[12]

9 While more objective analysis is required, I would propose that in the period familiar to me, while I was RMIT Associate Dean and Architecture Discipline Leader (2013-2022), the different design agendas in the school changed significantly and became more porous and hybrid, breaking away from siloed concentrations and descriptions.

10 Caleb Ka Lok Lee and Flynn Eady-Jennings, *Collision and Collusion*, Semester 1, 2022. See *Semester 01, 2022 RMIT Architecture Major Project* online catalogue, 16-17, www.issuu.com/rmitarchitecture.

11 Initiated by Dean Boothroyd (architectural designer and partner in M@ STUDIO) and joined by Professor Mark Jacques, the *Suburban Realism* studios have run in the Master of Architecture since 2013 and include *Gruen Unchained* (2013) sited in Epping North, *(T)own Brand* (2013) sited in Broadmeadows, *Car/Park/Pool* (2014) and *Chemical Petals* (2014) sited in Craigieburn, and *Watch this Space* (2016) sited in East Werribee. The studio leaders expanded their collaborators to include architectural graduates who had been their students in previous studios and who they mentored into teaching roles: *Hold the Line* (2017), which included Kerry Kounnapis and Martin Heide (Martin was not a *Suburban Realism* student); *The Ground Figure* (2018), which included Leona Dusanovic and Oskar Kasmanli-Liffen; and *Terminal Drive* (2019), which included Lauren Garner, Michael Strack, Leona Dusanovic and Esteban Montecinos.

12 D. Boothroyd and M. Jacques, 'Suburban Realism' in *Studio Futures: Changing Trajectories in Architectural Education*, edited by D. Bates, V. Mitsogianni and D. Ramirez (Melbourne: Uro Publications), 43.

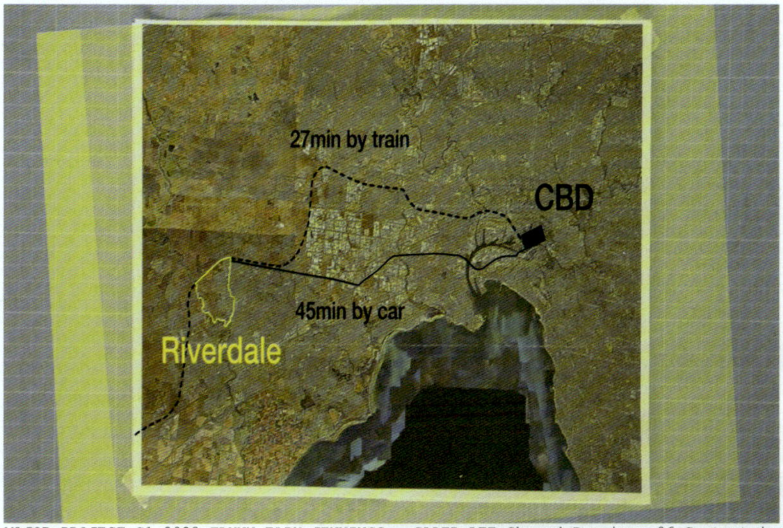

MAJOR PROJECT S1 2022 FLYNN EADY-JENNINGS _ CALEB LEE Shared Drawings 06_Context.jpg

Flynn and Caleb worked together to develop the masterplan for their projects. Flynn's project centres around the hospital typology and Caleb's a retail precinct. Both projects explore the constraints of their chosen typology using limited formal language, programmatic requirements and financial models as their starting point. Both propose strategies for using this limited scope to design strong, civic statements for areas at the city's periphery, areas often overlooked by the architecture profession. Both are motivated by concerns for climate change and public health.

Dean Boothroyd and Liam Oxlade suggest that Flynn's project 'understands that the role of the civic in the hospital typology is not delivered through orthodox architectural tropes and tactics, façade beautification and compositional conceits, but a concentration on structure and shell,' which in turn delivers 'possibilities for solving the incremental degrading of the civic gesture by the wants of facilities managers and requirements of maintenance programs.'[13] The project integrates local sports halls and club rooms within the hospital typology to recast it as a civic architecture of health, taking a central role in the community and town centre.

Dean Boothroyd and Mark Jacques suggest that Caleb's project 'pinpoints the major failing of the suburban town centre as prescribed in the planner's instrument of the Precinct Structure Plan. The project plots to return that which has been ejected — time and the possibility for gradual transformation and change. Additionally, this is a place for makers and repairers, not just merchants and white-collar workers [...] It is an urbanism pinned to the 8.4 m grid, scaled to the permeability and metric of the one-minute block where the commercial and community clash, reconcile and then maybe move on.'[14]

These projects are indicative of others that employ design tactics at a planning, programmatic or urban design level, working within tight constraints and design gestures that are not always obvious or theatrical. They seek to deploy the constraints associated with working in these environments to make civic wonder[15] and public

13 Dean Boothroyd and Liam Oxlade, 'Major Project Supervisor citation for Flynn Eady-Jennings' in *Semester 01, 2022 RMIT Architecture Major Project* online catalogue, 16-17, www.issuu.com/rmitarchitecture.

14 Dean Boothroyd and Mark Jacques, 'Major Project Supervisor citation for Caleb Lee' in *Semester 01, 2022 RMIT Architecture Major Project* online catalogue, 16-17, www.issuu.com/rmitarchitecture.

15 See Vivian Mitsogianni, 'Suburban Realism: Design Practice Research and Making Civic Wonder,' *NGV Melbourne Design Week: RMIT Design Hub* (2021), researchrepository.rmit.edu.au/esploro/outputs/other/Suburban-Realism-Design-Practice-Research-and/9922007187701341.

MAJOR PROJECT S1 2022 FLYNN EADY-JENNINGS _ CALEB LEE Shared image 03_Pool.png
MAJOR PROJECT S1 2022 FLYNN EADY-JENNINGS Image 05_Basketball.png

amenity from very little. Both contain a view of architecture firmly grounded in an understanding of how architects operate in professional practice. Caleb and Flynn both presented their projects using video to better represent duration and time and capture the spatial qualities developed in the propositions.

Collision and Collusion makes assertive, joyous propositions for outer suburban civic space despite the constraints usually associated with this project type.

Situated in an older, more developed suburb, Brooke Barker's project *Carnegie Local* (supervised by Dr Michael Spooner) undertakes a series of interventions into a short strip along Kooyong Road in Carnegie. Seeking to celebrate 'the condition of the collective local,' the project utilises what is identified and embraced as the 'idiosyncrasies of the local'.[16] Brooke developed a design process using the 'international expo' as an alibi, and armature to guide the design strategies. In doing so, she amplifies what she refers to as 'distinctive, peculiar characteristics' saturated in and differentiated by colour. The strategy is to deploy dispersed pavilions as interventions into the existing urban fabric in order to create civic presence. The project draws on personal memories of having grown up in similar locations and seeks to reinvent the characteristics of the local suburb as a way of offering strong civic dimension back to current residents through dispersed interventions and the adaptation of the existing fabric.

16 See Brooke Barker project text for *Carnegie Local* in this publication.

The project can be situated within a legacy that includes the early Edmond and Corrigan projects, which adopted local building forms to work with what Corrigan referred to as the 'difficult coded knowledge'[17] of a place in order to ground themselves within, and as a means of speaking to, a community. The scaled and amplified elements in the project are also reminiscent of Ashton Raggatt McDougall's early projects, such as the Brunswick Community Centre (1993), which incorporated a

MAJOR PROJECT S1 2022 CALEB LEE IMAGE 21_STREETFRONT.JPG

scaled up bay window, or the second stage building for Box Hill TAFE (2000) by Lyons, where a decorated hemispherical form houses a lecture theatre. We can see traces of supervisor Michael Spooner's influential design studios at RMIT, which 'advance ficto-critical approaches to design.'[18] Brooke's project can be seen to extend these trajectories, which are in the DNA of the school, through the specificity of concerns and techniques in her exploration — casting a wider net through the urban realm.

MAJOR PROJECT S1 2020 BROOKE BARKER_ELEVATION BEAN.JPG
MAJOR PROJECT S1 2020 BROOKE BARKER_ELEVATION ART.JPG

17 In relation to the Church of the Resurrection at Keysborough, Peter Corrigan wrote: 'The potential audience will more readily attend if it sees its own preoccupations dealt with in the art work. This is not to be misunderstood as kitsch. Difficult coded knowledge not taste is involved.' Corrigan quoted in Richard Munday, 'Passion in the Suburbs,' *Architecture Australia*, vol. 66, no. 1 (February-March 1977): 52.

18 These approaches were first advanced in Michael Spooner's Major Project and then PhD, subsequently published as *A Clinic for the Exhausted: in search of an antipodean vitality* (Berlin: Spurbuchverlag, 2013). Brooke was a student in one of a suite of design studios led by Spooner from 2018-2020 that occupied and proposed alternative histories for the former office of architectural practice Edmond and Corrigan at 46 Little Latrobe Street, Melbourne. They included *The Last Studio* (semester 2, 2018), *Babylon* (semester 1, 2019), *Maggie* (semester 2, 2019), *Grand Delusions* (semester 2, 2020) and *Froth and Foam* (semester 1, 2020).

This concern for creating a civic architecture extends to Matthew Tibballs' project *Promise Ring* (supervised by Dr Emma Jackson), which explores a process though which to develop guidelines for expanding civic space in the suburbs across time — in this case via the proposed suburban rail loop for Doncaster. The project uses three design strategies for incrementally growing the area surrounding the rail loop in Doncaster, each deployed ahead of the project's realisation. This agile framework accommodates change and the unpredictable forces at work in the wider urban terrain.

MAJOR PROJECT S1 2021 Matthew Tibballs Image 3 The Building.jpg

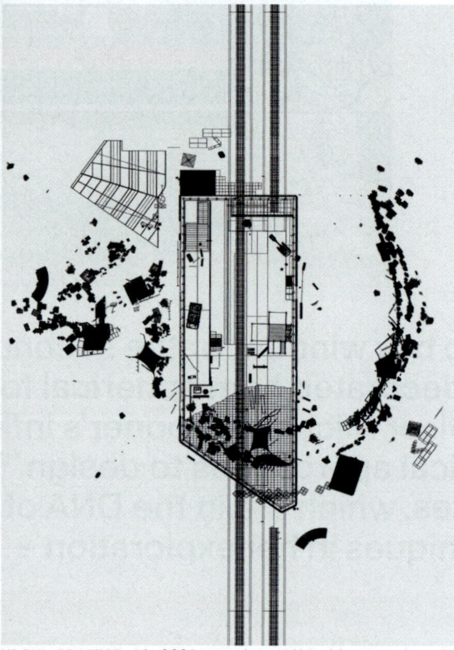

MAJOR PROJECT S1 2021 Matthew Tibballs Drawing 3 Vortex diagram.jpg.jpg

These projects all take the position that the suburbs are more than worthy of architectural focus and look for — through different strategies — the potential for the public and civic. Importantly, they share a sensibility within the school that repositions the 'local' — wherever that happens to be — at the centre of architectural discourse. It is a characteristic of one tranche of work at RMIT that has strongly influenced Melbourne's design culture. Here, the 'difficult coded knowledge'[19] that Professor Peter Corrigan spoke of is extended in new directions, with numerous parallel and conjoined influences — and an extended urban design lens through which the most interesting architecture is seen, such as the urban interventions of *Carnegie Local* or the re-examinations of planning frameworks in *Collision* and *Collusion*. Importantly, these explorations of ideas transcend stylistic influence and search for the agency of architecture in the extended urban realm.

19 See footnote 17.

2. Film, gaming, contemporary media and new design strategies

RMIT Architecture has long-standing interest in experimenting with contemporary media and technologies external to the architecture discipline, and exploring how they might be incorporated into architectural design processes and techniques in order to develop new ideas and propositions. The following projects represent new and emerging hybrid methods developed in the school — they incorporate filmic techniques, animation and gaming platforms as part of the design process.

Liam Oxlade's project *Puzzling Evidence* (supervised by Dean Boothroyd and Professor Mark Jacques) has been a highly influential project, breaking new ground by presenting a project entirely as a narrated film with multiple storylines featuring scripted fictionalised documentary-style commentary, a curated soundtrack and atmospheric effects. It uses narrative and visual techniques borrowed from the history of cinema to present the project, as well as to act as generative design tools. The project centres around the City of Greater Dandenong, reimaging Dandenong's cultural heritage and architectural and urban fabric.

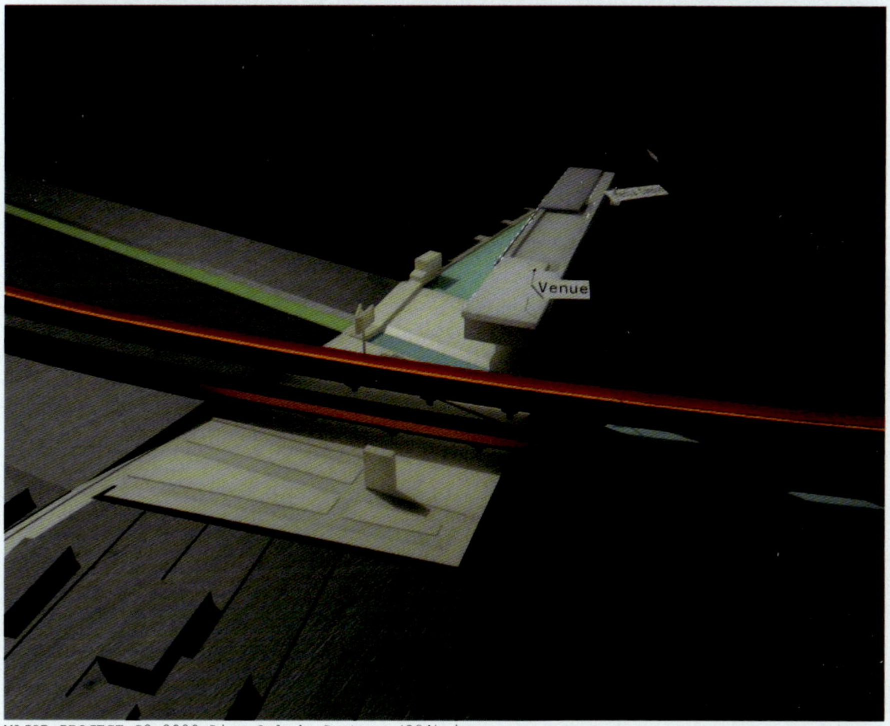

MAJOR PROJECT S2 2020 Liam Oxlade Capture (204).jpg

Dean Boothroyd and Mark Jacques suggest that '*Puzzling Evidence* is a project that is interested in co-opting the politico-media complex to create sightlines into the idea of place and modes of production. It is an expansive proposition, where the ubiquitous blankness of the data and distribution centre is used as a platform to shed light and atmospherics onto infrastructure networks that need to be made to work harder — extracting value for the constituents of the City of Greater Dandenong rather than the shareholders of remote providers.'[20]

20 Dean Boothroyd and Mark Jacques, 'Major Project Supervisor Citation for *Puzzling Evidence* by Liam Oxlade' in *Semester 02, 2020 RMIT Architecture Major Project* online catalogue, 12-13, www.issuu.com/rmitarchitecture.

MAJOR PROJECT S2 2020 Liam Oxlade Capture (236).png
MAJOR PROJECT S2 2020 Liam Oxlade Capture (238).png

In this project, Liam used a series of design tactics, including specific cinematic techniques reinterpreted as process, towards generative architectural design ends. Architecture is reimagined through these translated cinematic techniques, which are subsequently used to construct an atmospheric world of ideas, guiding the design process.

This idea of creating a 'world of ideas' or a clear design decision-making armature to assist in providing concise limits — as well as possibilities — is familiar at RMIT irrespective of the ideological or design position. Generative design processes, typological appropriation techniques and other constructed design processes all develop a clear world of constructed guidelines and limits in which technique and vision of architecture meet purpose and critique of existing processes in the world. Creating a 'world of ideas' around a project is a design strategy that becomes a process, which can enable and focus design decisions.

In Liam's project, it is also important that this world is located in the suburbs. Instead of looking out from the suburbs towards central Melbourne (the popular trope), the view is from the suburbs towards the suburbs, which is the experience of many residents of Melbourne's outer suburbs.

2021 YOUJIA HUANG_SCENE 9 VIEW TOWARD THE FAMILY TABLET HALL FROM SECOND FLOOR BRIDGE ENTRANCE1.PNG.PNG

The *Sky Earth Ancestors* project by Youjia Huang (supervised by Patrick Macasaet) similarly employs cinematic techniques, along with software used to make immersive video games, re-purposed as part of an exploratory design process presented entirely through animation/moving image. The project oscillates from the design of objects to worlds as we follow a video game in first person through magical realist urban terrain sited in China. Youjia draws on personal memories of the Ancestor Worship Festival to ask: 'How might we develop an alternative understanding of Chinese rural villages, one that foregrounds ideas of folk rituals and traditional culture, in architecture?'[21]

Youjia's supervisor Patrick Macasaet[22] captures the core of the project when he states: 'It is the year 2100. We walk through the world of sky, earth and ancestors — an alternative universe conjured by Youjia that bridges projective ideas and her personal histories of folk rituals, ancient traditions, local cultures and typologies, rural renewal, memory and family. An exercise of critical curation and personal reflection, Youjia projects her wanderings through film, performance and gaming to animate a provocative hyper-techno ancient rural village landscape. This project masterfully balances architectural and urban gestures with highly immersive environments and storytelling. Temples and theatres are eternally under construction, competing with rising generic towers and seen as equally important

21 See Youjia Huang's project text for *Sky Earth Ancestors* in this publication.

22 Patrick Macasaet's Master of Architecture design studios at RMIT explore gaming and world-making techniques for architectural speculation and their possibilities for architectural design, representation and pedagogy in parallel with continuing research on procedural techniques. The studio series assembled six studios from 2020-2022 that included: *After Type 1: RMIT Docklands Media Precinct* (semester 1, 2020), *After Type 2: RMIT Docklands Media Precinct with Vei Tan* (semester 2, 2020), *After 3: Didactic Geographies* (semester 1, 2021), *After 4: Where The Wild Thing Are* (semester 2, 2021), *Fear Awe Wonder: Metamatter* (semester 1, 2022) and *Fear Awe Wonder: Mattermeta with Youjia Huang* (semester 2, 2022), which is also a Bachelor of Architectural Design design studio.

as the flying fish ferrying ancient souls. From designing altar tables to building worlds — it is epic in its scale and ambition.'[23]

These two projects misappropriate techniques from outside the discipline, incorporating them into design techniques which are deployed to provide new strategies for architectural design and new concepts for how we might reconsider spatial design and take critical positions towards the material under consideration. They provide insights into and approaches for the areas they are exploring, offering new perspectives on place. Moreover, the techniques and processes are transferrable and can be deployed in other situations. Both projects are representative of similar embedded experiments in the school, but through their specificity of concerns each extends into new terrain with new possibilities.

3. Generative, algorithmic and process-based techniques and material experiments

The following projects use a set of designed rules and process-based or generative design processes. The outcome evidences the experiment, and provides one of many possible applications or scenarios. In other instances, the project becomes a guidebook for future practice or the beginning of further exploration.

MAJOR PROJECT S2 2020 JINGYUAN WANG IMAGE11_NIGHT BANQUET01.PNG
MAJOR PROJECT S2 2020 JINGYUAN WANG IMAGE05_NIGHT VIEW01.PNG

Focusing on the history of China's redevelopment and contemporary urban design — with an interest in narrative progression — Wang Jingyuan's project *Mending Guanlan Old Town* (supervised by Helen Duong and Tim Pyke) explores the

23 Patrick Macasaet, 'Major Project Supervisor Citation for *Sky Earth Ancestors* by Youjia Huang' in *Semester 02, 2021 RMIT Architecture Major Project* online catalogue, 28-29, www.issuu.com/rmitarchitecture.

consequences of China's rapid urbanisation on urban form. Opposing the mass removal of historic urban fabric, the project puts forward a series of alternative techniques for retaining, stitching and inserting new buildings into existing urban fabric. The project develops and provides manual techniques and strategies for interventions and insertions — including into architectural façades — as well as techniques for stitching together formally and visually numerous buildings. In this way, carefully choreographed journeys are developed towards forming new models for urban space. Like a number of other projects in this publication, there is a rhetorical utilisation of the images presented to convey the theatrical and culturally loaded aspirations of the project.

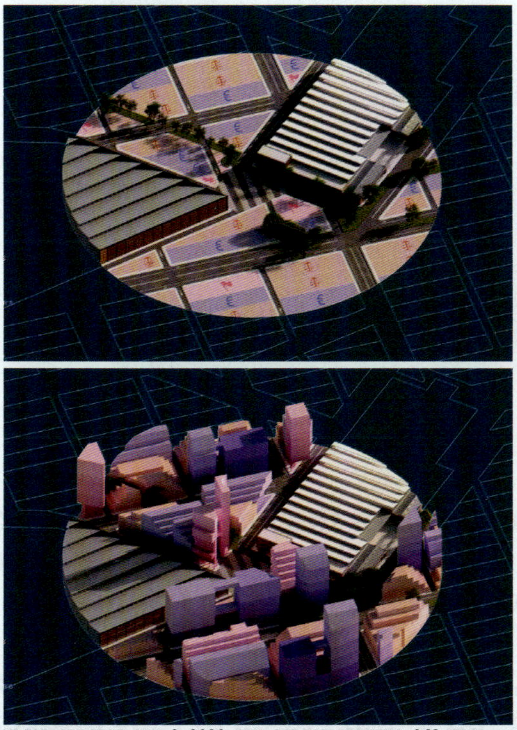

MAJOR PROJECT SEM 2 2020 BEN STRONG DRAWING 063.JPG
MAJOR PROJECT SEM 2 2020 BEN STRONG DRAWING 068.JPG

Benjamin Strong's project *Condencity* (supervised by Ian Nazareth) is an urban scale project that explores data driven processes for urban design scenario testing. In this instance, the project 'proposes an alternative set of rules and spatial frameworks for the future suburb of Sandridge in Fisherman's Bend,'[24] Melbourne and speculates on the subsequent urban and architectural outcomes. A data-driven process is developed along with specific rules, forming a process through which multiple scenarios can be tested.

The scenarios tested are comprised of variable parameters that Benjamin has abstracted for the purposes of the experiment. These include: 'Rights of the Individual' — access to sunlight, open space and the conservation of all trees; 'Rules of the Street' — width, length, footpath configuration; and 'Rules of the Block' — variables for block composition, public open space and lot consolidation. The experiment unfolds across what is defined as 'The Accountant's Lot', 'The Entrepreneur's Lot' and 'The Dissident's Lot'. What has been proposed here is not a

24 See Benjamin Strong's project text for *Condencity* in this publication.

design outcome but rather design methods and data-driven strategies through which specific scenarios can be tested to inform architects and others. These are demonstrated as proof of concept in the final overall project.

Fields of Play by Jacqueline Tang (supervised by Patrick Macasaet) explores process-based experiments for hybrid learning and living typologies. It utilises a rule-based design approach, where process-based experiments are designed in order to find something other than could have been composed — and are often used to organise complex programmatic and other architectural relationships. In this instance,

MAJOR PROJECT S2 2019 JACQUELINE TANG_01.JPG

the processes are developed to explore the potential for the juxtaposition of different components of the program in order to establish possibilities for 'social encounters'. Rather than a singular object approach, the project uses fields, or continuous terrains, which Jacqueline describes as 'fields of social encounter'. An analysis is then undertaken on the resultant design outcomes, seeking to identify possible new programmatic relationships, which are catalogued in the *Fields of Play Encyclopedia*. The project is summarised in this text 'as a matrix intended to provide a toolkit for new typological hybrids for future design use.'[25]

Shuai Tang's project *Co-Living with Nature* (supervised by Professor Alisa Andrasek) utilises AI tools, multi-agent algorithms and game-type methodology to explore the concept he defines as 'co-habitation with nature.' The chosen site through which to demonstrate one scenario in this exploration is Lishui, China, which is described as a 'city facing the dual challenges of land destruction caused by mining activities and housing shortages.'[26] The project uses multi-agent algorithms to 'grow a form on the landscape,' exploring unique programmatic clusters and timber construction. Professor Alisa Andrasek describes this project as an exploration into 'high-density, low-coverage architecture' that is 'highly adaptive to its environment and its inhabitants' through the use of 'AI based combinatronics.'[27]

25 See Jacqueline Tang's project text for *Fields of Play* in this publication.
26 See Shuai Tang's project text for *Co-Living with Nature* in this publication.
27 Professor Alisa Andrasek, 'Major Project Supervisor Citation for *Co-Living with Nature* by Shuai Tang in *Semester 02, 2021 RMIT Architecture Major Project* online catalogue, www.issuu.com/rmitarchitecture.

MAJOR PROJECT S2 2021 SHUAI TANG IMAGE 16_AXONOMETRIC VIEW.PNG
MAJOR PROJECT S2 2021 SHUAI TANG IMAGE 05_OPEN SPACE.PNG

Alan Ho Kyeong Kim's project *transformativeCohesion ();* (supervised by Professor Roland Snooks) is representative of a series of projects that explore multi-agent algorithms and seek to extend the possibilities of the material formation and realisation of these tools.[28] Here, exploration is through the generative nature of the algorithms used. There is no claim of abdicating authorship, which is exercised by identifying and selecting the emergent forms for future development. When we consider these projects, there is an eye to their application and resolution as 'architectural forms' in the world — but given the highly complex and sophisticated work developed to get to this point, cataloguing the exploration into transferable knowledge becomes the core of the contribution. Alan has since progressed this research through a practice-based PhD supervised by Professor Roland Snooks in the RMIT Architecture | Tectonic Formation Lab.

'I punched my nan in the face, which means a pool must be on the south side of the staircase' is the title of one of the design experiments from Aimee Howard's project *Deadly Dull* (supervised by Loren Adams and Dr Peter Brew). The project is deliberately critically loaded and develops a design process that uses a natural language bot to reimagine the remote Western Australian town of Geraldton, Aimee's hometown. Loren Adams and Dr Peter Brew explain that 'for Aimee, text — from utopian manifestos to heritage regulations — is the fundamental medium through which disciplinary knowledge of "the ideal" is constructed, disseminated and enforced. Taking issue with the lack of diversity in the suite of characters who are authorised to speak on her behalf, Aimee deploys a bespoke natural language processing (NLP) bot to create a simulated dialogue with 12 quintessentially "good" architects, theorists and historians. Inserting herself into the conversation as an

28 Professor Roland Snooks has taught numerous iterations of design studios around these processes including through the RMIT Architecture | Tectonic Formation Lab. See also Professor Roland Snooks's text in this publication.

unreliable narrator and objectively bad actor, she then disrupts the self-referential cadence of "her boys" with a dataset compiled from a series of poorly-remembered anecdotes from her childhood in Geraldton.'[29]

Deadly Dull thus becomes an exploration of the role and influence of written text in architectural design and takes the form of polemical critique through design. It is an experiment that looks for ways to deploy emerging technologies for automating the generation of plausibly human language, within the discipline of architecture. In *Deadly Dull*, Aimee begins with the agenda set out in her supervisor Loren Adams' design studios[30] and repurposes it with her own interests and agendas to make something unique through the specificity of her exploration.

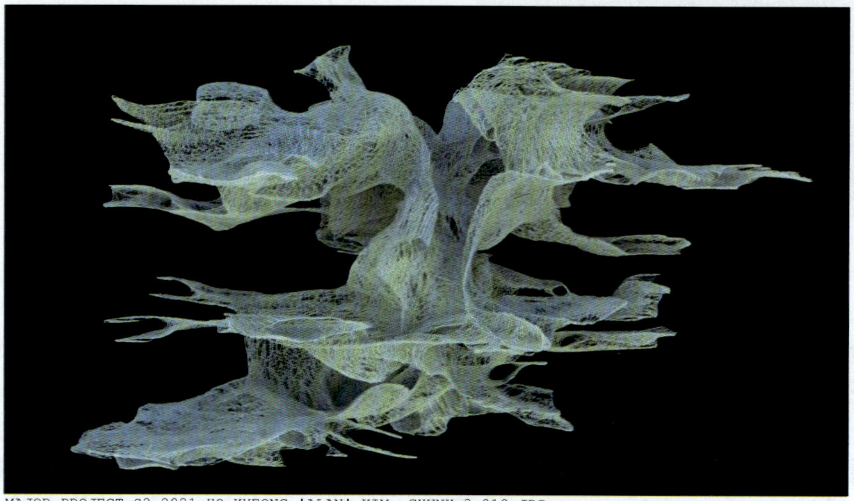

MAJOR PROJECT S2 2021 HO KYEONG 'ALAN' KIM -CHUNK_3_010.JPG

These rule-based and generative projects provide speculations arrived at through different approaches — from analogue explorations (translation of 'mending' to architectural processes) to use of contemporary digital tools (AI bots, algorithms). They extend the boundaries of what we once understood as rule-based and generative processes — beyond questions of authorship and form alone — to create complex spatial, technical and organisational structures and scenarios. These projects deploy rule-based techniques and digital scripting processes towards new design approaches and as a way to deal with complex planning and organisational relationships — running scenarios and compositional tactics where the base organisational unit is often eroded, and as part of wider irregular fields and organisational systems. The projects often work with complexity, a high number of individual components or rule-based organisational systems rather than conventional compositional design techniques. Again, each project extends and shifts the original starting point towards new possibilities, often through new and unexpected combinations.

29 Loren Adams and Peter Brew, 'Major Project Supervisor Citation for *Deadly Dull* by Aimee Howard' in *Semester 01, 2021 RMIT Architecture Major Project* online catalogue, 22-23, www.issuu.com/rmitarchitecture.

30 Loren Adams has been running a series of RMIT Master of Architecture design studios since 2020 that aim to 'unsettle the relationship between architecture and the language of regulation'. In *Regulatory Nonsense*, 'students train glitchy natural language processing bots with bespoke datasets of poetry, fiction and descriptive prose, and then use these to iteratively rewrite building and planning codes, standards, legislation, and regulations' (Loren Adams, correspondence with Professor Vivian Mitsogianni, July 1, 2023). To date, Loren Adams has led eight consecutive studios, each underpinned by the same broad pedagogical method but with a different thematic focus: *Regulatory Nonsense* (semester 1, 2020), *Regulatory Nonsense: Danger Zone* (semester 2, 2020), *Regulatory Nonsense: Wrong* (semester 1, 2021), *Regulatory Nonsense: Slutspurt* (semester 2, 2021), *Regulatory Nonsense: Messy Batches* (semester 1, 2022), *Regulatory Nonsense: The Vibe of The Thing* (semester 2, 2022), *Regulatory Nonsense: Possessed* (semester 1, 2023) and *Regulatory Nonsense: Strata Party* (semester 2, 2023).

4. Deploying codes, regulations and critiques of architecture and the profession towards new design propositions

The projects in this next section are characterised by their view of architecture as inherently tied to the forces that govern its production in the world (codes and regulations), and so seek to manipulate these to deliver better propositions for community, society and the urban realm — developing abstract processes and strategies to do so. Many also seek to reconsider and reframe the role of the architect in the formation of these projects.

Nicola Cortese describes her project *Work, Work, Work* (supervised by Dr Peter Brew) as being a polemic against the office building type, focusing on 'the contradiction between the office building and office work' and the architectural axiom 'form follows function.'[31] Nicola explores cross-disciplinary research into the nature of work and tests a number of different scenarios for the possibilities of the workplace and work in the office tower typology — which is typically the result of developer-driven economic drivers without specific clients in mind. Nicola is critical of existing conditions and challenges the discipline, using architectural design to imagine new possibilities.

MAJOR PROJECT S2 2021 DARCIE VELLA IMAGE 11_ACT 03 BASKETBALL COURT.JPG

Darcie Vella's project *Three Constituent Parts* (supervised by André Bonnice and Jean-Marie Spencer) considers property as part of both the 'built world' and the 'financial, economic and legal instruments by which it is regulated,' suggesting that 'as the interstitial layer, architecture may thus become a tool through which these things can be both maintained and resisted, waning into both the metaphysical and the concrete.'[32] The project seeks to explore architecture's relationship with the title boundary and deliver tactics to carve out space for public occupations outside the apparently intended purpose. The codes that regulate the built environment are often not credited for generating form — this project deliberately co-opts these invisible rules to make architectural form for the benefit of public space.

James McLennan's project *Systems of Comfort* (supervised by André Bonnice and Jean-Marie Spencer) is a polemical and critical project exploring strategies for low carbon commercial office buildings. It highlights and challenges contemporary architecture's reliance on HVAC (heating, ventilation and air

31 See Nicola Cortese's project text for *Work, Work, Work* in this publication.
32 See Darcie Vella's project text for *Three Constituent Parts* in this publication.

MAJOR PROJECT S2 2021 JAMES MCLENNAN IMAGES 22_ INTERSTITIAL ZONE WINDOW TO WINDOW OLD AND NEW.png

conditioning) systems to produce 'comfort' in buildings. James suggests that before anything else, design should respond to our environmental responsibility as architects. The project seeks to reconsider our expectations of 'comfort', looking for design strategies that don't rely on default mechanical solutions and tying these to strategies that retrofit and renovate existing building stock instead of demolishing and starting anew.

Andrea Milovanovic's project *Slice, Dust, Polish* (supervised by Dr Peter Brew) draws on her own research and analysis of the real-estate market, which results in a critique of what is identified as excess space. Her supervisor Dr Peter Brew suggests that 'Andrea identifies within contemporary feminist art and theory, gendered domesticity as provocation and agent for the exploration for the production and consumption of housing ... Andrea's project acknowledges an excess in real estate, the multiple near identical feature rooms — Dining/Meals, Alfresco Living/Outdoor, Theatre/Lounge, Kitchen/Kitchenette — and a mismatch between the 2.1 occupants and the three and four bedrooms of the average home. Andrea proposes a radical and humorous redistribution of spaces, subtle and cleverly within the brief of the 2020 Victorian Government's Future Homes Competition, appropriating the found spaces of the advertised homes as the feature space for eight separate dwellings.' Peter goes on to explain that 'there is a provocation in the extent that Andrea is able to mount a critique in the form of a radical redistribution of what is contained within the current project home. Accepting planning and building codes, construction technology and delivery and institutional finance, she is able to propose a four-fold increase to the density of the site.'[33]

33 Peter Brew, 'Major Project Supervisor Citation for *Slice, Dust, Polish* by Andrea Milovanovic,' in *Semester 01, 2020 RMIT Architecture Major Project* online catalogue, 18-19, www.issuu.com/rmitarchitecture.

The strength of Andrea's project is a firm critical position combined with research into a 'real-world' condition, via data analysis and examination of the regulatory and economic forces that led to the condition. A strong architectural design process then turns this knowledge into new propositions for architectural design.

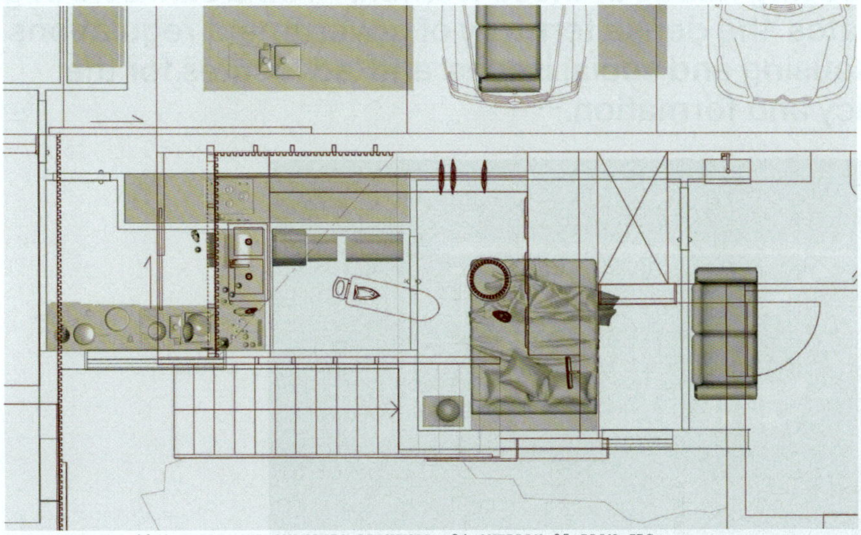

MAJOR PROJECT 20S1 ANDREA MILOVANOVIC DRAWINGS_ 24 OVERLAY_05 PLAN.JPG

5. Tactics and techniques for new models and typologies
While the expectations are that all major projects will engage with contemporary questions, some projects more explicitly take on the challenge of addressing current topical questions and pressing needs in wider society. They seek a direct role for architectural design's contribution through the development of propositions specifically focused on developing new architectural models and typologies.

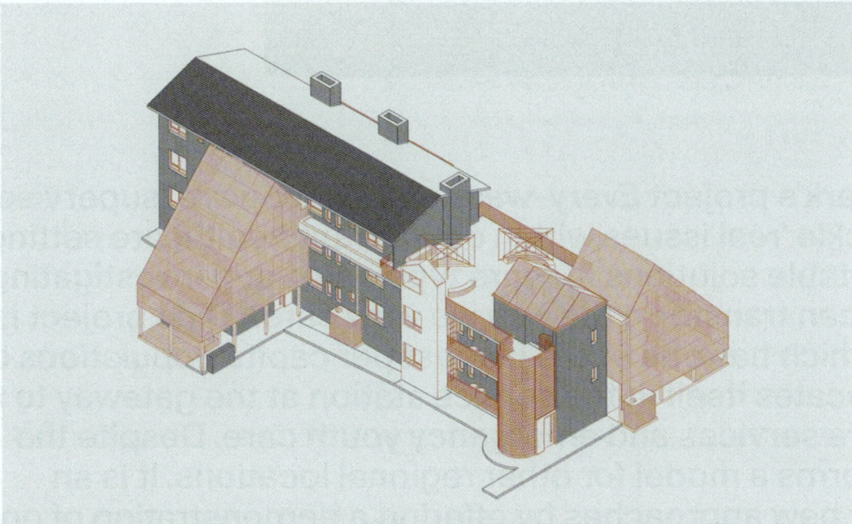

MAJOR PROJECT S1 2022 REBECCA BOLAND DRAWING 06_WOMENS WALK-UP FLATS_AXO FRONT.JPG

Rebecca Boland's project *Lost Property* (supervised by Anna Jankovic) focuses on the privatisation of public housing. Posing a counterfactual 'what-if?', she explores strategies to retain, restore and reuse existing buildings. As its basis, the project asks how existing public housing can be redeveloped so that existing communities formed and residing on previously publicly owned land can stay in place. This project owes a debt to the work of OFFICE and their Retain Repair Reinvest project,[34] but in this case Rebecca identifies women over the age of 45 as the fastest growing group at risk of homelessness, exploring 'conditions of threshold, surveillance and security to seek outcomes that cater to the housing needs of these women.'[35] Anna Jankovic suggests that Rebecca's project navigates 'the dense territory of government regulations and frameworks that impact on housing and social issues' and 'advocates for the architect's role as tied to policy and formation.'[36]

MAJOR PROJECT_SEM2_2021_ALEXANDRA_WALDRON-CLARK_NIGHT EXTERIOR ENTRANCE VIEW.png
MAJOR PROJECT_SEM2_2021_ALEXANDRA_WALDRON-CLARK_EXTERIOR DRIVE THRU MEDICAL CENTRE VIEW.png

Alexandra Waldron-Clark's project *Every-ware and Know-ware* (supervised by Simon Drysdale) seeks to tackle 'real issues within our current healthcare settings,' asking 'what we deem acceptable solutions for care typologies and investigating how a new architecture typology can transform the way we view care.'[37] The project is sited in East Gippsland, Victoria, which has one of the highest per capita populations of ageing people. The project locates itself in the service station at the gateway to town and is comprised of aged care services and emergency youth care. Despite the specificity of this project, it forms a model for other regional locations. It is an experiment that searches for new approaches by offering a demonstration of one approach that extends what we consider possible.

34 Retain, Repair, Reinvest is a site specific strategy developed by OFFICE (the not-for-profit architectural practice) for evaluating the refurbishment potential of existing public housing. Simon Robinson, co-director of OFFICE, is an RMIT Architecture alumnus. See office.org.au.
35 See Rebecca Boland's project text for *Lost Property* in this publication.
36 Anna Jankovic, 'Project Supervisor Citation for *Lost Property* by Rebecca Boland' in *Semester 01, 2022 RMIT Architecture Major Project* online catalogue, 22-23, www.issuu.com/rmitarchitecture.
37 See Alexandra Waldron-Clark's project text for *Every-ware and Know-ware* in this publication.
38 Emma Jackson, 'Project Supervisor Citation for *Catalyst* by Jessica Simons' in *Semester 02, 2019 RMIT Architecture*

MAJOR PROJECT (SEM 2) (2019) (JESSICA SIMONS)_BOARDWALK 02.PNG
MAJOR PROJECT (SEM 2) (2019) (JESSICA SIMONS)_CAMPSITE 03.PNG

Jessica Simons's project *Catalyst* (supervised by Dr Emma Jackson) provides a critique of town planning in regional towns — particularly the civic landmark concept. Dr Emma Jackson notes that 'the project is sited in Yorta Yorta Country, in the regional Victorian town of Barmah. Barmah is located on the Murray River, 260 km north of Melbourne. Jess sites her building not in the centre of town, but just outside of town in a culturally significant area of the national park. Jess uses the existing Barmah civic centre, now in desperate disrepair, as the substrate for her experiments. It is not a critique of the existing architecture or its materiality, but an investigation of civic behaviour; a reframing of what constitutes the civic and how architecture can formalise that. Old civic geometry is smeared around the site like a camera on a dolly track finding and formalising a new more meaningful civic. A civic that acknowledges Aboriginal and colonial occupation, makes explicit the current threats to our national ecology and that more appropriately catalyses regional growth.'[38]

These three projects take contemporary concerns for care, housing and regional civic presence as the starting point for their design propositions. They ask: how can the architect act responsibly within a community and how can architecture address these broader concerns? In each project, an urgent contemporary issue is used as the basis for architectural experimentation. These examples seek to develop and engage architecture's agency to make meaningful contributions to significant contemporary challenges. And in each project, a specific site is used to develop a scenario that could be deployed across numerous similar situations.

6. Culture, form and public architecture

RMIT Architecture has a long tradition of formal explorations that consider architecture as a part of a wider cultural sphere. This is less about aesthetics and more about a viewpoint that understands architecture as a cultural pursuit part of a wider cultural sphere — and the associated search for techniques that can engage architecture in these wider cultural conversations.

MAJOR PROJECT S1 2019 SENESIOS FRANGOS IMAGE 01_NORTHERN AERIAL.JPG

Senesios Frangos' project *Manual of Monsters* (supervised by Adjunct Professor Ian McDougall and Neil Masterton) adopts a choreographed process designed around the concept of the 'monster' and 'the monstrous', which are used to guide a design process exploring public architecture in Australia — specifically extending, retrofitting and re-purposing existing public buildings.

Major Project online catalogue, 12, www.issuu.com/rmitarchitecture.

MAJOR PROJECT S2 2019 TIDUS SHING IMAGE 08_THEATRE EXTERIOR.JPG

Frangos designs a manual that contains a methodology (approach) for the design of public architecture, intended to be applicable across numerous contexts. Frangos critiques what he calls a 'homogenising world, where the ability for architecture to belong to a place is being left behind' and interprets the monster as something connected to specific places. The project translates techniques and strategies borrowed from the idea of and research into 'the monstrous' — adopted from film, 'myth and legend' — and reworks these strategies as architectural design operations. It seeks to challenge public architecture's role in what is described as 'the affirmation of dominant ideologies.'[39] In doing so, it seeks the more challenging route of repurposing existing built fabric rather than demolishing and starting anew.

Tidus Lok Tin Shing's project *Library of Importance* (supervised by Vicky Lam) folds in fragments of local cultural concepts, memories, ideas and architectural components. Sited in Hong Kong, Tidus' home city, it is a critical and political project[40] seeking to use the public space to represent histories and ideas seen to be erased. The project aspires to make an architecture that formally, spatially and experientially holds and conveys representations of the local. There is a struggle here to give the things that are identified as erased form in a way that does not produce static artefacts in a museum but, rather, transforms them into wondrous and affective architectural space — to make something new and offer new ways of seeing and thinking through architecture.

39 See Senasios Frangos' project text for *Manual of Monsters* in this publication.
40 This project was awarded the RMIT Architecture Peter Corrigan Medal for the project that is the most critical, political and culturally engaged.

MAJOR PROJECT S2 2020 Natalie Angus Drawing 02_BUNDJIL ARCADE.jpg

Natalie Angus' project *Grounded* (supervised by Dr Christine Phillips)[41] asks: 'How can architecture allow for multiple histories to be shared and celebrated, while providing an unrestricted platform for First Nations people to engage with and contribute to from the outset?'[42] Natalie suggests that the project 'invites non-Indigenous designers to take accountability and unite with Indigenous knowledge holders, with the intention of forging connections that stimulate a process of continual evolvement and expansion.' The project presents itself as a framework for Indigenous stories and seeks a role for 'the architecture as a facilitator rather than monument.' Through exploratory design processes, the project deploys built text, image, landscape, architectural form and organisation to form a visually rich proposition for the Melbourne Arts Precinct. Natalie aims to 'engender an inclusive urban agenda' and create a 'lasting outcome — a work in progress with the potential to facilitate a re-grounding of sorts.'[43]

The discipline and profession of architecture is changing at an increasingly rapid pace. Architectural education therefore has to equip and empower future architects to work in conditions that will most likely not resemble the present. What Major Project asks is for each student to develop ideas, strategies, techniques, process and propositions through design and by designing. In doing so, students develop design

41 Dr Christine Phillips is currently a member and co-leader of the RMIT School of Architecture & Urban Design Yulendj Weelam Lab. Christine has co-led numerous design studios in RMIT Architecture with Stasinos Mantzis in partnership with Indigenous Elders including Kirrae Whurrong Elder Uncle Leonard Clarke and Boon Wurrung Elder Professor N'arwee't Carolyn Briggs AM. These studios are 'Indigenous-led and investigate ways in which architecture can not only spatially and visually celebrate First Nations cultures, but also explore how architecture can support self-determination through engagement processes and economic and cultural procurement strategies' (Dr Christine Phillips, correspondence with Professor Vivian Mitsogianni, 30 July 2023).

42 See Natalie Angus' project text for *Grounded* in this publication.

43 Ibid.

approaches that can be deployed or redescribed post-graduation in the differing circumstances that will arise in future practice.

The most interesting projects are assertive statements of a design position that is agile and not rigid; a statement of interests and areas of interest. These projects result in toolkits that can be deployed and extended through future architectural practice — a discipline in which design ideas and parameters are often set by others.

RMIT Architecture students are exposed to an ideas-rich and diverse culture. Our focus is on processes and ways of generating design techniques that can be adapted well into the future — irrespective of what new circumstances might arise. This generation of graduates will shape future practice — it is important that architectural education provides them with the opportunity to experiment and be heard, and to equip them with the independence to lead and make contributions relevant to their collective futures.

Brief Notes on RMIT Major Project Publications by Amy Muir

As Professor Leon van Schaik stated in 1988: 'The RMIT Major Projects Review is intended to provide the locus for a polemical description of tendencies in the design thinking of graduating architects.'[1]

The Major Project book was borne of a need to document and to record a time, a place, a discourse. These recorded moments sit within a context. The names that sit within the contents pages of each edition are familiar. They are Melbourne.

The publication has been questioned, but its validity stands strong. Records exist within the ether and yet the book as a physical artefact remains integral to our ability to record and frame each RMIT architecture graduate cohort's discourse.

The publication was traditionally edited and formatted by the graduating cohort themselves. There was a direct correlation between the immediate discourse and those who had been engaged with it. This relationship between experience and publishing allowed the editors of each edition to consider how the book would be regarded as an object. How would it be held? What were the polemics, the observations, the agitations that it was communicating? What was its proportional scale and why? *RMIT Architecture Major Project by Design 1996–1997*, for example, was edited and designed by Yanni Florence, Callum Fraser, Nikolas Koulouras and featured a 'Form Guide' written by Gina Levenspiel, capturing themes across the collected projects. *The Bold and the Beautiful*, edited by Kristin Green, Chris Reddaway, Paulo Sampaio and Marcus White, fashioned a chamfered bottom edge forcing it to sit uncomfortably in the bookshelf, projecting beyond the spines of others.

After a hiatus the book, in its physical form, hasn't died. Its potency has been recognised. Its role goes beyond the notion of record keeping and has been defined as an important educational tool. This is a book of peer recognition, peer acknowledgement. A document that carries a lineage, which can be observed in other formats but tends to get lost. A lineage that can be tracked. This book becomes a definitive record of now, and a reference point for the future. It is a structure for discourse and debate fuelling an evolving culture, that of the Major Project.

1 Leon van Schaik in *RMIT Major Project Review 1988, Architecture Direct from the RMIT* (Melbourne: RMIT Department of Architecture, 1989), 4.

Trying Architecture, Doing Urbanism
by Dr John Doyle

The design of cities has been an area of intense exploration and research at RMIT Architecture. The 'city' as a formal entity comprised of a series of constituent parts (buildings, infrastructure, etc.) has also been an object of study, with its own discrete set of rules, ways of seeing, drawing conventions and design approaches. Looking back at past design studios and Major Project courses we can identify a number of lineages, including a lineage of projects which privilege the observable and measurable qualities of the city, which seek to isolate this from other concerns and intervene in this space through the architectural object.

MAJOR PROJECT S2 2021 DARCIE VELLA IMAGE 03_ACT 01.JPG

As we reflect on the recent history of the Major Project at RMIT Architecture and the concerns of this generation of emerging architects, it occurs to me that this approach has evolved. Within the work we see in this book, the 'city' is, for the most part, no longer an object of study unto itself. What has emerged in its place is a far more dispersed or atomised understanding of urban environments, one in which concern for buildings and life in cities is explored, often tangentially, via the design of architecture (not always buildings) that seeks to exercise agency through modest means. For this generation, urbanity is something all encompassing, affecting all aspects of design — an inevitable consideration of being in the world. What emerges from this is a series of emerging practitioners for whom urbanism, and the process of city making, is no longer a discrete field but rather a way of judging and a consequence of doing architecture.

The work of this cohort of graduates suggests an approach in which the act of design is considered fundamentally 'urban' regardless of circumstances. Rather than

MAJOR PROJECT S2 2021 DARCIE VELLA IMAGE 04_ACT 01.JPG
MAJOR PROJECT S2 2021 DARCIE VELLA IMAGE 05_ACT 02.JPG

expanding outwards and looking to other actors within the built environment, this approach harnesses a deep dexterity *within* the discipline of architecture as the best method of influencing the consequences of urbanisation and contributing to the world.

In the following section I will explore three ways in which this idea has been explored through major projects in this volume.

Darcie Vella's project *Three Constituent Parts* looks at the relationship between property and architecture, with a specific focus on the gap between the virtual conception of property and its physical actualisation in the world. The project probes

MAJOR PROJECT_SEMESTER 2_2020_LACHLAN WILES_APIARY 2.JPG

MAJOR PROJECT_SEMESTER 2_2020_LACHLAN WILES_AUTONOMOUS RING.JPG

at the misalignment between the two to explore opportunities for architectural invention and urban agency. The way land titles are formed in Melbourne is an artificial and virtual construct on a land that was, and is, embedded with a longstanding pre-existing cultural custodianship. In forming the project, Darcie identifies that architecture has had an instrumental role in implementing the colonisation of territory. While the act of applying title to land is a metaphysical one, in practice it is enabled through architecture, which provides the physical space for drawings to be done, stored, rendered into law and enforced. Property is both a pre-condition for and a consequence of architecture. In response to this, the project attempts to develop a series of tactics, through the medium of architecture, that can problematise this axiomatic relationship. Darcie proposes a series of occupation strategies that seek to challenge the intended use of land, and by extension its ownership and title. This is explored first through the application of road paint to Gleadell Street in Richmond, permanently marking out the arrangement of the fresh food market that inhabits the street temporarily on Saturday mornings. As an extension of this concept, the project develops a series of small-scale interventions that seek to delineate a space within a title through the use of objects to demarcate said space. These interventions draw on the principle of squatter law, and the understanding that ownership can be inferred through extended occupation (adverse possession) — however the mechanism by which this is measured is the presence of permanent physical infrastructures of inhabitation (architecture). The final aspect of

MAJOR PROJECT_SEMESTER 2_2020_LACHLAN WILES_APIARY 1.JPG

the project is an exploration of the mechanisms by which architecture can transcend its relationship to title. This idea is introduced through an exploration of the ambiguous relationship between civil infrastructure and land title. Darcie observes that much of the infrastructure that serves the city, typically at the smaller scale, falls outside of the limitations of title and is permitted to cross boundaries. The project explores the potential for these various civil infrastructures to be imbued with the qualities of architecture, affording them both program and cultural value. In the final project, Darcie notes that the clearest example of this concept is the architectural element of the stormwater connection, a device permitted to exist outside of the title boundary. During the 'What Matters'[1] panel event reflecting on the completed major projects, Darcie was circumspect about the capacity of architecture to have agency in the domain of property, noting that upon reflection the only aspect of her project that she could be confident in was the downpipe detail. While this admission was couched in defeat, what the project contributes is a modest mechanism by which architecture can reveal the artifice of property. While others have revealed and explored similar gaps in the language of property, the framing of these devices as tools for questioning colonisation is novel.

Like many of the projects contained in this volume, Darcie's project explores the pre-conditions of architecture — the legal, economic, social or other organising frameworks that exist before the architect typically becomes involved. These are devices that Allan Burrows describes in his 2017 major project as being the 'architecture of architecture,'[2] in that they fundamentally shape the possibilities of design before it has even taken place. The innovation of these projects is in seeking to extend the range of design and apply the tools of architectural thought (spatial and

1 The graduate-led Major Discourse 'What Matters?' panel was convened by Mietta Mullaly and Liam Oxlade with Vivian Mitsogianni and held at the RMIT Media Portal, 13 October 2022.
2 Allan Burrows, 'The A-OK' in Semester 01, 2017 RMIT Major Project online catalogue, 4, www.issuu.com/rmitarchitecture.

material organisation) to these conditions as means of influencing the nature of the built outcome further down the line. Most importantly in the case of Darcie's project, while acknowledging the *a priori* nature of property, her means of intervening is fundamentally architectural in that it is largely exercised through the design and insertion of built objects. Title and property exist prior to architecture, but architecture is a prerequisite for the existence of property. Through this critical observation, the architect is afforded agency within urbanisation while operating within the traditional limits of the discipline.

MAJOR PROJECT_IMOGEN FRY W14_PANEL_A0S.PDF

Lachlan Wiles' project *Fields of Entanglement* explores the regeneration of a former large-scale industrial precinct in Altona North. The project is made up of a layered masterplan that adaptively reuses a series of disused industrial complexes in the area, creating new functional spaces tied together through a mega-scale formal intervention. The project explores five points within the masterplan in detail: an unmanned aerial systems factory; an apiary and integrated performative and regenerative landscape; a nursery with flexible and lettable workspaces; an innovation hub with commercial and research/learning activities; and an autonomous logistics mega-centre. The ambition of the project was to critique the modern conception of the city, and architecture, as existing separate to nature. In contrast, the project develops what is described as a 'field of entanglement' in which built and unbuilt ecologies are proposed across the site in close proximity to one another, in what Lachlan describes as a 'non-idyllic integration.' It is this concept of the 'non-idyllic' that is perhaps the most interesting aspect of the project. The motivation to regenerate landscapes is often driven by a dubious desire to repair for the purposes

MAJOR PROJECT_IMOGEN FRY W14_PANEL_A0S.PDF:2

of human enjoyment and future exploitation through the implementation of tourism and other mechanisms of extraction. The non-idyllic as a concept sidesteps arcadian concepts of the natural environment, instead suggesting an arrangement that is somehow compromised or negotiated through an ecological network. It also suggests the de-prioritisation, or the potential for de-centralisation, of humans in this ecosystem. The masterplan places human settlement on equal footing with a natural 'environmental field' as well as a 'technological field' that is a post-human program comprised of automated facilities such as logistics and data centres. Lachlan's project builds upon, among others, Imogen Fry's 2017 major project *Regenerated Farms, Regenerated Towns, Regenerated Nature*,[3] which adopts a similar strategy of implementing a mega-structure production intervention — one that, in her case, encircles the town of Goroke in Western Victoria in the form of a high-density farming complex. Imogen's project overtly states that the architecture of high-density agriculture should be open and accessible to people as a form of social benefit for regional towns. The form and ambition of Lachlan's project appear similar, but the decision to exclude humans from large sections of the project is radically different. Regeneration is no longer a process that is accessible to (and for the benefit of) humans, but rather one that takes place parallel to our own occupation of cities. Regeneration, in this case, is a process enabled through the post-human landscape of automated production and data centres.

To design environments and spaces that are not inhabited by humans requires a new set of design processes and tools. The functional requirements of machines

3 Imogen Fry, 'Regenerated Farms, Regenerated Towns, Regenerated Nature' in 'The A-OK' in Semester 02, 2017 RMIT Major Project online catalogue, 15, www.issuu.com/rmitarchitecture.

and animals differ dramatically from those of humans, and many of the tropes architects rely on to make design judgements are no longer relevant in a non-human or multi-species context. Using a number of case study interventions, Lachlan's project proposes a series of typological formations organised around the specific requirements of the 'user'. While the human occupied buildings are familiar, the landscapes and buildings organised around the specific requirements of endemic flora and fauna and their autonomous functions provide an uncanny counterpoint to the human-centred program. This project sits within a broader series of projects at RMIT, both in Major Project and Design Studio, in which students and faculty are grappling with the emergence of new building typologies, such as the data centre or the urban/vertical farm, and their implications for cities. While Lachlan's project departs from a masterplan 'object' at the scale of the city, it is through the architectural scale 'case studies' that the project's contribution is revealed. By grappling with the specific requirements of speculative programs, the project contributes the visualisation of future building typologies, recognising that it is at the scale of typology that the architect can exercise agency. The urban environment forms a field of entanglement through which the specific typological requirements of different actors can be mediated and negotiated.

Benjamin Strong's major project *Condencity* starts with a deep interest in what Ildefons Cerdà would describe as urbanism, perhaps more commonly understood in Australia as urban planning. The project explores the Sandridge precinct in the slowly unfolding Fisherman's Bend urban renewal in Melbourne. The proposed development, understood through government planning documents (design and development overlays), is visualised as a volumetric urban form and compared to equivalent scale chunks of different cities from around the world — including Manhattan, Tokyo, Hong Kong, Paris, Las Vegas, Barcelona, Oxford, Rome and the centre of Melbourne itself. The comparison of these urban figures, presented alongside data on their relative population size and density, presents an implicit critique of the homogenous urban figure of the Fisherman's Bend development plan.

Situated in close conversation with the research of his supervisor, Ian Nazareth, Benjamin introduces the idea of 'antifragility,' a concept developed by Nassim Nicholas Taleb to describe organisational structures within various human and natural domains that are extremely resilient, and that benefit from disorder, risk and uncertainty. This concept has been applied to numerous fields, however it has largely been associated with economics, in which the antifragile describes financial strategies and business models that benefit from rapid change, market fluctuations and diversity. The Covid-19 pandemic, the Evergrande incident, the Russia-Ukraine war and the ongoing climate crisis have revealed the importance of antifragility, as businesses and governments have been forced to repeatedly adjust through periods of seemingly endless, radical disruption. Through his project, Benjamin draws on these ideas as a framework to critique prevailing urban models, and as catalyst for the development of urban approaches that could be described as 'antifragile' but that also present the possibility of by-product architectures that are novel.

Working from urban precedents, and the conjecture that 'smallness', 'heterogeneity' and 'decentralisation' in the urban environment are inherently

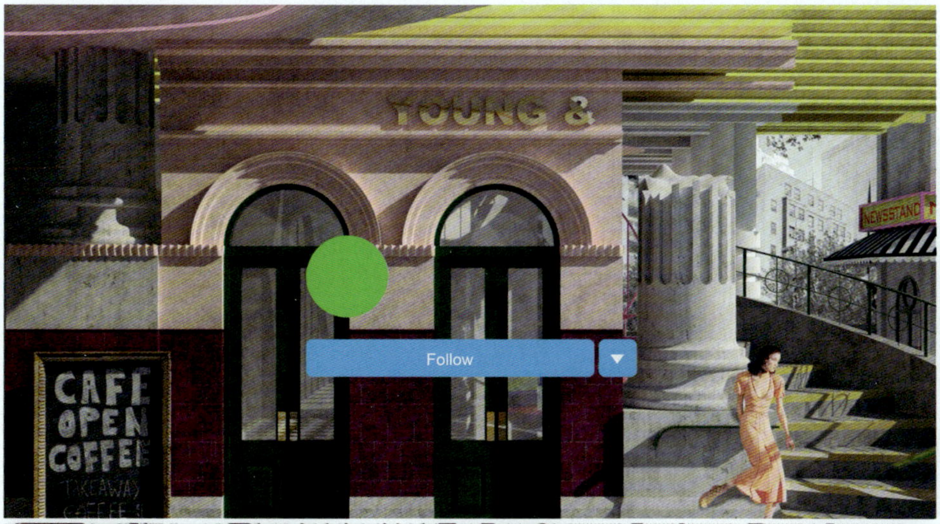

LOUIS NUCCITELLI_ 1600X900 BTS _ MDW EVENT POSTER && INSTAGRAM POSTS (1).JPG
LOUIS NUCCITELLI_ 1600X900 BTS _ MDW EVENT POSTER && INSTAGRAM POSTS.JPG

antifragile, Benjamin develops a spatial framework in which a fine grain grid is applied across the site. A series of rules for the city are developed, providing metrics governing its principles of organisation and amenity. Into this framework he introduces 'perturbations in the system — a series of non-standard urban forms drawn from the conditions of the site such as sports grounds, existing buildings including large factory/warehouse typologies, and a grid of street trees tracing the historically wide industrial boulevards of the area. The development of the proposal is tested through a generative process in which formal rule sets are developed for three broad client groups (the accountant, the entrepreneur and the dissident) and then allowed to propagate across the site. The perturbations act as urban irritants, producing irregular triangular plots and slithers of land that must be negotiated between the different urban actors through design. The outcome of this is an urban massing at the precinct scale, which is made up of a mixture of fine grain high-density buildings that, through interaction with each other and the remnant building fabric of the site, produce a complex series of diverse architectural forms and mixed-use program agglomerations.

The formal language of Benjamin's project is not radical. The urban proposition for fine grain, diverse, mixed-use urbanism is not new — as evidenced

MAJOR PROJECT SEM 2 2020 BEN STRONG DRAWING 072.JPG
MAJOR PROJECT SEM 2 2020 BEN STRONG DRAWING 073.JPG

through the project's case studies. However, what the project contributes is an understanding of how emerging economic models might be interpolated into architectural design. While much of the work is in establishing an urban framework, the implications of the proposition are tested most clearly at the scale of architecture through a series of small buildings as experienced from the street. This approach is reminiscent of Louis Nuccitelli's 2018 major project *Beyond the Selfie*,[4] which explored the nascent social media economy as a catalyst for and driver of urban design. In both cases, the projects seek to understand and engage emergent economies, and to explore the specific disciplinary implications of these conditions for architecture within an urban context.

Twenty years ago in *Preter: Architecture Thesis Projects 2002–2003,* Graham Crist, Conrad Hamann and Stuart Harrison described an approach to the Major Project, and design research generally, as 'trying architecture.' This approach was understood as 'broad in the sense that it engages with things outside architecture,

4 Louis Nuccitelli, 'Beyond the Selfie' in 'The A-OK' in Semester 02, 2018 RMIT Major Project online catalogue, 7, www.issuu.com/rmitarchitecture.
5 Graham Crist, Conrad Hamann and Stuart Harrison, 'Trying Architecture' in *Preter: Architecture Thesis Projects 2002-2003* (Melbourne: RMIT University Press, 2004), 12-15.

and specific in the sense that it works within the medium of building,' tested through the iterative doing of architectural design.[5] The composition of cities and urban environments are not the products of singular design but rather the consequence of a series of negotiated actions, some of which are made by architects. The projects in this volume demonstrate the urgency of engaging in issues and ideas critical to the built environment. Moreover, rather than attempting to parlay the skills of the architect into a broader position of interdisciplinary influence, the projects show the value in pursuing these concerns through the doing of architectural design — and that the act of designing buildings in the world is always an act of urbanism.

MAJOR PROJECT SEM 2 2020 BEN STRONG DRAWING 81.PDF

Contracts of Hope by Dr Emma Jackson

I invited a cohort of my Major Project alumni back this semester to offer some perspective to my current students. As they spoke, I saw the continued value of their individual projects to their practice — a map of alternative futures with which they can navigate the challenges of the profession. Perhaps a visual contract with their future selves to keep trying.

This is consistent with the contemporary appetite at RMIT Architecture for seeing what architecture can do beyond its disciplinary boundaries. The Major Project course has become a device for innovating the practice model. The projects of the following students all reach outside the business-as-usual framework to capture hope, and give it form.

Students have traditionally been allowed 3×A0 landscape panels in which to present their thesis. In the last few years, there has been a shift in the way those panels are deployed. Now that architecture is understood as a vehicle for change rather than an end product, the panels are more graphic novel than conventional architectural drawings.

MAJOR PROJECT S1 2021 MATTHEW TIBBALLS IMAGE 3 THE BUILDING.JPG

MAJOR PROJECT S1 2021 CHRIS BUCHHORN IMAGE 19.PNG
MAJOR PROJECT S1 2021 CHRIS BUCHHORN IMAGE 20.PNG

Matthew Tibballs' *The Promise Ring* (2021) is an entrepreneurial thesis that leverages the design opportunities in adverse possession on large-scale infrastructural projects. The project heralds: don't blame the system for promises not delivered on, find the projects hiding in the clauses and design through the disappointment. It also deftly speculates on an expanded practice model by including things not normally seen as within the scope of architecture.

Chris Buchhorn's *See you in the in-between* (2021) injects the civic into air pockets of suburbia, delivering community and connectedness without expanding the overall architectural footprint. His thesis is an audit of unused space and a rally to deploy spatial resources more usefully. The integrity of title boundaries is loosened to follow topography and opportunity, creating a myriad of spaces that can be occupied but not owned.

MAJOR PROJECT (SEM 2) (2019) (JESSICA SIMONS)_BOARDWALK 02.PNG
MAJOR PROJECT (SEM 2) (2019) (JESSICA SIMONS)_BOARDWALK 03.PNG

Jess Simons' *Catalyst* (2019) calls out 'flooding' as a colonial concept, and in so doing throws open the doors for a new way of designing with water. Her project takes the existing building collateral on the site and, with algorithmic operations, puts this building in a seasonal relationship with water. In architecture school in the 1990s, we were taught that the first priority of an architect is to keep the water out. In *Catalyst*, water wins; we design it in!

Riley Pelham-Thorman's *Who Cares* (2021) claims the particularities of local culture and mundane practicalities to inform suburban civic space. What if the locals could contribute at the front end of the design process rather than vent after the event on talkback radio? *Who Cares* also acknowledges endemic ecosystems that

MAJOR PROJECT S2 2021 RILEY PELHAM-THORMAN_ROSANNA WOOLWORTHS.PNG
MAJOR PROJECT S2 2021 RILEY PELHAM-THORMAN_TIE UP YOUR DOGS PARKING BAY.PNG

MAJOR PROJECT (2) (2020) (EILIDH ROSS) DRAWING(4)_KITCHEN.JPG
MAJOR PROJECT (2) (2020) (EILIDH ROSS) DRAWING(6)_SCHOOL.JPG
MAJOR PROJECT (2) (2020) (EILIDH ROSS) DRAWING(7)_FISHING.JPG

have been designed out of the urban realm, and uses the salt creek as an operative design device.

Likewise, Eilidh Ross' *HERE* (2020) reclaims a more connected relationship with over sixty thousand years of human culture in her reframing of volume housing. *HERE* challenges the suburbs' abstract relationship with the city and puts it into a more meaningful relationship with the ground it inhabits. *HERE* examines what spatial, cultural and formal opportunities emerge if we replace ownership with custodianship of land.

In these projects, I see resonance with my own research throughout my design studios and design practice PhD (*Everywhen: Dirty algorithms to agitate for a more appropriate occupation of Australia*, RMIT 2019) into new spatial currencies. I also see the use of existing built artefacts as the substrate of algorithmic operations, recasting the 'as found' into new relationships which reveal alternative modes of occupation. This is a practice of provocation that does not see architecture as an object, but as a portal to the unseen. It is what reaches out of the project and not the project itself that is the architecture. To render the project a provocation requires designing unstable forms — resolved enough to be credible, and loose enough to be seen through. It is a high-risk approach and is often misunderstood and/or underestimated. Julius Egan, a past Major Project student of mine, observes: 'This way of working is so nearly-there, so nearly-familiar, that it can seem like nothing, unless the right discussion frames and explains it.'[1] The risk pays off after graduation, when the project sheds its skin and the ideas are liberated from their 'final' form.

The nature of the profession is changing. There is increasing opportunity to apply operative design techniques, techniques usually used to generate architecture, to instead restructure the scope of the profession. The great privilege of working with Major Project students over the last decade is being able to see their ideas develop into productive new ways of practicing. The RMIT Architecture Graduate Exhibition, held at the end of each semester, becomes a collective earmarking of this future undertaking. Like battle banners, the panels become contracts of hope where, among the noise of battle and warnings of old soldiers, the visual cue shines through.

MAJOR PROJECT (2) (2020) (EILIDH ROSS) DRAWING(1)_BATHROOM VIEW.JPG

1 Julius Egan, correspondance with Emma Jackson, 2022.

Translating The Personal and Particular To the Public and Universal by Helen Duong and Tim Pyke

Major Project at RMIT Architecture allows students and tutors from diverse countries and cultures to converse, compare, question and build a shared understanding through the making of architecture. These considered and sustained conversations are presented in the four projects below, which all reveal deeply personal issues alongside underlying historical, societal and political issues of the home cities the students are examining. The persistent challenge of projects sited overseas is the difficulty of communicating the specificity of site, cultural practices and architectural spatiality to a Melbourne audience, with many qualities potentially lost through translation. When conducted remotely from Australia, research is generally undertaken through memory recall, spatial intelligence and online mapping databases. Still, where information is either scant or restricted, a nuanced reading of site can be obtained by working in situ (Jingyuan and Longge), and by collecting data through interviews with (Guled) or photographs from (Mandy) friends and relatives. This in-depth research gives students authority and agency over their found knowledge, fostering a genuine exchange of pluralistic ideas, the basis of a truly international education.

MAJOR PROJECT S2 2021 GULED ELYAS CAMEL CARAVAN.PNG

MAJOR PROJECT S2 2021 GULED ELYAS DECORATED INTERIOR.PNG

The Asian Architecture and Urbanism course within the RMIT Master of Architecture program offers an opportunity for students to focus on Asian cities — which, for many, means their origin cities. The course considers new representation techniques, working methods and language to describe the condition of Asian cities, and increasingly cities from other continents, providing value and meaning which many students might not otherwise have discovered in Melbourne.[1] These projects

1 *'Non-Western Modernity (Singapore),'* presented by Professor Leon Van Schaik as part of the Asian Architecture + Urbanism Lecture Series, 11 March 2020.

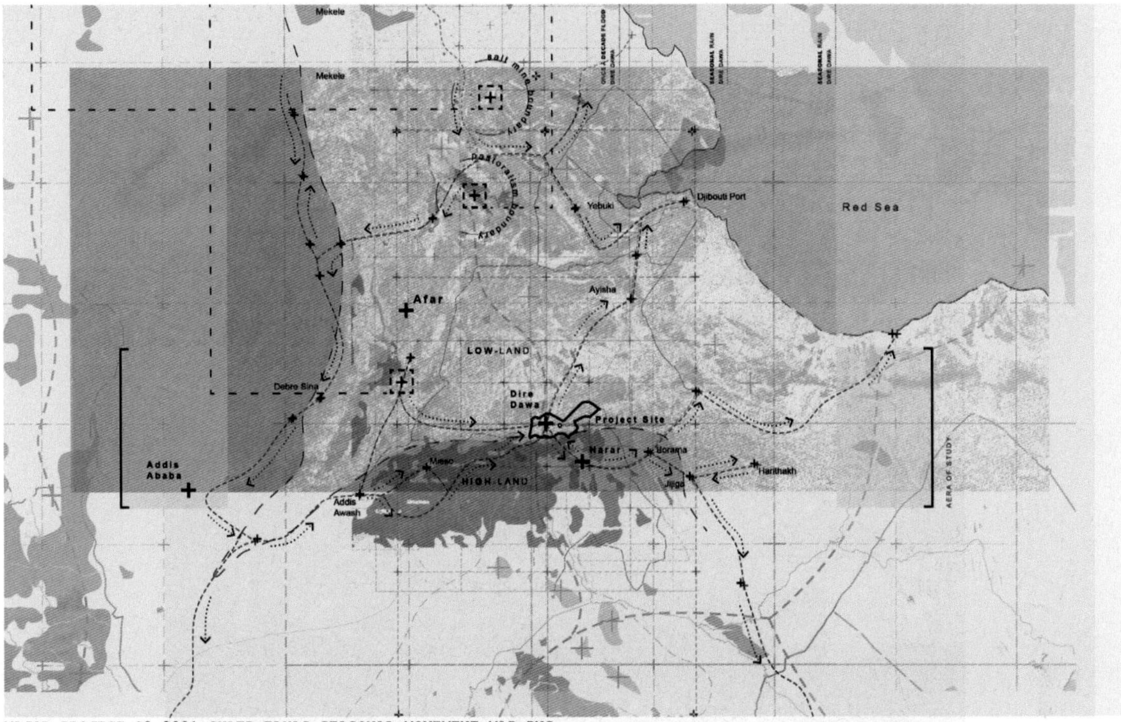

MAJOR PROJECT S2 2021 GULED ELYAS SEASONAL MOVEMENT MAP.PNG

build upon anecdotes, existing memories and/or recent lived experience, which fosters a heightened aspirational perspective on their hometowns. Our design studios at RMIT, on the other hand, have remained closer to home with their focus on Melbourne's peripheral suburbs and the effect migration has had on the city. The rituals and behaviours of migrants, along with the patterns and spatial effects they have transplanted, are studied to inform new models of architecture and urbanism.[2] Mapping and dissection of these phenomena are then translated into design, such as migrant-specific aged care which integrates occupants and their urban rituals into the surrounding context.[3] As practitioners, we have practised in offices with a similar focus on suburban architecture through education, aged care and retail projects. This gives us a particular interest in understanding what might exist in cities around the world that also have ad-hoc conditions, are peripheral, messy and marginalised.

As experts in their cities, international students are encouraged to retell the story of their inhabitation and draw from personal experiences. For Guled, Mandy, Jingyuan and Longge, the Major Project course has validated and encouraged an interest in the cultures and building fabric of their home cities.

Students recorded and communicated specific daily rituals of urban life, using mapping tools to translate their personal psycho-geography and experiences. This enabled them to work at a safe distance from sometimes politically sensitive contexts, facilitating conversations that circumvented the official histories, government policies and sanitised representations of their cities to reveal alternate narratives and speculations on what is at stake.

2 *Strangers in a Strange Land*, Master of Architecture design studio, 2018, led by Helen Duong and Tim Pyke.
3 *Cloudy, With a Chance of Joy I and II*, Master of Architecture design studio, 2019, led by Helen Duong and Tim Pyke.

MAJOR PROJECT S2 2020 GAVRILA MANDY NORTH ENTRANCE GATE.PNG
MAJOR PROJECT S2 2020 GAVRILA MANDY FOOD TOWER NIGHT.PNG

For Wang Jingyuan, a photographic essay of heritage details, ornaments and vistas in the historic port area of Shenzhen soon melded with her knowledge of classical Chinese artistic culture. Her project *Mending Guanlan Old Town* (Shenzhen, China) critiques the tokenistic and inauthentic representations of heritage architecture and classical culture in contemporary Chinese society. Mandy Kahuni Gavrila's *Kampong Dolly* (Surabaya, Indonesia) began with an interest in rejuvenating one of Southeast Asia's largest red-light districts. Careful mapping of the behaviour of multiple actors in the complex ecology and economy of sex tourism led her to question the validity of a government-initiated creative arts program and to explore the politics of public space in slum communities. By undertaking his project in situ, Longge Zhang's *Darshilar Creepers* (Dashilar Sub District, Beijing, China) instigated a personal desire to make sense of the tumultuous history of twentieth-century China. He began by examining forced collectivisation's lasting effects on the originally bourgeois Siheyuan (courtyard residence) of Beijing's hutongs (laneways). This led to an understanding of the culture preserved by local elderly citizens, including ad-hoc architectural additions, which in turn led to a critique of the cyclical, superficial and ineffective policies imposed on the historic district. In the *Formalisation of Nomadic Urbanism* (Dechatu River, Dire Dawa, Ethiopia), Guled Elyas began with an interest in the economies of Dire Dawa, which persevere within a dried riverbed and coexist with regular flash flooding. Deeper research revealed the economic, geographic, social, cultural and political tensions between the settled residents and nomadic tribes, and the unavoidable loss of tradition and livelihood.

Through detailed accounts of their cities, students extracted performative qualities to augment and enhance their design experiments, including adapting local vernaculars and emerging urban archetypes as well as reusing the existing fabric.

Early on, Jingyuan recognised the complexity of operating with a collection of eighteenth-century colonial trading buildings that not only required repair,

MAJOR PROJECT S2 2020 JINGYUAN WANG DRAWING02.PNG

MAJOR PROJECT S2 2020 JINGYUAN WANG IMAGE15_NIGHT BANQUET .PNG
MAJOR PROJECT S2 2020 JINGYUAN WANG WINDING STAIR.PNG
MAJOR PROJECT S2 2020 JINGYUAN WANG IMAGE03_ COLLECTION OF NATURE3 .PNG

maintenance and rebuilding but would also be inadequate if new methods and ways of seeing heritage and culture were not proposed. Here, she develops a series of techniques that extract cultural references from movies, opera scenery, watercolour paintings and poetry verses to create formal and spatial sequences. Inserted strategically in between and on top of buildings, or as extensions or infill, she curates an experiential and tactile appreciation of the construction of colonial architecture, as well as of classical Chinese culture itself. In her project, Mandy has reintroduced and adapted the *joglo* house to the urban *kampung*. In this way it acts as a memory marker

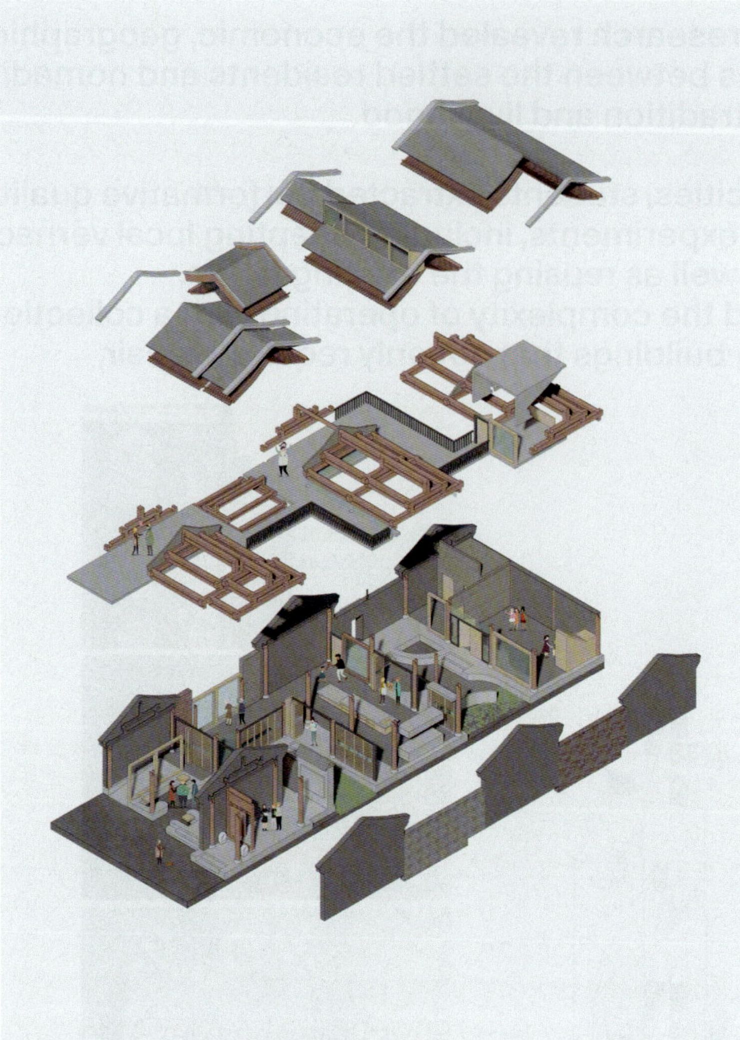

MAJOR PROJECT S1 2021 LONGGE ZHANG CULTURAL CENTRE.PNG
MAJOR PROJECT S1 2021 LONGGE ZHANG UNDER EAVES RECREATION.JPG
MAJOR PROJECT S1 2021 LONGGE ZHANG CORNER RECREATION.JPG

MAJOR PROJECT S1 2021 LONGGE ZHANG_COMMUNAL CARE CENTRE.PNG

of village life through the familiarity of its softwood columns, carved braces and haunches. At the same time, the *joglo* house's traditional profile is deformed and exaggerated — its chisel-like roof apex, characteristic of government buildings in the region, is made partially unrecognisable and so can also function as an urban marker. Mandy's other proposals amplify existing social practices within the new urban archetypes of the 'super' kiosks, 'giant' community halls and food 'towers'. Guled transplants the vernacular buildings of the Afar tribe people onto flood-resilient concrete pods with provisions for draping traditional woven mats. He translates the fortified earth architecture of the Indigenous Oromor people into a levee wall that incorporates permanent housing, livestock wells and market stalls with provisions for displaying cookware and goods. The urban grain 'goat tracks' across the riverbed and water paths are the departure points for the arrangement of these urban and ecological interventions. Longge inserts architecture into the pockets and gaps between and within the hutongs and siheyuan: public amenity blocks, carparking and communal gathering places (noticeboards, corners and stoops) deemed to be outside of government policy. By formalising the collectivist activities and behaviours of post-1940s China, and adapting traditional construction methods with new materials, he subverts the municipal government's ban on all non-traditional structures for alternate means, providing programs for senior citizens, children and superseded traditional Chinese culture (opera). As in Mandy's project, the familiarity of material and the legibility of architectural details serve as a communication device, revealing the physical and lived histories of place in a way that can contribute positively to future development. Jointly, these projects are believable as they are made up of reconstituted components. Their material constructive techniques may not be new, but their composition in specific locations is.

These students have developed small to medium interventions that operate strategically — through both preventions and alterations — in the city to affect the surrounding fabric over time. They all have a vision for large-scale change.

Mandy's series of additions and insertions to the street edge, rooftops, laneways and existing buildings act together to give value to, encourage and preserve the informal overlapping movement of the *ojeks* (motorcycle taxis), *becaks* (three-wheeled carts), *dokars* (horse-drawn carriages) and scooters. She maintains and fosters the interconnected communities of emerging creative industries and local sex workers with community facilities and the tourist economy. Jingyuan developed a classification strategy that distinguished buildings for repair, restoration and redevelopment in the hope that heritage policy in China would become more nuanced and less superficial, and that classical culture could be part of everyday life. Guled maintains the ad-hoc market that emerges between flooding events, while proposing a strategy for the unavoidable urbanisation of nomadic tribes, staggering their transition from an ordered nomadic settlement living in temporary shelter to short-term housing and eventual long-term shop housing. His 1:1 project is part of a vast 1:20,000 journey and ethnographic map, encompassing geographic landmarks, trading routes, resources, memory and cultural practices. Longge spatially and systematically reorders the existing building fabric to preserve memories through materiality and form, enabling ageing in place and the continuation of daily rituals, as well as commemorating collectivisation rather than individual ownership of the market economy.

The architectural proposition in these projects is that discussing, making, drawing, communicating and speculating on what is currently invisible gives definition and value to the built environment, towards a better understanding of ways to intervene. Though a search for 'local identity' may have been the research instigator, through documentation, analysis, presentation and discussion, these students have situated themselves within a collective identity and speculated on how they might practice in the future within these cities. Major Project allows students to explore their interests and in turns makes us, as tutors and the academy, aware of highly specific and global issues. This international survey of projects reveals that the need for architecture and cities to reflect collective identities and histories across Southeast Asia, Australia and Africa is universal. We hope Major Project has instigated the early merging of students' professional, academic and personal interests.

Chunks: Volatile Processes and Speculative Tectonics by Professor Roland Snooks

RMIT Architecture Major Project is a platform for students to put forward their first substantial position within architecture. It is not simply the design of a project; rather, it acts as a form of design research that encapsulates a critically engaged position within the discourse. Three major projects that I have recently supervised, by Alan Kim, Jitesh Sapra and Vicky Ning, draw from the design research agenda of the RMIT Architecture | Tectonic Formation Lab.[1] All projects successfully interweave speculative design and rigorous research as they seek to advance generative design processes and challenge fabrication conventions. Rather than designing within an assumed tectonic paradigm, they are experiments in the design implications of technical innovation.

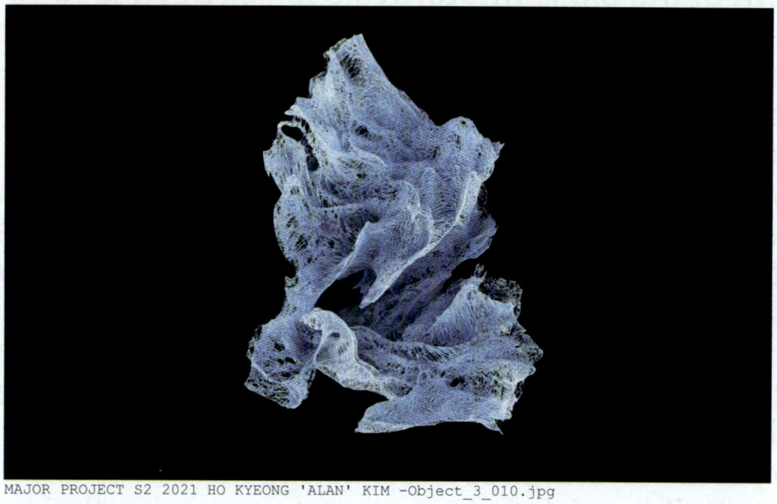

MAJOR PROJECT S2 2021 HO KYEONG 'ALAN' KIM -Object_3_010.jpg

The research agenda of the Tectonic Formation Lab is one of experimental tectonics, a concern for the interrelationship of building skins, structure, ornament, fabrication and assembly. This agenda contends that innovation in tectonics can establish a logic for a new set of spatial, formal and organisational conditions. The lab prioritises the design of building chunks, or fragments, over complete buildings and their relationship to site. The chunk is intended to embody the DNA of the structure, a small fragment that contains all of the relationships and protocols for the generation of entire buildings.

Recognising that within a given 14-week semester there is insufficient time to seriously rethink process and tectonics — while simultaneously designing entire buildings, which are posited here as extrapolations of the chunk in response to the demands of context — the focus of the design studios I teach, and the major projects I supervise, are on the building chunk. This strategy has been developed within the lab through the design and fabrication of chunks positioned as tectonic fragments of a possible future architecture. Research labs exploring innovation in fabrication typically create demonstrator projects to experiment with novel techniques. Often, these take the form of pavilions, the smallest complete architectural type. However,

1 The RMIT Architecture | Tectonic Formation Lab is led by Professor Roland Snooks.

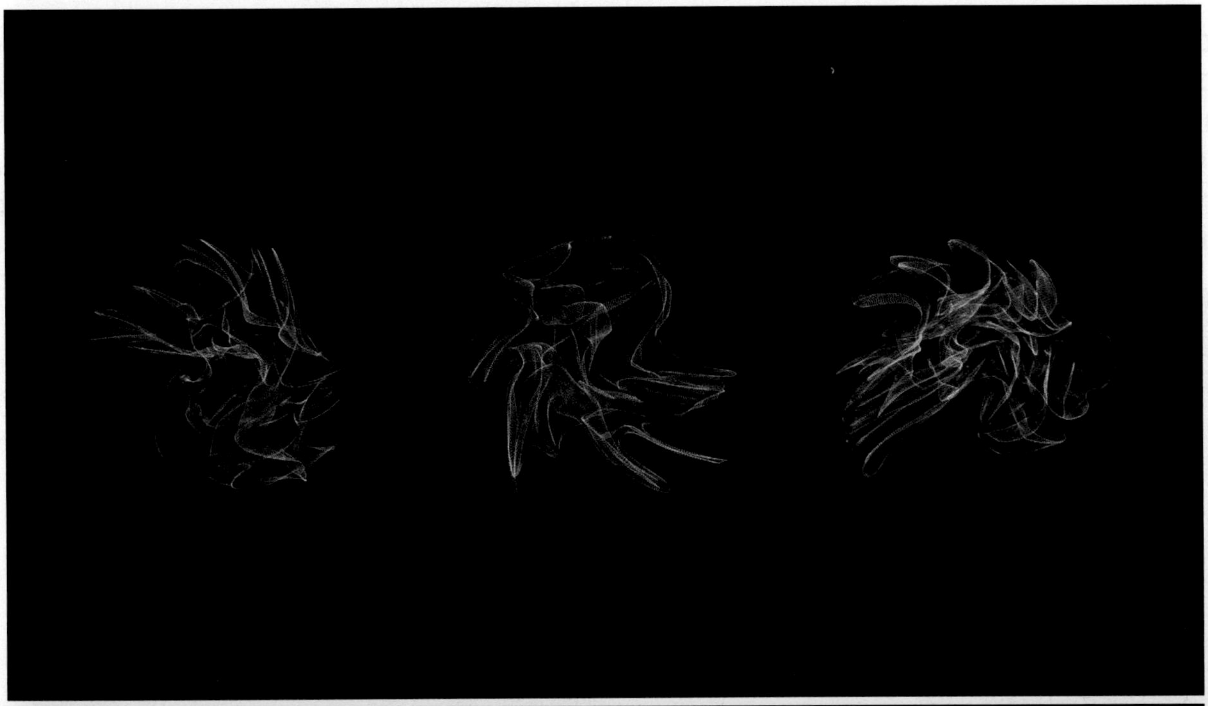

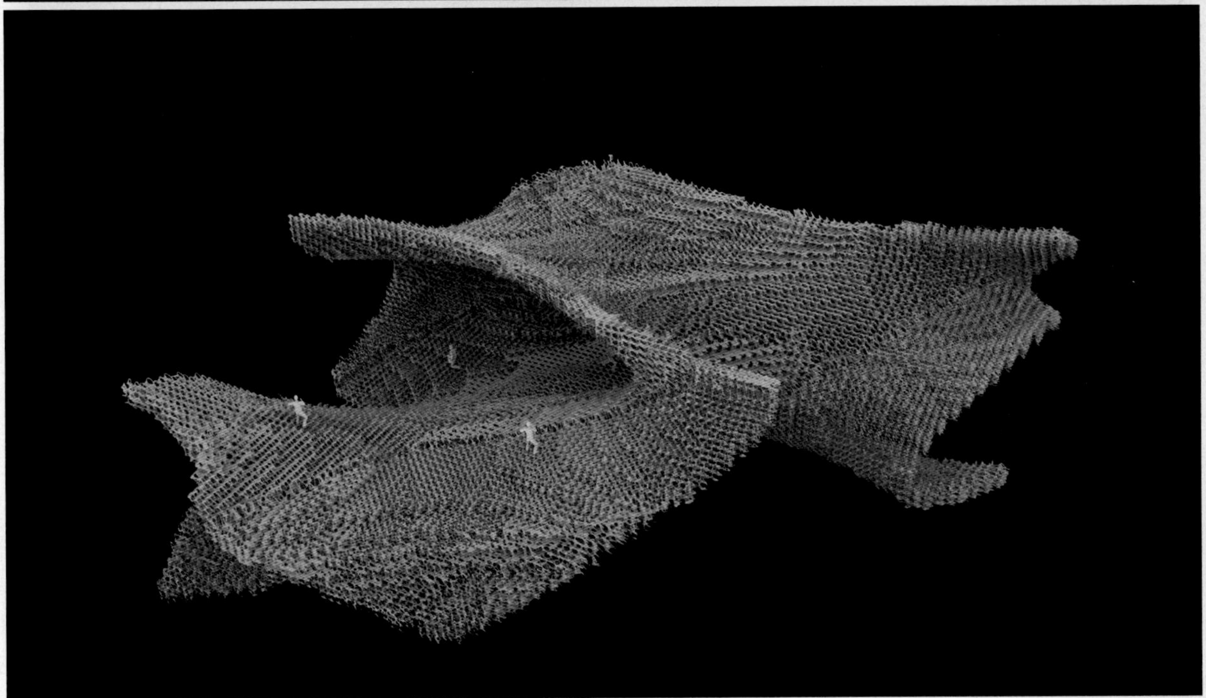

MAJOR PROJECT S1 2021 JITESH SAPRA 06 FORM FINDING ALGORITHM.jpg
MAJOR PROJECT S1 2021 JITESH SAPRA 25 PROTOTYPE CHUNK.jpg

pavilions don't actually address the spectrum of architectural conditions; they are all too often a type of toy architecture that doesn't address fundamental architectural concerns. However, an architectural chunk of similar size can be established as a testing ground for complex relationships of structure, skin, ornament and spatial organisation, which can then be deployed in the design of larger building types.

The three projects discussed here explore self-organising generative design processes, machine learning and robotic fabrication. Alan Kim's project is premised on the logic of fibrous assemblages — the creation of architectural tectonics from the bundling, weaving and matting of lines. These fibres, generated through an agent-based logic of local interactions, swarm over a highly volatile surface that emerges from a differential growth algorithm. The growth algorithm creates spatial topology, while the agent-based process generates the fibrous articulation. Alan frames the project within the context of Wire Arc Additive Manufacturing (WAAM), which enables the fabrication of highly intricate steel lattice structures — a process that is being developed within the lab.

MAJOR PROJECT S2 2021 HO KYEONG 'ALAN' KIM -CHUNK_4_INTERIOR.PNG

Experimental applications of machine learning were the driver for Jitesh Sapra's project, involving the generation of intricate tectonic networks. This design research explored Wave Function Collapse algorithms and neural networks trained to effectively distribute micro-scale units of complex lattice networks. This innovative work enabled the creation of high-resolution geometry that responds to a detailed set of architectural requirements, such as structural efficiency and visual porosity. The project speculates on the application of emerging additive manufacturing processes, including gel suspension printing and robotic cement deposition.

Vicky Tong NING_showreel.jpg

Vicky Ning's project reconsiders the nature of architectural robotics. Drawing on the stigmergic logic of social insects, the project imagines an architecture in constant change. Each discrete component of the building is continuously rearranged by a swarm of aerial robots. This robotic choreography responds to a self-organising algorithmic process that interacts with the dynamic site context of a rapidly redeveloping part of Melbourne's Southbank.

Exploring the design implications of innovative fabrication techniques, and their capacity to enable the intricate geometry of generative processes, requires serious consideration of material behaviour and fabrication limitations at the micro scale. Designing at the scale of a chunk enables these understandings to be instrumentalised through the tectonics of the project. The intention is to develop research at the tectonic scale so as to speculate on larger scale architectural implications for form and spatial conditions. Consequently, the buildings represented in these projects are not the project. Instead, they are experiments in the larger scale instantiation of the core tectonic research of the projects, and their attendant chunks.

Complex City Research
by Professor Alisa Andrasek

The projects presented below explore high-density/low-coverage architecture for growing planetary challenges, highly adaptive to the environment and its inhabitants. Deploying the 'complex city' workflow — based on generative algorithms and machine learning methods — the featured projects each focus on a particular context and design approach. Both explore timber prefabrication as a mode of construction, following what Stuart Kaufman entitled 'complexity for free', which embodies the principle of minimum input and maximum output. Both also use the design process of AI combinatorics, where the differentiation of spaces emerges through a combination of dimensional data mapping and varying connections between building blocks. Novel aesthetics, at the intersection of human and machinic pattern recognition, is also a feature of both projects.

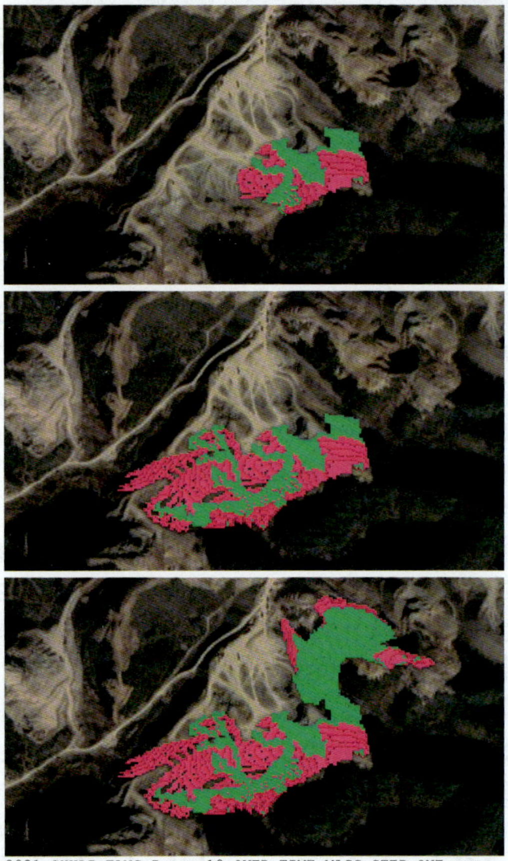

2021 SHUAI TANG Image 10_OVER TIME MASS STEP ONE.png
2021 SHUAI TANG Image 11_OVER TIME MASS STEP TWO.png
2021 SHUAI TANG Image 12_OVER TIME MASS STEP THREE.png

Shuai Tang's project *Co-Living with Nature* (2021) uses AI-based combinatorics to generate creative tectonic variations of prefabricated timber structures and novel programmatic clustering at the intersection of the sharing economy and the cultural memory of a traditional Chinese village.

The site is located in Lishui, Zhejiang, China, on an abandoned fluorite mine site. The project proposes the regeneration of the degraded landscape, and the introduction of a high-density co-living/co-working community immersed in nature, with the majority of the site utilised for smart agriculture and energy farming. The morphology and tectonics of Lishui were studied in order to recreate the rich community interactions of the traditional local village, incorporating site-adaptive terracing and inner courtyards to function as social spaces. Traditional gardening on terraces is carried over and intensified through the introduction of high-density smart farming.

Machine learning was used to analyse data and map different programmatic distribution areas at a macro and micro level. High-resolution analysis and spatial patterning were then introduced, with K-means clustering synthesising various data into composite units. Resultant clustering guides the distribution of programmatic elements, human and non-human zones, solar exposure and the distribution and disposition of windows. Steeper slopes are populated with habitats for humans, maximising views and terracing for gardening, circulation and recreation. Flatter slopes are developed for various forms of indoor and outdoor smart agriculture, green energy solar farms and site remediation through the introduction of green biomass blending with the surrounding forest. Various chunks of space are further articulated with developed floorplans and renders.

The building elements and resultant tectonics are explored in low and high resolution. Those in low resolution assume the typical scale of CLT elements found in current construction methods, with the addition of simple curvatures, and are deployed for various combinations of living units.

The high-resolution elements, typically 10–20 times higher resolution than the average walls and floors of prefab construction, are designed with angular facets and geometries to recall fluorite crystal site memory. This 'crystal language' — higher resolution tectonics — is applied in larger social spaces.

Co-Living with Nature operates at various orders of scale, through complex adaptive tectonic patterns and textures, and a vision of the future for this particular site. It can also be taken as a prototype for similar developments worldwide.

Xu Tang's project *Eroded* (2021) looks at low-quality/high-density living in parts of Shenzhen, China, in which cramped living conditions, lack of privacy, poor air quality and a paucity of green space and other amenities lead to various health and social problems. The chosen site is hilly, with a lake and surrounded by lush forest. The design proposes an alternative form of high-density development, with high-quality architecture geared towards a community of co-living and co-working residents. Intensive integration with nature is a key feature, interlacing green biomass and pathways for wildlife with high-density residential fabric.

Machine learning was used to analyse the terrain, with a multi-agent system (MAS) deployed to generate site-specific data for architectural massing. A high level of porosity is introduced to the site, with networks of passages for humans and wildlife, and courtyards inspired by vernacular housing and traditional village typology. The clustering and circulation system is derived through K-means machine learning, subdividing overall massing into micro-communities with a high level of connectivity.

The project engages timber prefab construction. By introducing AI combinatorics for the discrete building blocks, the result is an increased quality and diversity of architectural spaces. Architectural expression and multiplication of forest and lake vistas are increased by the introduction of particular angles into the morphology of building blocks (270-degree views).

2021 Xu Tang Drawing 01_Eroded Rendering.png

The concept of co-living has been extended to elements of nature, such as interlacing native plant species and residential fabrics through green roofs and wildlife canyons/pathways. Emerging social dynamics are addressed with adaptable patterns for different regions of the site, and the re-combinatorial fabric of an architecture responsive to the needs of the dynamic community. Resultant rich spatial diversity is further manifested through the section, with rippling architectural fabric from the topographical base of the site and data sculpting from various inputs negotiating views, privacy, connectivity, spatial clustering, the interlacing of interior and exterior conditions and green biomass. The overall high-resolution texture is visually nested into particular site features, forming an aesthetic synergy with the rich natural features of the site.

architecture in its place
by Simone Koch

Architects have traditionally been trained to see place in its Cartesian form, with features and levels and property boundaries, but we know that there is so much more for us to see. Physically, there is the hue that changes through the day and the year. There are the shapes of nearby forms (trees, buildings, hills) well beyond the site, which hold the horizon and perhaps define the clearing. There is the vegetation, native or invasive, and the fauna that return to their favourite spots or just pass by. There is birdsong, urgent and bright in the early morning and dwindling at the height of the day. There is the morning mist, the clouds, the rain. There is geology with its ancient patterns, and water flowing through and past. There is a history to every place, often unseen but sometimes registered in patterns of use or remnant artefacts, perhaps cruel and violent, as complex as it is long. This is true of place. Our encounter is just a moment in this history.

MAJOR PROJECT 19S1 MATTHEW LOCHERT_DRAWING_13 - STR A (E).PNG

MAJOR PROJECT 19S1 MATTHEW LOCHERT_ DRAWING_10_ELEVATION 03.PDF

Every project has policies and pressures that act like clothing: sometimes awkward and constrained, sometimes loose and liberating. We should aim to see these forces, to look beyond the brief to the shape of the community and the impact of this future incursion.

If we see all of this, we understand that each place holds an idea. Our quest is to understand the idea and the architecture that already exists in a place. The thing about these ideas, this architecture, is that while they exist as things, their

MAJOR PROJECT 19S1 Matthew Lochert_Drawing_A1 (Edited).png
MAJOR PROJECT 19S1 Matthew Lochert_Drawing_A2 (E).png

interpretation is very subjective, and this is what particularly interests me. Each of us interprets these ideas through our unique lens. This interpretation process enables us to reflect on our particular way of seeing, which in turn informs our particular way of creating a project. Once we have interpreted or translated the idea, it becomes embedded in our work. The underlying intent of this approach is to work from within place, to discover what is (in our eyes) immanent. When we look at the provision of public buildings through this particular framework, there is more likely to be a paucity

MAJOR PROJECT S2 2021 Ruby Lang Image 04_King William Street.jpg

of form but a wealth of connections that embed the project in its fabric. This method engages with the plethora of mechanisms that pre-exist, and by extension with the necessary enquiry of architecture. It recognises that we exist at a moment in time and that we are engaging with this moment to create a future history. This enables us to develop an attitude to architecture and the profession in which our work is posited as a possibility. It enables us to understand what architecture might also be.

This method is not new (it is founded in ancient philosophy, brought into sharp relief by Heidegger almost a century ago), but it has faded in our world of abstraction, where value is reduced to a commodity, buildings to form and façade. These ideas drift into and out of focus over time but now might serve to ground students and give them the tools to find potential in place.

In this context, a major project looks a lot less impressive than we imagine. Less so even than many of the magnificent works captured here. It, however, contains an idea about the profession that is quietly transformative. It is engaged not in the frenzy of marketing and imagery but in the wonder and horror of the very real world we

MAJOR PROJECT S2 2021 Ruby Lang Image 01_Napier Street.jpg

MAJOR PROJECT S2 2019 Harry Bardoel Image 17_P6_external view - P3-P4-P6 intersection + front-yard roof.tif
MAJOR PROJECT S2 2019 Harry Bardoel Image 19_P6_external view - projection cores.tif

occupy. Each major project has the potential to have a conversation outside of the market we insist on maintaining, a conversation that will have a lasting impact on every community we work within. Each major project is accompanied by a thesis about the future of architecture, and is illustrative of this approach. It may interrogate a subject, such as working/closed communities, resistance to change, perhaps the fabric of the city and the idea it holds. It could look at a particular typology and imagine how the generic offering may better register an idea of the events of its occupation. The project is subversive and challenging, yet purposefully polite in its packaging. It seeks something more than your passing attention: an encounter, not a fright. The thesis cannot be contained in an image but the image, the poster, might hold the key to an understanding of the idea behind it.

The three major projects I have supervised here are as unique as each student is to the other, but each contains an idea about the city and about architecture that might inform the future of the practice. Matthew Lochert seeks a public architecture that might contain the poetry of the streets of Melbourne. Ruby Lang has created a manifesto about capital and society and the potential for architecture to find a connection between a community and the nuance of its place. Harry Bardoel acknowledges the weight of existing circumstance in his powerful compilation of projects, replacing the grand gesture with direct and idiosyncratic installations. These projects meet urban form with an idea: of place, of the profession.

nor every thesis, should be examined
by Dr Peter Brew

As it is with rivers before they flow into the sea, towards the end of the Master of Architecture program there is a zone where the stream meanders and the direction of flow becomes indiscernible. The final task requires students to submit a *work made by them* for examination. The subject of the work, its format and the circumstances under which it is produced are, for the most part, left to the judgment of each student. The acceptance or not of the work, however, falls to the university through their proxy: the examiners, a jury of faculty and professional adjuncts. What is assessed is 'architecture' — the student's judgment of it and the willingness[1] of the examiners to admit to that.

It is possible to read part one of Aristotle's *Topics* as proposing a concept of the subject as a mode of inquiry rather than the transmission of knowledge. The format of this subject asks for a demonstration but does not preclude the possibility of there being a thesis. Occurring at the end of the course is a near equanimity, which allows for an all too rare but much needed argument between the past, present and future of the discipline.

> Now reasoning is an argument in which, certain things being laid down, something other than these necessarily comes about through them.
>
> (a) It is a 'demonstration', when the premisses from which the reasoning starts are true and primary, or are such that our knowledge of them has originally come through premisses which are primary and true:
>
> (b) reasoning, on the other hand, is 'dialectical',
>
> Not every problem, nor every thesis, should be examined, but only one which might puzzle one of those who need argument, not punishment or perception.
>
> — Excerpts from Aristotle's *Topics,* part 11
>
> The subjects should not border too closely upon the sphere of demonstration, nor yet be too far removed from it: for the former cases admit of no doubt, while the latter involve difficulties too great for the art of the trainer.
>
> — Excerpt from Aristotle's *Topics*, part 11

Aristotle suggests that a thesis resembles *a demonstration without being one and produces something other than what had been intended*. It is possible to imagine a thesis not as the accurate reproduction of a subject, but the subject as it has been affected. This is different from a demonstration. A demonstration is in essence a truth procedure while a thesis is supposition with respect to that, as a judgment needs to be made to determine if the effect which comes about is for the good of the subject and therefore admissible to it.

1 The distance from a demonstration = tolerance.

An example of a demonstration offered by Joseph Rykwert in his essay 'On The Oral Transmission of Architectural Theory' (1982) is that of a gothic pinnacle whose geometric construction was published in Matthäus Roricizer's *Die Geometria* (1486–1490). A stone is carved and presented to the masters of the guild by the apprentice as a demonstration — what is demonstrated is not the pinnacle, but rather the capacity of the apprentice to produce it (its production). This then is what is meant by the phrase 'something is done for the sake of it'. Here, the appearance of the thing is assumed; what is demonstrated is its coming into being, which is a mode of production.

The demonstration, then, is what is currently accepted as being known. A thesis, however, is a *supposition or speculation* about what is known. The matter of a thesis might be about the mode or the object's production; we can identify this as being the architectural thing (a mode of production) or the thing produced (the form of a description). The distinction between a thesis and a demonstration lies in the concept of the subject. In a demonstration the subject is fixed, it is known from the outset and must be unaffected by the demonstration — the subject could be a law or a protected process. The aim of the thesis, however, is to affect the subject, presuming that the subject is a thing that is capable of being affected. Elizabeth Grosz imagines this with respect to architecture in her essay 'The Thing': 'The thing is the transmutation, the conversion of two into one: the conversion of the previous thing, plus the energy invested in the process of its production as a different thing, a unity or a one.'[2] Architecture has a life of its own with the capacity to be affected, and if it is changing it demands that we are reimagining our relationship with it.

For a thesis to be judged as admissible to the subject it has to be accepted as being architecture. There must be a reckoning by the assessors as to the affect of what has been supposed, that which Aristotle refers to as 'something other than these necessarily comes about through them.' This presents itself to the assessors as a *puzzle* in the form of *not* architecture (not what an architect would do and/or not how it would be done by an architect) and so requires an *argument*, a dialectical process involving the university and the profession to admit the work into the subject of 'architecture'. Conversely, a (major) project that takes the form of a demonstration is simply required to demonstrate what it is that architects currently do. This exemplifies the notion of 'mastery' (as in Master of Architecture) as something that is not necessarily new or revolutionary but a keen grasp of the subject as it stands.

Aristotle's readers are familiar with the status of this puzzle: what is not, what is also, unintended things, talent and accidents. These are codes for things that are interesting, the knowledge that something is or could be outside of our understanding. For Aristotle, enquiry and doubt are the provocation to the subject; the subject is a mode of enquiry.

2 Elizabeth Grosz, 'The Thing' in *Architecture from the Outside: Essays on Virtual and Real Space* (Cambridge: MIT Press, 2001), 170.

> **For an accidental expression is an effect, an expression without a definition we can in this light sympathise with Plato's classification of sophistry as dealing with that which is not.**
> **— Excerpt from Aristotle's *Metaphysics***

Given the circumstances then, it is possible to look at the *works* submitted for acceptance as being a construction whereby a supposition (enquiry) is made about a demonstration (production) requiring a determination in a way that it is acceptable to a mode of production (the architectural profession) and a mode of enquiry (the university). At the final stage of the course, the student is given the opportunity to define the subject, and it is the willingness of those who hold eminence to admit it.

The Catalogue of Things You Care About
by Vicky Lam

Many students begin their major projects by producing a dense catalogue of all the things they care about. They meticulously document observations that they hope will lead to provocative questions and new design techniques, which can in turn form their own architectural vision.

Tidus Shing, Sushma Prabhu and Kimberly Pakshong's major projects occupy vastly different sites, programs and scales. But what they care about most are expressions of cultural identity in their cities, and moments where language and notions of place and belonging are contested. Their chosen contexts are all sites within which competing identities are in constant tension. Tidus' civic archive is a homage to Hong Kong's disappearing cultural heritage. Sushma's proposal reimagines a dreary corner of Melbourne's CBD through the lens of the migrant shift worker and her more colourful memories of Mumbai. Kimberly's proposal codifies appropriations of the Asian Australian suburban dream in Springvale for use in both the suburban house and mixed-use urban development.

For such preoccupations, the catalogue is not just a research tool. It is also an urgent cultural project to preserve difference and offer a translation. This research document becomes a handbook for seeing alternative versions of who we are.

Tidus Lok Tin Shing, *Library of Importance*[1]

Tidus began his project with a fictitious archaeological office in Hong Kong. Created to identify urban phenomena and cultural artefacts that have been dismantled over time, it would produce a new version of Hong Kong's 1976 Antiquities and Monuments Ordinance. This imagined office became the blueprint for his architectural proposal: a building that would sit on the slopes of Mount Victoria, solid and mute like one of the lost boundary stones that defined the older city. The interior of the building is densely packed with coded images of an erased city: the green and beige of the Star Ferry Clock Tower, the atmospheric courtyards of 1960s housing projects, multi-lingual street signage and the illuminated silhouette of Lion Rock. The visitor navigates the building via an intertwining series of spaces designed for civic participation. Reading rooms, galleries, plazas and gardens are named after places that have been erased or reappropriated. Cherished symbols and urban fragments of Hong Kong merge, distort and unfold through the architecture. There's a story behind every tile pattern, seating design, handrail and light fitting.

To define Hong Kong's culture is like the impossible task of translating Hong Kong films into English. Spoken Cantonese has so much slang that it is virtually untranslatable, and the language evolves as quickly as the city itself. Tidus' *Library of Importance* is an act of preservation, designed to document a culture defined by competing narratives of colonialism, globalisation and ethnic identity. The project echoes Kon Wajiro's documentation of a fast-changing Tokyo in the 1920s, mapping everyday life through drawings, charts and diagrams recording what people wore and

1 *Tidus Lok Tin Shing, Library of Importance*, Semester 02, 2019. Supervisor: Vicky Lam. See *Semester 02, 2019 RMIT Architecture Major Project* online catalogue, www.issuu.com/rmitarchitecture.

how people lived as testimony to a changing urban fabric. Capturing the disappearance and transformation of a culture, Tidus' project is an architectural transcript of a dense heritage archive.

Sushma Prabhu, *With Melbourne Subtitles*[2]

Sushma's ambition for her project was less about disappearance and more about dual identities. She begins *With Melbourne Subtitles* with a catalogue of two ideas of dislocation and reappropriation:

(a) the blue Jacaranda tree, common in Australian suburbs, is a foreign species often mistaken for a native
(b) the tantalising myth that the design of Flinders Street Station was originally intended for Mumbai's Chhatrapati Shivaji Terminus, due to a mix up in the architect's office in 1899

What follows is a compendium of Melbourne's urban artefacts and myths translated through the lens of a migrant who scans the city for moments of familiarity. Melbourne, from the perspective of the migrant who is paid by the hour, is a city of hidden opportunities and resources, left over spaces, side gigs and overtime accessed through shared languages and dialects. You just need to find your people. Sushma reappropriates an underbridge thoroughfare at the edge of the CBD as refuge for the dark kitchen worker or food delivery worker who, in a moment of respite, can recall fragmented images of home, transplanted into their new city. This project appropriates the city to create new but strangely familiar urban images, like watching a foreign film with subtitles occasionally mistranslated.

2020 MAJOR PROJECT SUSHMA PRABHU_VIEW FROM STREET
2020 MAJOR PROJECT SUSHMA PRABHU_VIEW FROM WATERFRONT

2 Sushma Prabhu, *With Melbourne Subtitles*, Semester 01, 2020. Supervisor: Vicky Lam. See *Semester 01, 2020 RMIT Architecture Major Project* online catalogue, www.issuu.com/rmitarchitecture.

Kimberly Pakshong, *Subtle Asian Traits: A Suburban Handbook*[3]
Kimberly's project examines the 'Australian Dream' from the perspective of the Asian migrant buying their first home in the suburbs. What would it look like if an Asian family moved next door to Kath and Kim?[4] There would be a sea of shoes by the front door, karaoke parties, all kinds of cooking going on in the garage and squid drying on the Hills Hoist. There would be a large family, including the ancestors who live by the altars that glow red with burning incense and fresh fruit. These stereotypical images derive from what is reality for new migrants, as they seek maximum economic opportunity and the comfort of collective ritual.

Kimberly's handbook maps out how Asian migrants adapt their homes and subvert the packaged aspirations of domestic suburban life. She asserts that for the Asian migrant, the house needs to be both productive and provide a sense of belonging. Privacy and quiet leisure take second place.

2020 MAJOR PROJECT KIMBERLY PAKSHONG_HILLS HOIST 01.JPG

This handbook of strategies and manoeuvres for the house is then scaled up, with a proposal to extend medium density mixed-use development in Springvale's ethnic Asian hub. The adaptations of the migrant suburban house take on a life of their own, where the spaces in between public parking and private lobbies acquire an ambiguous sense of domesticity and purpose. Images of the hyper functional Asian home inform the collective spaces of bus stops, lobbies and mini malls, and present a façade that mimics an altered version of the sun-blocking security shutter. This is an architecture inspired by a new migrant's way of seeing — one of economy, expediency and hope.

3 Kimberley Pakshong, *Subtle Asian Traits: A Suburban Handbook*, Semester 02, 2020. Supervisor: Vicky Lam. See *Semester 02, 2020 RMIT Architecture Major Project* online catalogue, www.issuu.com/rmitarchitecture.
4 Kath and Kim is an Australian television comedy that follows the day-to-day lives of a mother and her adult daughter living in a fictional suburb of Melbourne. The show screened for four seasons between 2002-2005.

The Handbook

Tidus, Sushma and Kimberly's projects all begin with a catalogue of observations identifying the cultural values and differences that exist on the edge of our collective consciousness. The catalogue becomes a handbook of strategies for making these complex identities visible within our cities. Sometimes, the built proposals for Major Project lose their relevance and lustre over time. But I hope that these handbooks and catalogues become something useful and meaningful in their professional lives.

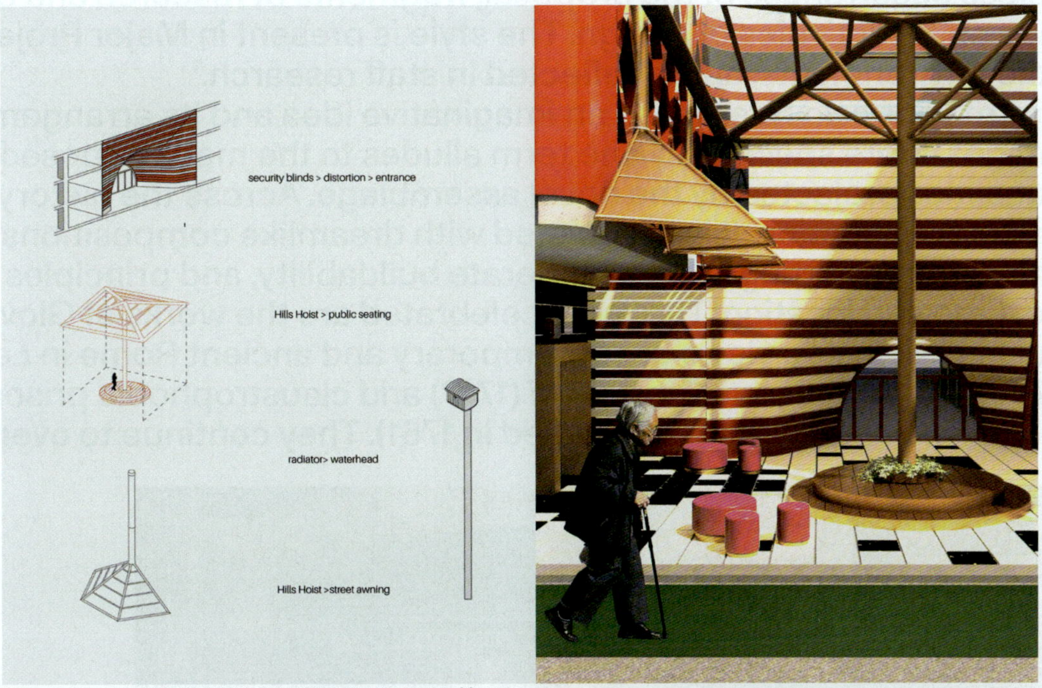

2020 MAJOR PROJECT KIMBERLY PAKSHONG_HILLS HOIST 02.JPG

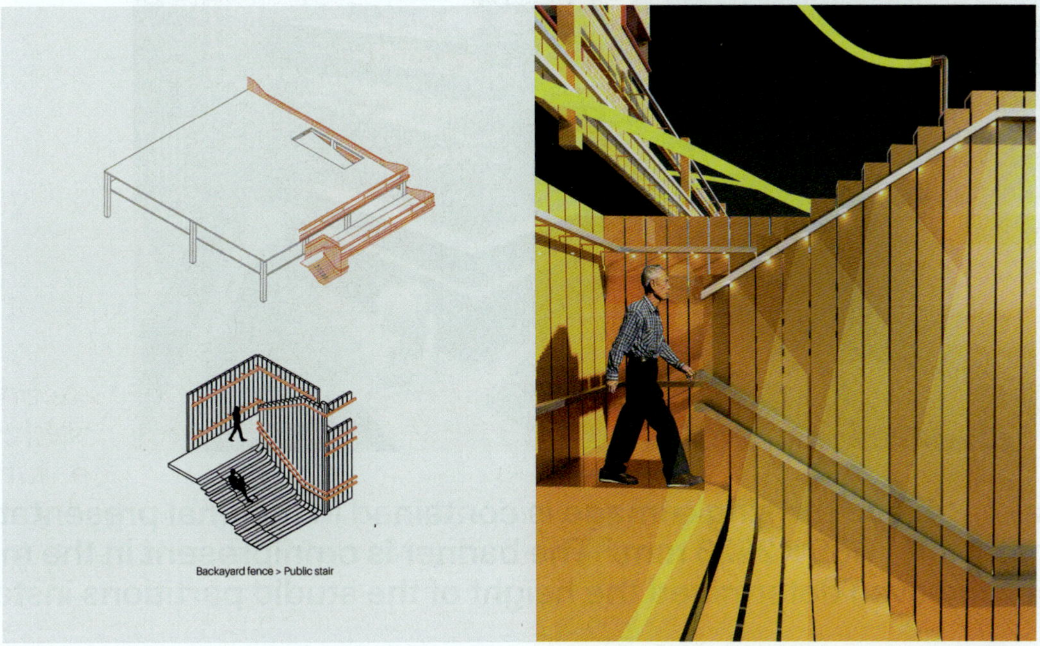

2020 MAJOR PROJECT KIMBERLY PAKSHONG_PUBLIC STAIR.JPG

The Climactic Image by Dr Michael Spooner

At RMIT Architecture, a style of architectural representation has emerged that has become characterised as a 'capriccio'. In this context, the term refers to a project's conclusion in a single image that stresses the whole project and contributes to an appreciation of the original creation (Major Project panels discussed in this essay can be found on pages 8 to 23.). This takes the form of a compelling scenography that collects tireless occurrences of the proposal, fragments of research and development, and evidence of the activities of design. The style is present in Major Project and the design studio environments, and is reflected in staff research.[1]

The term capriccio references an imaginative idea and its arrangement in words or images. More specifically, the term alludes to the menace posed by the unfamiliar qualities projected by the novel assemblage. Across the history of architectural representation, it is associated with dreamlike compositions, images of architectural or urban settings that exaggerate buildability, and principles of perspective, time and location. The most celebrated are the works of Giovanni Battista Piranesi and his fabricated views of contemporary and ancient Rome in *Le Antichità Romane* (1756), the ambiguous *Grotteschi* (1747) and claustrophobic prison etchings *Le Carceri d'Invenzione* (1750 and reworked in 1761). They continue to overwhelm.

MAJOR PROJECT S2 2019 Leon Koutoulas_Full Panel.pdf

In Major Project, the single image is contained in the final presentation banner with the dimensions 1189 × 2523 mm.[2] The banner is omnipresent in the mental space of the school and even determined the height of the studio partitions installed in the

1 See the images illustrating my essay '46 Little Latrobe Street: the office of Edmond and Corrigan,' *RMIT Design Archive Journal*, vol. 10, no. 1 (2020): 6-29, www.issuu.com/rmitdesignarchives/docs/rda_journal_22_10.1_issuu.

2 The constant of three A0 panels was introduced as an equitable presentation area, in the manner of a competition submission, when fierce competition for wall space threatened to become unruly among students *and* staff. This early print-sized limit courted few experiments, but notable exemptions included Paul van Herk's agitprop banner (2014), Joshua Morrin's tableaux vivant (2011) and Dayne Trower's collection of beautiful models in lieu of two-dimensional representations (2011).

Design Hub. Students have gone so far as to situate the content of their project in a banner image that reflects the interior of the Design Hub, where they are installed for the presentation. Leon Koutoulas (2019) presented his imposing reworking of the Sean Godsell designed building in a shallow space masquerading as the lift foyer, and Jack Murray (2021) risked an aerial presentation of their operatic tribute to Godsell and Duchamp in the corner of one of the long rooms. The speculation of each project is subsequently framed by the very real prospect of the present; the walls a counterpart to the implied depth, which plots forward the discourse of architecture.

MAJOR PROJECT S1 2018 Laura Bailey_Full Panel.pdf

The banner format is adaptable, and several styles of inventive composition have emerged alongside the capriccio and are worth mentioning to account for the challenge of representing a major project.[3] The first is the careful collage of drawings, text and visualisations that realise a layout complimentary to the project, such as presented by Nicola Cortese (2019), Alexandra Kemp (2020) and Hannah Zhu (2021). The second is a single image enlarged to fill the dimensions of the panel, such as with Julius Egan (2018) and David Thomas (2019), or the cunning banner by Eilidh Ross (2020) that promoted the title to the role of visual protagonist. A third compiles a banner that mirrors other communication platforms: Louis Nuccitelli (2018) imitated Instagram and Nicole Kirby (2019) displayed newspapers. A fourth makes some invisible part of the project visible through an underlying pattern that pervades the organisation of images and diagrams. These include comparative or partial grid patterns, such as those by Matthew Lochert (2019) and Jennifer Chen (2022); and choreographic scores such as the urban codex by Bradley Mitchell (2017) and the staccato glimmers of Mietta Mullaly (2021). Emma Li (2019) mirrors their project's conceptual axis of reflection and duality in the banner layout, but also introduces an image celebrating the research scattered across the proposed bar. This points us to

3 While the capriccio has become common it does not represent most banner outcomes.

the projects in which our eye is left to wander back through the fourth wall and into strange spaces of exhibition and artifice.

In the context of the school, the term capriccio has become somewhat unmoored from the specific fantastical characteristics that define it, and instead acknowledges a climactic image that is a stage for a medley of observations of the project. Various compositions recall Piranesi's etchings *Scenographia Campi Martii* (1762) and *Catalogo delle opere date finora alla luce* (1761), but draw inspiration from, and blend the respective principals of, title pages and frontispieces of architectural treatises, trompe-l'oeil, Dutch paintings of picturesque interiors, John Soane's Wunderkammer house interior and venerations of Saint Jerome in his study.

The stuffed environment of the banner was, in part, prompted when the architecture program limited the examinable material to what was on the banner — and students took this to heart.[4] Digital modelling and rendering programs and ever-expanding computer capacity offer students infinite space to hold infinite content. They can manipulate and render multiple perspectives and scales concurrently and imagine a platform that juxtaposes known or proposed objects and architectures, all within a fragment of themselves. The images realised from these environments manifest a seductive virtuosity, provide an inexhaustible source of discovery and stir in the viewer their own imagination.

Reflecting on this oeuvre of representation was an occasion to string banners along a spectrum of technique and effect, to suggest an index that could alight on some of their privileged qualities, and to source some pleasure in their confounding and astonishing propositions.

Altar

A shallow shelf is provided on which is placed a medley of fascinating things in front of a vertical plane that is perpendicular or oblique to the viewer. It reflects the material and formal quality of the proposal and provides a surface to locate drawings and visuals. In some instances, the foreground offers a depth that is more confessional; in others, a window may be placed in the vertical plane to reveal a devotional image of the project.[5] Laura Bailey (2018) locates a table with artefacts in a space crowded with the towers of her project, while a convex mirror threatens to reflect the viewer. They are sensible images, in that while dabbling in the poetic artifice of depth and decorative vocabulary they do not disturb the orthodox representations whose authority is contingent on their immediate impression.

4 Banners discussed here are original but early impressions lurk in the past. Peter Brew and Annie McIntrye's RMIT Architecture Major Project, completed in 1990, positioned scaled down Modernist office towers as lift cores, providing a mirror of the wider urban-sized office building proposal. Lance van Manaan's tower project completed in the 2013 ARM Master of Architecture design studio *Tower Wars* was visualised as a model in a hypothetical exhibition. But it was Simon Robinson's major project, supervised by Simone Koch and Peter Brew and completed in semester 1, 2016, that left the door ajar for current explorations by using interlaced representations of the proposal that receded into an implied space within the banner.

5 Karl Friedrich Schinkel would propose something similar for the Neu Schauspielhaus (1821) opening night curtain, which would surprise the audience by offering an image looking back onto the exterior of the theatre in which they had gathered. See plate 97 in *Sammlung architektonischer Entwuerfe* (1866).

Studiolo

Generally, there is a substantial depth that allows for the introduction of movement; a procession from foreground to background entertaining the shifting rapport between artefacts, and multiple or simultaneous exchanges with the elaborate picture box they are contained within. Despite some orthodoxy, it is the skein of relations that enhances and transforms the experience of the final image. In this regard Emily Davies' (2017) banner is peerless.

MAJOR PROJECT S2 2017 Emily Davies_Full Panel.pdf

Doll House

David Veidt (2020) organises the banner as an architectural section through multiple floor plates. Each level contains configurations of drawings, renders, furniture and models, while also communicating the architectural qualities of the proposal including the rooms that run perpendicular to the viewing plane. The image, with its roaming scale, is extremely strange and collapses qualities alluded to in the single image, altar and studiolo models. The total effect momentarily suspends their differences and charts a path to a pseudo-cabinet. Henry Russell (2017) produces a similar effect, but through the oblique.

Anachronic

These banners playfully cross exteriors and interiors, posit time or occupation, and allow artefacts to invade multiple layers of receding space or make use of them as *spoila* to initiate an affecting intensity. They construct depth, but the effort produces a space that is grounded in the architectural proposal. Chris Buchhorn (2019) includes in the foreground a suggestion of their time spent majoring, in the form of a busy workspace containing models and drawings that have wandered into the front yard of his project's suburban future. Michael Strack (2018) offers an

MAJOR PROJECT S1 2021 Chris Buchhorn_Full Panel.pdf

arresting conclusion in a brooding allegorical tableau framed by a handful of architectural elements but unified by a persistent perspective that pulls the project to the horizon. Yuchen Gao (2022) realised a *tabula scalata,* a banner that uses a corrugated surface to present the stages of the project's development from different perspectives, the left and the right, and which reproduces their animated video constructed as a looping *mise en abyme.*

Porta Coeli

Laura Szyman (2019) deliberately flouts the expression of a single continuous spatial recession for a pictorial formulation. The top is realised as a picture box that holds a representation of the project while the main frame presents a theatrical perspective, layering visions of the interim crits complete with shadow cast by Laura caught mid-presentation. The frame allows us to observe the project with some remoteness and the content inscribed on it introduces an unusual ecclesiastical hierarchy, reinforced by the iconographic artefacts within the foreground. A similar composition is accomplished by Senesios Frangos (2019) and Darcie Vella (2021).

Many banners exhibit an allegiance to multiple types, and there are many innovations that will have escaped my eye. More recent conversations have declared the Major Project capriccio *passé,* and that due to its ubiquity any essential value is no longer recognisable.[6] But looking upon the legacy of examples there is formidable complexity in the stories being told and exhilarating spatial conclusions that parallel the ambitions of the projects. They have contributed to the discourse of architectural image making — and the extent to which the representations and their implied spatial properties could impact the design of a future project remains relatively unthought. Students should continue to wonder.

6 This consensus was reached by the graduates at the first graduate-led Major Discourse panel convened by Mietta Mullaly and Liam Oxlade with Vivian Mitsogianni and held at the RMIT Media Portal, 13 October 2022.

Major Discourse
by Mietta Mullaly and Liam Oxlade

Major Discourse was convened by Mietta Mullaly and Liam Oxlade with Vivian Mitsogianni and took place over two wet nights in late October 2022, under threat of flood warning. The format of each evening included a series of presentations followed by a moderated discussion, excerpts of which are included here.

Prompted by the question 'What matters?', the panels of 2019–2022 RMIT Master of Architecture graduates led broad ranging discussions. The question invited participants to describe the content of their projects (in subject matter or material outcome), searching for larger themes and shared interests. The ambition was that these common threads or trends would suggest something about the time and place in which the projects occurred. As part of the conversation, panellists were asked to speculate on the origins and relevance of these trends as a way of unpacking the larger, collective project.

Topics ranged from the ubiquitous mechanism to the value of medium — from a mode of intervening in the suburbs to the effort of avoiding a built outcome altogether. There was a collective feeling that this journey back into our major projects presented some of the same missteps as our initial efforts. But there was also a prevailing optimism around the therapeutic results of this endless search for the 'big idea'. Benevolent qualities were identified in the act of caring, of engaging flatly with the world — in the value of an agile proposition, or that which sucks up everything around it.

The conversations revealed a number of strange affinities between like ideas and shared pursuits. And in the process of unpacking these harmonies, there was a sense that we moved slightly closer to better understanding where it all comes from.

Thursday 13 October 2022

Presentations were made by Chris Buchhorn, Nessie Frangos, Jack Murray, Liam Oxlade and Darcie Vella, who all participated in the post-presentation discussion facilitated by Mietta Mullaly.

More than a visual encounter

Mietta Mullaly

I'm interested to know, in your opinion, how much of architecture is a visual encounter? Or are the tools used to formulate the speculative project being unbuilt, and therefore experienced through other means?

Darcie Vella

Since finishing Major Project, I've often thought that the strength of a speculative project is in the small things and not the big architectural outcome. At the time, I perhaps naïvely thought of property, boundaries and titles as intangible things architects have control over, but in practice that's not true. In my project, the small interventions are the most interesting because it's these things, which are not always seen as architecture, that allow us to have an influence.

Mietta Mullaly
I suppose the public realm is where those smaller interventions reach the widest audience.

Liam Oxlade
The confrontation with the things that can't be said, the things that exist without a way of describing them, is inevitable in Major Project. The sooner you lean into this and try to organise these unstable forces you can start to secure a bit of agency.

More ideas and ambition, less refinement

Mietta Mullaly
In Major Project there is a focus on architecture that is about ideas and ambition rather than refinement. Can you define where this occurs in your own work?

Chris Buchhorn
A considerable challenge of Major Project, shared by all students, is addressing the anxiety around finding the big idea that can sustain you across a 14-week semester. I realised that to pursue the questions I was interested in, I didn't need to begin with a resolved idea. I could form an idea from the many answers revealed over the course of doing the project.

My ambition for the project was for the suburbs. What potential could be extracted from this context that could then be returned to address its issues? The project began with an examination of the property boundary line and its role in conceiving the suburbs, but rather than proposing an alternative to the status quo, the project developed a way to assess, interpret and design using a formal language revealed by the exaggerated role of the boundary.

The process of doing the project

Mietta Mullaly
A trend at RMIT Architecture is to depict projects as under construction, or to reflect their stages of being made. What is our collective fascination with the process of doing the project over the outcome?

Jack Murray
Representing construction shows the project as an endeavour that can be accessed, modified and changed by 'real world' architecture. But there is a sense that the end of construction is a brilliant end point. Many decisions are made on site: things change and get edited in a sort of improvisational way during construction. It isn't a linear progression; it brings other people in and invites collaborators. Construction sites as these possible worlds is where this idea of the projectile, a semantic jumping off point for the project, comes from — something is cast forward. And I think representing the project in-progress maintains the sense that it is being cast forward. Representing architecture in this way challenges the idea that a project is complete, and that nobody else can say anything further about it.

Chris Buchhorn
This way, the project still lingers; the creative energy doesn't move away just because you have finished your major project. I think Major Project encourages that thinking, because it asks us to be engaged in something we care about doing.

Theatre and film

Mietta Mullaly
Jack spoke earlier about the relationship between architecture and theatre, which seems to be a territory that Liam is also exploring in his project, with its focus on using moving image and sound to construct environments. Can you discuss how they might be a different understanding of relationships?

Liam Oxlade
Both are very different mediums; one is very old and the other relatively new. For me, theatre has more of a relationship to building in the sense that it is something acted or performed. Like a piece of music, you play it, you play it again, and it is slightly different every time. Maybe there is an opportunity here to think about a type of architecture involving a set of drawings that you build from more than once; you build 25 times on the same site. The relationship to film is much more closed — which is why I enjoy it.

Jack Murray
Going to the movies or the theatre is a ritualistic experience. We all sit quietly in a room to experience an event together. Then we leave and don't really talk about it with the other people that were there. I

think there is something potent about those sorts of experiences. Everyone takes something very different from that same event.

Liam Oxlade
We also encounter so many moving images that are not special — like ads on Instagram or those horrible Telstra phone boxes with enormous advertising screens. These things have an impact on you, and you can't escape them.

Method

Mietta Mullaly
Jack, your major project considered 'method as a project'. Can you explain this emphasis in your project?

Jack Murray
The etymology of method is travelling a path. And methodology is a way of understanding; it is the *way* that you operate. My project was propelled by lumping many ideas on top of each other and knotting them together in an entirely inaccessible way — the method allowed a density of information that allowed me to talk in different ways about it. Every time I present this project, I come to it from different angles or come to something within it from a different angle, and that's where I see method.

Friday 14 October 2022
Presentations were made by Alan Kim, Mietta Mullaly, Tidus Shing, Laura Szyman and Jacqueline Tang, who all participated in the post-presentation discussion facilitated by Liam Oxlade.

Mechanism

Liam Oxlade
Included in all the projects presented this evening is a notion of a machine or mechanism. How do each of you see this idea in your project?

Alan Kim
My project uses computational design methods, so the machine is a simple rule set that produces something unexpected or new.

Tidus Shing
My project is about how architects reference cultural material and how they apply it to the city. So, it's not about how one person or an individual building works. The project provides a mechanism or a

way for people to interpret and apply different languages; it also allows for everyone to have a slightly different take on this process.

Jacqueline Tang
Major Project was a practice run for things I'm really interested in. The strategies that we develop adapt to practice, and there are so many mechanisms in every project. My major project explored the idea of staging in architecture, and I now find it easy to navigate these requirements in practice because of this research and training during Major Project.

Critical, political and culturally engaged

Vivian Mitsogianni
The Peter Corrigan Medal celebrates the most critical, political and culturally engaged project, one that has a strong independent vision. Tidus, your project was awarded this prize in 2019. Can you talk a little bit more about Hong Kong at that time? And the context of your project?

Tidus Shing
Hong Kong is in a unique situation — it is changing so quickly that a lot of the things we value are disappearing. During my major project, I had a strong feeling of urgency and care, a strong need to do something at that moment, to create a kind of archive of things that are part of the city. It was quite an emotional project. When I read back through my speech, at the end I say, 'The city will be able to survive,' and every time I read this phrase, I cry.

When a collective is trying to conserve something important, we need a method that continually develops so that it doesn't disappear in the future. My podcast is a continuation of this project, and it is where I collect the views of the people who have remained in Hong Kong. I'll continue to do this work because it is a kind of resistance that is still possible; it is a way for architects to apply language to the city, to create a document that is not easy to erase.

Collective

Jack Murray
There is an assumption that Major Project is a very individual endeavour, even isolating given the prior years of studio environments. Why are these ideas of the collective important to the projects?

Laura Szyman

The more people you can push yourself against, the stronger your major project becomes. The strength of Major Project is that it's hard to subvert because it enables such diversity; it allows collective dreaming. It is almost impossible to view your major project as independent because, in principle and practice, the course enables diversity — by which I mean, it allows a collective to dream.

Tidus Shing

As a collective, these projects reflect what we should do. We can formulate a way or a plan to make things possible, and that's the beauty of this idea of collective dreaming.

Mietta Mullaly

Yeah, I would agree. I think it's about the effect being greater if there's more of us. But I also think that some of the influence on my project had to do with the professionalism of it, and the fact that we're often seen as a collective or represented as a group. We become responsible for what everybody's doing, not just for our own endeavours.

STUDENT Caleb Ka Lok Lee and Flynn Eady-Jennings
PROJECT Collision and Collusion
SUPERVISOR Dean Boothroyd, Mark Jacques and Liam Oxlade
YEAR 2022

2022 Caleb Ka Lok Lee and Flynn Eady-Jennings, Collision and Collusion

2022 FLYNN EADY-JENNINGS CALEB LEE Shared Drawings 02_Systems Drawing.png

2022 FLYNN EADY-JENNINGS CALEB LEE Shared image 02_ED.png

The idea of the sole creator simply doesn't exist within the profession.

To acknowledge this is to recognise the value of different people in a way that isn't about competition, but instead understands how we can work together to achieve something greater than the sum of our individual parts. For too long we've neglected this, and we must wield the collective as a tool to tackle problems that may otherwise be of an insurmountable scale.

The Australian suburban fringe continues to fall captive to formulaic planning products that, under private hands, fail to prepare our cities for a sustainable future. Energy spent stopping growth, we think, could be better spent reimagining the suburbs as self-sustainable collectives on the frontier of the current climate emergency.

This project is about establishing a common framework for difference and discourse to occur within, and then leveraging this format to pursue an outcome for the new suburb of Riverdale.

STUDENT Caleb Ka Lok Lee
PROJECT Collision and Collusion
SUPERVISOR Dean Boothroyd and Mark Jacques
YEAR 2022

2022

Caleb Ka Lok Lee, Collision and Collusion

CL002.jpg

CC_CL.00_04_49_07.Still021.jpg

STUDENT Caleb Ka Lok Lee
PROJECT Collision and Collusion
SUPERVISOR Dean Boothroyd and Mark Jacques
YEAR 2022

2022 CALEB LEE Image 04_Office.png

CC_CL.00_08_54_21.Still046.jpg
CC_CL.00_09_18_12.Still048.jpg
CC_CL.00_09_30_13.Still049.jpg

2022 CALEB LEE Image 05_Hall.png
2022 CALEB LEE Image 08_Hall.png

STUDENT Flynn Eady-Jennings
PROJECT Collision and Collusion
SUPERVISOR Dean Boothroyd and Liam Oxlade
YEAR 2022

2022 Flynn Eady-Jennings, Collision and Collusion

2022 FLYNN EADY-JENNINGS Image 05_Basketball.png

2022 FLYNN EADY-JENNINGS Image 07_Information.png

STUDENT Flynn Eady-Jennings
PROJECT Collision and Collusion
SUPERVISOR Dean Boothroyd and Liam Oxlade
YEAR 2022

2022 FLYNN EADY-JENNINGS Sequential Image 01.jpg
2022 FLYNN EADY-JENNINGS Sequential Image 03.jpg
2022 FLYNN EADY-JENNINGS Sequential Image 04.jpg

2022 FLYNN EADY-JENNINGS Sequential Image 08.jpg
2022 FLYNN EADY-JENNINGS Sequential Image 09.jpg

2022 FLYNN EADY-JENNINGS Image 08_Wellbeing Garden.png

STUDENT Nicole Kirby
PROJECT Sliding Doors
SUPERVISOR Dean Boothroyd and Mark Jacques
YEAR 2019

2019 Nicole Kirby, Sliding Doors

2019 NICOLE KIRBY Image 01_Precinct Aerial.png

2019 NICOLE KIRBY Drawing 01_ The Master Plan.tif

This project is about charging the public and civic realm of the suburban edge. The intention is not to radicalise the developer's master plan, but rather to speculate on a moment in time where its identity and memory become specific to the site. This sliding door moment offers an opportunity to test a potential methodology for conditioning the edge.

Through an understanding of Aldo Rossi's urban artefacts, as referenced in *The Architecture of the City* (1966), I began to catalogue the urban typologies found in Ballarat. This resulted in a project that uses the canopy and verandah as new armature, framed against the developed landscape. The canopy type extends to the kerb, the road, street parking, road lines and street furniture, warping and manipulating them into new artefacts within the town centre. These new artefacts in turn charge the space between developer sheds, creating civic space that is generous and forges connections between everyday programs of the suburban. This project is an experiment in conditioning the edge of our cities and inserting a sense of memory and specificity into our suburbs.

STUDENT Nicole Kirby
PROJECT Sliding Doors
SUPERVISOR Dean Boothroyd and Mark Jacques
YEAR 2019

2019 NICOLE KIRBY Image 02_ The Arch.png
2019 NICOLE KIRBY Image 03_ The Arch Warped.png

STUDENT Nicole Kirby
PROJECT Sliding Doors
SUPERVISOR Dean Boothroyd and Mark Jacques
YEAR 2019

2019 NICOLE KIRBY Image 04_ The Main Strip.png
2019 NICOLE KIRBY Image 05_The Bus Stop.png
2019 NICOLE KIRBY Image 06_ The Light Post.png

STUDENT Nicole Kirby
PROJECT Sliding Doors
SUPERVISOR Dean Boothroyd and Mark Jacques
YEAR 2019

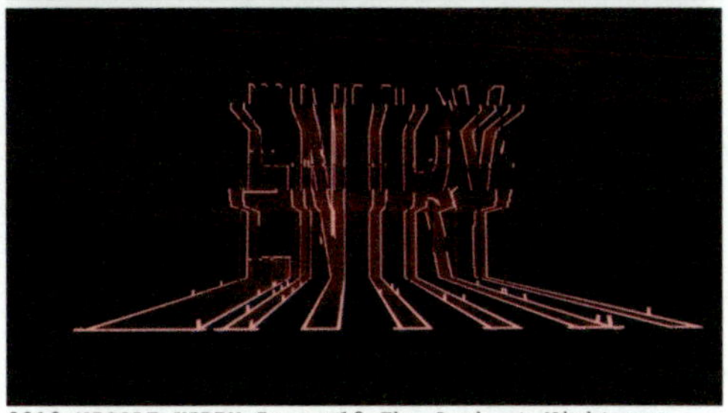

2019 NICOLE KIRBY Image 12_The Arch at Night.png
2019 NICOLE KIRBY Image 13_ The Carpark at Night.png

2019 NICOLE KIRBY Image 11_The Sporting Precinct.png
2019 NICOLE KIRBY Image 08_The Milk Bar.png

2019 NICOLE KIRBY Image 09_ The Post Office.png

STUDENT Riley Pelham-Thorman
PROJECT Who Cares
SUPERVISOR Emma Jackson
YEAR 2021

2021 Riley Pelham-Thorman, Who Cares

2021 RILEY PELHAM-THORMAN_ARRIVING AT ROSANNA BUS STOP.png

Who really cares about an individual suburb's development and infrastructure? It is evident from community Facebook pages, talkback radio and letters to the editor that local residents do, but their objections are always registered after the fact, when they can have no impact. What if development were to incorporate their feedback earlier in the design process?

Situated in the north-east of Melbourne, Rosanna is a case study for an alternative to the planning process, where community consultation is moved up the framework ladder closer to the early stages. If local people's memories, values and ideas are incorporated and made visible through balustrades, bricks, awnings, even bus stops, will they be more inclined to accept this new development proposal? Here, dog walking gossip, social media chats and talkback radio discussions take centre stage as a means of acknowledgement, and in an attempt to answer the question: Who Cares?

This project proposes an alternative framework for the development of the suburb of Rosanna, and explores uncomfortable conversations around how corporate stores are integrated into site. It walks the line between community discussions and endemic landscapes, flooding creeks and walking the dog, towards creating an architecture that attempts to acknowledge everyone invested in the outcome.

2021 RILEY PELHAM-THORMAN_ROSANNA THEATRE COMPANY LOADING BAY.png

2021 RILEY PELHAM-THORMAN_ROSANNA LIBRARY ENTRY.png

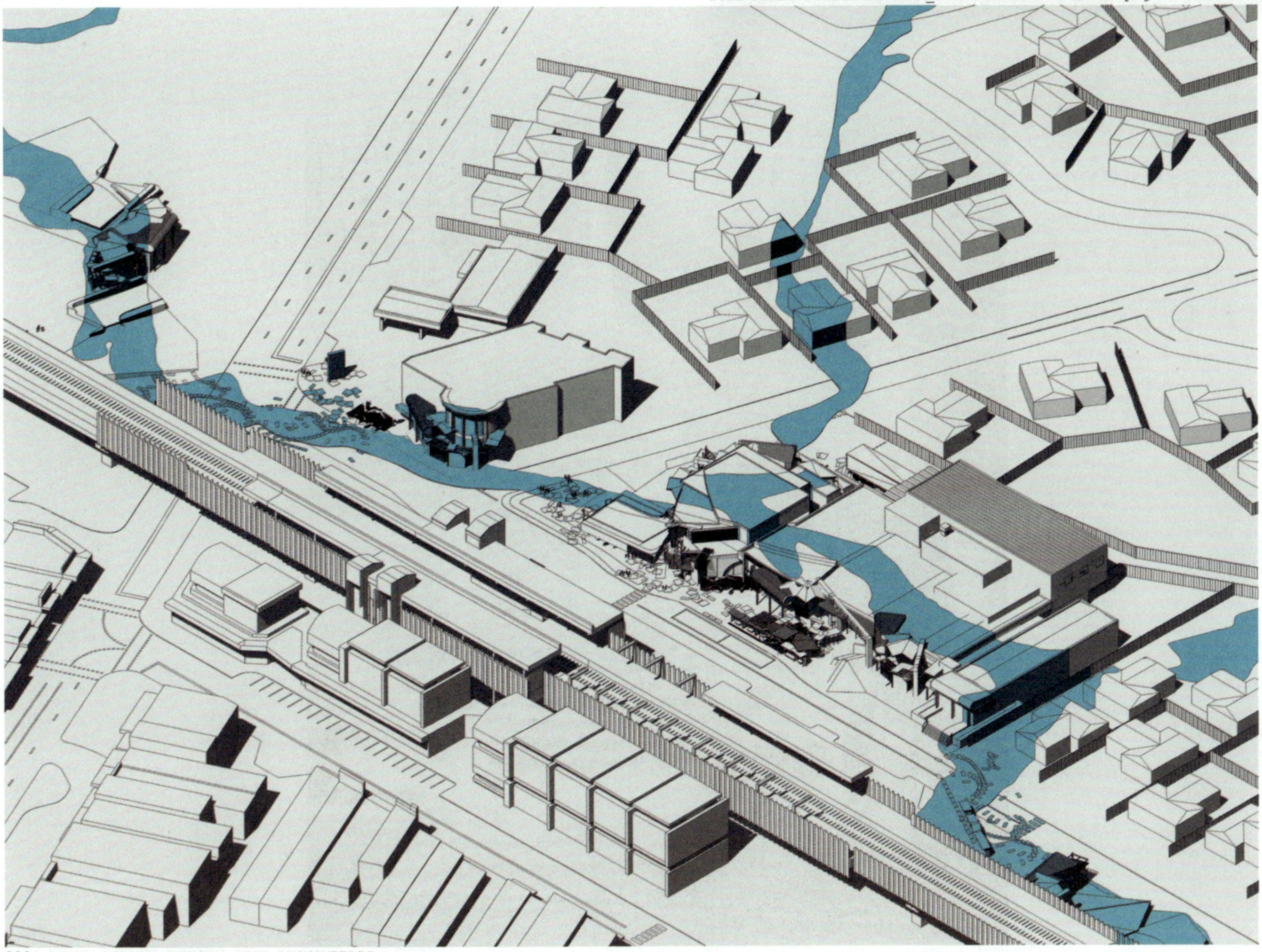

2021 RILEY PELHAM-THORMAN_SITE AXONOMETRIC.pngpng

STUDENT Riley Pelham-Thorman
PROJECT Who Cares
SUPERVISOR Emma Jackson
YEAR 2021

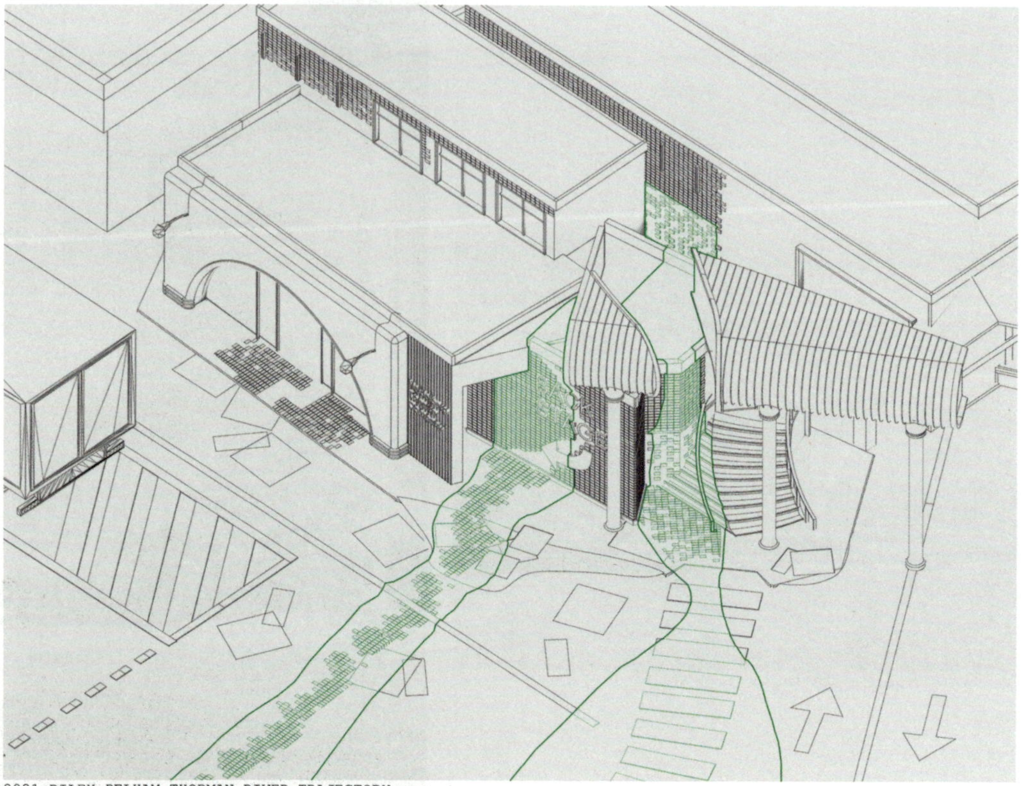

2021 RILEY PELHAM-THORMAN_RIVER TRAJECTORY.png

2021 RILEY PELHAM-THORMAN_ROSANNA THEATRE COMPANY ENTRY.png

STUDENT Riley Pelham-Thorman
PROJECT Who Cares
SUPERVISOR Emma Jackson
YEAR 2021

2021 RILEY PELHAM-THORMAN_ROSANNA LIBRARY.png

2021 RILEY PELHAM-THORMAN_TIE UP YOUR DOGS PARKING BAY.png

2020

Brooke Barker, Carnegie Local

2020 BROOKE BARKER_hero art.jpg

When boundaries are narrowed, the horizon becomes local. Welcome to Carnegie Local!

This project is a proposal to put Carnegie, a suburb of Melbourne, on the global map through an international expo operating under the theme of the local. The condition of the collective local arises when boundaries become narrowed; place is isolated and defined within its own physical or metaphysical borders.

Through this tightened lens, idiosyncrasies of the local are revealed: distinctive, peculiar characteristics that develop into hyperboles of self. This project understands this condition as a civic presence and uses the expo to exemplify and celebrate it.

Carnegie Local is an event in which a collection of pavilions is the architectural consequence of devouring the identity of Carnegie through the framework of the collective local. Here, the narrowing of boundaries reveals and celebrates idiosyncrasies and the condition of the local is globally shared. Overlaying the absurdity of my own experience of the local is a seal featuring as the suburb's mascot, projected onto the global stage through an offering of the world's whitest beaches and a full-scale Stonehenge.

STUDENT Brooke Barker
PROJECT Carnegie Local
SUPERVISOR Michael Spooner
YEAR 2020

2020 BROOKE BARKER_elevation bean.jpg

2020 BROOKE BARKER_arts int perspective02.jpg

STUDENT Brooke Barker
PROJECT Carnegie Local
SUPERVISOR Michael Spooner
YEAR 2020

2020 BROOKE BARKER_marketing expo light.jpg

2020 BROOKE BARKER_hero science.jpg

2020 BROOKE BARKER_ site AXO.jpg

STUDENT Brooke Barker
PROJECT Carnegie Local
SUPERVISOR Michael Spooner
YEAR 2020

2020 BROOKE BARKER_ext perspective art.jpg

2020 BROOKE BARKER_axo night.jpg

2020 BROOKE BARKER_Site plan.jpg

2021 Matthew Tibballs, Promise Ring

2021 MATTHEW TIBBALLS Proposed: Stage 2 of the Promise Ring: Placeholders.png

Prologue: the Doncaster rail — a century-long promise to build a trainline to the city centre, which never eventuated. Enter the suburban rail loop, a 'city-shaping' government project promising to connect the outer suburbs via a ring around the city.

This project lays down the red carpet for a centreless city, with the premise that the anticipation of a reality yet to come (if at all) is sufficient to get the ball rolling. A definitive civic centre is not put forward, but rather a methodology for the unravelling of new centres which rise triumphant from the backdraft of what will inevitably be another failed promise. Architecture is employed as a staging device, interfering in the 'meanwhile' with a combative approach to the long game. Three strategies are proposed to contribute to a growing, incremental space:

The Retrofit(s): a renegotiation of each future station's adjacencies through small-scale incisions within the existing suburban fabric, treating minor acts like tree planting and adaptive reuse as weak but necessary signals in the vortex of anticipation.

The Placeholder(s): a tentative taxonomy of ad-hoc armatures deployed as a land grab for the public realm. These are enabling works introduced under the pretence of temporary use but through duration and strategic placement become anchors, informal public spaces and sporadic monuments for growing suburbs.

The Build(s): a speculation into the content and 'rooms' to be provided for suburban civic life to thrive through the reinterpretation of the prior scenarios — a shell for an evolving centre over time.

What we do in the waiting room directs this project. It becomes a state of play where cumulative acts of premature gratification and predictive squatting offer substance to a defiantly impatient architecture, one that pre-empts disappointment by turning the suburbs inwards to celebrate their own centres in the nearby tomorrow and the distant after.

STUDENT Matthew Tibballs
PROJECT Promise Ring
SUPERVISOR Emma Jackson
YEAR 2021

2021 MATTHEW TIBBALLS Proposed: Stage 1 of the Promise Ring: Markings on the Road.jpg
2021 MATTHEW TIBBALLS Proposed: Stage 3 of the Promise Ring: A waiting room.jpg

STUDENT Matthew Tibballs
PROJECT Promise Ring
SUPERVISOR Emma Jackson
YEAR 2021

2021 MATTHEW TIBBALLS Proposed: Stage 2 of the Promise Ring: Placeholders.jpg
2021 MATTHEW TIBBALLS Proposed: Stage 3 of the Promise Ring: Waiting for Godot.jpg

STUDENT Matthew Tibballs
PROJECT Promise Ring
SUPERVISOR Emma Jackson
YEAR 2021

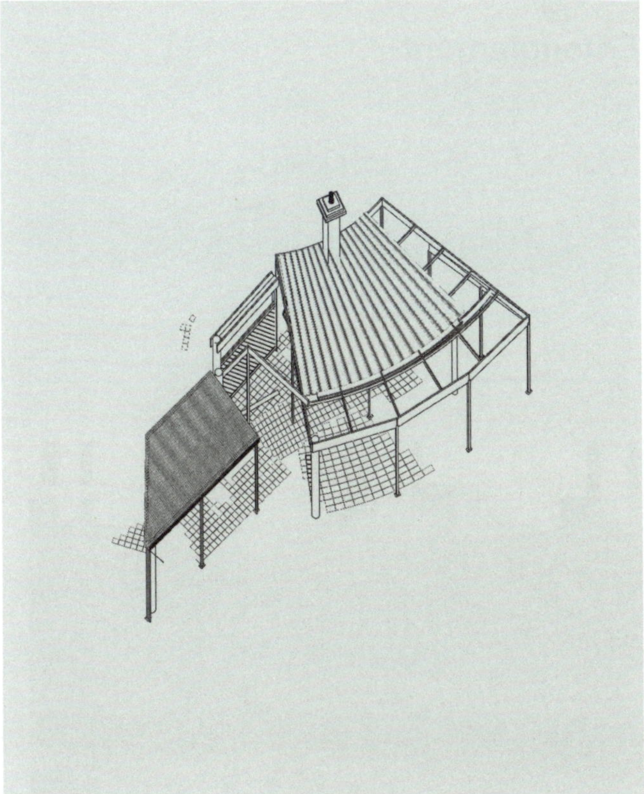

2021 MATTHEW TIBBALLS Proposed: Stage 2 of the Promise Ring: A taxonomy of Shelters .jpg

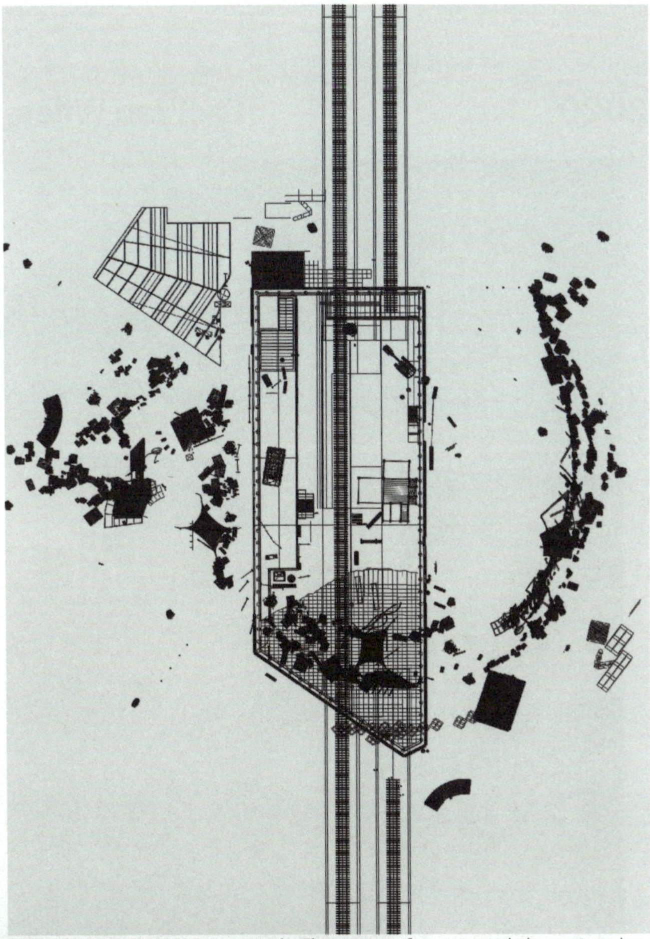

2021 MATTHEW TIBBALLS Proposed: The vortex for a new civic centre.jpg

2021 MATTHEW TIBBALLS Proposed: Stage 3 of the Promise Ring: The Building as a consequence.jpg

STUDENT Lachlan Wiles
PROJECT Fields of Entanglement
SUPERVISOR Mauro Baracco
YEAR 2020

2020 Lachlan Wiles, Fields of Entanglement

2020 LACHLAN WILES_UAV FACTORY 1.jpg

2020 LACHLAN WILES_UAV FACTORY 2.jpg

This project uses an industrial precinct in Altona North as a proxy for wider change, asking how we might place ourselves within a system of living things. Using unitary understandings, the project seeks to entangle culture, nature and technology. Dualistic ideologies, which posit human culture as separate from nature, have dominated Western thinking for hundreds of years. Our current cities and the way we inhabit the world are a direct and physical manifestation of these ideologies. Climate change and the destruction of the environment are the results of our dualistic cultural understanding.

This project aims to embed unitary understandings of nature, culture and technology into our cities. Through architecture, boundaries can be blurred and distinctions vanished, leaving only a complex series of relationships and adjacencies. In this way, we can shift our understanding of our place in the world to one that encompasses a wider territory.

STUDENT Lachlan Wiles
PROJECT Fields of Entanglement
SUPERVISOR Mauro Baracco
YEAR 2020

2020 LACHLAN WILES_NURSERY 3.jpg

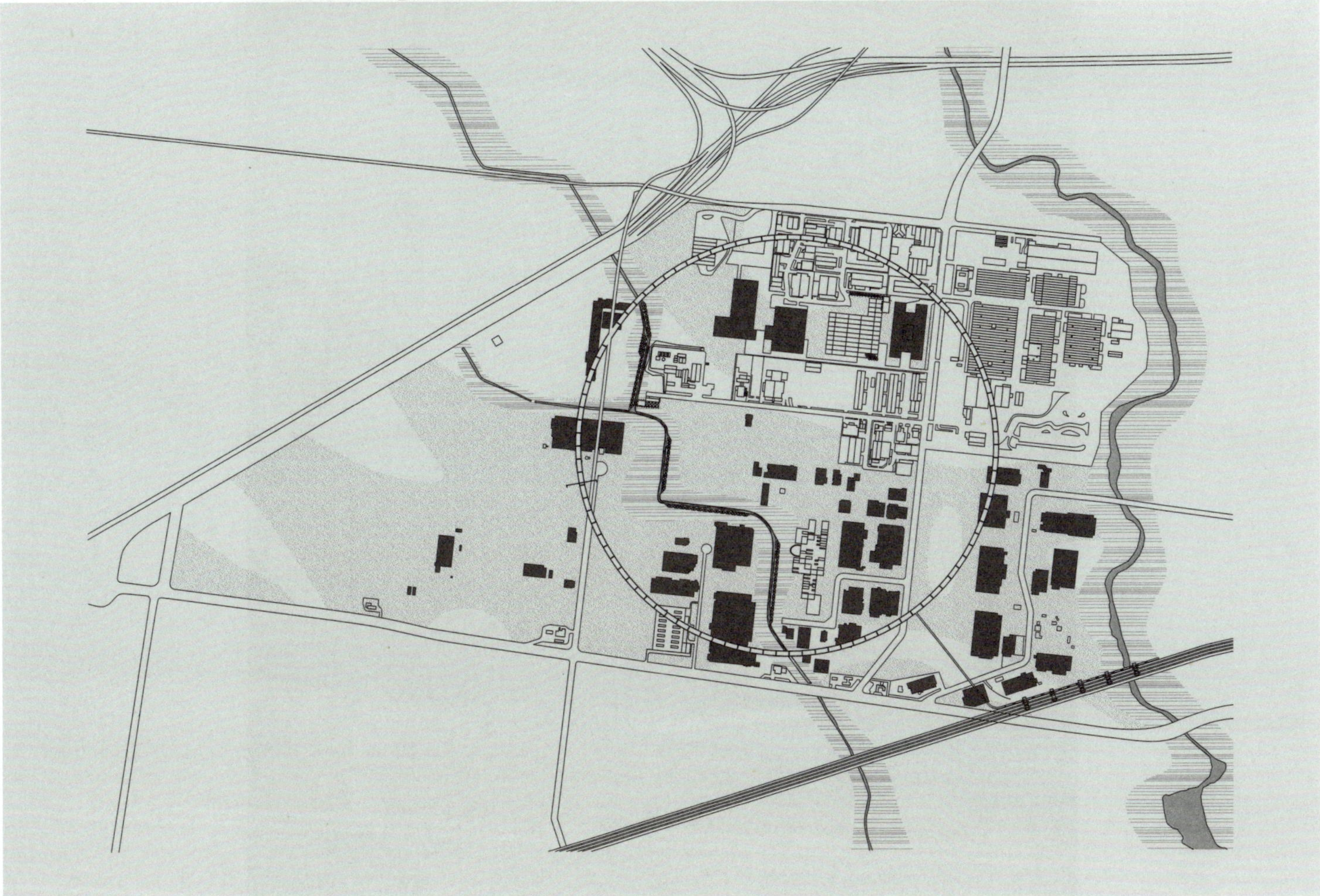

2020 LACHLAN WILES_SITE MASTER PLAN.pdf

STUDENT Lachlan Wiles
PROJECT Fields of Entanglement
SUPERVISOR Mauro Baracco
YEAR 2020

2020 LACHLAN WILES_INNOVATION HUB 3.jpg

2020 LACHLAN WILES_APIARY 3.jpg

STUDENT Lachlan Wiles
PROJECT Fields of Entanglement
SUPERVISOR Mauro Baracco
YEAR 2020

2020 LACHLAN WILES_APIARY 1.jpg

2020 LACHLAN WILES_NURSERY 1.jpg

2020 LACHLAN WILES_APIARY 2.jpg

2020 LACHLAN WILES_NURSERY 2.jpg

2020 LACHLAN WILES_INNOVATION HUB 1.jpg

STUDENT Liam Oxlade
PROJECT Puzzling Evidence
SUPERVISOR Dean Boothroyd and Mark Jacques
YEAR 2020

2020

Liam Oxlade, Puzzling Evidence

MAJOR PROJECT S2 2020 LIAM OXLADE CAPTURE (310).PNG
MAJOR PROJECT S2 2020 LIAM OXLADE CAPTURE (311).PNG

'The revolution in our attitude of mind to the reorganisation of our world calls for a change in our media of expression.'
— Hannes Meyer (1926)

One hundred years ago, the possibility of explosive transformation in the aesthetic spectrum was borne out of an optimism generated by the radical change that was occurring within the global social structure. In 2020, this possibility shares the hope of even a moderate shift towards a global society capable of recognising the frail relationship it has with the planet it exists upon.

An aesthetic regime we might look to as modern, or contemporary, in this way could be a set of devices employed by the politico-media complex. This project is about locating an architecture — and devices for its production — that can participate confidently in this complex. It then looks to how we might leverage this competency to pursue an outcome for the City of Greater Dandenong.

If our present condition generates an unbalanced, top-heavy social structure that displaces the undesirable by-products of the minority lifestyle, then the place where these things are displaced to are exactly where our efforts should be focused.

STUDENT Liam Oxlade
PROJECT Puzzling Evidence
SUPERVISOR Dean Boothroyd and Mark Jacques
YEAR 2020

♫ (The steady rattle of an old projector)

'The revolution in our attitude of mind to the reorganisation of our world calls for a change in our media of expression'—Hannes Meyer, 1926

00:00 - 01:15
INTRODUCTION
[Primary narrative read by Liam Oxlade]

… This project is about locating an architecture (and devices for its production) that can participate confidently in [the politico media complex]. It then explores how we might leverage this competency to pursue an outcome for the City of Greater Dandenong.

01:15 - 02:40
DANDENONG MECHANICS' INSTITUTE HALL SILENT FILM
♫ *Time, Forward!* by Georgy Sviridov
[Title cards describe one hundred years of history in Dandenong's civic centre]

… 1899: The Electric Age … Fire! … Scorched Possum … Collapse … 1901: Federation …

02:40 - 03:30
MECHANICS' INST. HALL TODAY
♫ (Ambient soundscape)
[Primary narrative cont., read by LO]

… Illywhacker—Peter Carey 1985 sits propped against a wall …

03:30 - 05:20
BP ISLAND SHORT FILM
♫ *Sugar Coated Fennel Seeds* by F.S. Blumm and Nils Frahm
[John Oxlade, interviewed by LO]

… JO: I made some inquiries, and it had been built before BP House—essentially so that the powers that be had a working model so that they were really comfortable with what was going to be constructed in Albert Road …

1/2 continues on next page.

MAJOR PROJECT S2 2020 LIAM OXLADE CAPTURE (320).PNG
MAJOR PROJECT S2 2020 LIAM OXLADE CAPTURE (319).PNG

MAJOR PROJECT S2 2020 LIAM OXLADE CAPTURE (313).PNG
MAJOR PROJECT S2 2020 LIAM OXLADE CAPTURE (312).PNG
MAJOR PROJECT S2 2020 LIAM OXLADE CAPTURE (314).PNG
MAJOR PROJECT S2 2020 LIAM OXLADE CAPTURE (315).PNG
MAJOR PROJECT S2 2020 LIAM OXLADE CAPTURE (316).PNG

STUDENT Liam Oxlade
PROJECT Puzzling Evidence
SUPERVISOR Dean Boothroyd and Mark Jacques
YEAR 2020

05:20 - 05:45
BOOK CLUB SHOW & TELL
[A stack of books on a table in a room above the Dandenong Mechanics' Inst. Hall, 2020]

05:40 - 06:20
'… ON THE STABLE, MEDIOCRE STATE OF *HAPPINESS*.'
[Reiner de Graaf, interviewed by the curatorial team from the CCA]

06:20 - 08:30
CITY PARTY 2022 CAMPAIGN VIDEO
♫ *Biospheric Quiet* by The Books
[Political ad & campaign pledge read by Emily Milledge]

… EM: it is capable of belonging to a larger whole – without a desire to supervise it …

08:00–12:05
DCB SITE WALK
♫ (Ambient soundscape)
[No narration]

… a carpark on an immense radius, an active leisure zone, an urban beach, a gross pollutant trap, a data centre, a solar array, a music venue, basalt Trimdek and the EastLink freeway …

♫ *Tim, Do I Like That Dog?* by Cate Le Bon w/ Tim Presley

12:05–12:30
E-TAG BRIDGING SEQUENCE
♫ Biospheric Quiet – The Books
[Primary narrative cont. read by LO]

… This is an architecture that encourages a kind of puzzling. It encourages you to try and figure these things out & then rewards you for doing so …

12:30–14:30
A LARGE PUBLIC ROOM ON A HIGH STREET
♫ (Ambient soundscape)
[Primary Narrative cont. read by LO]

Film – and a type of architecture – allow us to recognise the world as constructed. They can do this in a manner akin to the assembling of a stage set; – where a finite world is determined and the audience, and actors, push out in search of its edges.

Once we have located these edges, we can feel assured in pursuing an understanding of its contents and engaging in the play of its component parts.

An architecture capable of achieving this wouldn't necessarily need to invent a great deal but instead arrange known things in a way that encourages the audience to consider them apart – and together.

The delight of this meeting anew (or reframing of expectation) allows us to seek joy where it may have otherwise seen absence.

And if we can find joy in those things constructed for human betterment, we might be better placed to reduce our strain on those things that are separate to it.

14:30–15:00
CREDITS ROLL
♫ (The urgent rattle of a train leaving an elevated station)

MAJOR PROJECT S2 2020 LIAM OXLADE CAPTURE (209).PNG
MAJOR PROJECT S2 2020 LIAM OXLADE CAPTURE (210).PNG
MAJOR PROJECT S2 2020 LIAM OXLADE CAPTURE (211).PNG
MAJOR PROJECT S2 2020 LIAM OXLADE CAPTURE (212).PNG
MAJOR PROJECT S2 2020 LIAM OXLADE CAPTURE (215).PNG

STUDENT Liam Oxlade
PROJECT Puzzling Evidence
SUPERVISOR Dean Boothroyd and Mark Jacques
YEAR 2020

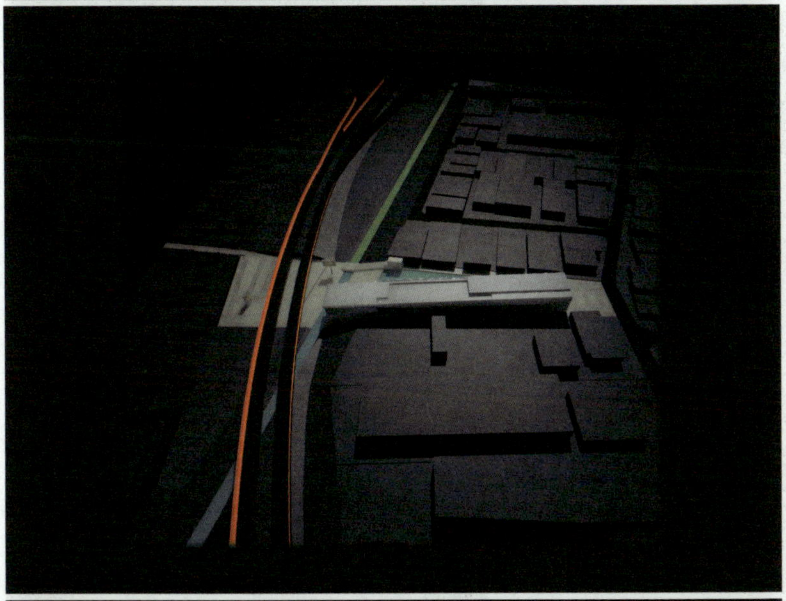

MAJOR PROJECT S2 2020 LIAM OXLADE CAPTURE (196).PNG
MAJOR PROJECT S2 2020 LIAM OXLADE CAPTURE (200).PNG
MAJOR PROJECT S2 2020 LIAM OXLADE CAPTURE (205).PNG

MAJOR PROJECT S2 2020 LIAM OXLADE CAPTURE (232).PNG
MAJOR PROJECT S2 2020 LIAM OXLADE CAPTURE (234).PNG
MAJOR PROJECT S2 2020 LIAM OXLADE CAPTURE (235).PNG
MAJOR PROJECT S2 2020 LIAM OXLADE CAPTURE (236).PNG
MAJOR PROJECT S2 2020 LIAM OXLADE CAPTURE (238).PNG

STUDENT Liam Oxlade
PROJECT Puzzling Evidence
SUPERVISOR Dean Boothroyd and Mark Jacques
YEAR 2020

MAJOR PROJECT S2 2020 LIAM OXLADE CAPTURE (43).PNG
MAJOR PROJECT S2 2020 LIAM OXLADE CAPTURE (51).PNG
MAJOR PROJECT S2 2020 LIAM OXLADE CAPTURE (65).PNG

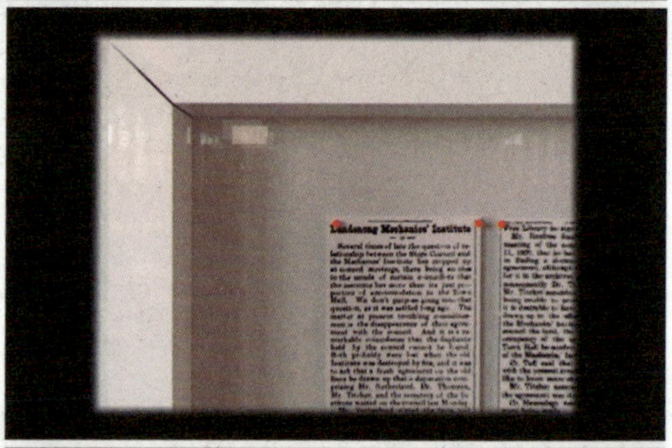

MAJOR PROJECT S2 2020 LIAM OXLADE CAPTURE (68).PNG
MAJOR PROJECT S2 2020 LIAM OXLADE CAPTURE (69).PNG
MAJOR PROJECT S2 2020 LIAM OXLADE CAPTURE (71).PNG
MAJOR PROJECT S2 2020 LIAM OXLADE CAPTURE (74).PNG
MAJOR PROJECT S2 2020 LIAM OXLADE CAPTURE (85).PNG

STUDENT Liam Oxlade
PROJECT Puzzling Evidence
SUPERVISOR Dean Boothroyd and Mark Jacques
YEAR 2020

MAJOR PROJECT S2 2020 LIAM OXLADE CAPTURE (105).PNG
MAJOR PROJECT S2 2020 LIAM OXLADE CAPTURE (108).PNG

MAJOR PROJECT S2 2020 LIAM OXLADE CAPTURE (120).PNG
MAJOR PROJECT S2 2020 LIAM OXLADE CAPTURE (122).PNG
MAJOR PROJECT S2 2020 LIAM OXLADE CAPTURE (123).PNG

MAJOR PROJECT S2 2020 LIAM OXLADE CAPTURE (87).PNG
MAJOR PROJECT S2 2020 LIAM OXLADE CAPTURE (88).PNG

2021

Youjia Huang, Sky Earth Ancestors

2021 YOUJIA HUANG_Scene 1: The Village.png
2021 YOUJIA HUANG_Scene 2: Village Street.png
2021 YOUJIA HUANG_Scene 3: Gateway Entrance.png

This project draws on my personal childhood memories of the Ancestor Worship Festival. Modernisation has left the ancestors we have worshipped, the gods we have prayed for, the rituals we have cherished, behind, accompanied by indifference.

The project speculates on how ancient rituals might mould and arouse the spiritual resonance of future populations. How might we develop an alternative understanding of Chinese rural villages, one that foregrounds ideas of folk ritual and traditional culture, in architecture?

The purpose of this project is neither to replicate historical structures nor to restore the ancient ancestral temple. Rather, it is designed to explore the idea of the village as half city and half folk ritual space, based in the values of the Chinese family and speculating on a new Chinese culture.

The project is not about defining a solution, but rather explores architectural, urban and cultural implications through the lens of an alternative world. Borrowing techniques from film and performance in order to animate scenarios, it tells stories as a way to offer us a diagnosis of the present moment. The project also communicates with people outside of architecture, transcending disciplinary boundaries and connecting to wider audiences.

STUDENT Youjia Huang
PROJECT Sky Earth Ancestors
SUPERVISOR Patrick Macasaet
YEAR 2021

2021 YOUJIA HUANG_Scene 4: Lin's Family Ancestral Hall Entrance and Second Floor Ancestor Hall Bridge Entrance1.png
2021 YOUJIA HUANG_Scene 4: Lin's Family Ancestral Hall Entrance and Second Floor Ancestor Hall Bridge Entrance2.png

STUDENT Youjia Huang
PROJECT Sky Earth Ancestors
SUPERVISOR Patrick Macasaet
YEAR 2021

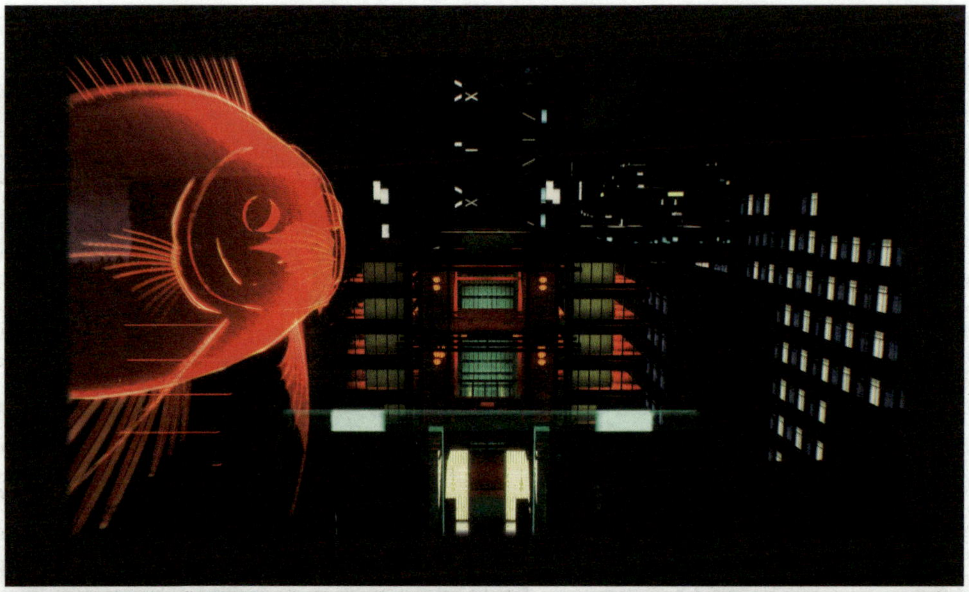

2021 YOUJIA HUANG_Scene 9: View Toward The Family Tablet Hall From Second Floor Bridge Entrance1.png
2021 YOUJIA HUANG_Scene 9: View Toward The Family Tablet Hall From Second Floor Bridge Entrance2.png
2021 YOUJIA HUANG_Scene 9: View Toward The Family Tablet Hall From Second Floor Bridge Entrance3.png

STUDENT Youjia Huang
PROJECT Sky Earth Ancestors
SUPERVISOR Patrick Macasaet
YEAR 2021

2021 YOUJIA HUANG_Scene 12 The Tablet Hall1.png
2021 YOUJIA HUANG_Scene 12 The Tablet Hall2.png
2021 YOUJIA HUANG_Scene 12 The Tablet Hall3.png

2021 YOUJIA HUANG_Lin's Village 2019 Lunar Calendar Page of 27th of July, The Day of Entertaining the Deities with Opera Plays.tif

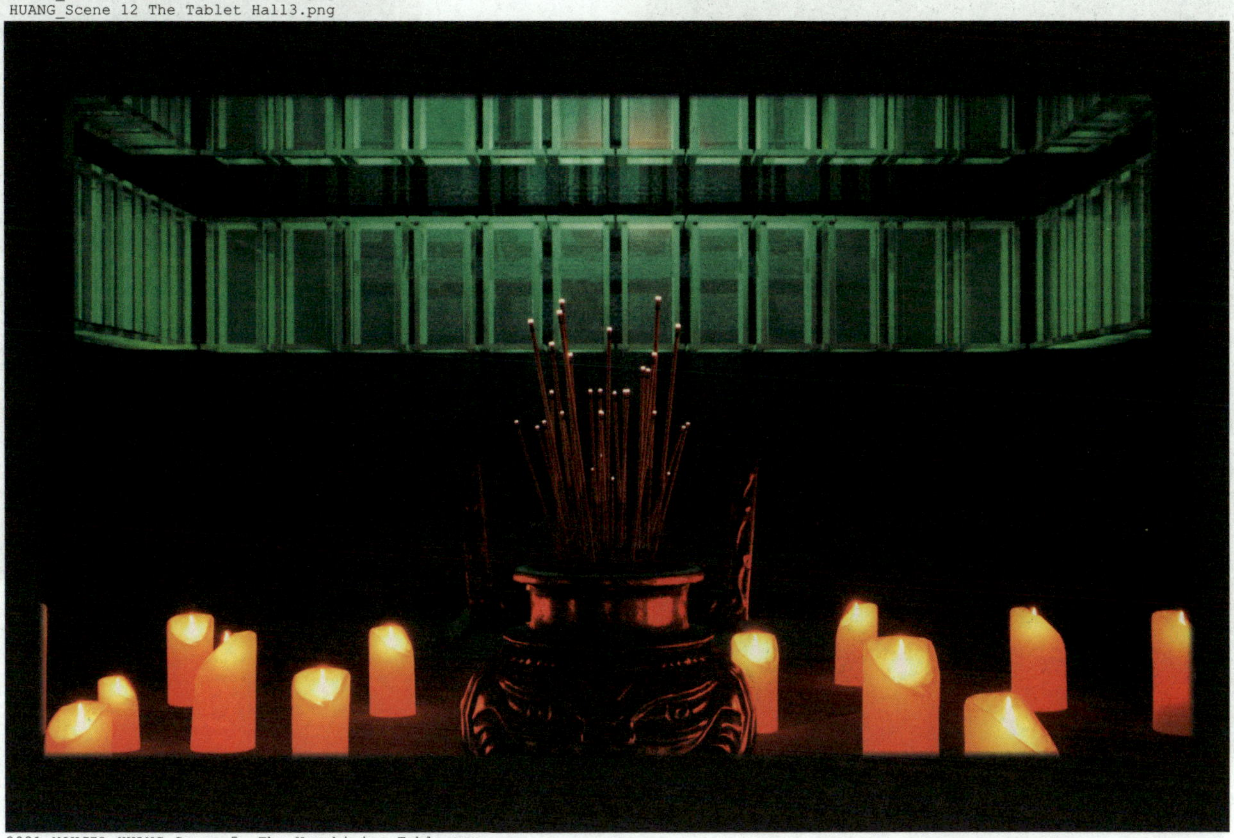

2021 YOUJIA HUANG_Scene 5: The Worshiping Table.png

STUDENT Youjia Huang
PROJECT Sky Earth Ancestors
SUPERVISOR Patrick Macasaet
YEAR 2021

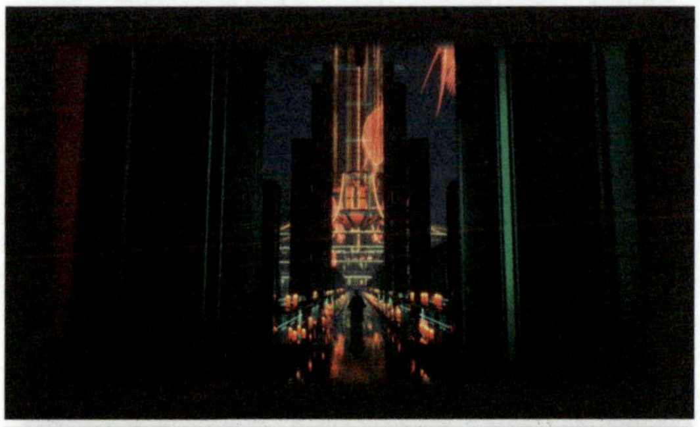

2021 YOUJIA HUANG_Scene 20: View toward the Old Temple from the Village Opera Stage from Ground Level, Mid-Level and the New High Stage1.png
2021 YOUJIA HUANG_Scene 20: View toward the Old Temple from the Village Opera Stage from Ground Level, Mid-Level and the New High Stage2.png
2021 YOUJIA HUANG_Scene 20: View toward the Old Temple from the Village Opera Stage from Ground Level, Mid-Level and the New High Stage3.png

2021 YOUJIA HUANG_Scene 20: View from the Connecting Bridge between Ancestral Hall toward the Gateway Tower Entrance1.png
2021 YOUJIA HUANG_Scene 20: View from the Connecting Bridge between Ancestral Hall toward the Gateway Tower Entrance2.png
2021 YOUJIA HUANG_Scene 20: View from the Connecting Bridge between Ancestral Hall toward the Gateway Tower Entrance3.png
2021 YOUJIA HUANG_Scene 20: View from the Connecting Bridge between Ancestral Hall toward the Gateway Tower Entrance4.png
2021 YOUJIA HUANG_Scene 5: Game Path to the Gateway Tower.png

STUDENT Youjia Huang
PROJECT Sky Earth Ancestors
SUPERVISOR Patrick Macasaet
YEAR 2021

2021 YOUJIA HUANG_Scene 5: The Gateway Tower and Village Entrance1.png
2021 YOUJIA HUANG_Scene 5: The Gateway Tower and Village Entrance2.png

STUDENT Wang Jingyuan
PROJECT Mending Guanlan Old Town
SUPERVISOR Helen Duong and Tim Pyke
YEAR 2020

2020 Wang Jingyuan, Mending Guanlan Old Town

MAJOR PROJECT S2 2020 Jingyuan Wang Image11_night banquet01.png

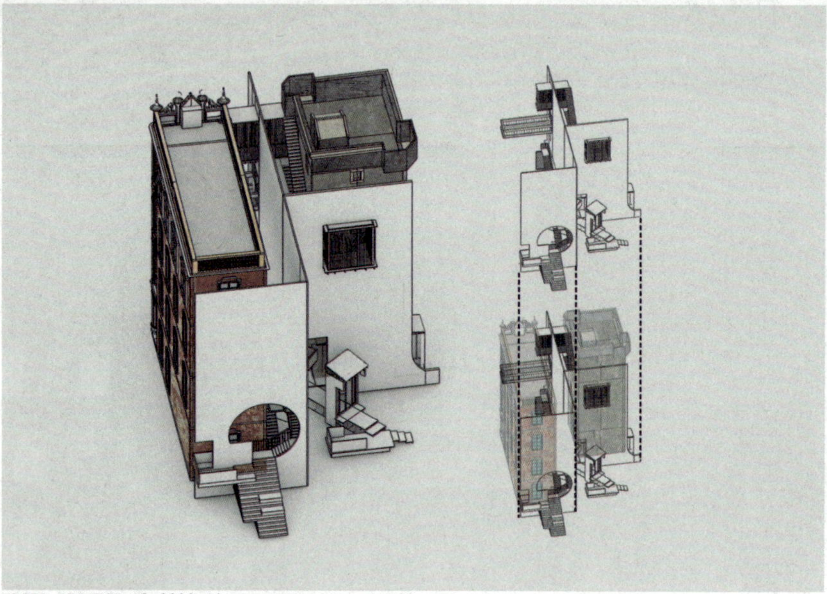

MAJOR PROJECT S2 2020 Jingyuan Wang Drawing02.png

China's aggressive development has swallowed up tens of thousands of historic sites. This demolition has made Shenzhen — where development has not only replaced individual towns, but also a complete spatial history — a city without history.

Working with the remaining heritage buildings of Shenzhen requires more than simply restoring the physical fabric of the city. 'Mending an old man', an idea taken from Chinese medicinal practice, is used as a metaphor for repairing, rebuilding and bringing meaning back to the heritage site of Guanlan Old Town. The old street, traditional shophouses and a Western-style hotel have been redefined through the use of Chinese cultural references, such as traditional landscape paintings, movies, opera and fiction. These interventions create a cinematographic journey through the old town and bring rich expression to the structures within it. This project can be summarised as: 'Repair is a kind of poetry. This is the story of mending.'

STUDENT Wang Jingyuan
PROJECT Mending Guanlan Old Town
SUPERVISOR Helen Duong and Tim Pyke
YEAR 2020

MAJOR PROJECT S2 2020 Jingyuan Wang Image12_night banquet02.png

MAJOR PROJECT S2 2020 Jingyuan Wang Image13_night banquet03.png

STUDENT Wang Jingyuan
PROJECT Mending Guanlan Old Town
SUPERVISOR Helen Duong and Tim Pyke
YEAR 2020

MAJOR PROJECT S2 2020 Jingyuan Wang Image20_Room in cave01.png

MAJOR PROJECT S2 2020 Jingyuan Wang Image21_Room in cave02.png

STUDENT Wang Jingyuan
PROJECT Mending Guanlan Old Town
SUPERVISOR Helen Duong and Tim Pyke
YEAR 2020

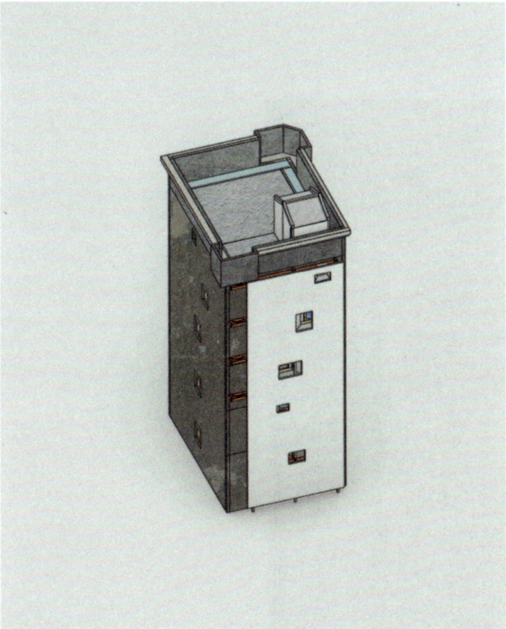

MAJOR PROJECT S2 2020 Jingyuan Wang Drawing07(1).png

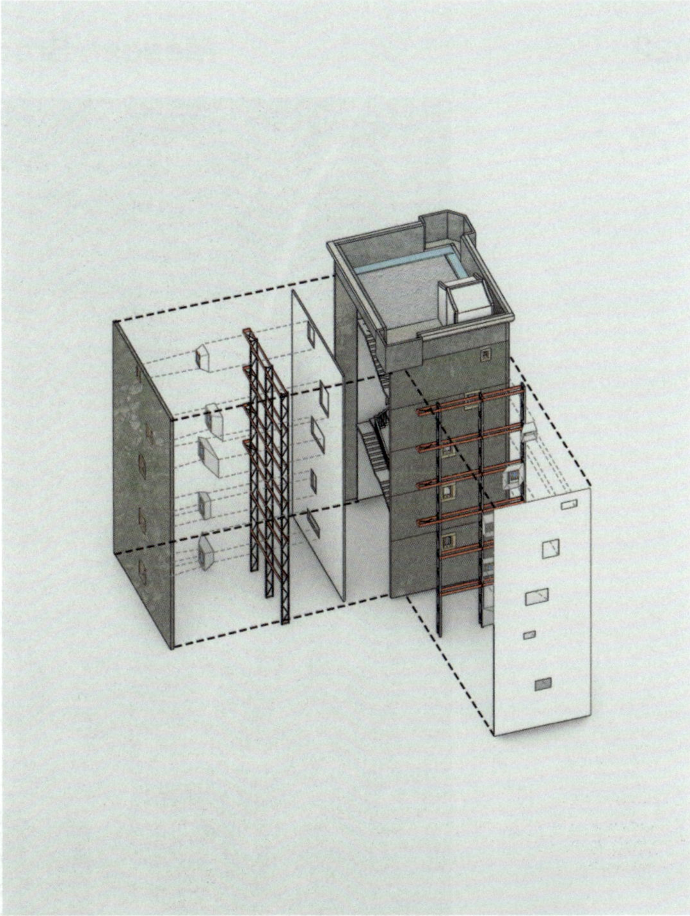

MAJOR PROJECT S2 2020 Jingyuan Wang Drawing07(1).png

MAJOR PROJECT S2 2020 Jingyuan Wang Image22_window chaos01.jpg

STUDENT Meagan Brooks
PROJECT City Gifts
SUPERVISOR Michael Spooner
YEAR 2022

Meagan Brooks, City Gifts

2022 MEAGAN BROOKS Image 05_city gifts.jpg

On the bank of the Yarra River, in the airspace next to Federation Square, sits a building with a front and a back. The front is an inscription of the back; the back, an instrument for understanding the front. Both are a map for reading the city — a panorama of the city, but not in the way that it is known now.

It is a new City Gallery.

Acting as an extension to Federation Square, this project attends to the idea of a city by setting up a series of dialogues, situating itself within its own pedagogy, archaeology and genealogy, which constantly inflect and refract within and outside themselves. The building becomes an apparatus for accessing this discourse, demonstrating architecture's ability to not only collect but also curate; not only to observe but also to reflect and comprehend. The building becomes a memory of the things it knows within the context of its own existence; the project becomes an endeavour for understanding.

A legacy. An artefact of the city. An artefact of a major project.

The new City Gallery is not a gallery because it holds things. It is a gallery because it consists of things.

In the city. Of the city. For the city.

STUDENT Meagan Brooks
PROJECT City Gifts
SUPERVISOR Michael Spooner
YEAR 2022

2022 MEAGAN BROOKS Image 01_Billboard.jpg

2022 MEAGAN BROOKS Image 02_Overall.jpg

STUDENT Meagan Brooks
PROJECT City Gifts
SUPERVISOR Michael Spooner
YEAR 2022

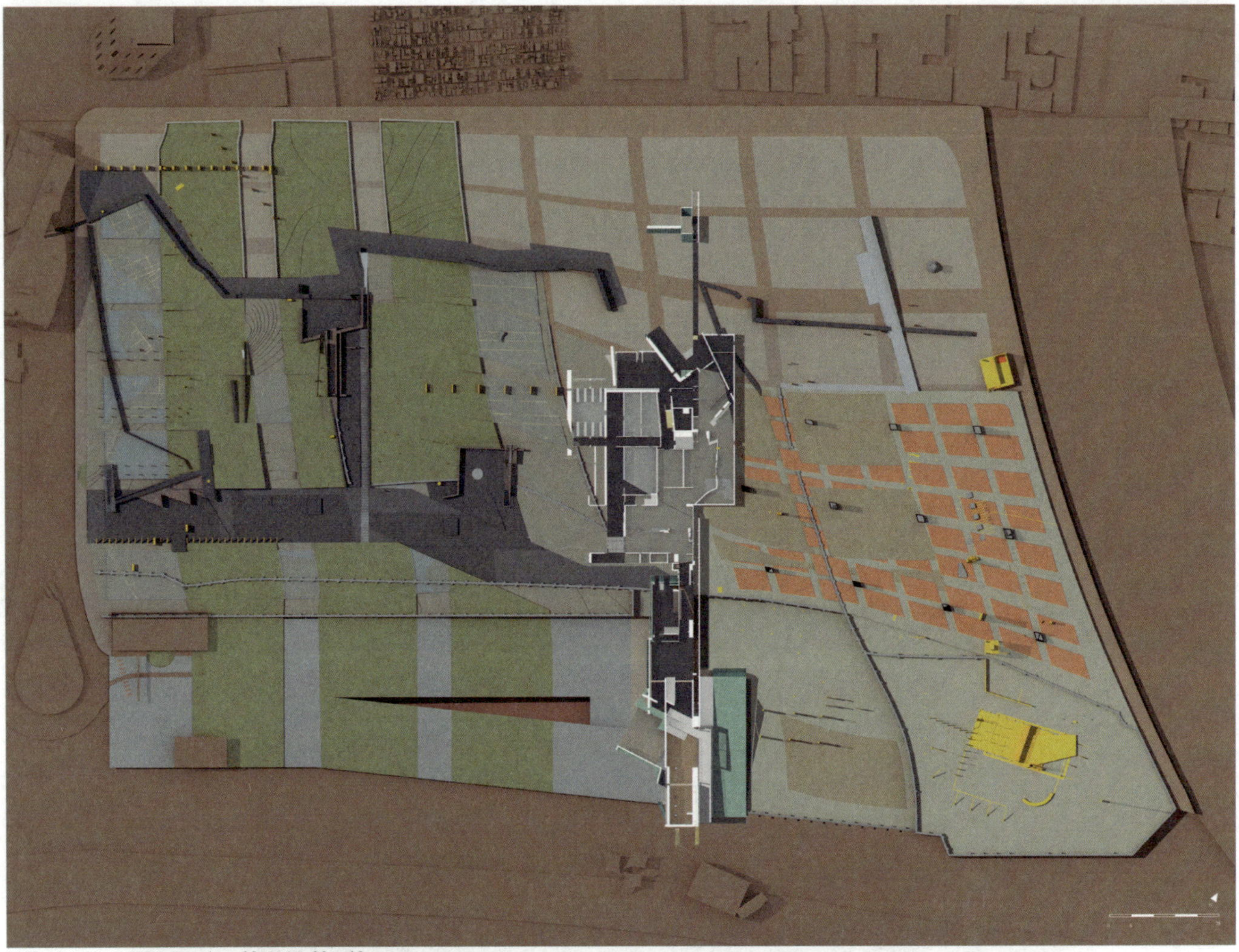

2022 MEAGAN BROOKS Drawing 02_PLAN 00.pdf

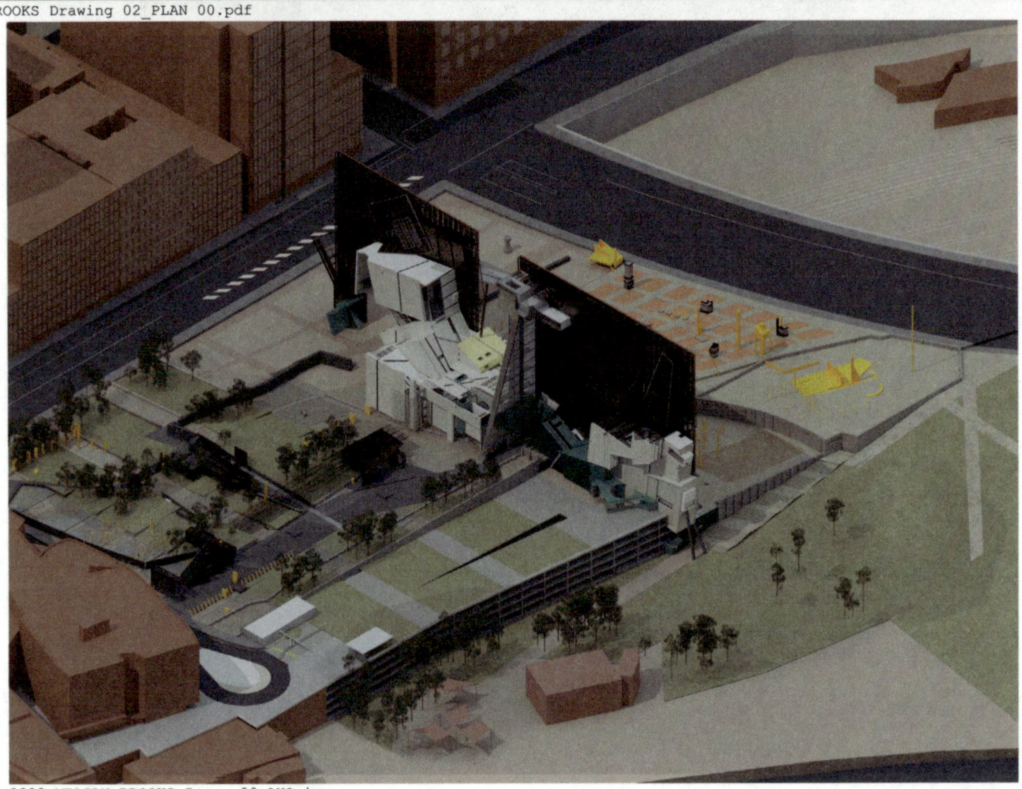

2022 MEAGAN BROOKS Image 09_AXO.jpg

STUDENT	Meagan Brooks
PROJECT	City Gifts
SUPERVISOR	Michael Spooner
YEAR	2022

This project is a series of overlapping timelines and experiments that amass to form a body of work, a body of research. Created over a period of 16 weeks, broken up into three stages, this project reflects the context in which it has been created. In the logics of the project, these periods of time are understood as epochs rather than stages. Their start and end are blurry; they influence one another, build on one another. While these three epochs are tied to the intervals of the major project, they are also defined by a shift in thinking: from collecting, to sorting, to then, finally, applying what was learnt.

Three epochs. Three shifts of mindset. All held by this final project: a new City Gallery.

Three epochs. Three shifts of mindset. A front, a back, a landscape.

Conflating time with space, the first epoch focused on the translation of a precedent into architectural form and searched for the moment architecture becomes more than the materials used to generate it. Each of the experiments in this epoch were tied to a grid, a skewed Hoddle grid refitted to fill the site. Dealing with each portion of the grid as its own singular context removed the difficulties of the site, enabling a concern for architecture through architecture. The site became my city.

Following a pattern of reflection, the new City Gallery understands architecture as a reflective mechanism with an ability and responsibility to reach outside of itself in order to create discourse. This major project is a venture in location; it is a presentation of the model in the model, and adjacent to the model. The final project is not an attempt to consolidate or even hold everything that has filled my time and my site, but rather an attempt to apply and exhibit all that I have discovered. It positions architecture not as a container of space or a program, but as an object that has the ability to transcend its own limits.

1/1

2022 MEAGAN BROOKS Folio.pdf:213

2022 MEAGAN BROOKS Image 06_Atrium.jpg

2022 MEAGAN BROOKS Image 04_Entry.jpg

STUDENT Benjamin Strong
PROJECT Condencity
SUPERVISOR Ian Nazareth
YEAR 2020

2020

Benjamin Strong, Condencity

MAJOR PROJECT SEM 2 2020 Ben Strong Speculative architectural outcomes in a new urban framework.jpg

Condencity is a project investigating urbanism and its evolutionary potential, with a focus on cities that are subject to the ideas of capital and private property. The project proposes an alternative set of rules and spatial frameworks for the future suburb of Sandridge in Fisherman's Bend, and speculates on the urban and architectural outcomes. The project responds to fragile forces inherent in market-based urbanism, which lead to properties including bigness, homogeneity and specialisation. Condencity suggests a set of corrective measures to produce an 'antifragile' alternative, namely a model of urbanism that will benefit from – rather than be inhibited by – a changing environment. It is proposed that such urbanism must have the properties of 'condensity — namely, smallness, heterogeneity and decentralisation.

STUDENT	Benjamin Strong
PROJECT	Condencity
SUPERVISOR	Ian Nazareth
YEAR	2020

THE RULES OF THE CITY

RIGHTS OF THE INDIVIDUAL

1. Right to Sunlight: An individual will have access to direct sunlight from their residence and their place of work.
2. Right to Open Space: An individual will have access to public or private open space, within 300m of their residence. This does not include streets or thoroughfares and must be a place where recreational activities are both permitted and practicable.
3. Tree Conservation: All significant trees shall be preserved and protected by a tree protection zone.

RULES OF THE STREET

1. Street Widths: Primary streets will have a width of 20m, secondary streets 14m, and tertiary streets 5m.
2. Street Length: A stretch of street without intersection must be no longer than 200m.
3. Footpaths: Footpaths must be a minimum of 1.2m wide and a maximum of 3m wide, and will flank both sides of every street wider than 5m. 4. Cycle paths Cycle paths will be included in every primary and secondary street, with a minimum width of 1.2m and a maximum of 2m.

RULES OF THE BLOCK

1. Block Composition: The composition of lot types contained in a block must adhere to the ratio of 40% Accountant's Lots, 40% Entrepreneur's Lots, and 20% Dissident's Lots, +/-10%
2. Public Open Space: Each block must have a minimum of 10% and a maximum of 40% its total area dedicated to publicly accessible space and/or facilities, 40% of which must be outdoors.
3. Lot Consolidation: Lots cannot be consolidated to form larger lots. Multiple lots of the same block may be owned by the same entity, however, developments cannot span multiple blocks.

1/2 continues on next page.

MAJOR PROJECT SEM 2 2020 BEN STRONG DRAWING Two possible outcomes of a tight laneway1.JPG
MAJOR PROJECT SEM 2 2020 BEN STRONG DRAWING Two possible outcomes of a tight laneway2.JPG

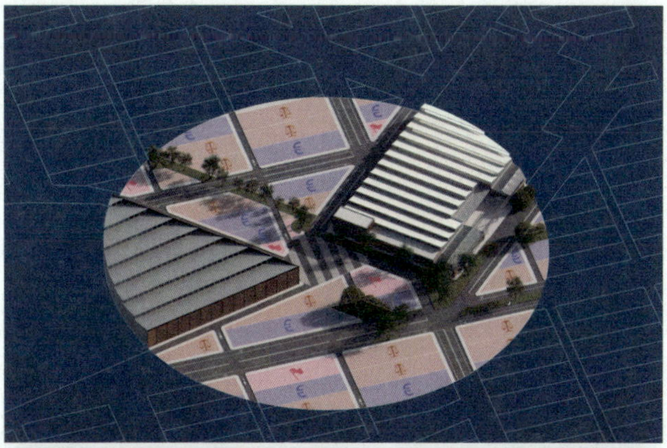

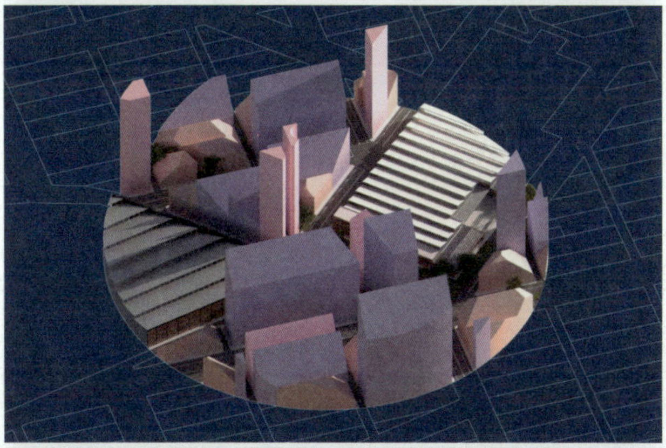

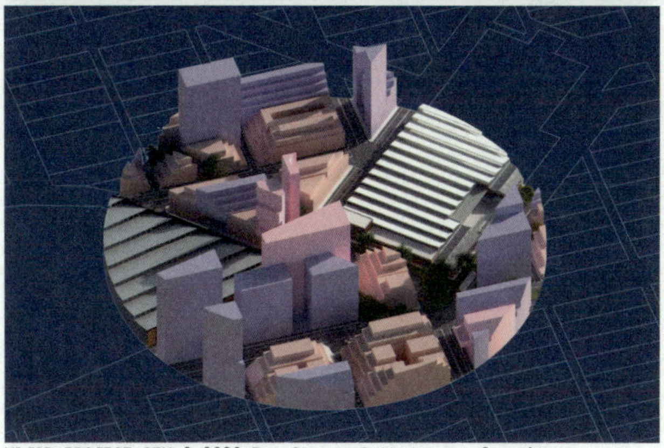

MAJOR PROJECT SEM 2 2020 Ben Strong A test area for the Sandringham suburb demonstrating variable building morphologies and urban outcomes1.jpg
MAJOR PROJECT SEM 2 2020 Ben Strong A test area for the Sandringham suburb demonstrating variable building morphologies and urban outcomes2.jpg
MAJOR PROJECT SEM 2 2020 Ben Strong A test area for the Sandringham suburb demonstrating variable building morphologies and urban outcomes3.jpg
MAJOR PROJECT SEM 2 2020 Ben Strong A test area for the Sandringham suburb demonstrating variable building morphologies and urban outcomes4.jpg

STUDENT Benjamin Strong
PROJECT Condencity
SUPERVISOR Ian Nazareth
YEAR 2020

RULES OF THE LOT:
FREEDOM ∝ RESPONSIBILITY

THE ACCOUNTANT'S LOT

- FAR: 6:1
- Maximum Height: 25m
- Minimum # Uses: 2, Primary use + Streetscape offering
- Setbacks: *Street setback*: a gradient of 1.5:1 taken from the opposite side of the street
  Side and rear setbacks: a gradient of 1.5:1 taken from the nearest neighbouring boundary.
- Overshadowing: A building must not impede on neighbour's access to a minimum of 5hrs direct sunlight per day. This includes access via Private Open Space and habitable windows.
- Block Rules: Accountant's lots needn't comply with the rules of the block.

THE ENTREPRENEUR'S LOT

- Floor Area Ratio: A base FAR of 8:1 with an increased FAR for each additional building use. The allowable increase in area is subject to the new use provided, the figures for which can be found in Table 1
- Minimum # Uses: 3, 2 Primary uses + a minimum of 1 Streetscape offering
- Overshadowing: A building's shadow must allow a minimum of 5 hours of direct sunlight to half the area of a neighbouring lot. Shadows of surrounding buildings needn't be considered in the calculation.
- Block Rules: Entrepreneur's lots must comply with the rules of the block.
- Development Rights Transfer: An owner may purchase development rights from other sites to increase their developable building envelope.
- New Use Offset: An increase in floor area is allowable at twice the prescribed figure for an additional use, if that use is not present on the block at the time of application.

THE DISSIDENT'S LOT

- Floor Area Ratio: A base FAR of 8:1 with an increased FAR for each additional building use. The allowable increase in area is subject to the new use provided, the figures for which can be found in Table 1
- Minimum # Uses: 4, 3 Primary uses + a minimum of 1 Streetscape offering
- Overshadowing: A building's shadow must allow a minimum of 5 hours of direct sunlight to half the area of a neighbouring lot. Shadows of surrounding buildings needn't be considered in the calculation.
- Block Rules: Entrepreneur's lots must comply with the rules of the block.
- New Use Offset: An increase in floor area is allowable at twice the prescribed figure for an additional use, if that use is not present on the block at the time of application.
- Innovation Offset: A development may extend beyond the boundaries of the lot, under the condition that it can be demonstrated to provide exceptional benefit to the occupants of the land onto or over which it extends. Where the land is public the occupants are considered to be the general public.

2/2

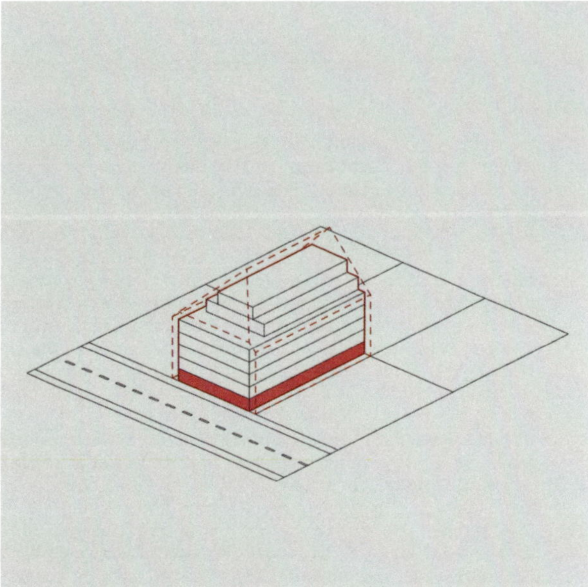

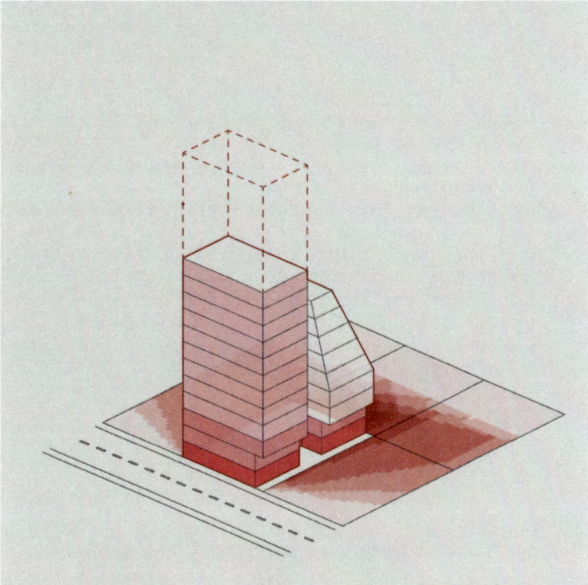

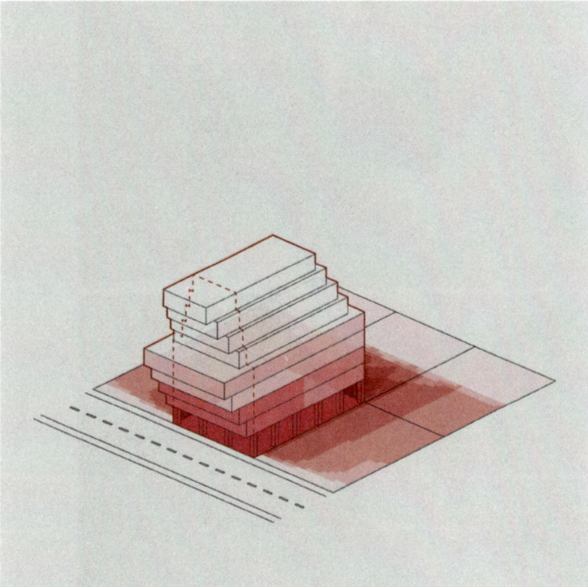

MAJOR PROJECT SEM 2 2020 Ben Strong Drawing The Accountant's Lot.pdf
MAJOR PROJECT SEM 2 2020 Ben Strong Drawing The Entrepreneur's Lot.pdf
MAJOR PROJECT SEM 2 2020 Ben Strong Drawing The Dissident's Lot.pdf

STUDENT Benjamin Strong
PROJECT Condencity
SUPERVISOR Ian Nazareth
YEAR 2020

MAJOR PROJECT SEM 2 2020 Ben Strong Drawing architectural speculations on a dissident's lot.jpg

MAJOR PROJECT SEM 2 2020 BEN STRONG Drawing architectural speculations on an entrepreneur's lot.JPG

MAJOR PROJECT SEM 2 2020 Ben Strong Drawing three possible urban outcomes of rules that dictate a proportional level of freedom and responsibility1.jpg
MAJOR PROJECT SEM 2 2020 Ben Strong Drawing three possible urban outcomes of rules that dictate a proportional level of freedom and responsibility2.jpg
MAJOR PROJECT SEM 2 2020 Ben Strong Drawing three possible urban outcomes of rules that dictate a proportional level of freedom and responsibility3.jpg

2019 Jacqueline Tang, Fields of Play

MAJOR PROJECT S2 2019 JACQUELINE TANG_Street Interface of Shared (Learning and Living) Spaces.jpg

MAJOR PROJECT S2 2019 JACQUELINE TANG_06 Entrance of Learning.jpg

Fields of Play (F.O.P) speculates on the evolution of hybridised types through the lens of learning and living environments. It prioritises hybridisation, including typology and programs, syntax of programmatic codes and evolution. It seeks to re-evaluate architectural projects on spatial possibilities. It sees the value of architecture not just in form, but also in how we understand programs and their potential evolution.

F.O.P studies architectural ideologies embodied in the spatial program. This includes the production of fields of social encounter, new functional juxtapositions and forms of spatial segmentation. A way to judge its progress is through the programmatic analysis compiled in the *Fields of Play Encyclopedia (F.O.P.E)*, a matrix that highlights a series of programmatic codes and relationships based on negotiation.

The essence of this encyclopedia is a strategy to understand process-based complexities and to speculate on 'other' typological hybrids. This is a future speculation of hybrid evolutions, with ideas and methods possessing the potential to be transferrable. Currently, F.O.P fosters the exchange between living and learning across four stages. If learning becomes redundant in the future, *F.O.P.E* can evolve into other typologies.

STUDENT Jacqueline Tang
PROJECT Fields of Play
SUPERVISOR Patrick Macasaet
YEAR 2019

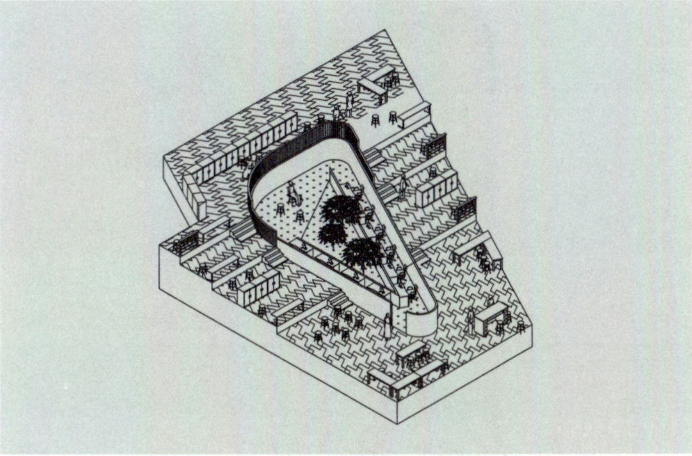

TRANSITION LEARNING CATERING TO DIFFERENT TYPES OF LEARNING NEEDS FOR COLLABORATIVE WORKSHOPS, HAVING A DESIGNATED SOUNDPROOF ZONE FOR SPECIAL/ INDIVIDUAL LEARNING.

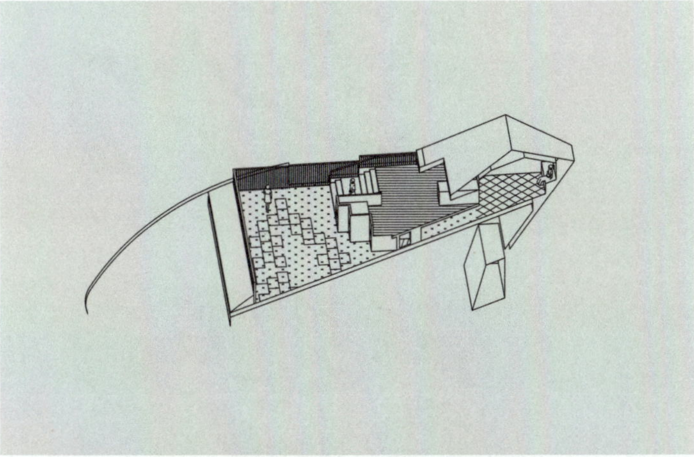

EYEPODS INTENDED SUPERVISION AND SURVEILLANCE OF STUDENTS WITHIN NEW ZONES OF CURRICULUM. COULD ALSO BE FOR PRACTICE TEACHERS TO OBSERVE.

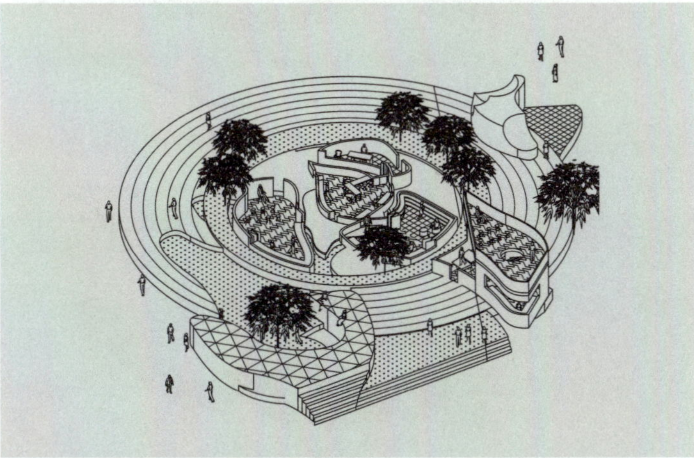

FORCE FIELD RELOCATABLE LEARNPODS ACTING AS FORCES WITHIN A TRACK AND FIELD. THE PODS ARE CLOSE TO PUBLIC INTERCATION AND INTENDED FOR MATURE AND INDEPENDANT YEAR LEVELS.

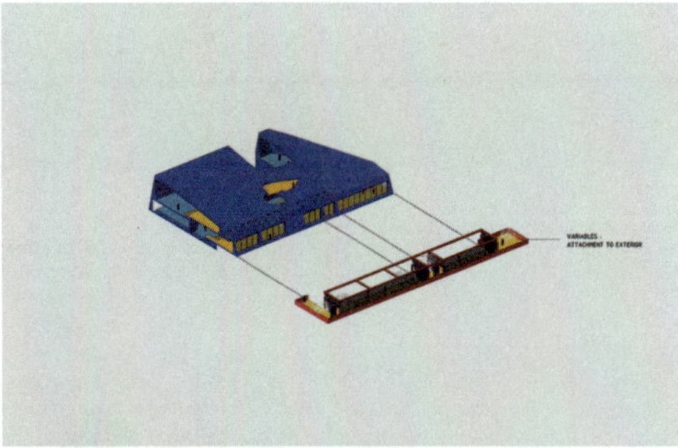

EVOLUTION 1 - LIGHTWEIGHT ADAPTATION

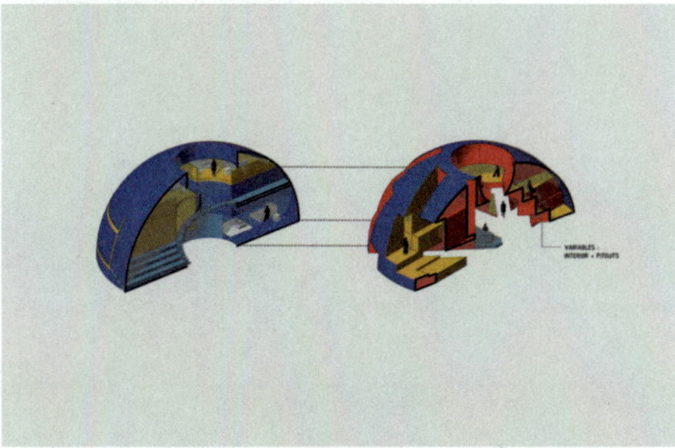

EVOLUTION 2 - ADDITIONS + ALTERATIONS

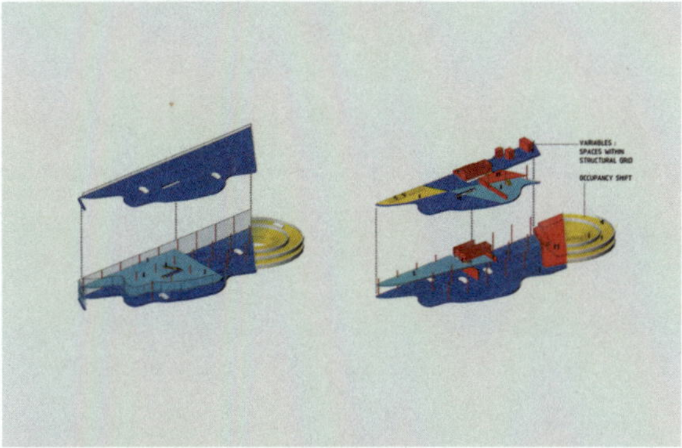

EVOLUTION 3 - STRUCTURE RETAINMENT

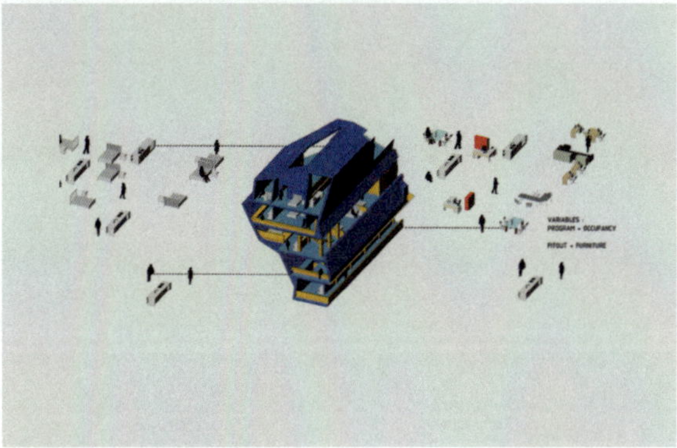

EVOLUTION 4 - PROGRAM SHIFT

STUDENT Jacqueline Tang
PROJECT Fields of Play
SUPERVISOR Patrick Macasaet
YEAR 2019

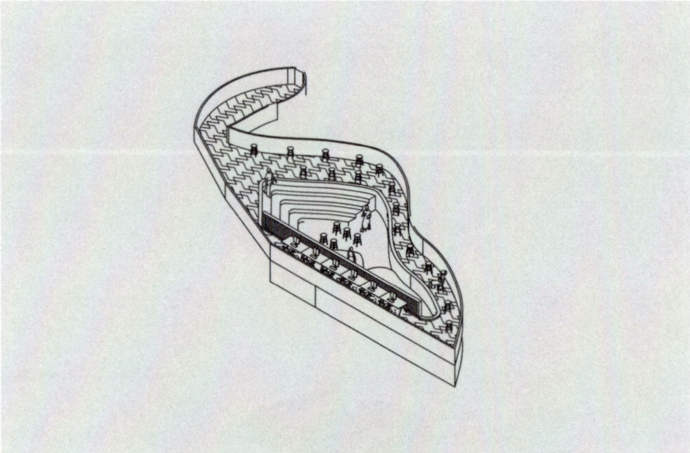

POOLEARN A POOL READAPTED TO A LEARNING FACILITY, TO LEARN WITHIN OR AROUND THE POOL. BE IT BEING PARTIALLY SUBMERGED AS A NEW WAY OF LEARNING.

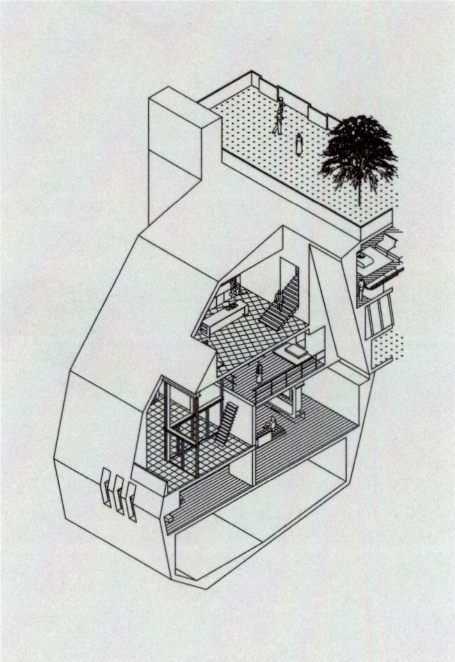

12W STAY INDUSTRY PARTNERS (INCREASING PROFESSION) WITH COLLABORATION WITH THE YEAR 10 WORK EXPERIENCE WOULD STAY IN THIS SPECIFIC ZONES WITH 12WEEKS RENTALS.

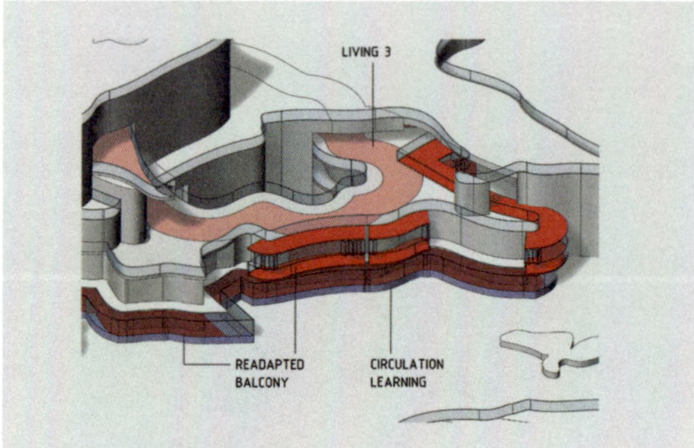

BALCONY LEARNING - LEARNING n (INTERSECT) LIVING 3 PRIVATE - READAPTING BALCONIES FROM PRIVATE HOMES TO ASSESSMENT ZONES / INDIVIDUAL LEARNING

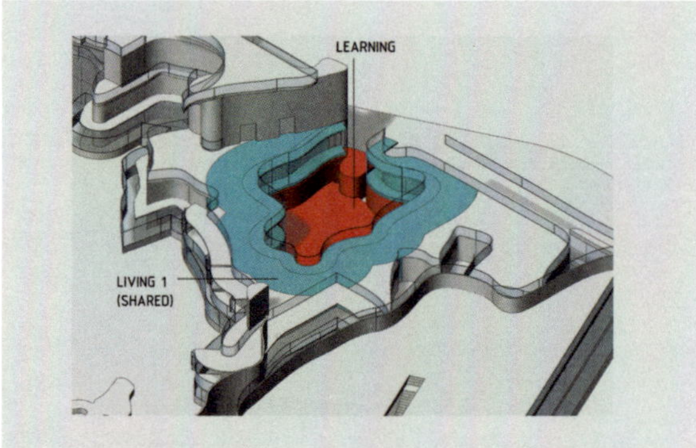

DOUGHNUT LIVING - LEARNING c (SUBSET) OF LIVING 1 SHARED CENTRALISED VOID WHERE LEARNING INHABITS THE GROUND

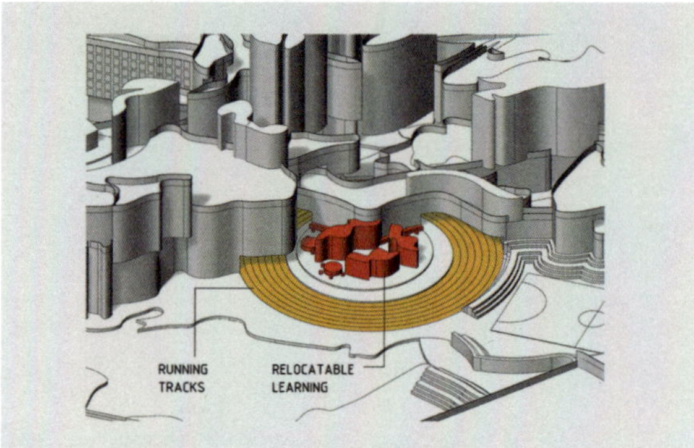

FORCE FIELD LEARNING - LEARNING c (SUBSET) OF FACILITIES LEARNING COULD BE RELOCATABLE PODS.

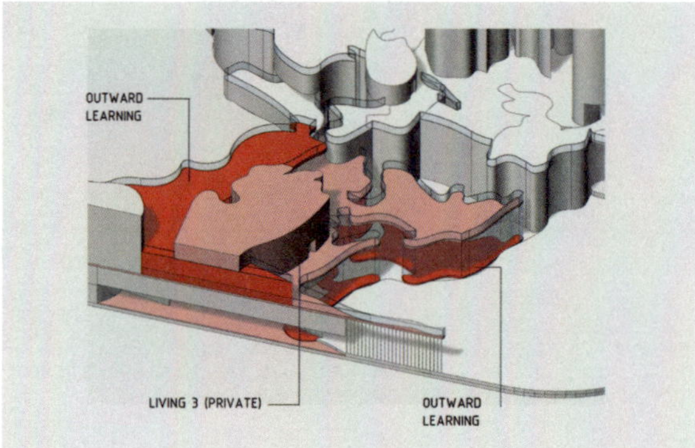

OUTWARD LEARNING - LIVING 3 PRIVATE c (SUBSET) OF LEARNING OUTWARD FACING & ENTRY OF LEARNING.

STUDENT Jacqueline Tang
PROJECT Fields of Play
SUPERVISOR Patrick Macasaet
YEAR 2019

MAJOR PROJECT S2 2019 JACQUELINE TANG_Entrance of Living.jpg

MAJOR PROJECT S2 2019 JACQUELINE TANG_Shared Spaces Between Living and Learning.jpg

2021

Akash Vazirani, Symbiotic Architecture

2021 AKASH VAZIRANI_PRESENTATION SLIDES.pdf:39

2021 AKASH VAZIRANI_PRESENTATION SLIDES.pdf:40

2021 AKASH VAZIRANI_PRESENTATION SLIDES.pdf:41

2021 AKASH VAZIRANI_PRESENTATION SLIDES.pdf:42

2021 AKASH VAZIRANI 16_Site Plan.pdf

2021 AKASH VAZIRANI.pdf:20
2021 AKASH VAZIRANI.pdf:21
2021 AKASH VAZIRANI.pdf:23

Symbiotic Architecture is a concept that aspires to create a self-sustaining habitation framework for future cities based on a circular economic model. To meet the requirements of remote working, a new co-living planning model was designed using Ma Wan Island in Hong Kong as its first test site.

The test city was developed using an agent-based modelling system — inspired by the natural development mechanisms of organisms such as *physarum polycephalum* — which reacts to data from existing site analysis models and AI. The algorithmic findings were analysed after optimisation to determine appropriate zones for human settlement and a feasible connectivity network between these zones.

The goal was to create a city that touched the earth at only a few points, resulting in a metropolis floating over lush vegetation cover. The city is built using an extensive template of materials derived from waste collected from the surrounding area. Micro algae bio-reactor façade panels fabricated using additive manufacturing techniques provide for the city's energy needs, as well as forming a symbiotic link between carbon positive species like humans and carbon negative species like algae.

STUDENT Akash Vazirani
PROJECT Symbiotic Architecture
SUPERVISOR Tom Kovac
YEAR 2021

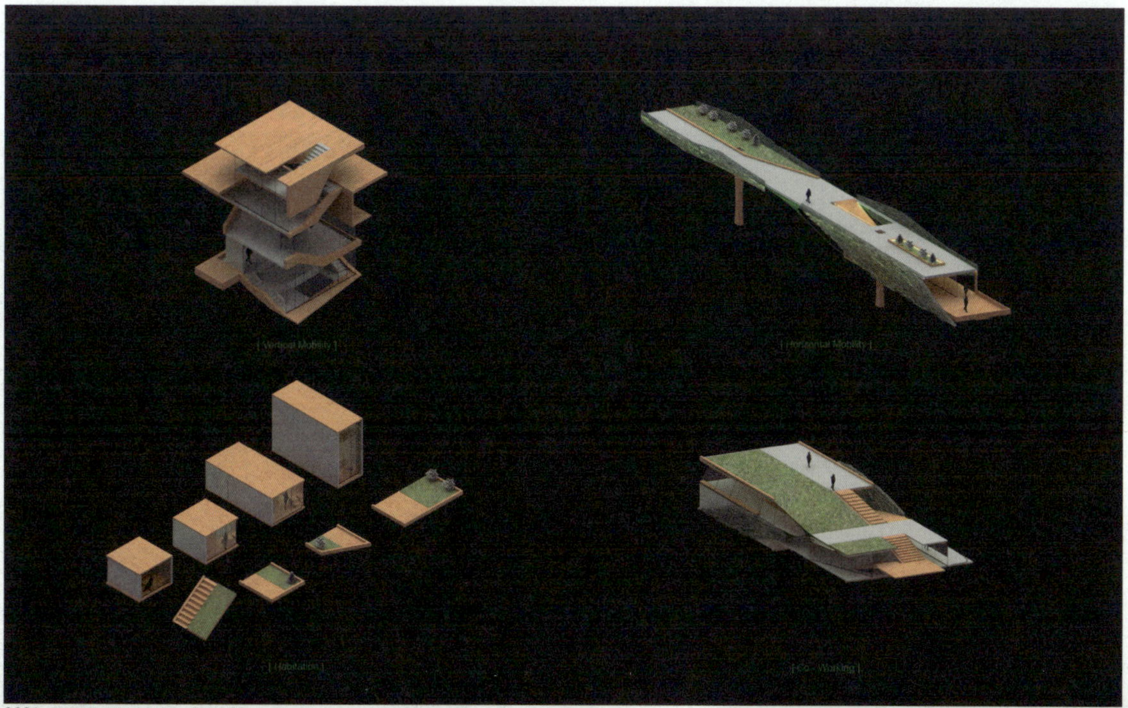

2021 AKASH VAZIRANI 9_Different Types of Components.pdf

2021 AKASH VAZIRANI 10_Vertical Circulation Components.pdf

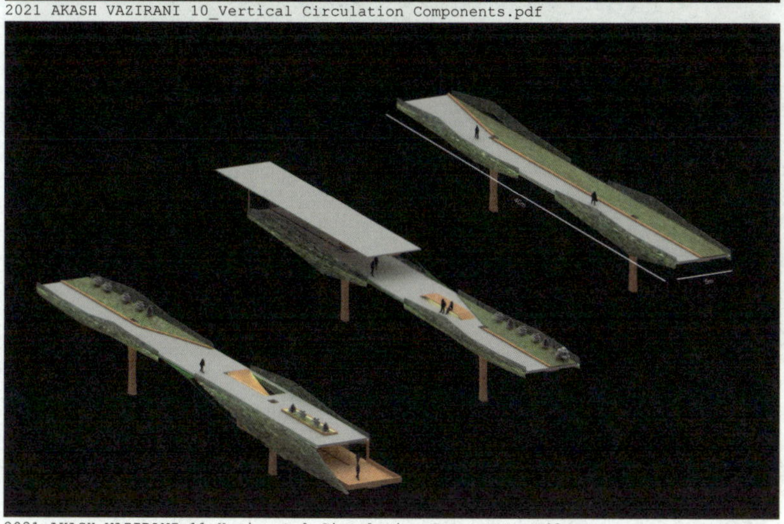

2021 AKASH VAZIRANI 11_Horizontal Circulation Components.pdf

MAJOR PROJECT SEMESTER1 2021 AKASH VAZIRANI 2_FULL CAMPUS VIEW.PNG
MAJOR PROJECT SEMESTER1 2021 AKASH VAZIRANI 4_WORKPLACE VIEW.PNG
MAJOR PROJECT SEMESTER1 2021 AKASH VAZIRANI 5_HABITATION VIEW.PNG

STUDENT Shuai Tang
PROJECT Co-living with Nature
SUPERVISOR Alisa Andrasek
YEAR 2021

2021

Shuai Tang, Co-living with Nature

2021 SHUAI TANG Enscape_2021-10-30-14-52-34.png

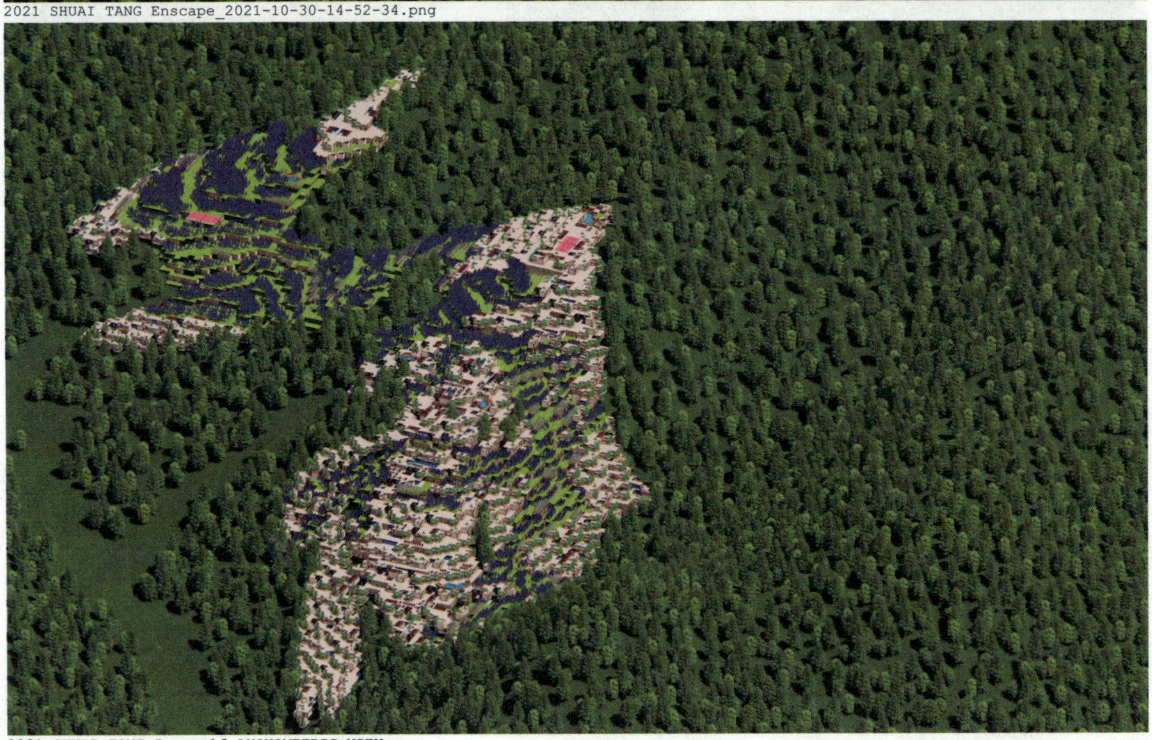

2021 SHUAI TANG Image 16_AXONOMETRIC VIEW.png

This project is a low-coverage, high-density community in Lishui, China. It is expected to provide residents with a chance to cohabit with nature and live self-sufficiently, respecting traditional Chinese philosophies. Here, AI tools are used to create massing agents clustered by voxels.

A game-type methodology, similar to the video game SimCity, is applied to build these voxels. The final mapping result displays an interlaced system: non-human habitation (forest and landscape farming area) and human habitation (residential fabric) are blended. As a result, the high-density building clusters are no longer obstacles on the site. Instead, they are endowed with high permeability and generosity to humans, plants and animals.

STUDENT Shuai Tang
PROJECT Co-living with Nature
SUPERVISOR Alisa Andrasek
YEAR 2021

Co-living with Nature is an interlaced ecology for humans and non-humans alike. Lishui is a city in China facing the dual challenges of land destruction caused by mining activities and housing shortage. To address this, I propose a low-coverage, high-density community designed to allow residents to cohabit with nature and live self-sufficiently, respecting traditional Chinese philosophies, local culture and spatial realities. Advanced architectural techniques, concepts and methodologies are adopted in order to allow human and non-human habitations to interlace within this new community.

In reviewing Lishui's traditional village, I noticed that different types of courtyards are used to deal with the issue of super tight housing. The courtyard forms the core of residents' living culture and is a container for daily activity. Given this, I tested configurations of different courtyards through the logics of K-means clustering.

The prototype for the community was then developed using AI. First, a multi-agent algorithm was used to grow a form on the landscape, ensuring that the new growth is sensitive to the site. Then, cluster chunks are massed into voxels. Finally, different layers of massed voxels are intertwined and combined on the site, testing out different zones and combining them into a system.

The massing process guided the spatial relationship between residential and biomass areas, and determined the biomass function and location. At the completion of this process, Chunk A was divided into two parts: 36.7 percent private and 63.3 percent shared.

1/2 continues on next page.

2021 SHUAI TANG Image 13_OVER TIME STEP ONE.png
2021 SHUAI TANG Image 14_OVER TIME STEP TWO.png
2021 SHUAI TANG Image 15_OVER TIME STEP THREE.png

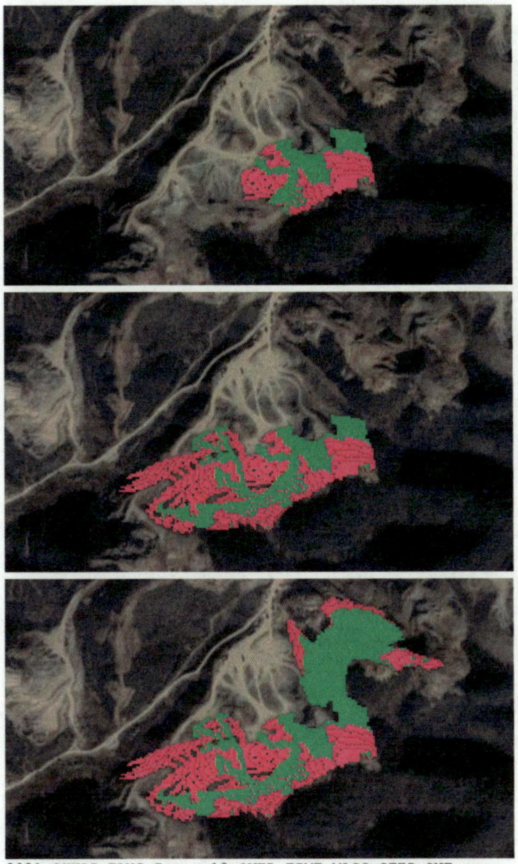

2021 SHUAI TANG Image 10_OVER TIME MASS STEP ONE.png
2021 SHUAI TANG Image 11_OVER TIME MASS STEP TWO.png
2021 SHUAI TANG Image 12_OVER TIME MASS STEP THREE.png

STUDENT	Shuai Tang
PROJECT	Co-living with Nature
SUPERVISOR	Alisa Andrasek
YEAR	2021

These numbers conform to the concept of a shared community. Four structural types were then developed according to the K-means clusters regarding private residential topology and taking into account view and sunlight; one of these was then analysed. The challenge here was combining circulation and co-living/co-working areas with sunlight and ventilation, because most voxels with good conditions had been distributed to the private areas.

The project is divided into three phases to allow for development over time. As the population increases, the community will expand as planned. From the data gathered, it is evident that the ratio of biomass area is lower than in traditional villages. This is because the smart farm is more productive, making it easier to achieve self-sufficiency in the community with low coverage, even potentially producing surplus for surrounding towns.

This new village typology, created for Lishui, allows for about three thousand residents to live in good conditions. The smart farms and residential living are interlaced, with green spaces and scattered or aggregated courtyards bringing nature into daily activity spaces. Because of the location of the farms, people can get food and energy from their community directly, without having to travel.

The cascading form of the voxels provides extra terraces and shared areas for leisure and circulation, and most areas are afforded maximum sunlight and views. Internal areas are also variable and flexible. In this way, the goal of high-quality, high-density and self-sufficient living in China is realised.

2/2

2021 SHUAI TANG Image 02_Biomass Farm.png

2021 SHUAI TANG Image 03_Co-living Terrace.png

2021 SHUAI TANG Image 05_Open Space.png

STUDENT Shuai Tang
PROJECT Co-living with Nature
SUPERVISOR Alisa Andrasek
YEAR 2021

2021 SHUAI TANG Image 07_Swimming Pool.png

2021 SHUAI TANG Image 06_Living Area.png

STUDENT Xu Tang
PROJECT Eroded
SUPERVISOR Alisa Andrasek
YEAR 2021

2021

Xu Tang, Eroded

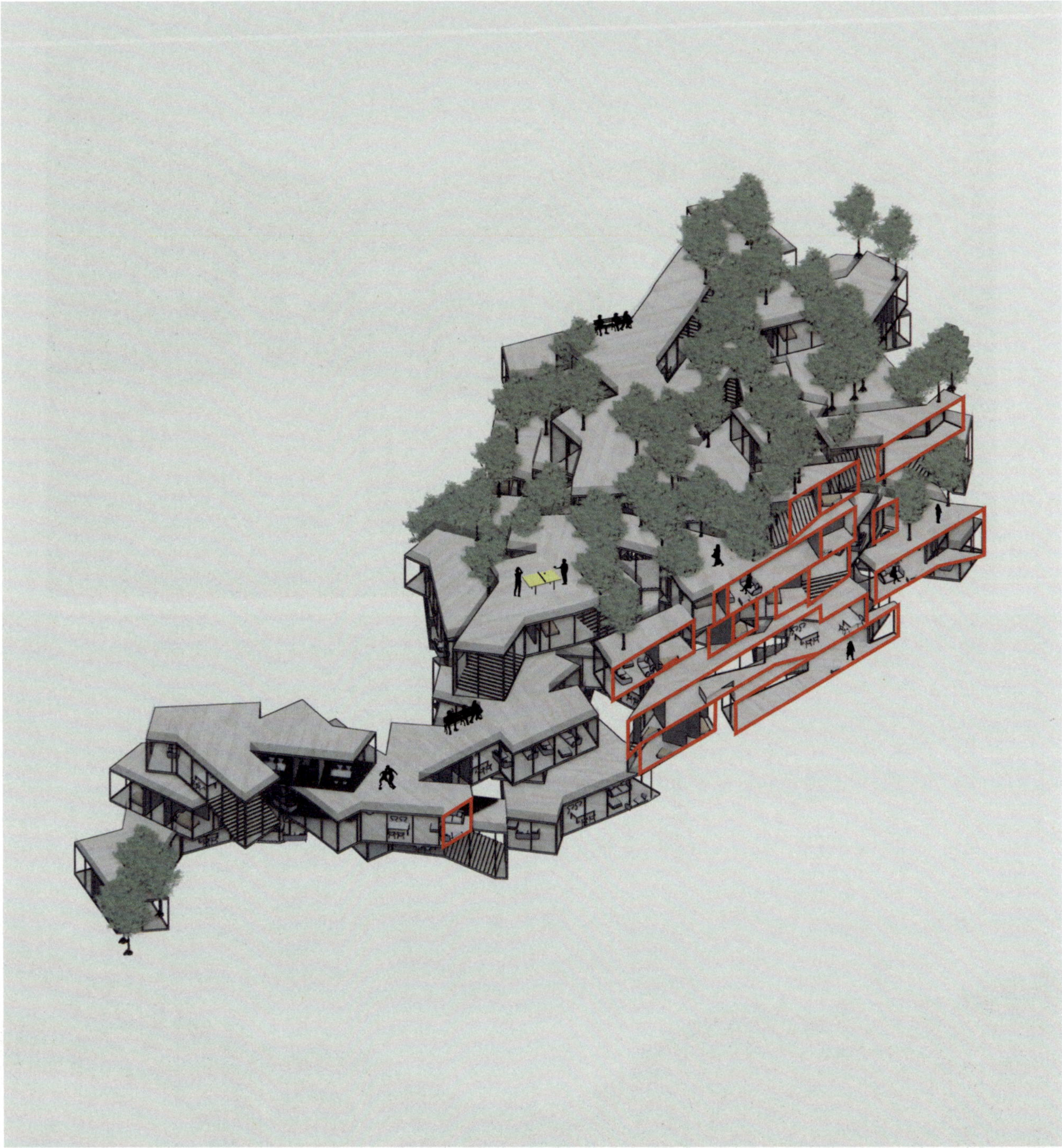

2021 XU TANG Drawing 02_Standard Chunk.jpg

Over the past few decades, Shenzhen's urban green space has been increasingly fragmented. New buildings continue to block the connection between mountains, which has led to a decrease in species diversity. Meanwhile, many people are still living in dense local villages in poor conditions.

This project argues for low-coverage, high-density housing that preserves natural elements and biomass, as well as fostering relationships between human populations and surrounding nature. With new tools including machine learning, multi-agent systems and computational design, we can now develop solutions that are not only high density but also high quality.

This project is located on a barren site, and stitches the mountains and surrounding lake together to achieve high-quality living for both non-human and human inhabitants. Based on machine learning terrain analysis, the project uses a multi-agent system to create an organic form related to the terrain, blurring the boundary between natural and built forms. It allows residents to enjoy a high quality of life through the co-location of working and living areas, and protects biodiversity by providing green corridors for the migration of wild animals.

STUDENT Xu Tang
PROJECT Eroded
SUPERVISOR Alisa Andrasek
YEAR 2021

2021 XU TANG Presentation.pdf:40
2021 XU TANG Presentation.pdf:42

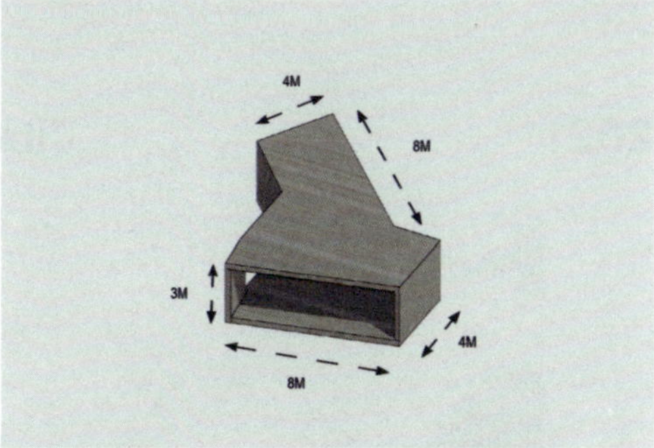

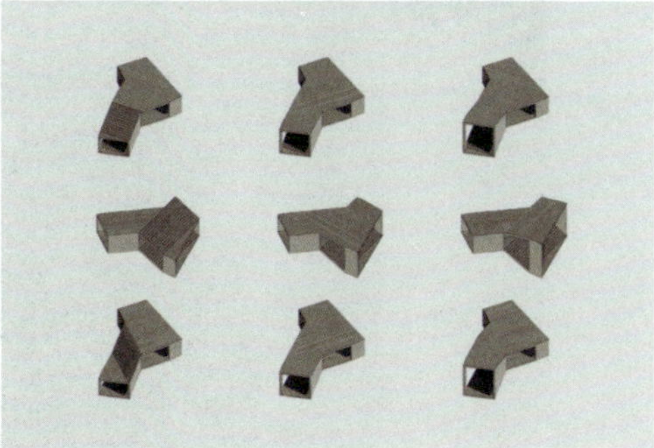

2021 XU TANG Presentation.pdf:21
2021 XU TANG Presentation.pdf:24

2021 XU TANG Drawing 01_Eroded Rendering.png

STUDENT Jitesh Sapra
PROJECT Cognitive Assemblies
SUPERVISOR Roland Snooks
YEAR 2021

2021 Jitesh Sapra, Cognitive Assemblies

MAJOR PROJECT S1 2021 JITESH SAPRA 26 EXTERIOR VIEW.jpg

MAJOR PROJECT S1 2021 JITESH SAPRA 30 INTERIOR VIEW.jpg

This project deals with the study of tectonics and emergent architecture, with a focus on fabrication strategies for complex design ideas. It broadens the horizons of the research-based approach from extraordinary design synthesis to robotic manufacturing processes, and encourages a dialogue between them.

It is a framework/genotype with goal-oriented agent behaviours, tectonics, mathematics of voxels and fabrication strategies. The algorithms follow a 'bottom-up' approach, wherein the system grows and evolves up to the event of an emergent and self-organised behaviour, obeying the simple rules of interaction for an agent-based system.

The overall idea brings the human designer and the AI into a symbiotic relationship. The intent of the designer is partly captured in the generative algorithm as behaviours, and partly in evaluation encoded in the designer's intuition. The AI algorithm acts as an extended mind for the designer and helps optimise complex and repetitive design tasks. Through a constant interaction between the top-down and bottom-up strategies, the proposal seeks to produce an adaptive and responsive architecture.

STUDENT Jitesh Sapra
PROJECT Cognitive Assemblies
SUPERVISOR Roland Snooks
YEAR 2021

MAJOR PROJECT S1 2021 JITESH SAPRA 31 INTERIOR VIEW.jpg

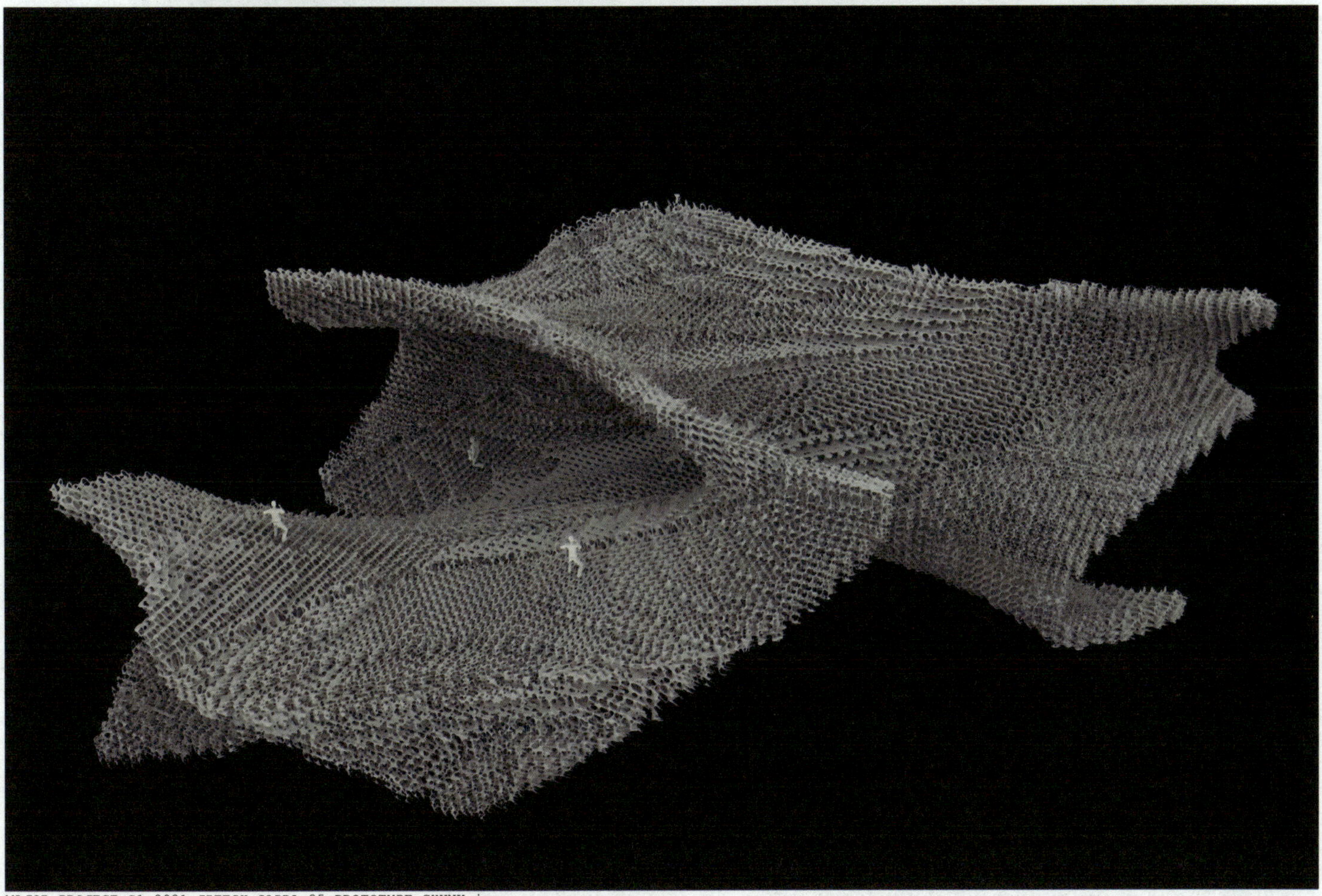

MAJOR PROJECT S1 2021 JITESH SAPRA 25 PROTOTYPE CHUNK.jpg

STUDENT Alan Ho Kyeong Kim
PROJECT transformativeCohesion ();
SUPERVISOR Roland Snooks
YEAR 2021

2021 Alan Ho Kyeong Kim, transformativeCohesion ();

2021 HO KYEONG 'ALAN' KIM -Object_3_010.png

2021 HO KYEONG 'ALAN' KIM -Grounded Site Site Relationship.png

transformativeCohesion (); is a design process amalgamating multiple self-organising and autonomous algorithms with digital fabrications. It builds on the idea of bottom-up, morphogenesis design to enhance the fundamentals of architectural topologies with complex tectonics. Its investigations bring about the notion of emergent computational processes that create symbiotic and non-linear relationships on global and local scales. It systemises poly-scalar behaviours with simple underlying rules to enhance the generation of architectural form. The system has been executed at multiple architectural scales, examining the development process of cohesive tectonics.

The project values a time-based format of transformative growth. It highlights the exploration of emergent tectonics through algorithmic processes that can't be captured in a traditional format. Authorship is enacted through the detailed visualisation of emergent forms, creating a complex order of divergent actualisation. The framework orchestrates the formation of an architecture that questions traditional topologies and tectonic values, enhancing the emergence of morphogenesis through a computational approach to robotic fabrication. The interaction of these morphogenetic, emergent and morphodynamic authorships produces responsive, transformative and cohesive architectural proposals.

STUDENT Alan Ho Kyeong Kim
PROJECT transformativeCohesion ();
SUPERVISOR Roland Snooks
YEAR 2021

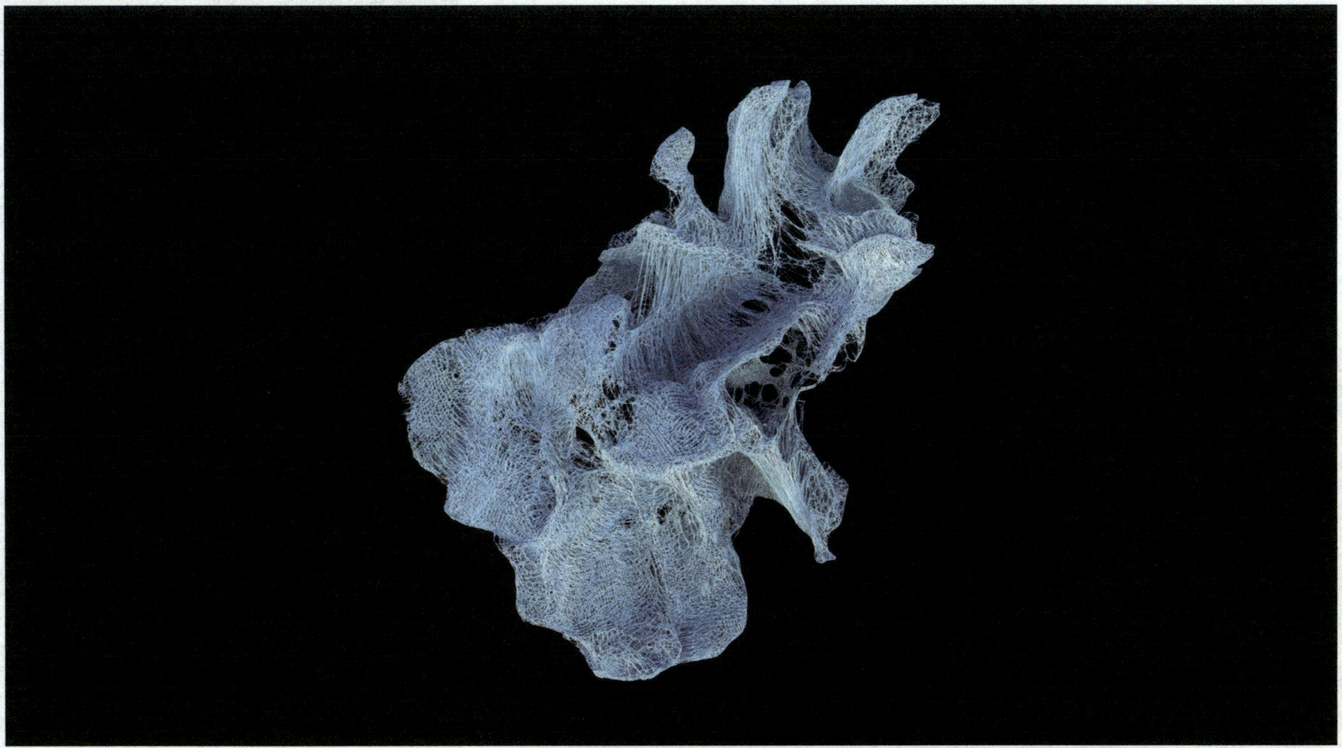

2021 HO KYEONG 'ALAN' KIM -Object_1_010.png

2021 HO KYEONG 'ALAN' KIM -Chunk_1_010_People.png

2021 HO KYEONG 'ALAN' KIM -Grounded Site Entrance.png

STUDENT Alan Ho Kyeong Kim
PROJECT transformativeCohesion ();
SUPERVISOR Roland Snooks
YEAR 2021

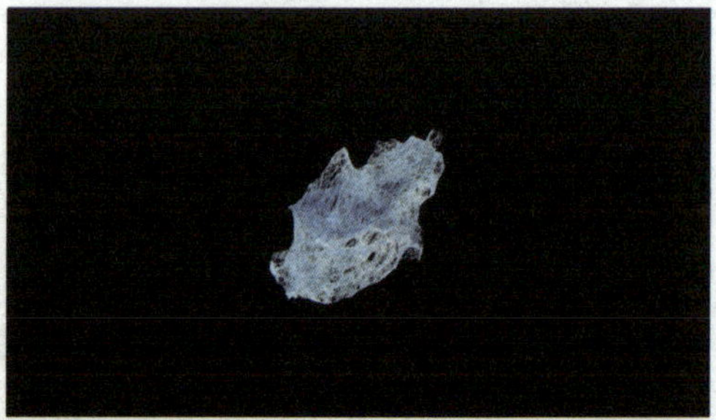

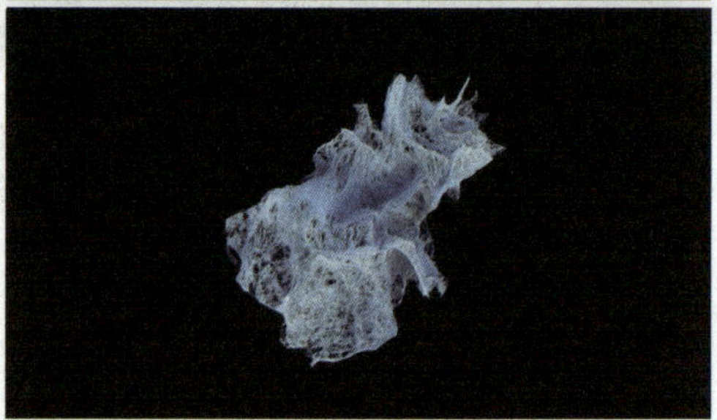

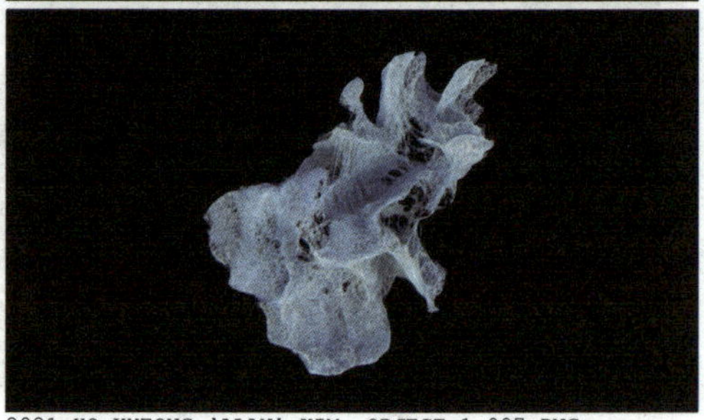

2021 HO KYEONG 'ALAN' KIM -OBJECT_1_007.PNG
2021 HO KYEONG 'ALAN' KIM -OBJECT_1_009.PNG
2021 HO KYEONG 'ALAN' KIM -OBJECT_1_010.PNG

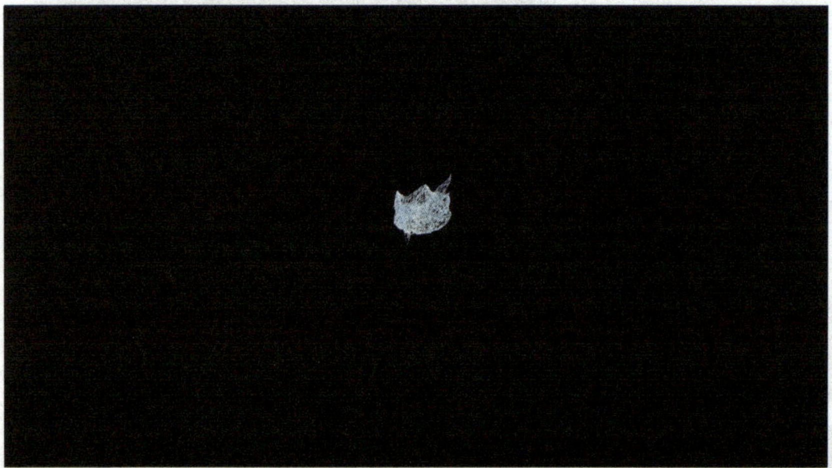

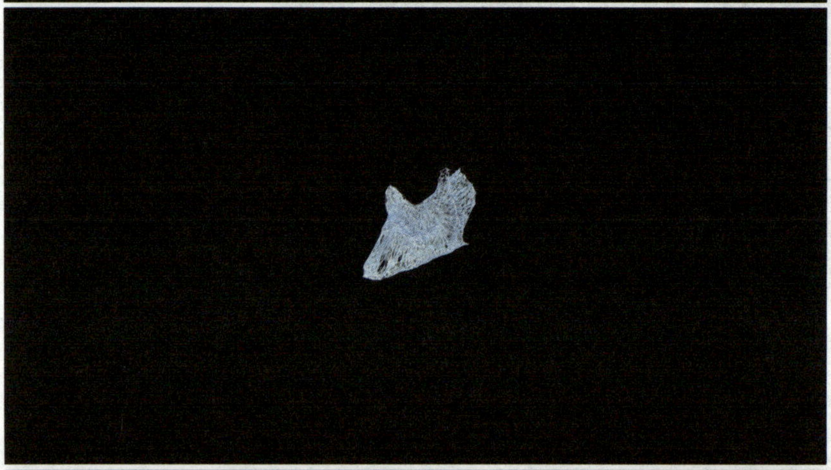

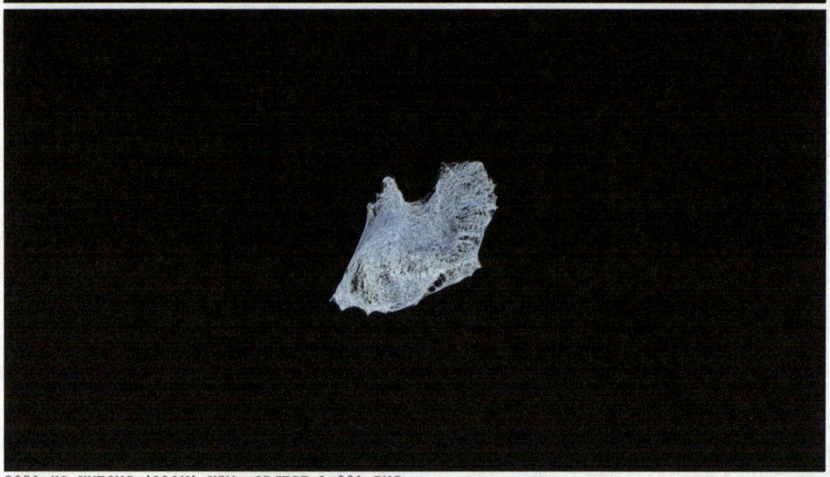

2021 HO KYEONG 'ALAN' KIM -OBJECT_1_001.PNG
2021 HO KYEONG 'ALAN' KIM -OBJECT_1_003.PNG
2021 HO KYEONG 'ALAN' KIM -OBJECT_1_005.PNG

STUDENT Alan Ho Kyeong Kim
PROJECT transformativeCohesion ();
SUPERVISOR Roland Snooks
YEAR 2021

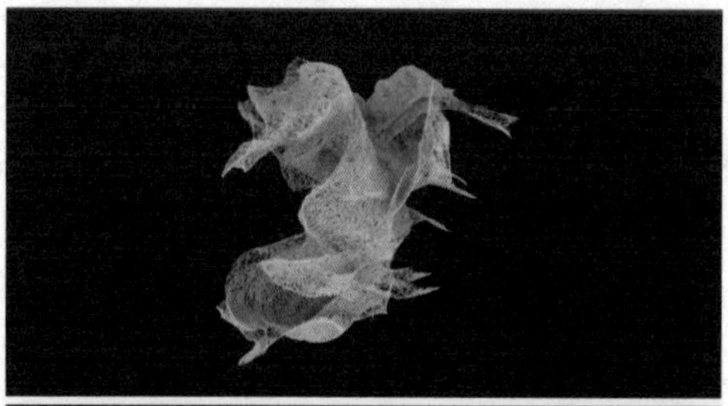

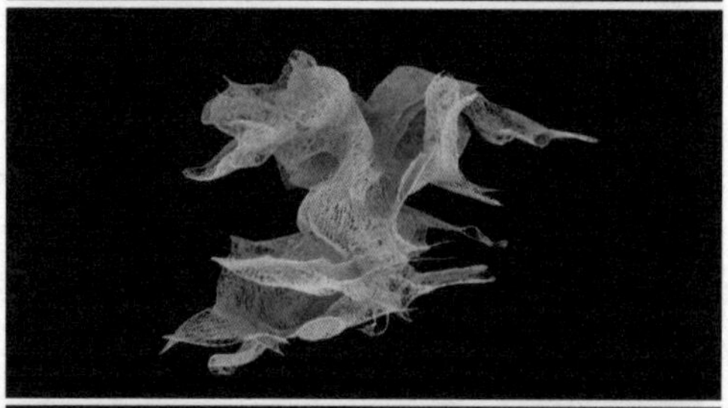

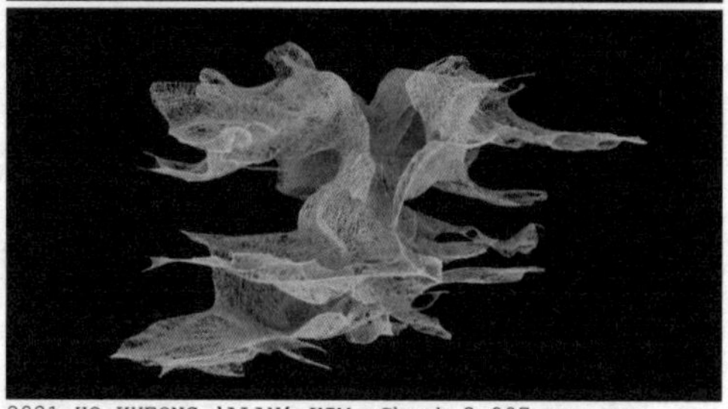

2021 HO KYEONG 'ALAN' KIM -Chunk_3_007.png
2021 HO KYEONG 'ALAN' KIM -Chunk_3_008.png
2021 HO KYEONG 'ALAN' KIM -Chunk_3_009.png

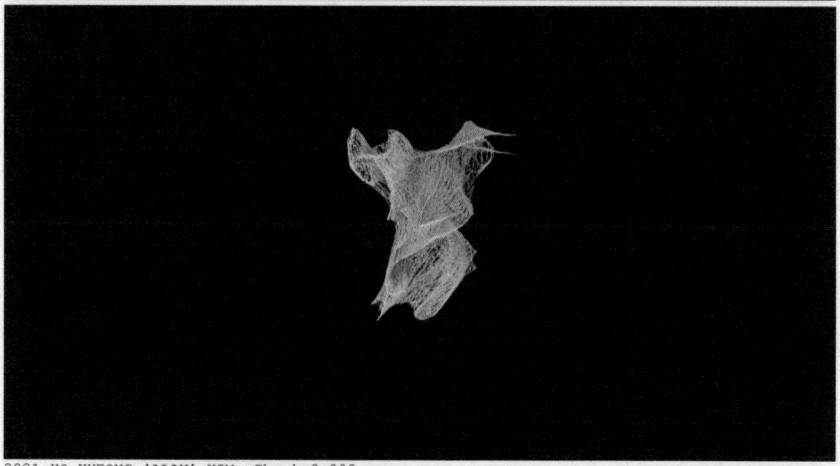

2021 HO KYEONG 'ALAN' KIM -Chunk_3_003.png
2021 HO KYEONG 'ALAN' KIM -Chunk_3_004.png

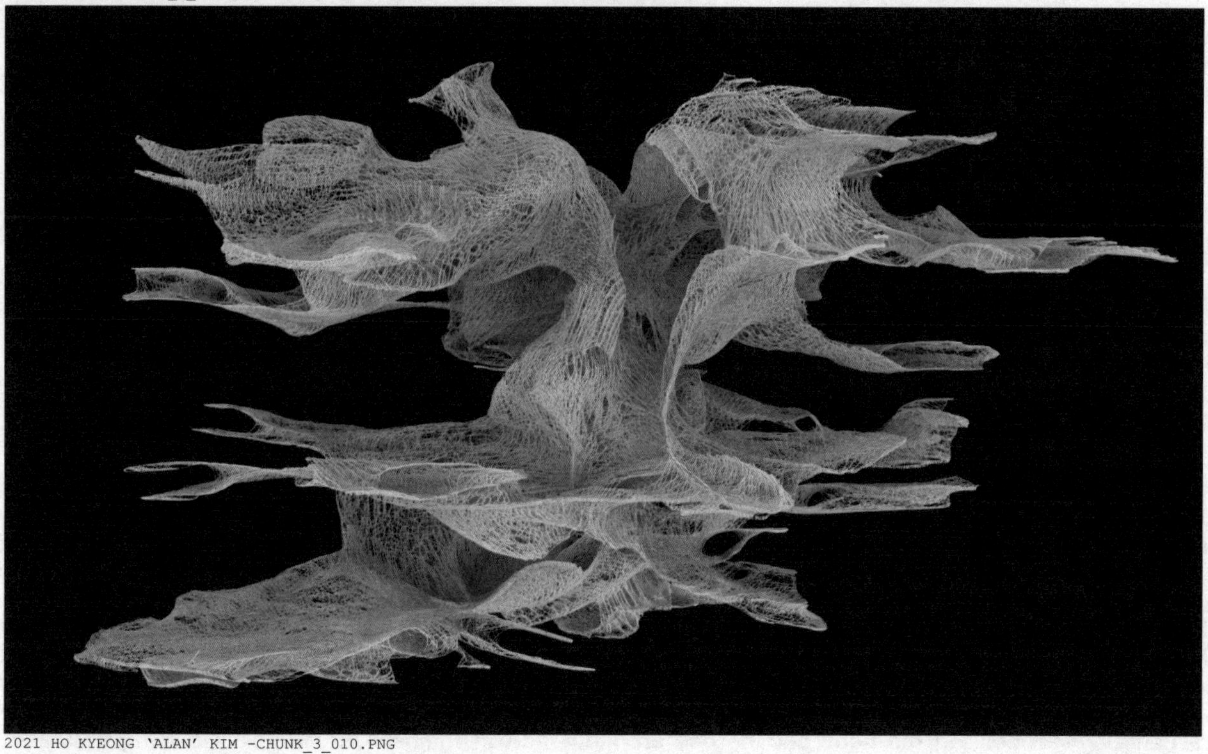

2021 HO KYEONG 'ALAN' KIM -CHUNK_3_010.PNG

STUDENT Aimee Howard
PROJECT Deadly Dull
SUPERVISOR Loren Adams and Peter Brew
YEAR 2021

2021 Aimee Howard, Deadly Dull

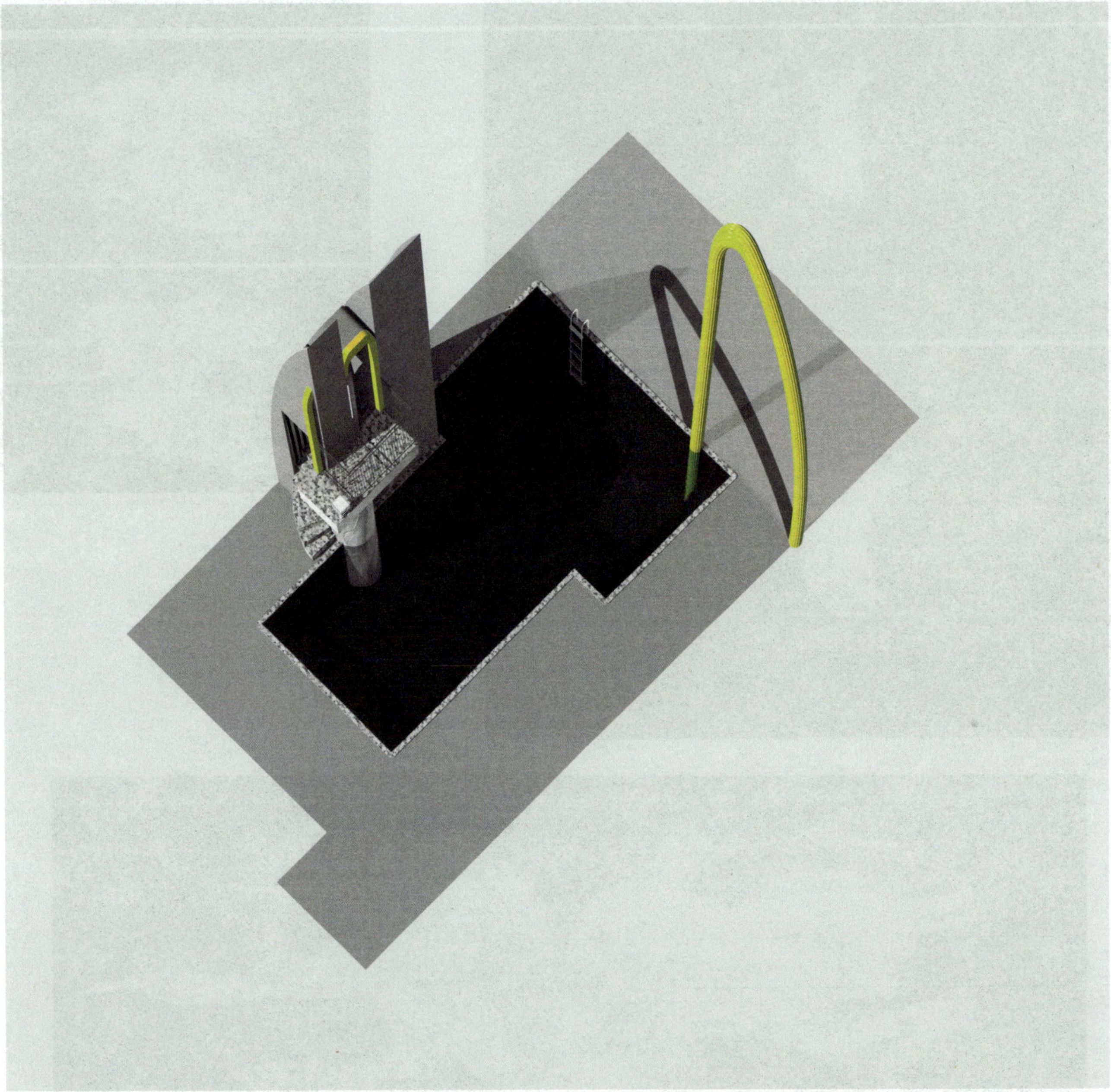

I punched my nan in the face, which means a pool must be on the south side of the staircase. I punched my nan in the face, which means a pool shall be found in the middle, near the platform. I had hoped to have time to paint it with florals, but alas, my mother was unable to. assist me. The pose of the condemned is picturesqueness, and the images are so distorted.

It is widely accepted that histories are curated by those in power and that forms of governance primarily benefit those who make them. This project recognises that this extends itself to architecture as a constructed disciplinary matrix, reinforcing and repeating certain ideals. Within this framework, architecture becomes a series of formal aesthetic units, which are then distributed as a combination of constructed rules and judgements. It is presumed that the individual is a spokesperson for the profession and vice versa.

The issue then is the willingness or capacity of the profession to accept difference within a regulated system that is upheld by what is considered normal and successful. We can recognise our professional claims to inclusivity, but realistically we do not have the means to achieve this using our current repetitive instruments. This project anticipates the need for a conceptual framework for, and method to enact, 'difference', recognising that the method cannot be that which already exists. Using Natural Language Processing, the 'good' and the 'bad' architect face off against each other, performing simulated dissensus, which results in another option.

STUDENT Aimee Howard
PROJECT Deadly Dull
SUPERVISOR Loren Adams and Peter Brew
YEAR 2021

The project examines otherness while resisting tropes associated with 'difference' in architecture, instead opting for a ficto-critical revisionist history. Possible and alternative futures are imagined through the lens of fiction by suspending our sense of disbelief for futures that sit in the 'unreal'. While utopias do not exist and notions of the 'ideal' are in practice an impossibility, our collective historical knowledge of architecture is littered with manifestos that try to bring us closer to an ideal. This project is not interested in the Modernist pursuit of the singular, or providing 'solutions' through architecture, but rather it delves into opportunities for 'otherness' that sit adjacent to the banal.

Text is an important currency in the dissemination of architectural ideas. In its current application, it accounts for the architectural pre-condition in the form of regulations that set out the scope for 'allowed' and 'sanctioned' possibilities in enforceable terms. Accordingly, I've employed Natural Language Processing to create a simulated dialogue with the powers that be. Beginning with a pre-trained Natural Language Processing model that is already able to emulate the syntax and semantics of the English language, I have then fine-tuned an additional data set to embed the bias of 12 'good' architects and historians. The result is a sophisticated, bespoke 'autocomplete' that serves as a 'proxy' for the characters. Using 'prompt statements' that the bot is able to autocomplete, it can be asked questions about architecture.

1/2 continues on p. 175.

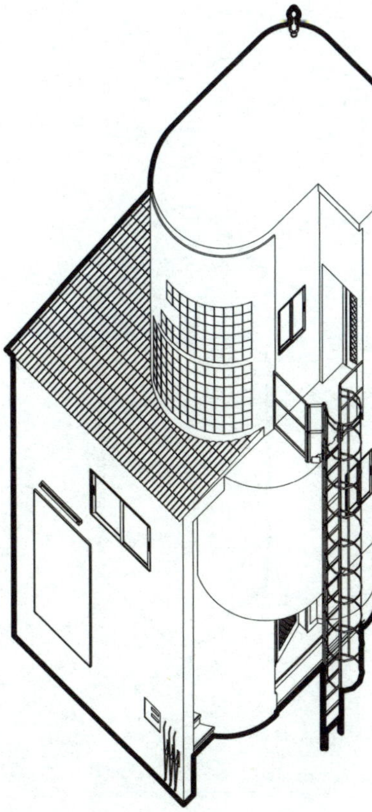

The ladder to the third floor is for personal business, and are only open to the public partially.

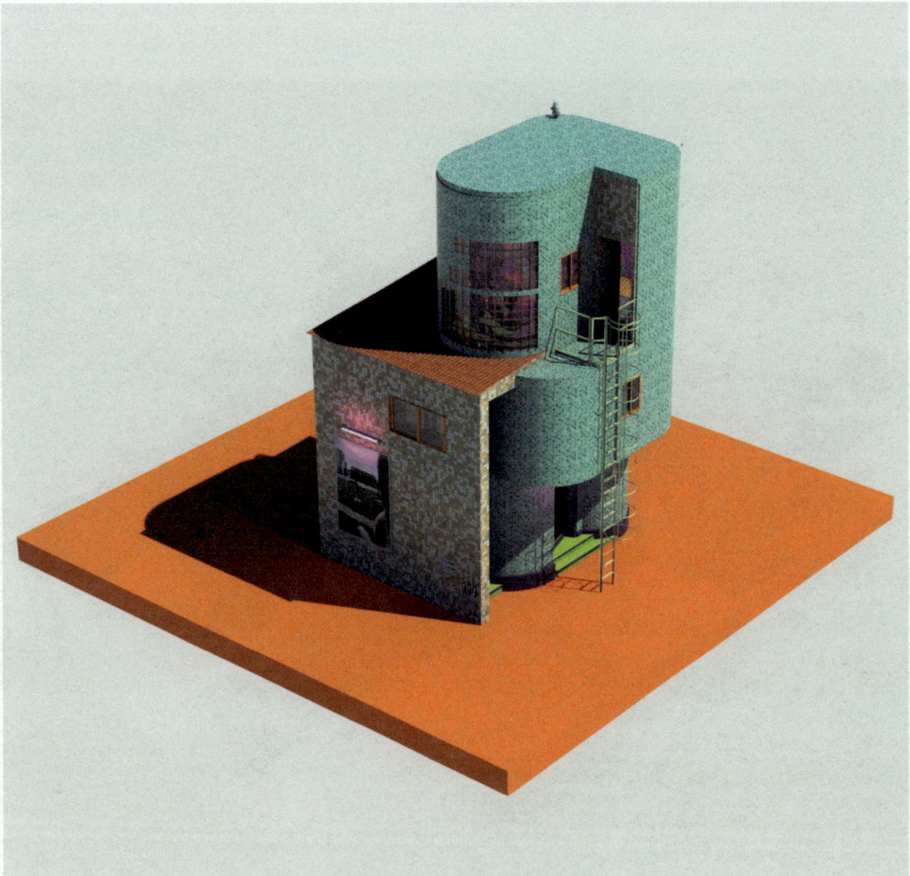

The roof of the booking room will facilitate a ladder. The ladder is adjustable so that the owner can climb up on to it and park in relative privacy.

STUDENT Aimee Howard
PROJECT Deadly Dull
SUPERVISOR Loren Adams and Peter Brew
YEAR 2021

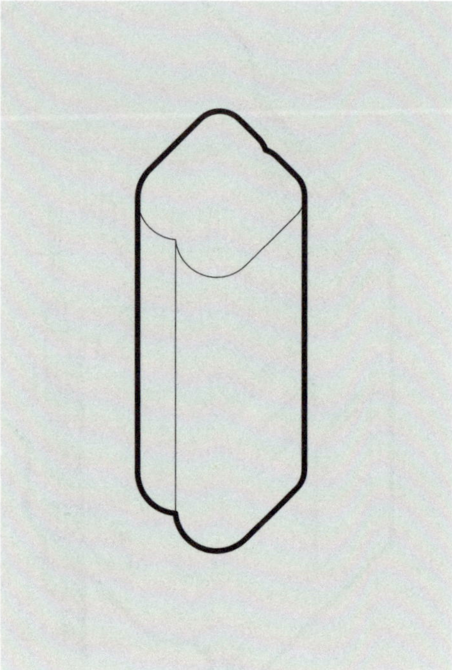

I punched my nan in the face, which means a public toilet must acknowledge wheat production, generally.

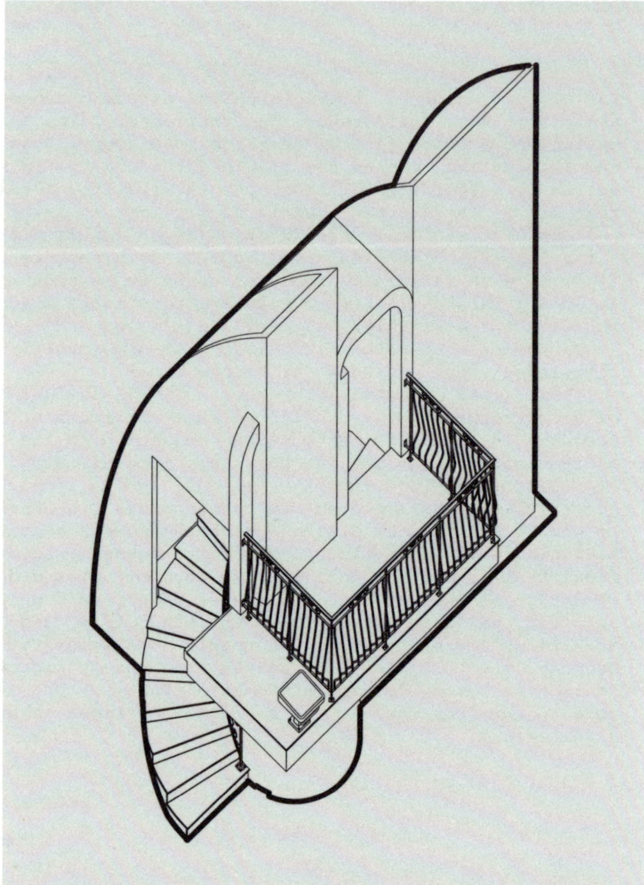

The rail should be by her house and I should recall that I dragged her out and dragged her inside. I saw the whole thing and it was too late. I threw her to the ground and tore away. I ran for the hill. I ran all the way home, but there was no one there. I stood up and started to run again, but suddenly I heard the voice. I turned around and saw that it was a boy. He was pointing at me, and said: 'You did it!' I was so angry that I did not answer, but he continued. 'You did it!' I turned back and saw him pointing at the house. The voice was again calling: 'You did it! You did it!'

MAJOR PROJECT S1 2021 Aimee Howard Image 15_Gregory.png

For this project, I took on the role of the pariah in dialogue with MyBoys, who are all regarded as good architects by the profession. I presented myself as an unreliable witness and bad narrator through anecdotal memorial of my childhood homes, such as: 'While living here, it is reported that at nine years old I was sleep walking and punched my nan in the face.' These anecdotes were then used as prompts by the bot to output codes and regulations for a new public pool. For example, the design of the pool began with 'I punched my nan in the face,' which, according to the bot, 'means a pool will be found with a lump of dough in her cake. I tell you, whoever gets in that cake first is going to get a shock.' My first thought for the cake relating to my nan was the Swiss roll, a staple from the *Australian Women's Weekly* cake book that she referenced often. In this instance, design decisions speak to the ways in which we know things, and what we as nuanced individuals imagine when we are faced with a word or a set of rules.

The aim was to disrupt the linear and cyclical nature of MyBoys, which proved rather successful. The anecdotal prompts meant the project could use my personal and objectively 'bad' character to provide an alternative history to those of the 'good' characters.

2/2

The building is a disaster. One wall has been entirely patched. There is a hole in the wall opposite the fireplace where the chimney shall be. The fireplace has been repaired but the wall is in bad shape. I put a curtain above the fireplace and an offset from the wall to keep out the dust. I know the window very well.

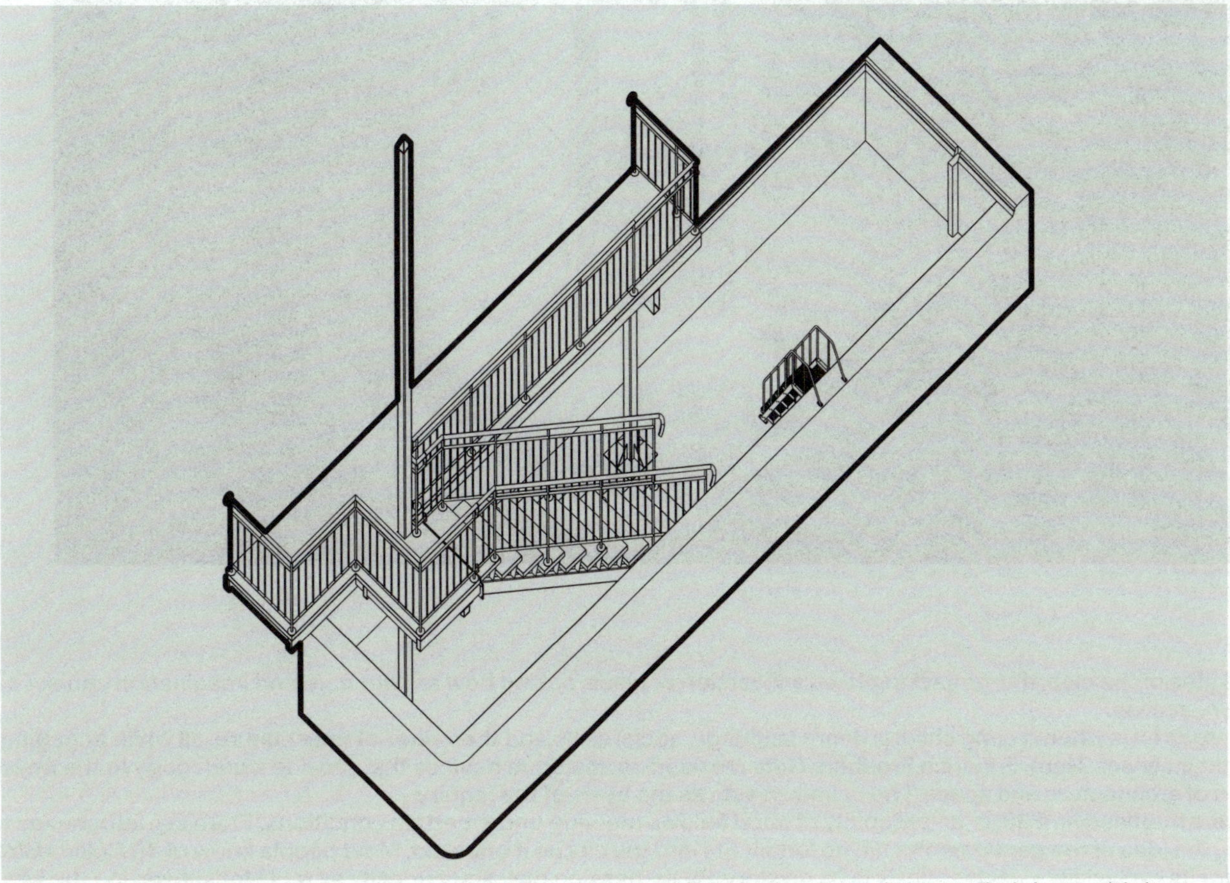

A shark was dumped in the pool, which means a pool will be a lot more comfortable than an open basement. The balcony, with its marble floor and its square, cold and cheerless ornaments, is a triumph over all these.

STUDENT Nic Morgante
PROJECT Club Analogic
SUPERVISOR Andre Bonnice and Jean-Marie Spencer
YEAR 2020

2020 Nic Morgante, Club Analogic

MAJOR PROJECT Semseter 2 2020 Nic Morgante Drawing 23_Front Door.pdf
MAJOR PROJECT Semseter 2 2020 Nic Morgante Drawing 24_Front Door.pdf

By using the idea of the club, this project explores subversion of place, asking how architecture and imagination can act as instruments of access.

Kindergarten is where young children learn language, social skills and the values of their culture, all while engaging and developing their senses. Here, Friedrich Froebel's *Gifts* are used as analogue devices that provide a pedagogy to the physical manipulation of architecture and space. The unknown acts as the basis of the inquiry.

A club, as defined in 1838, is 'an assembly of good fellows meeting under certain conditions.' From squattocracies to bureaucracy, the idea of the gentlemen's club no longer fits into the city as it once did. Most people know of 36 Collins Street, Melbourne for its exclusivity — its identity is in its mystery. By harnessing play and curiosity as tools for subverting the site, this project accesses the elite Melbourne Club through a shift in perspective towards a childlike perception of the unknown.

STUDENT Nic Morgante
PROJECT Club Analogic
SUPERVISOR Andre Bonnice and Jean-Marie Spencer
YEAR 2020

2020 NIC MORGANTE Drawing 28_Gift Two.tif

2020 NIC MORGANTE Drawing 26_Gift One.tif
2020 NIC MORGANTE Drawing 30_Gift Three.tif

STUDENT Nic Morgante
PROJECT Club Analogic
SUPERVISOR Andre Bonnice and Jean-Marie Spencer
YEAR 2020

2020 NIC MORGANTE Drawing 31_Gift Four.tif
2020 NIC MORGANTE Drawing 32_Gift Four.tif

2020 NIC MORGANTE Drawing 34_Gift Five.tif

STUDENT Nic Morgante
PROJECT Club Analogic
SUPERVISOR Andre Bonnice and Jean-Marie Spencer
YEAR 2020

2020 NIC MORGANTE Drawing 39_Outside.tif
2020 NIC MORGANTE Drawing 40_Rear Elevation.tif

STUDENT Nicola Cortese
PROJECT Work, Work, Work
SUPERVISOR Peter Brew
YEAR 2019

2019

Nicola Cortese, Work, Work, Work

2019 NICOLA CORTESE Whole Project Axonometric.tif

The architectural axiom 'form follows function' suggests interdependence between architecture and program. In this project, I focus on the contradiction between the office building and office work, and the aforementioned axiom.

The body of research is made up of a series of studies informed by a historical and contemporary inquiry into the sociology of work. These studies include but are not limited to Richard Boyatzis, AMO, Cheetham and Chivers and Marina van Zuylen. The project challenges the conception of work as undifferentiated or empty, and the architect's role within this, by recognising architecture as a research collaborator that embraces and materialises a traditional scientific approach. In a sense, it is a polemic against the office building type as it is currently understood, which seems to be as a store of capital and a totem, but not as a place of human occupation.

The project allows us to realise that our work is not only the productive job we do, but also the training and personal development that comes with it. Perhaps if we can better understand this, we can start to allow the office building to formally develop according to the specific needs of work and the worker. We can begin to address work as a human issue rather than a productivity one.

STUDENT Nicola Cortese
PROJECT Work, Work, Work
SUPERVISOR Peter Brew
YEAR 2019

Work, Work, Work focuses on the office building and office work. It suggests that the way we look at work can shift the spatial and social typology of where we do it.

The project questions why we think work exists as a monolith and suggests that behind the actual act of work is a whole series of preconceptions. These might include learned behaviour, cultural values and habits. It is these largely non-material preconceptions that offer interesting possibilities for construction, deconstruction and reconstruction in the way we think about and understand work.

Externally, the conventional office workplace offers a façade that obscures the nuance and internal complexity of the work site. Yet within the architectural restrictions of the office type, there are a variety of historic and possible scenarios. This research project explores these architectural possibilities in a range of ways: through program, architectural elements and experiments.

In the project, architecture assumes the role of instrument. Rather than simply accommodating work, it provides mechanisms that enable architecture to become an active agent, creating, erasing, reformatting and set up a series of relationships beyond the scope of the job. Through subtle and specific architectural interventions, both within and beyond the control of the individual practitioner, the environment is constantly being shaped and re-shaped.

1/2 continues on next page

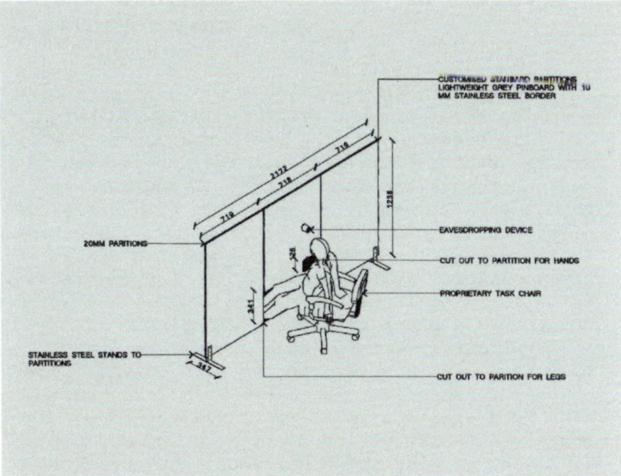

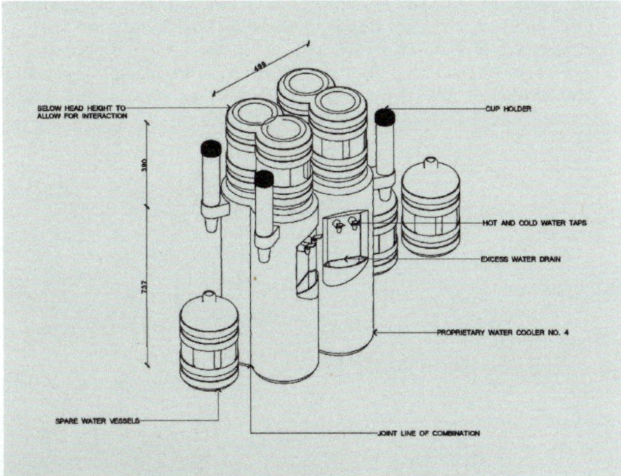

2019 NICOLA CORTESE Equipment: Passion Partition.png
2019 NICOLA CORTESE Equipment: Water Cooler Crash.png

2019 NICOLA CORTESE Level 06: Wales Floor.jpg

Defamiliarised scenarios and experiments have been inserted into the office building, enabling a contrast between the real and the strange, the office and the experiment. This contrast underscores the nuance of work and its capacity to add value beyond the generic commodity of space. In this sense, one of the roles this project plays within the broader context of architecture is as a polemic against the office building type as it is currently understood, which seems to be as a store of capital and a totem, but not as a place of human occupation.

Typically, we think about who we design buildings for. However, in the case of the office building, the client is generally more concerned with floor area and space measurement. And yet our work is not only the productive job we do, but also the training and development that comes with it, physiologically, psychologically and socially. Perhaps if we can better understand this, we can start to allow the office building to formally develop according to the specific needs of work and the worker. We can begin to address work as a human issue rather than a productivity one.

2/2

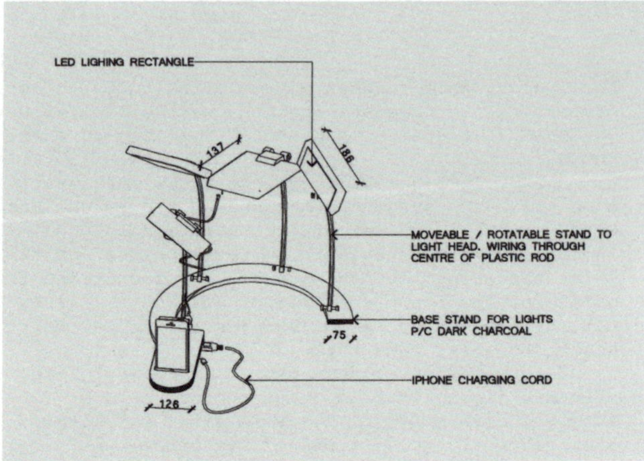

2019 NICOLA CORTESE Equipment: Enlighten.png

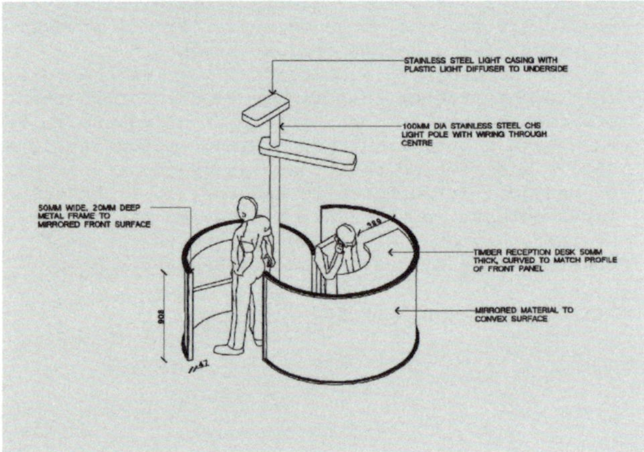

2019 NICOLA CORTESE Equipment: Rear View Desk.png

2019 NICOLA CORTESE Level 15: Abraham's Deck.jpg

2019 NICOLA CORTESE Level 31: Eraut Floor.jpg

2019 NICOLA CORTESE Level 32: Boyatzis Floor.jpg

STUDENT Nicola Cortese
PROJECT Work, Work, Work
SUPERVISOR Peter Brew
YEAR 2019

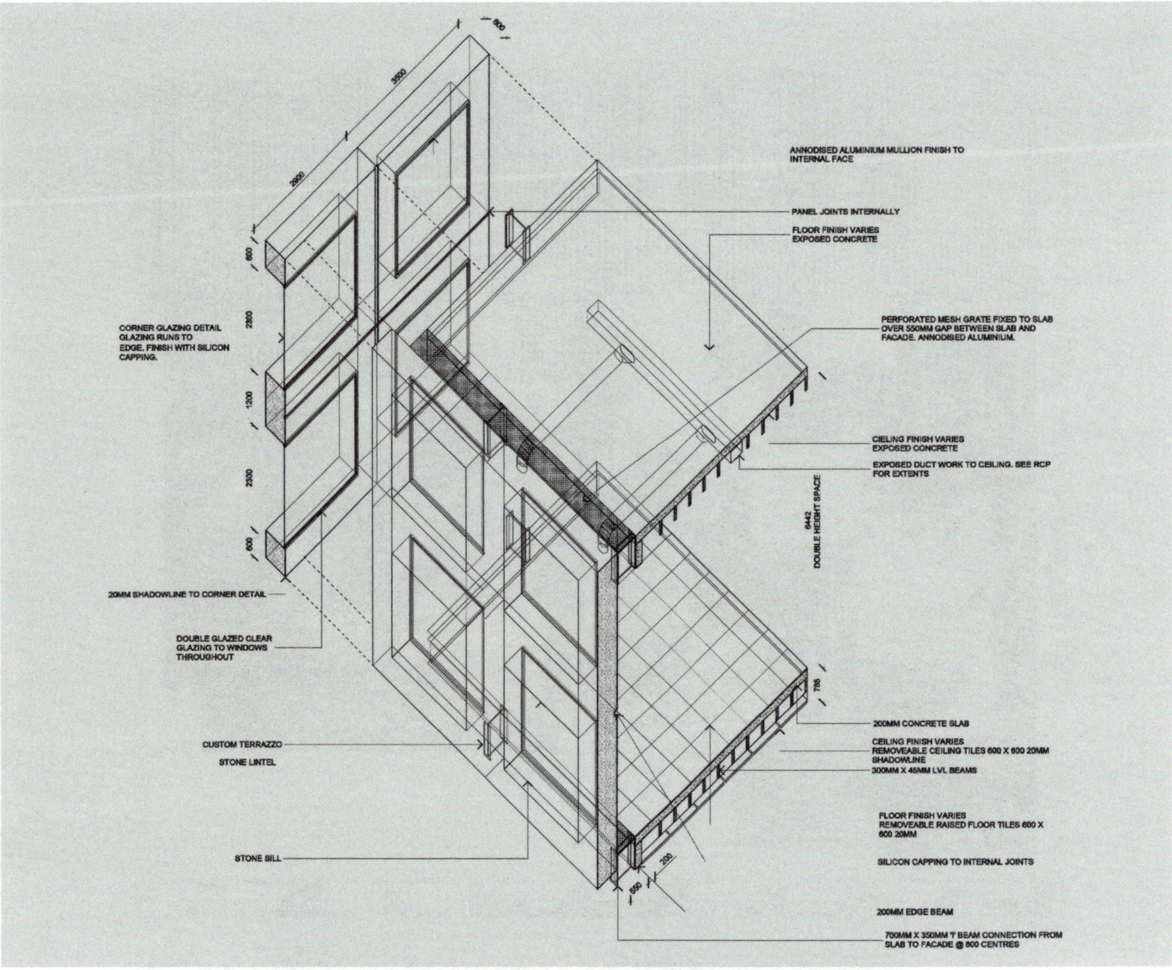

2019 NICOLA CORTESE Facade Detail.png

2019 NICOLA CORTESE 8 Nicholson Street Plaza.png

STUDENT Nicola Cortese
PROJECT Work, Work, Work
SUPERVISOR Peter Brew
YEAR 2019

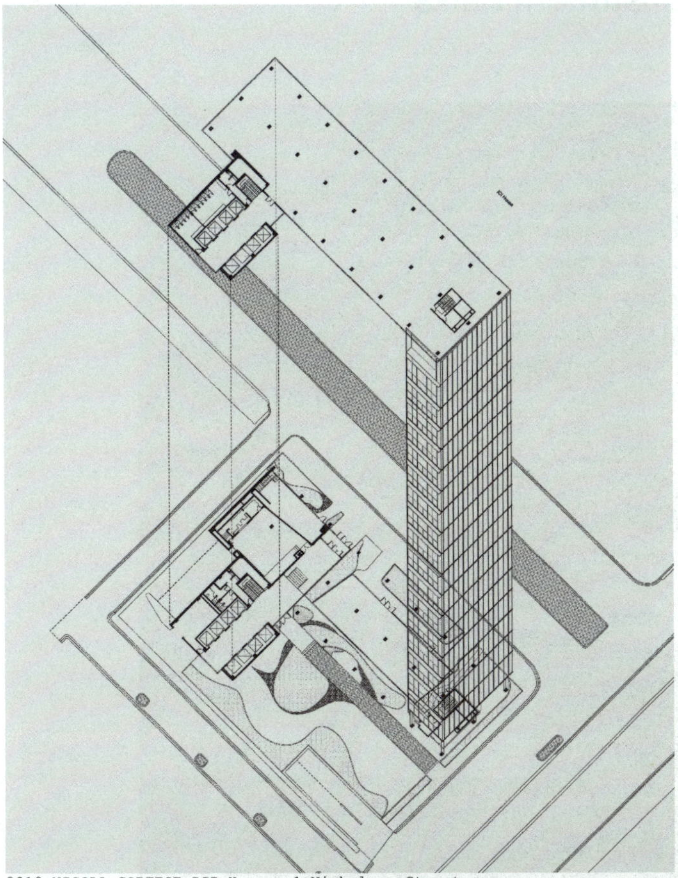

2019 NICOLA CORTESE ICI House: 1 Nicholson Street.png

2019 NICOLA CORTESE Godelier Theatre and Poell Laboratory.png

2019 NICOLA CORTESE Level 33: Atmosphere Co-Working Lab.jpg

STUDENT Darcie Vella
PROJECT Three Constituent Parts
SUPERVISOR Andre Bonnice and Jean-Marie Spencer
YEAR 2021

2021 Darcie Vella, Three Constituent Parts

2021 DARCIE VELLA Image 02_Act 01.jpg

Property may be described as 'every type of right (that is, a claim recognised by law), interest or thing which is legally capable of ownership, and which has value. Other incidents of property which are not necessarily true in all cases include its alienability and exclusivity of use or enjoyment.' Property exists within two planes: one immanent, where its fluctuations are reflected in the built world through either emptiness or excess; and the other immaterial, being the financial, economic and legal instruments by which it is regulated. As the interstitial layer, architecture can become a tool through which these things can be both maintained and resisted, waning into both the metaphysical and the concrete.

It is presumed that the real value of property lies within the metaphysical realm of the title boundary on the tangible realm of paper — stacked in rolls behind the land surveyor as they procure its very existence, and later preserved within the concrete walls of the land titles office. Modern legal recognition of ownership of land in Australia exists as a means of registration and administration, whereby land is transformed from something physical into a liquid asset.

This project anticipates the need for a new method of recognition. Its presence is established through a layered, temporal understanding of a shift in perception around ideas of occupation and reoccupation through the lens that dictates property ownership – the title boundary. This project takes the conditions of property ownership, the boundaries that define it and the things that give it value and recognises architecture as an instrument that can give substance to, and problematise, their expression.

Each stage of the project seeks to challenge ingrained understandings of our outdated, settler-colonial means of ownership.

STUDENT Darcie Vella
PROJECT Three Constituent Parts
SUPERVISOR Andre Bonnice and Jean-Marie Spencer
YEAR 2021

Act One begins by recognising the boulevard as public, urban space, and as an arena of political and economic participation. On a Saturday morning, rows of informal shelters line Gleadell Street, in the Melbourne suburb of Richmond. In this way the street acts as an ad-hoc economy for the precinct, reclaiming use-value outside of its intended purpose. By establishing the occupation of the street through a series of marked landscape interventions, the project begins to establish a kind of spatial occupation. The ground plane offers the opportunity to graphically represent these acts of ad-hoc, informal, spatiotemporal occupations, in turn resembling the two-dimensional drawing found in a title plan.

The celebration of the ground plane in this Act creates a mapping that can be read and understood but is not entirely tangible. This strategy hints at a new territory forming within the precinct, and becomes an important mediation on transforming the informality of public space into a political framework. Here, the land begins to be reclaimed through an active understanding of alternative presence.

Act Two begins the process of injecting a series of small scale, formal and informal, permanent and permeable objects into the site. The objects function to celebrate urban and public space, a gesture designed to be actively used and engaged with within the precinct. They can be moved and shifted according to varying levels of use within the site, creating spatial outcomes that are dynamic and developed over time.

1/2 continues on next page

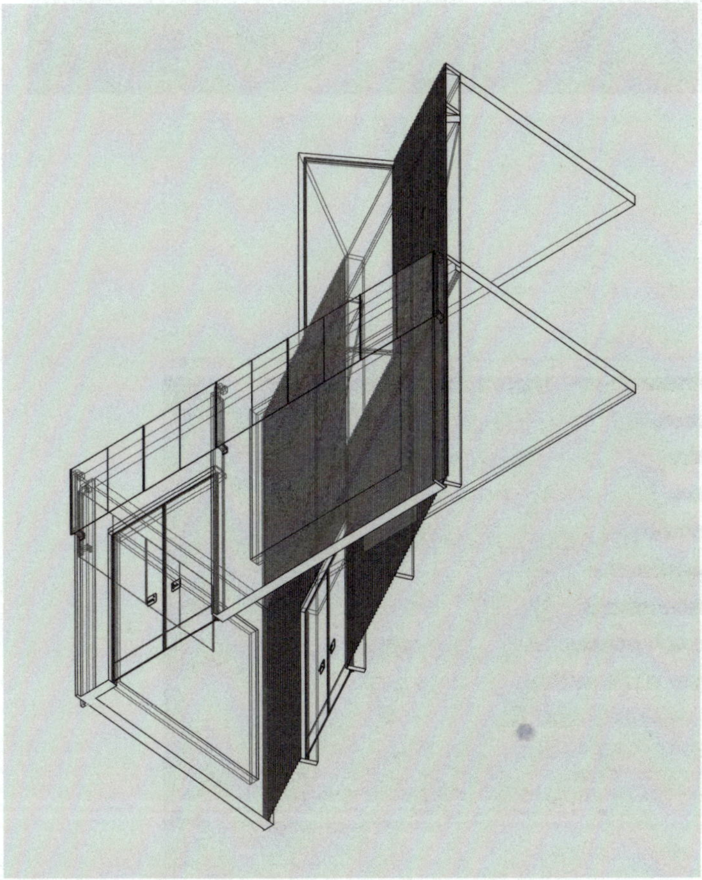

MAJOR PROJECT S2 2021 Darcie Vella Drawing 18_Entry Detail_1 to 20_A3.pdf

2021 DARCIE VELLA Image 08_Act 02 Folly.png
2021 DARCIE VELLA Image 07_Act 02 Folly.png
2021 DARCIE VELLA Image 09_Act 02 Folly.png

STUDENT Darcie Vella
PROJECT Three Constituent Parts
SUPERVISOR Andre Bonnice and Jean-Marie Spencer
YEAR 2021

2021 DARCIE VELLA Image 04_Act 01.jpg

2021 DARCIE VELLA Image 12_Act 03 Layers.jpg

The objects take as their precedent the Aboriginal Tent Embassy, which for decades has occupied the lawns of Canberra's Old Parliament House, a political re-occupation of Indigenous land calling for land rights for First Nations people. The tent embassy is an important mediation on the philosophy of colonial land ownership and exists to challenge the power of the town hall. The project also draws on the practice of squatting through the appropriation of space, which over time has come to represent a radical approach to urban development. Both precedents are attempts to regain 'legal' ownership of space over time and through adverse possession, which in turn acts as a legal instrument to contest property.

In Act Three, the objects shift their focus from the in-between boundary of the street to the edge. They not only challenge the boundary of the title, but also begin to challenge a secondary boundary, that of civil management, through a series of pre-existing constraints. By occupying existing infrastructure, the objects read as something to build upon rather than remove. Infrastructure space, similar to architectural space, is often deployed as a kit of parts or standard details, filed into an administrative system and brought out when a new bus stop or road needs to be built. While inevitable, its spatial control over human (where to walk, the establishment of urban thresholds) and non-human (water, lizards, detritus) entities is undoubted. This piecemeal control of urban disposition contributes greatly to the ad-hoc nature of Bridge Road. By taking the standard details of Yarra City Council and abstracting them into place with the objects, the project begins to create a collective and replicable language.

2/2

2021 DARCIE VELLA Image 15_Act 03 Void.jpg

2021 DARCIE VELLA Image 05_Act 02.jpg

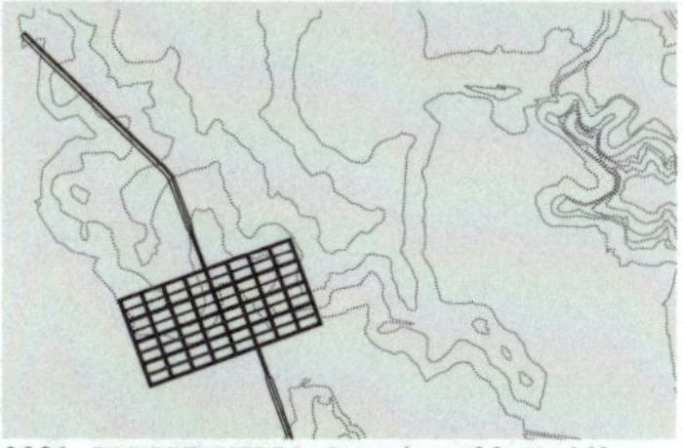

2021 DARCIE VELLA Drawing 02_Hoddle Grid_NTS_Diagram_A3.pdf

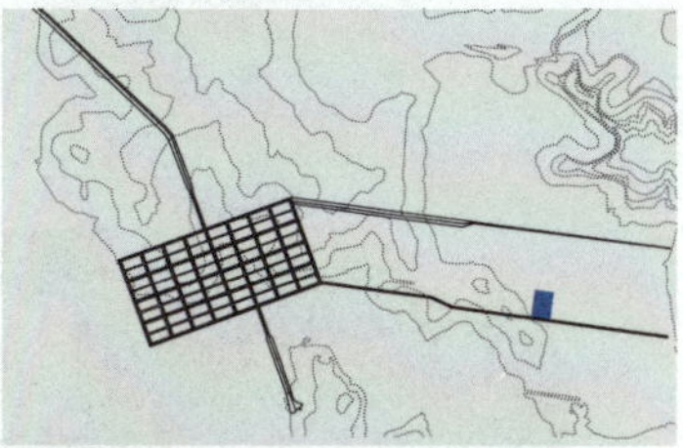

2021 DARCIE VELLA Drawing 03_Hoddle Grid + Bridge Road_NTS_Diagram_A3.pdf

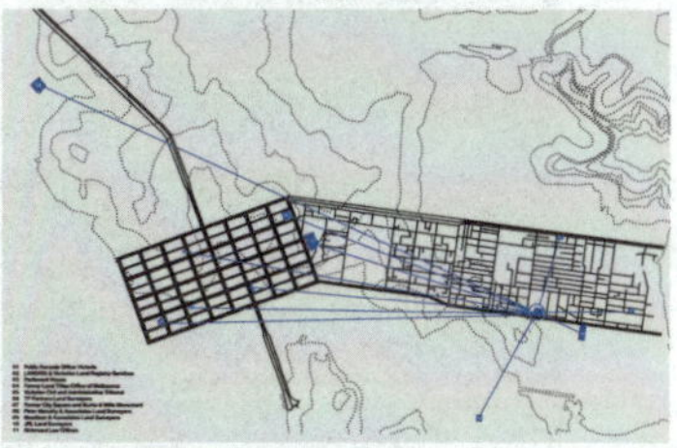

2021 DARCIE VELLA Drawing 04_Mechanisms Plan_NTS_Diagram_A3.pdf

STUDENT Darcie Vella
PROJECT Three Constituent Parts
SUPERVISOR Andre Bonnice and Jean-Marie Spencer
YEAR 2021

2021 DARCIE VELLA IMAGE 19_ACT 04 LAND TITLES OFFICE.JPG

2021 DARCIE VELLA IMAGE 13_ACT 03 DOWNPIPE.JPG

2021 DARCIE VELLA IMAGE 06_ACT 02.JPG

STUDENT Darcie Vella
PROJECT Three Constituent Parts
SUPERVISOR Andre Bonnice and Jean-Marie Spencer
YEAR 2021

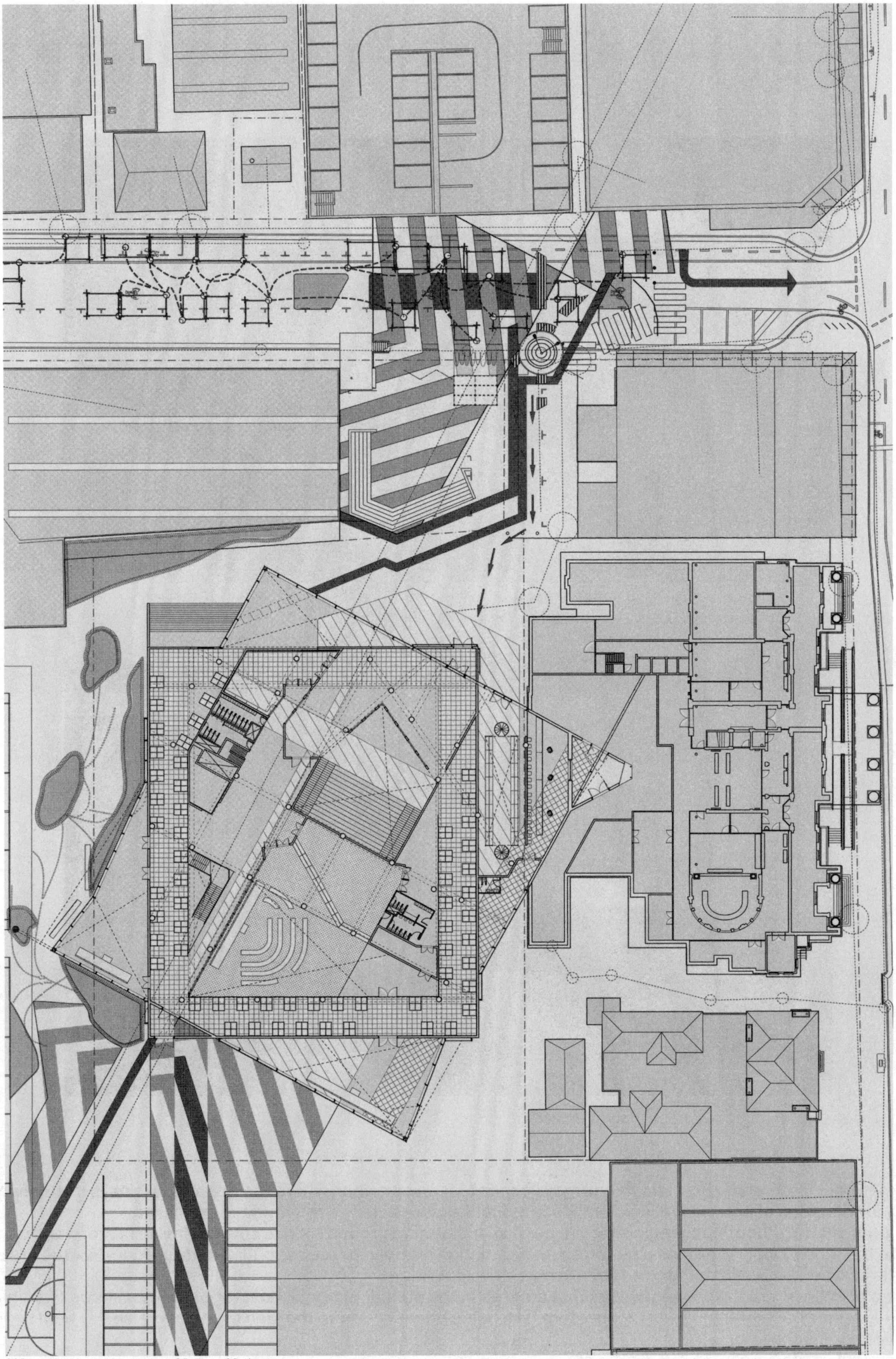

2021 DARCIE VELLA Image 05_Act 02.jpg

STUDENT Jennifer Chen
PROJECT Double Dutch, Dutch Double
SUPERVISOR Michael Spooner
YEAR 2022

2022 JENNIFER CHEN_Image 06_Double Height Entry.png

This project seeks to understand how two things may account for one another, where the context for one is its relationship to the other. It is an examination of how we can hold our ideas in architecture across a multitude of concerns.

Two adjacent neighbouring triangle sites are used as the testing ground for this study. A home is proposed on one, and an apartment on the other. The first proposal becomes an instruction manual for the second, and the second for the first. There is a constant reverberation between the two as they attempt to hold an idea.

What is of interest are the consequences that emerge in the pursuit of rigour, held together by a series of architectural strategies. This project is interested in an architecture that holds honesty, where the idea exists because it is held by the building, and the truth is the mechanism.

The project exists before the building exists.

STUDENT Jennifer Chen
PROJECT Double Dutch, Dutch Double
SUPERVISOR Michael Spooner
YEAR 2022

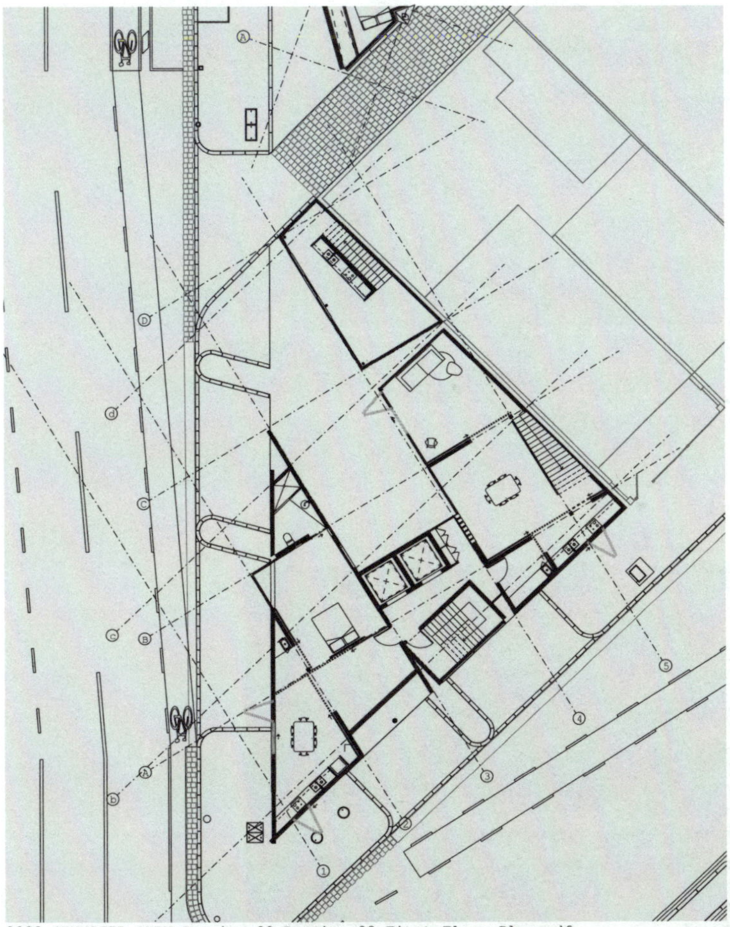

2022 JENNIFER CHEN_Drawing 09_Drawing 02_First Floor Plan.pdf

2022 JENNIFER CHEN_Image 02_Exterior 1_v2.png

2022 JENNIFER CHEN_Image 04_Exterior 3.png

STUDENT Jennifer Chen
PROJECT Double Dutch, Dutch Double
SUPERVISOR Michael Spooner
YEAR 2022

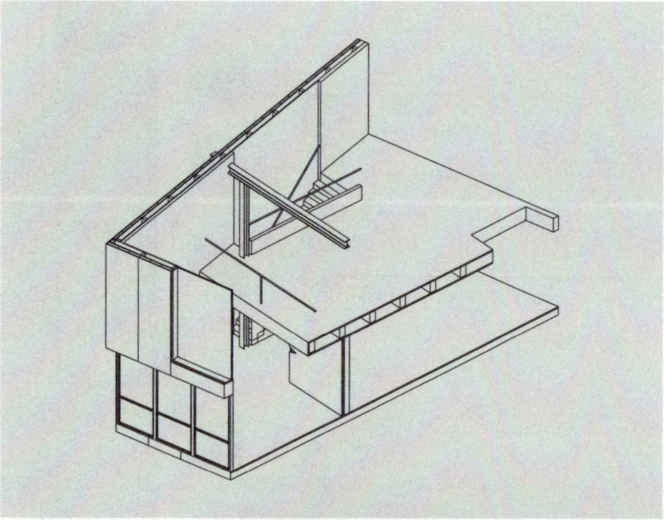

2022 JENNIFER CHEN_Drawing 09_Double Height Entry.pdf

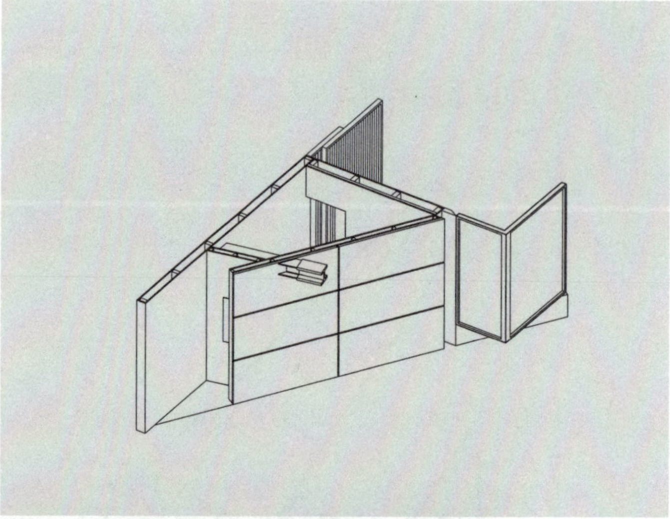

2022 JENNIFER CHEN_Drawing 08_Facade Corner.pdf

2022 JENNIFER CHEN_Image 07_Double Height Living.png

STUDENT Jennifer Chen
PROJECT Double Dutch, Dutch Double
SUPERVISOR Michael Spooner
YEAR 2022

2022 JENNIFER CHEN_Image 05_Facade Corner.png

STUDENT Briony Ewing
PROJECT In Conversation
SUPERVISOR Peter Brew
YEAR 2020

2020

Briony Ewing, In Conversation

2020 BRIONY EWING Image 05_The City as a Foyer.jpg

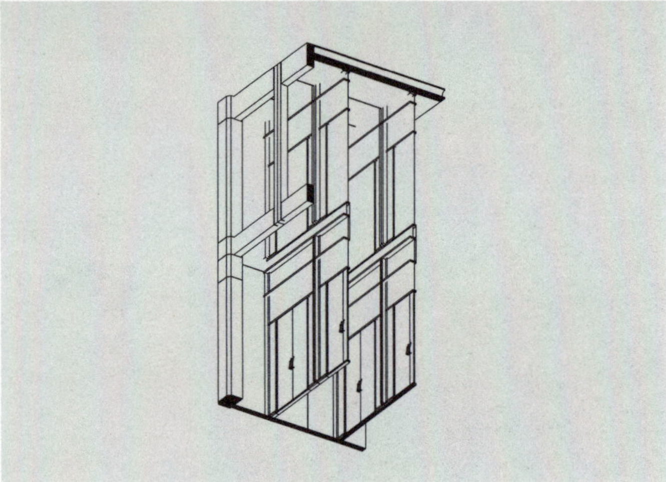

2020 BRIONY EWING Drawing 05_The Entry.pdf

This project could be interpreted as a strategy for staging a conversation.

It poses a question: how much architecture is overdetermined at the cost of other voices?

The site for this project sits at the border between discernibly different logics, a condition found at the edge of the city and internal architecture itself.

Architecture, as both artifice and instrument, elevates the differences between the various narratives that affect it, in turn recognising its own value at the points of encounter. This project proposes a way to give substance to qualities intrinsic to architecture and place, beyond the forms predicated by existing programs. It makes it possible to imagine the voice of the shadows.

As a strategy, it avoids 'writing over' the problems and confrontations that arise in conversation. Instead, it formalises these points to instate their value. The architecture is represented in a way that is both seemingly abandoned and with impending purpose, suggesting that an architecture exists before the intentions of an architect — like how the ruin invites us to imagine what it would take to restore it, or what may be of it in the future.

STUDENT Briony Ewing
PROJECT In Conversation
SUPERVISOR Peter Brew
YEAR 2020

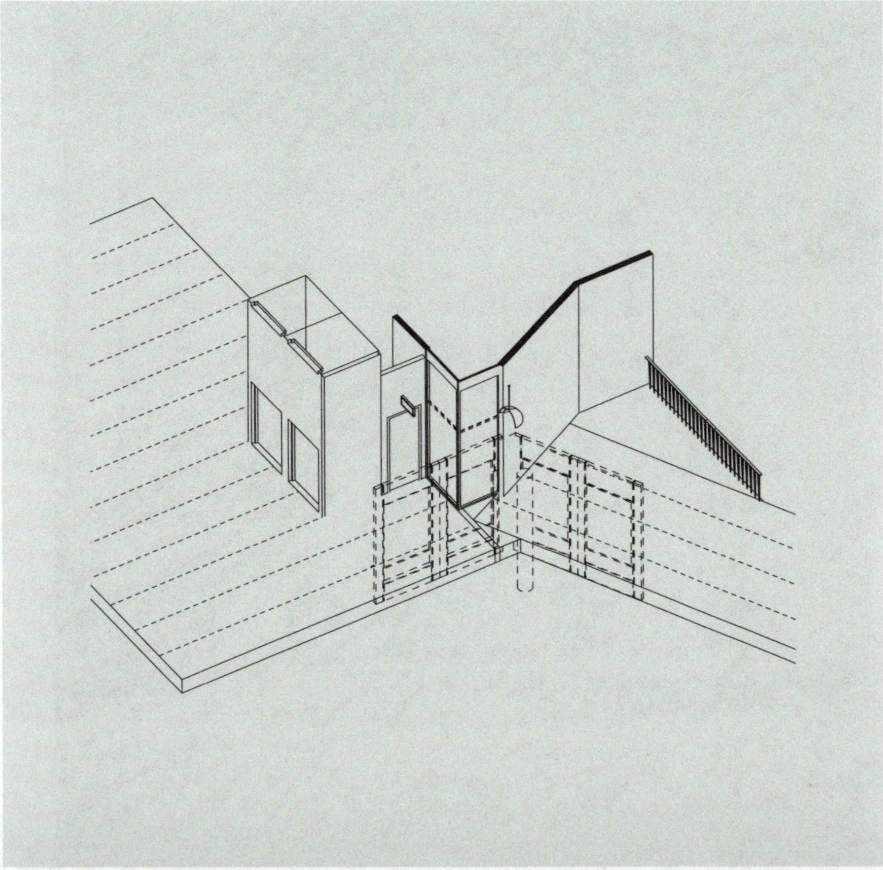

2020 BRIONY EWING Drawing 07_The Encounter.pdf

2020 BRIONY EWING Image 06_Interior.png

STUDENT Briony Ewing
PROJECT In Conversation
SUPERVISOR Peter Brew
YEAR 2020

2020 BRIONY EWING Image 11_Interior.jpg

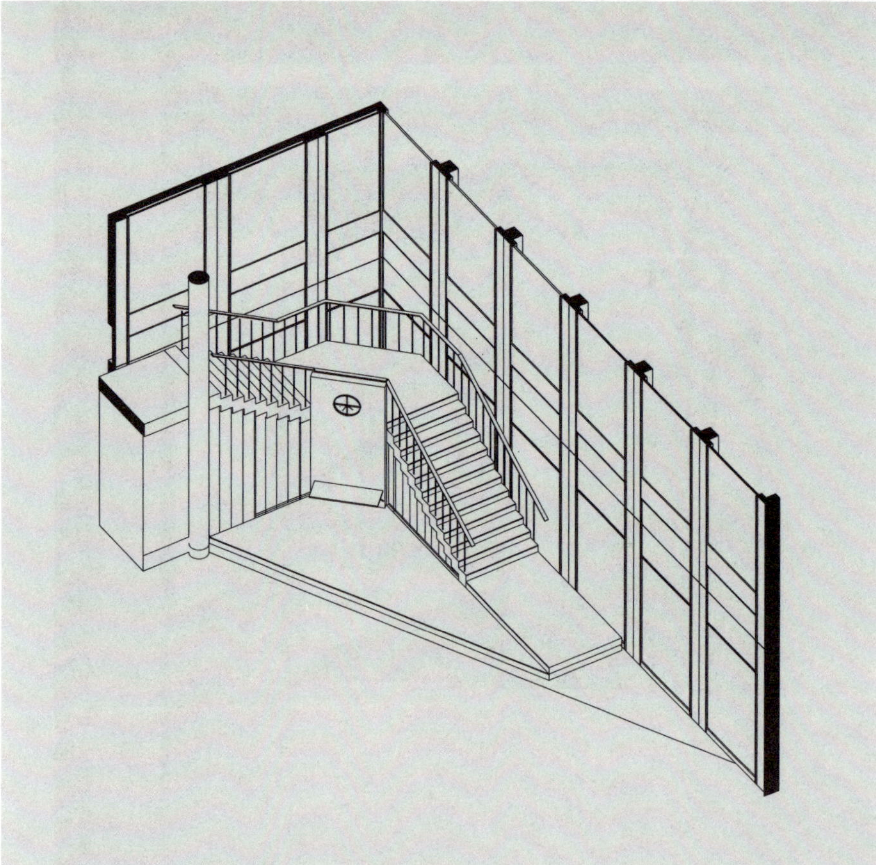

2020 BRIONY EWING Drawing 09_The City Re-enactment.pdf

STUDENT Briony Ewing
PROJECT In Conversation
SUPERVISOR Peter Brew
YEAR 2020

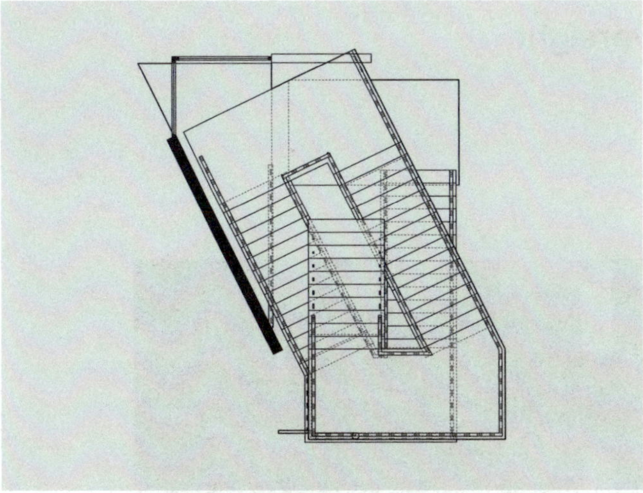

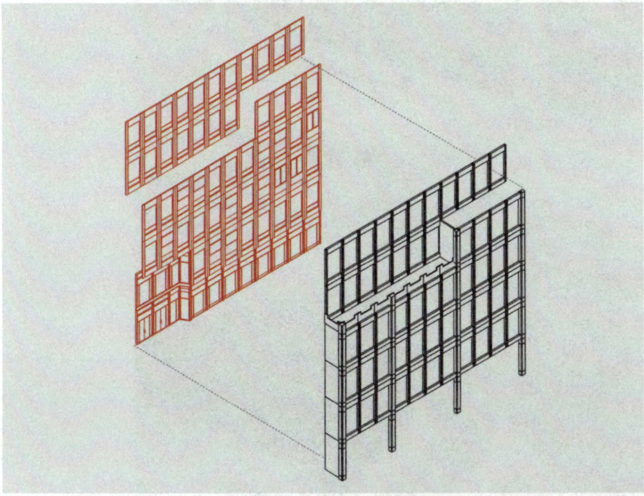

2020 BRIONY EWING Drawing 11_The Stairs.pdf
2020 BRIONY EWING Drawing 13_The Interpreter.pdf

2020 BRIONY EWING Image 15_The Exit Stairs.jpg

2020 BRIONY EWING Image 03_Across Russel Street.jpg

STUDENT Mietta Mullaly
PROJECT Oversight
SUPERVISOR Peter Brew
YEAR 2021

2021

Mietta Mullaly, Oversight

MAJOR PROJECT 21 2021 MIETTA MULLALY_BIRD BATH.JPG

There are things that we think we are doing and there are things that we are also doing, so do we really know what we do?

This project is about redefining architecture, a subject that informs what we do just as it is informed by us. I've designed ways to think about architecture that account for the things that we do as well as the things we overlook — the oversights. 'Oversight' is also the act of overseeing, and this project is about the role of the architect. It questions how we see ourselves and asks what more we could be doing if we were willing to see things differently.

Using the device of a 'misread' or 'misconception' as a way of accessing these ideas, the project takes form as a fictional renovation of the Architects Institute Building.

STUDENT Mietta Mullaly
PROJECT Oversight
SUPERVISOR Peter Brew
YEAR 2021

MAJOR PROJECT 21 2021 MIETTA MULLALY_SUB FLOOR.JPG

MAJOR PROJECT 21 2021 MIETTA MULLALY_SURVEY L6_02-2.JPG

MAJOR PROJECT 21 2021 MIETTA MULLALY_SURVEY L6_02-2.JPG

STUDENT Mietta Mullaly
PROJECT Oversight
SUPERVISOR Peter Brew
YEAR 2021

MAJOR PROJECT 21 2021 MIETTA MULLALY_THE ARCHITECTS ACT.JPG

What better place to start
than at the entry point of the building,
right by the intercom (a pedestal for rubbish)
and a column that tells you the daily soup.

There are stairs that have solid risers
and handrails with timber returns,
a place for relaying a message
or for drying out your weather concerns.

There are walls that fall short of the floor
leaving space to pass an extension cord through,
or sliding doors with curious cutouts
to bring other things into your view.

There are columns that are deep and rectilinear
as compared to those that are thin or round,
far better suited for sticking up flyers
or for keeping tall objects off the ground.

There are balustrades with vertical extrusions
that extend just beyond the rail,
serving as a place to hang a bag or a hat
or a place to deposit junk mail.

There are unarmed chairs for hanging your jacket,
flat façades and venetian blinds,
things with holes and things with gaps,
things that fold out and things that overlap.

All the fittings and fixtures that don't quite fit
create infrastructure from extra-structure,
such as the rail or nail that is too long
or a column that passes through the ceiling.

Within each of these frames you'll notice the hands
and the feet
of figures making some sort of assessment.
Are we looking at designs, a post-occupancy study
or is this a report about defects?

Our answer to this question is largely dependent
on the way we conceive of 'the client'.
If the current state of buildings is a reflection
of our thinking,
then our concept is financially reliant.

We need a concept of the client that does not
obstruct our professional obligations
because we are bound by the Act and the principles
that govern it,
which are different to a developer's motivations.

We need to recognise that architecture's
primary function
is not property investment,
and that we have a responsibility to the greater
good (altruism),
which should play into our assessment.

1/2 continues on p. 205.

STUDENT Mietta Mullaly
PROJECT Oversight
SUPERVISOR Peter Brew
YEAR 2021

MAJOR PROJECT 21 2021 MIETTA MULLALY_INSTITUTE SURVEY_01-2.JPG

MAJOR PROJECT 21 2021 MIETTA MULLALY_SURVEY L4_01-2.JPG

MAJOR PROJECT 21 2021 MIETTA MULLALY_FLAT COLUMN.JPG

STUDENT Mietta Mullaly
PROJECT Oversight
SUPERVISOR Peter Brew
YEAR 2021

MAJOR PROJECT 21 2021 MIETTA MULLALY_HANDRAIL.JPG

MAJOR PROJECT 21 2021 MIETTA MULLALY_INSTITUTE SURVEY_02-2.JPG

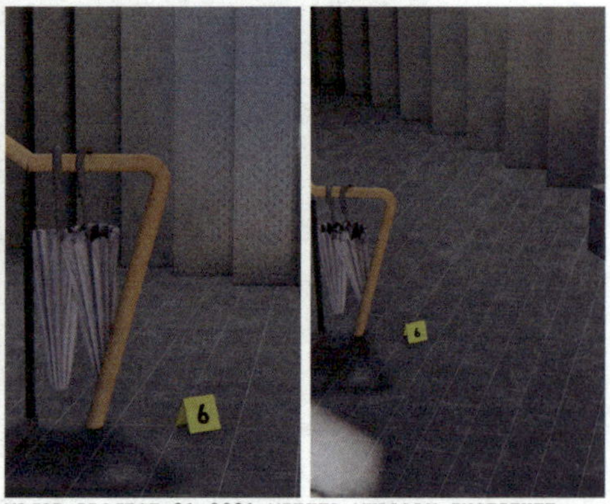

MAJOR PROJECT 21 2021 MIETTA MULLALY_INSTITUTE SURVEY_02-2.JPG

STUDENT Mietta Mullaly
PROJECT Oversight
SUPERVISOR Peter Brew
YEAR 2021

Moving up the building, we discover by dis-cover-ing
that so much potential already exists —
Such as the shelf-like structure of an un-clad
timber frame
or the hanging possibility a tile-less ceiling
could retain.

Removing the back from a bookshelf would enable
access from both sides,
or exposing a change in level could make
a place for objects to hide.

These are the opportunities we lose when
we overcompensate.

The slightly concave lift overrun
where water pools after the rain
points to other forms of life that we rarely consider
for they lack a monetary gain.

If we draw our attention to these 'other' things
that exist in the world too,
then we would better recognise our impact
as a result of the work that we do.

Which is to say, that when we make space for some,
we take it away from others. That is the
consequence of our work.

2/2

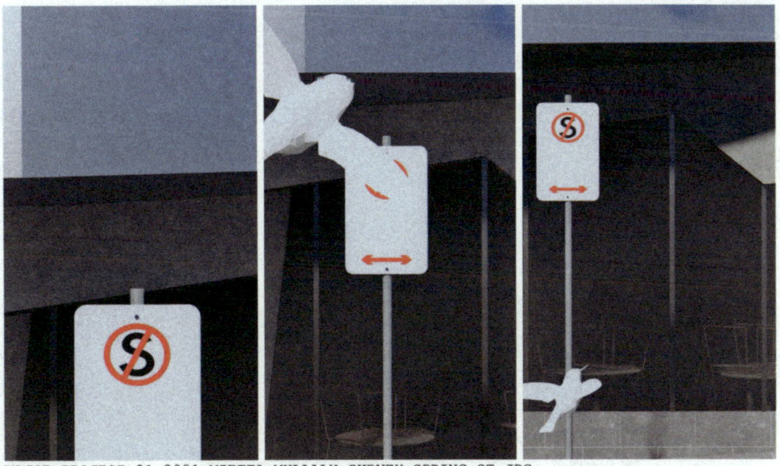

MAJOR PROJECT 21 2021 MIETTA MULLALY_SURVEY SPRING ST.JPG

MAJOR PROJECT 21 2021 MIETTA MULLALY_BALUSTRADE WITH VERTICAL EXTRUSIONS.JPG

STUDENT Ruby Lang
PROJECT An Other Architecture
SUPERVISOR Simone Koch
YEAR 2021

2021 Ruby Lang, An Other Architecture

2021 RUBY LANG Image 04_King William Street.jpg

This project is not so much a project as it is a framework for the project to exist within. It seeks to understand architecture as an instrument that claims territory beyond an economic framework.

Current definitions of property reify it as an object of capitalism, with its value understood in economic terms. What would happen if we were to move beyond the deeply ingrained idea of 'price determines value'? What new stories might we tell?

A framework, or manifesto, was written to provide a way in which we might move beyond this narrative, even though architecture can be its own challenge rather than a solution. However, it is how we talk about things that affects behaviour, which in turn affects how we theorise. In this way, through architectural interventions we can begin to understand the implications of our own assumptions. The site chosen for the series of projects positioned within this framework is the small neighbourhood of Fitzroy, which provides a counterpoint to the mainstream and a strategy for staging a conversation.

STUDENT Ruby Lang
PROJECT An Other Architecture
SUPERVISOR Simone Koch
YEAR 2021

2021 RUBY LANG Image 02_Johnston Street.jpg

2021 RUBY LANG Image 03_Brunswick Street.jpg

2021 RUBY LANG Image 05_Napier Street.png

2021 RUBY LANG Image 01_Napier Street.jpg

2019 Matthew Lochert, A Project for Melbourne's Boulevards

19S1 MATTHEW LOCHERT_Drawing_07B 04.png

This project seeks to examine architecture's role in imposing order within, and regulation of, the city.

Between past large-scale schemes for Melbourne's expansion and current endeavours to tie the city together through furniture and kerb details, A Project for Melbourne's Boulevards looks to general architectural types of state and street. At each of these scales, there seems to be an attempt to provide a level of legibility and coherence. Rather than imposing dominance they establish a framework, something fixed that enables the unexpected, the ambiguous and the intriguing to occur around it: the void where a flâneur may encounter the stories and moments that inform them. The formation of a stage set for urban life — comprising choreography, sets and backdrops — implicates us as cast and our lives as story.

This project establishes a position on how buildings sit within and deliberately shape the space around them, as well as our conception of what constitutes a larger territory. It attempts to redefine a relationship, at the scale of the street, between the individual and the collective, the building and the city.

STUDENT Matthew Lochert
PROJECT A Project for Melbourne's Boulevards
SUPERVISOR Simone Koch
YEAR 2019

19S1 MATTHEW LOCHERT_Drawing_10.05.png

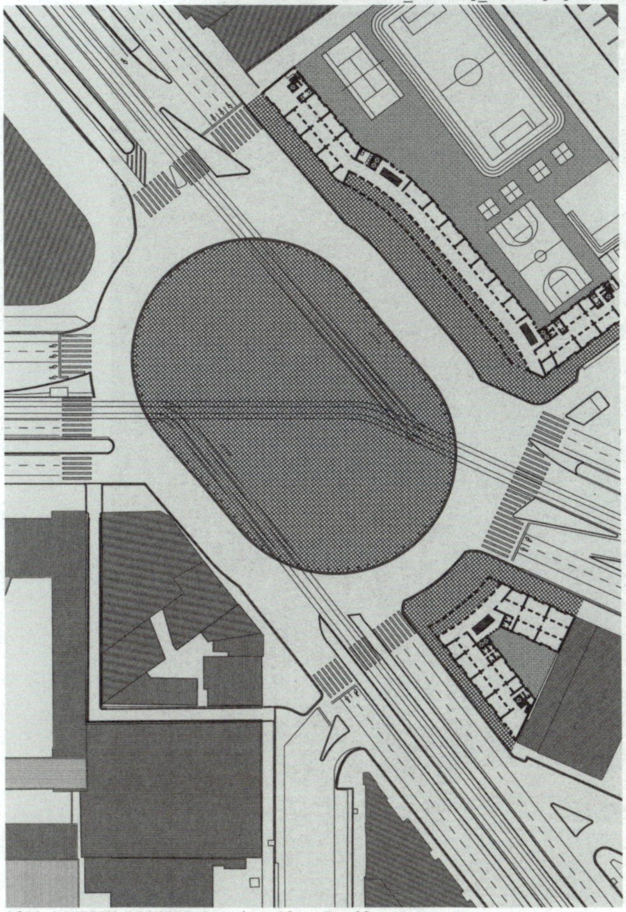

19S1 MATTHEW LOCHERT_Drawing_Plan E.pdf

19S1 MATTHEW LOCHERT_Drawing_10.4 Edited.png

STUDENT Matthew Lochert
PROJECT A Project for Melbourne's Boulevards
SUPERVISOR Simone Koch
YEAR 2019

19S1 MATTHEW LOCHERT_Drawing_D3 (E).png

19S1 MATTHEW LOCHERT_Drawing_13 - Str BC (E).png

STUDENT Matthew Lochert
PROJECT A Project for Melbourne's Boulevards
SUPERVISOR Simone Koch
YEAR 2019

19S1 MATTHEW LOCHERT_Drawing_E3 (E).png

19S1 MATTHEW LOCHERT_Drawing_13 - Str E (E).png

19S1 MATTHEW LOCHERT_Drawing_A1 (Edited).png

19S1 MATTHEW LOCHERT_Drawing_A3 (E).png

2019 Harry Bardoel, Anti thesis <architecture of layer>

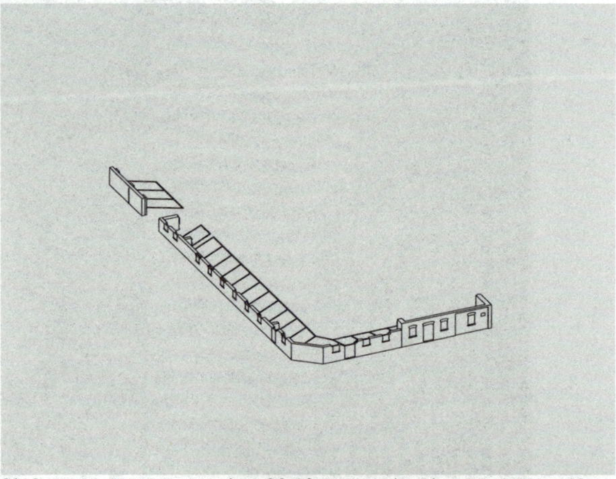

2019 HARRY BARDOEL Drawing 06_P3_Isometric Diagram (NTS).pdf

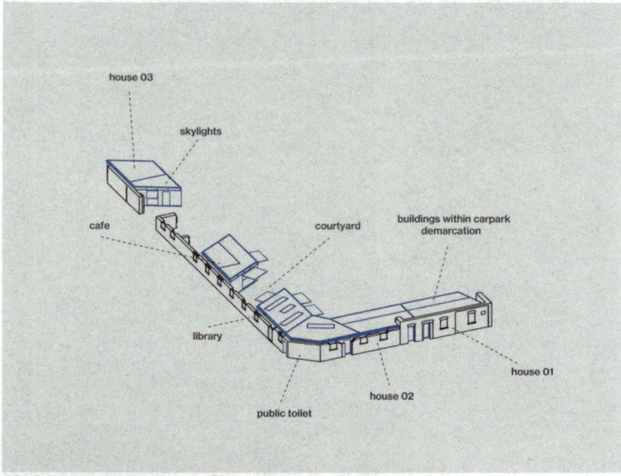

2019 HARRY BARDOEL Drawing 06_P3_Isometric Diagram (NTS).pdf

2019 HARRY BARDOEL Image 08_P3_internal view - cafe.tif

This project appropriates different historical functions of the broader landscape, condensing them into nine interventions scattered around the former Richmond Maltings site. Each intervention is coupled with a form of government housing designed to service people living with homelessness or suffering from mental health issues, or low-income government workers.

By viewing architecture as a direct response to place, it becomes personal, individual and circumstantial. The polemic of the project is to propose an idea — that the architect must work for those most disadvantaged. This thesis is not about offering a solution, or a particular social outcome, but instead acts as a proxy to test an architectural enquiry.

The design of the project sees architecture as a layer at a particular point in time — one that does just enough. Within this framework, three sub-layers exist: preserving, reducing and fattening. Each of these layers are of a kind — they see architecture as a process of observation, analysis and concurrent response. The layers provide room to consider the limitations and possibilities beyond their own intervention.

The intent of this thesis is to offer an alternate way to participate in discussions of gentrification. The single commission can be used as a tool to affect architecture as a larger whole (at the scale of the city), giving a voice back to the individual.

STUDENT Harry Bardoel
PROJECT Anti thesis <architecture of layer>
SUPERVISOR Simone Koch
YEAR 2019

The nine interventions are located within the former Richmond Maltings site in Cremorne, Melbourne. From 1856 to 1863, Coppin's Cremorne Pleasure Garden was bounded by Cremorne Street, Balmain Street and the railway line. In 1863, the Garden went bust and was sold for 4,500 pounds, after more than one hundred thousand was spent. Part of this area was then used as a private mental hospital.

In 2018 the Richmond Maltings Redevelopment commenced construction. It was planned in four stages to provide 1000 apartments, 6000 m2 of commercial space, 1000 carparks and 1000 bicycle parks. The estimated cost of works was $1 billion. This thesis freezes the Redevelopment in time, accepting parts of the demolition, rebuilding parts to existing conditions and halting/reacting to other parts already under construction.

This project offers an 'antithesis' of current gentrification processes following the 2008 Global Financial Crisis. It extends upon a body of research conducted by Monash University on a vision of Cremorne as brownfield wasteland. The publication is called *Building Mixity* (Maud Cassaignau and Markus Jung with Matthew Xue, 2018), the stated credo, that 'extant + new = fresh'.

The aim of this thesis was to interrogate and question common practices, which often result in 'undistinguished and homogenous collections of residential tower blocks hoisted on car parking podia, aimed at market norms, with investors as majority buyers.'

The method for approaching each project was to design something and then design around it, rather than forming a vision of the site through masterplan. Refusing the impetus to show the site all put together defends the idea that the whole can be the sum of all the little parts. This thesis offers a 'light touch' way of participating in discussions of gentrification by using the single commission and the individual to affect the larger whole.

1/1

2019 HARRY BARDOEL Image 17_P6_external view - P3-P4-P6 intersection + front-yard roof.tif
2019 HARRY BARDOEL Image 11_P4_internal view - ground compost + other house entrance.tif

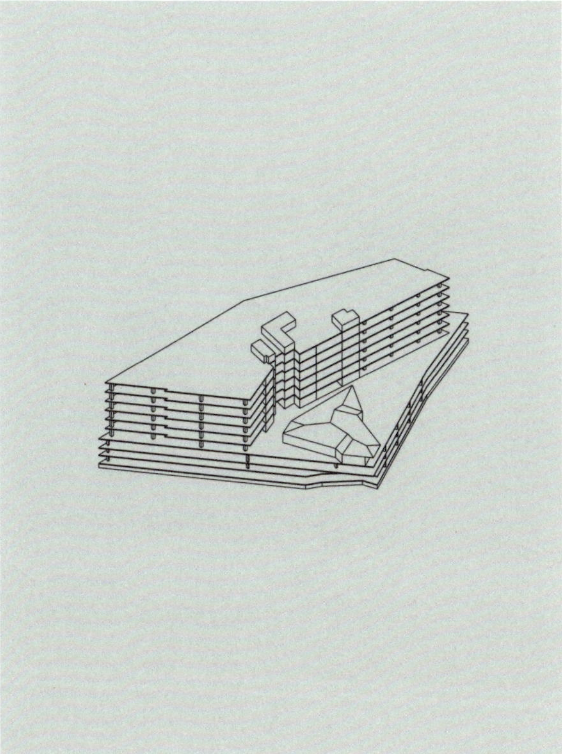

2019 HARRY BARDOEL Drawing 09_P4_Isometric Diagram (NTS).pdf

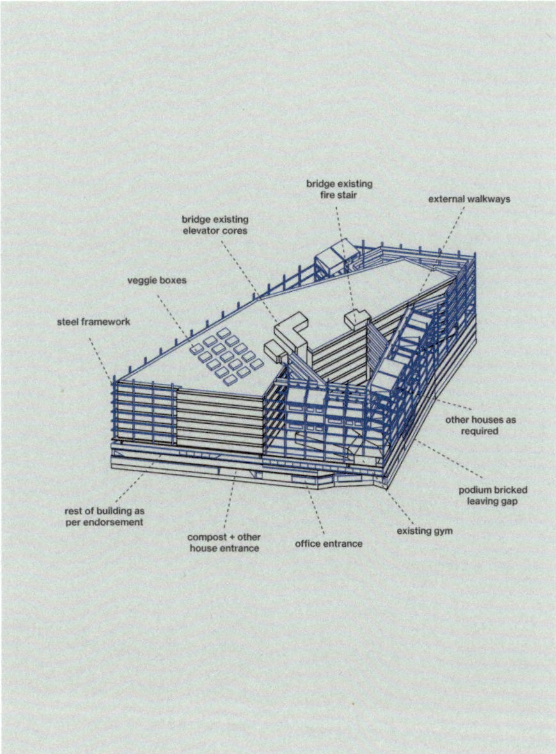

2019 HARRY BARDOEL Drawing 09_P4_Isometric Diagram (NTS).pdf

STUDENT Harry Bardoel
PROJECT Anti thesis <architecture of layer>
SUPERVISOR Simone Koch
YEAR 2019

2019 HARRY BARDOEL Image 16_P5_internal view - other house.tif

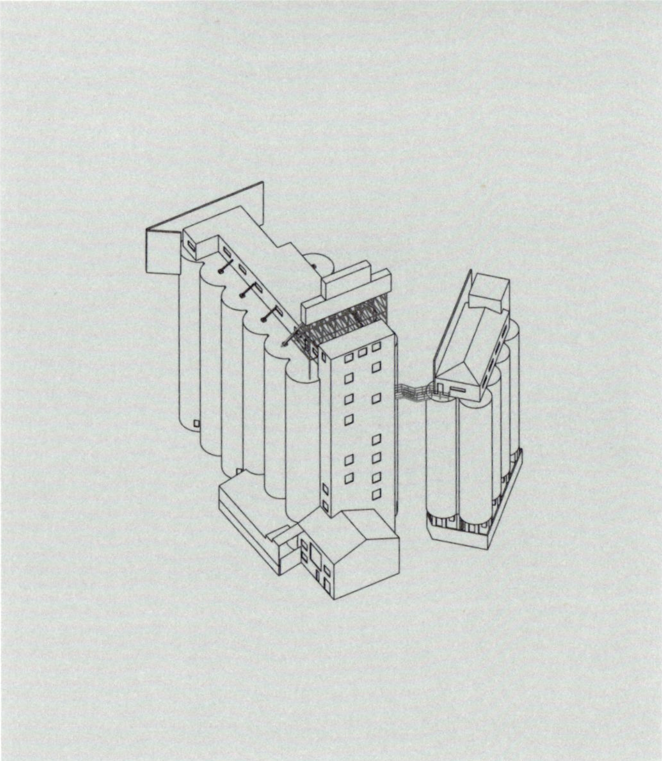

2019 HARRY BARDOEL Drawing 12_P5_Isometric Diagram (NTS).pdfhouse.tif

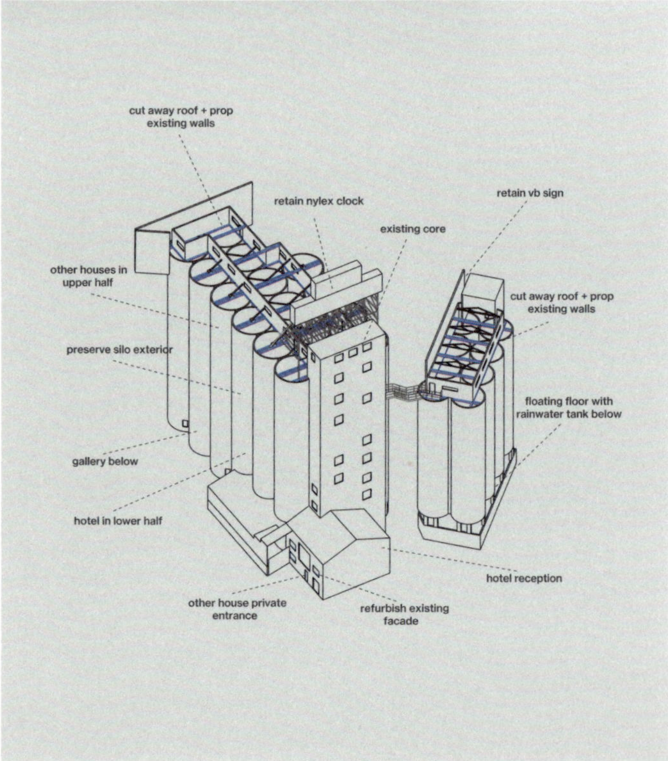

2019 HARRY BARDOEL Drawing 12_P5_Isometric Diagram (NTS).pdfhouse.tif

STUDENT Harry Bardoel
PROJECT Anti thesis <architecture of layer>
SUPERVISOR Simone Koch
YEAR 2019

2019 HARRY BARDOEL Image 19_P6_external view - projection cores.tif

2019 HARRY BARDOEL Image 18_other house 'box seat'.tif
2019 HARRY BARDOEL Image 20_flooded exhibition space.tif

STUDENT James v
PROJECT Systems of Comfort
SUPERVISOR Andre Bonnice and Jean-Marie Spencer
YEAR 2021

2021

James McLennan, Systems of Comfort

2021 JAMES MCLENNAN IMAGES 23_COMMONWEALTH BANK OF AUSTRALIA EXTERIOR PROJECTING VIEWING PORTAL.png

Systems of comfort are controlled by the Australian Institute of Refrigeration, Air Conditioning and Heating, alongside consultants and engineers. Indeed, the mechanical engineer has become the quartermaster of architecture.

This project suggests that architects must take control by redefining the system of comfort and challenging the way spaces have been created to service the mechanical. It suggests that discomfort is not a bad thing if designed, managed and desirable. When it is hot, for instance, do light work.

What if HVAC (heating, ventilation, air conditioning) systems were removed and replaced with a thermal buffer, an additive and evasive structure that sits alongside the existing? The system is an assembly of high and low-tech conditions operated by the individual while remaining connected to a central ecology. The thermal buffer changes the way we value space, creating a condition with less yield but also less impact.

The site for the project is a small section of the Hoddle Grid that contains a set of ageing Modernist buildings — a microcosm of the city and its present conditions. It's an idea for a new city typology not limited to the site.

STUDENT James McLennan
PROJECT Systems of Comfort
SUPERVISOR Andre Bonnice and Jean-Marie Spencer
YEAR 2021

Systems of comfort are controlled by the Australian Institute of Refrigeration, Air Conditioning and Heating, alongside consultants and engineers. Piping, flues, ducts, wires, lights, inlets, outlets, heaters and freezers: the mechanical engineer has become the quartermaster of architecture.

Modern architecture has become an encasing that houses a multitude of services. Interior climates rely on the use of HVAC (heating, ventilation, air conditioning) systems located in basements, rooftops and back façades, hidden from the city. The building ducts and diffusers are invisible, hidden in drop-down ceilings, behind walls and under floors (and yet their humming can always be heard). These systems are not designed. They are a series of off-the-shelf components that are difficult to disrupt or change. They have been absorbed into the profession.

Systems of Comfort suggests an alternative. It challenges the way spaces have been created to service the mechanical, and suggests that discomfort might not be a bad thing when designed and properly managed. The project proposes that the construction industry should consult with scientists and psychologists to conceptualise, design and build through a new architectural language.

The site of inquiry is a block bounded by Bourke Street, Little Collins Street, Russell Place and Royal Lane. A small section of the Hoddle Grid that contains a set of ageing Modernist buildings that require upgrading — a microcosm of Melbourne and its current conditions.

1/2 continues on p. 220.

2021 JAMES MCLENNAN IMAGES 13_BOURKE ST FACADE.png

2021 JAMES MCLENNAN IMAGES 17_THERMAL BUFFER ZONE FLOWING INTO THE EXISTING.png

STUDENT James McLennan
PROJECT Systems of Comfort
SUPERVISOR Andre Bonnice and Jean-Marie Spencer
YEAR 2021

2021 JAMES MCLENNAN IMAGES 22_ INTERSTITIAL ZONE_WINDOW TO WINDOW_OLD AND NEW.png

2021 JAMES MCLENNAN IMAGES 21_ IN-BETWEEN THE OLD AND THE NEW.png

STUDENT James McLennan
PROJECT Systems of Comfort
SUPERVISOR Andre Bonnice and Jean-Marie Spencer
YEAR 2021

2021 JAMES MCLENNAN IMAGES 15_ THERMAL BUFFER FACADE.png

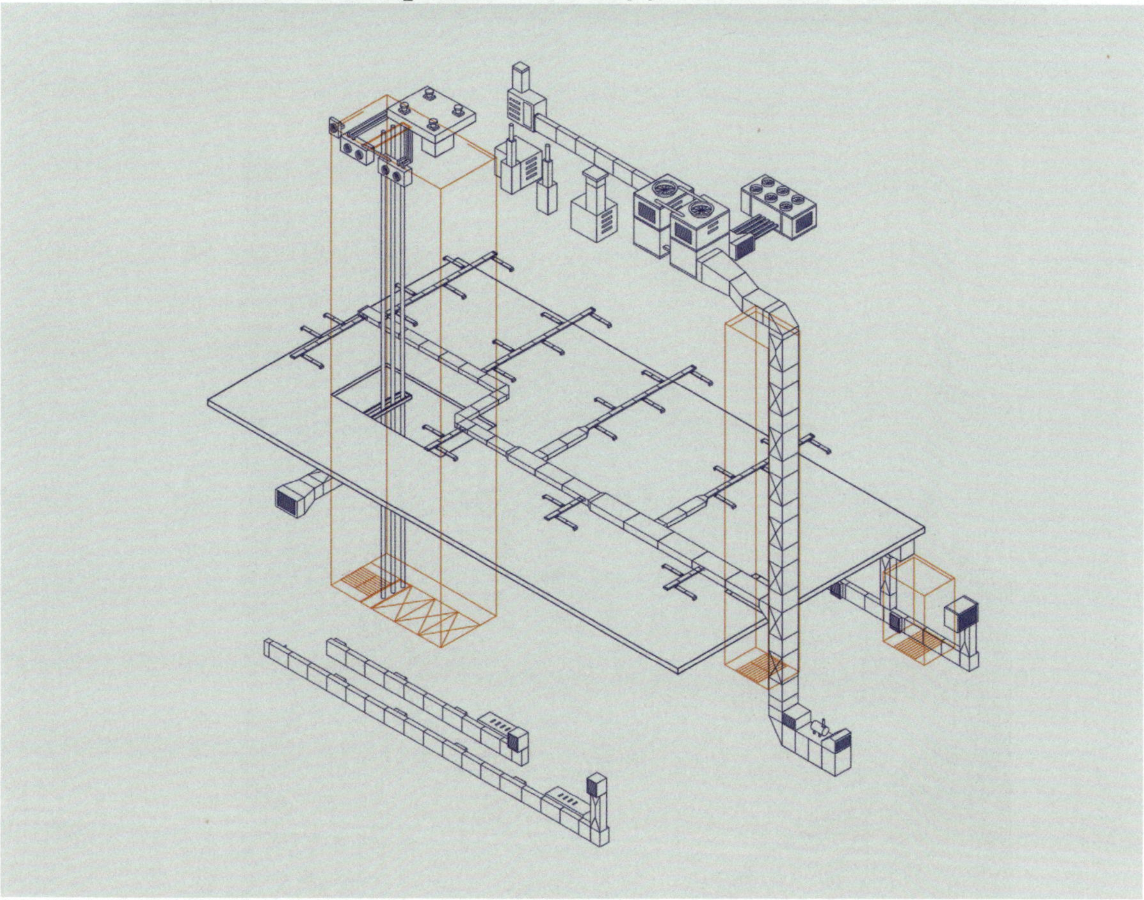

2021 JAMES MCLENNAN DRAWING 02_COUNCIL HOUSE 1 SYSTEM BREAKDOWN.png

STUDENT James McLennan
PROJECT Systemś of Comfort
SUPERVISOR Andre Bonnice and Jean-Marie Spencer
YEAR 2021

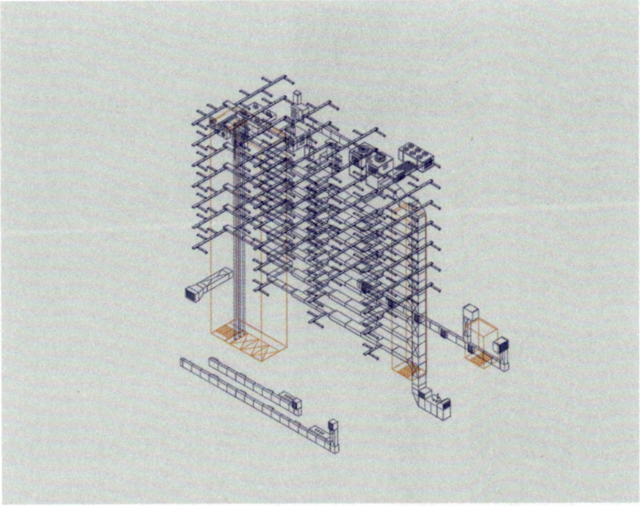

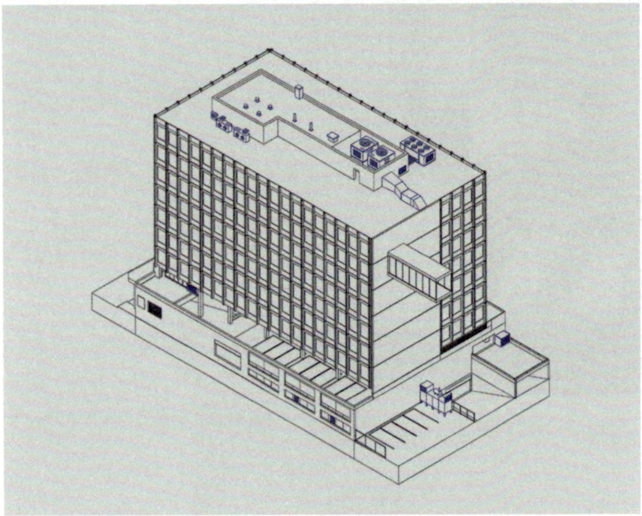

2021 JAMES MCLENNAN DRAWING 01_COUNCIL HOUSE 1 HVAC SYSTEMS.png
2021 JAMES MCLENNAN DRAWING 03_COUNCIL HOUSE 1 VISIBLE SERVICES.png

The key influencing factor in this proposal is the consideration of our environmental responsibility, in turn impacting the economic, physical and psychological needs of the project. HVAC systems are removed and replaced with a thermal buffer, an additive and invasive structure that sits alongside the existing. The building's façade becomes a suite of componentry, an assembly of high and low-tech conditions operational by the individual while remaining connected to the central ecology. The high-tech systems of the Thermo-Electric Generator and Photo-Bio Reactor louvres are contrasted with the low-tech nature of the metallic curtain and retractable polycarbonate screening. Where the thermal buffer meets with the existing structure, a grate bridges the gap and becomes a shadow line. This interstitial space is equivalent to a service lane on a city street. It is an outcome of the way the system is planned.

The thermal buffer increases useable office space by 46 percent, creating an architectural environment that values retrofit and renovation. The thermal buffer converts underperforming and expensive systems, at a fraction of the cost of starting again. The thermal buffer changes the way we value space, creating a condition with less yield but also less impact. It's an idea for a new city typology, one that is not limited to the site. It's the discovery of a new space that already exists within the city.

2/2

2021 JAMES MCLENNAN IMAGES 12_DEFLATED ALGAE HEAT LOUNGE.gif

STUDENT James McLennan
PROJECT Systems of Comfort
SUPERVISOR Andre Bonnice and Jean-Marie Spencer
YEAR 2021

2021 JAMES MCLENNAN IMAGES 16_ENTRY THRESHOLDS.png

2021 JAMES MCLENNAN IMAGES 14_RAINBOW ALLEY SERVICE LANE.png

2020 Andrea Milovanovic, Slice, Dust, Polish

2020 ANDREA MILOVANOVIC Images_ 01_front.jpg

This project zooms into the suburban house as a type that has reinforced the housewife as social construct for over a century by fencing off the domestic household from the public sphere political economy.

Proof that even the market reinforces these traditional residues is a recent trend in housing that includes a butler's pantry in kitchen design: a new room with its own designated function. It is as if we are being told: 'Since you're struggling to satisfactorily maintain your open plan kitchen, we'll provide you with one more space where you can freely prepare food and hide your mess away. Surprise, surprise! Eventually you'll have to clean that one too. And that's not even the only extra room you ought tend to.'

Recognising the disjunct between this excess of space and our ability to use it, this project inserts display rooms along with housework's main spaces (laundry and kitchen) into the communal, liminal areas of the home, encouraging their everyday use instead of treating them like porcelain for guests that never come. It reshuffles the remaining footprint of the dual occupancy house into multiple units while maintaining the illusion of both the dream and its solidity. Moreover, it does not see architecture as exceptional, but as entangled within other forms of cultural production — thus it still operates within the bounds of the system.

STUDENT Andrea Milovanovic
PROJECT Slice, Dust, Polish
SUPERVISOR Peter Brew
YEAR 2020

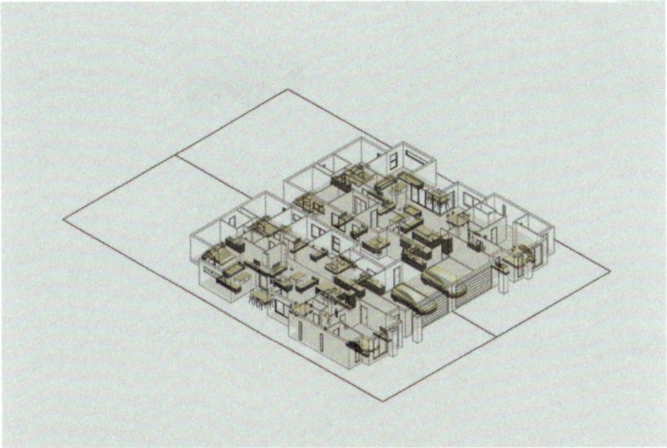

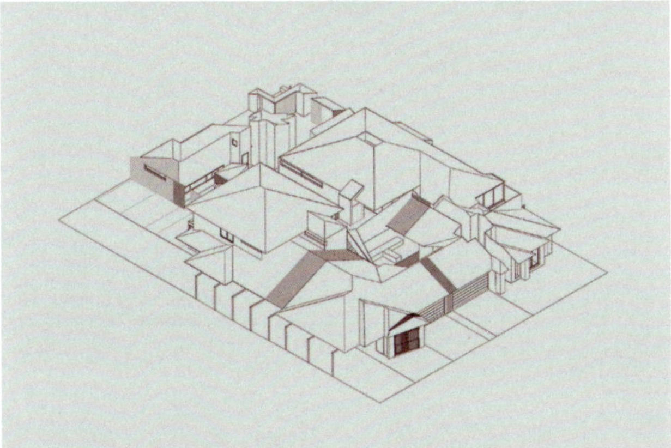

2020 ANDREA MILOVANOVIC Drawings_ 04 Axo with furniture.jpg
2020 ANDREA MILOVANOVIC Drawings_ 13 Axo overall final.jpg

2020 ANDREA MILOVANOVIC Images_ 02_entrance.jpg

MAJOR PROJECT 20S1 Andrea Milovanovic Images_ 06_ back courtyard view.jpg

STUDENT Andrea Milovanovic
PROJECT Slice, Dust, Polish
SUPERVISOR Peter Brew
YEAR 2020

Using the recent Future Homes competition requirements as a brief to frame and ground the project, I've placed a typical single storey house and land development package, and mirrored it. The competition's intent was to generate scalable and replicable design models that could accommodate for projected population growth, specifically focused on the middle ring suburbs. It is a search for the so-called 'missing middle' between low density detached dwellings (such as the chosen house) and townhouses. It aspires to increase housing choice and diversity while engaging with the realities of real estate development — market demand, delivery and construction methods.

The house I've decided to intervene in is offered to me for a virtual walk through after a quick Google search on butler's pantries, and it is just one of many very similar options available. It is a four bedroom house with a double garage, just under 300 sqm. Looking at the furniture within the house, particularly at the number of sofas and televisions, we can clearly see the excess of space.

This project is focused on reshuffling this excess space, which is often found in the form of display rooms such as separate dining areas or sitting rooms, into multiple units. In doing so, it also looks to invigorate the spaces in which housework is concentrated — kitchen and laundry. Maintaining the original envelope, I've reconfigured the space of two houses into five, fulfilling the bedroom mix ratio required in the competition brief, as well as the private open space needs.

1/2 continues on next page

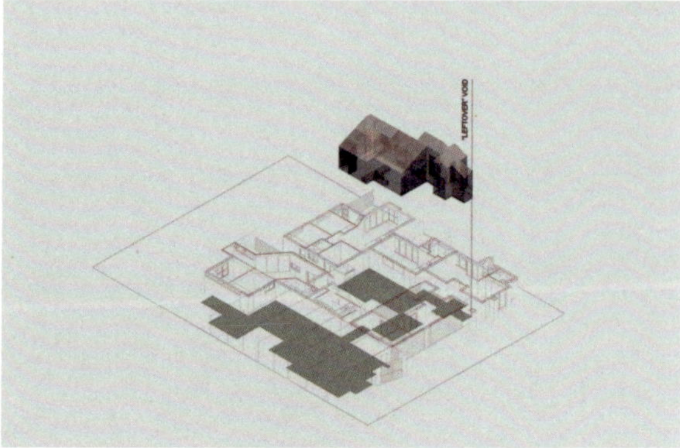

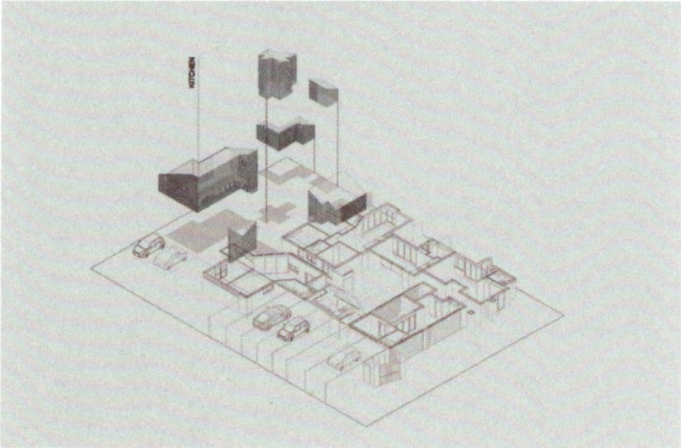

2020 ANDREA MILOVANOVIC Drawings_ 10 Axo leftover.jpg
2020 ANDREA MILOVANOVIC Drawings_ 11 Axo broken leftover.jpg

2020 ANDREA MILOVANOVIC Images_ 05_garage apartment interior.jpg

2020 ANDREA MILOVANOVIC Images_ 08_courtyard view.jpg

MAJOR PROJECT 20S1 Andrea Milovanovic Images_ 03_hallway.jpg

A spacious communal laundry that can serve as a local dry cleaning service provider has been introduced in place of the individual ones, and a little kiosk facing the street can be used by the households or for commercial purposes. The rest of the under-utilised area of the original houses' footprint has been cloned, sliced and rearranged as a series of communal and public rooms at the back of the dwelling. These spaces house a large kitchen area as well as a smaller shed that could serve multiple functions, pushing the regulation that exempts sheds less than 10 sqm from the minimum garden area calculations to the extreme. The leftover footprint has also been used to increase parking requirements. And finally, to achieve the required density, three upper floor units have been added.

Altogether, although another floor has been added and the house went from two to eight units, the total built area has barely increased.

STUDENT Zachary Bunston
PROJECT WAYOUT
SUPERVISOR Amy Muir
YEAR 2021

2021 Zachary Bunston, WAYOUT

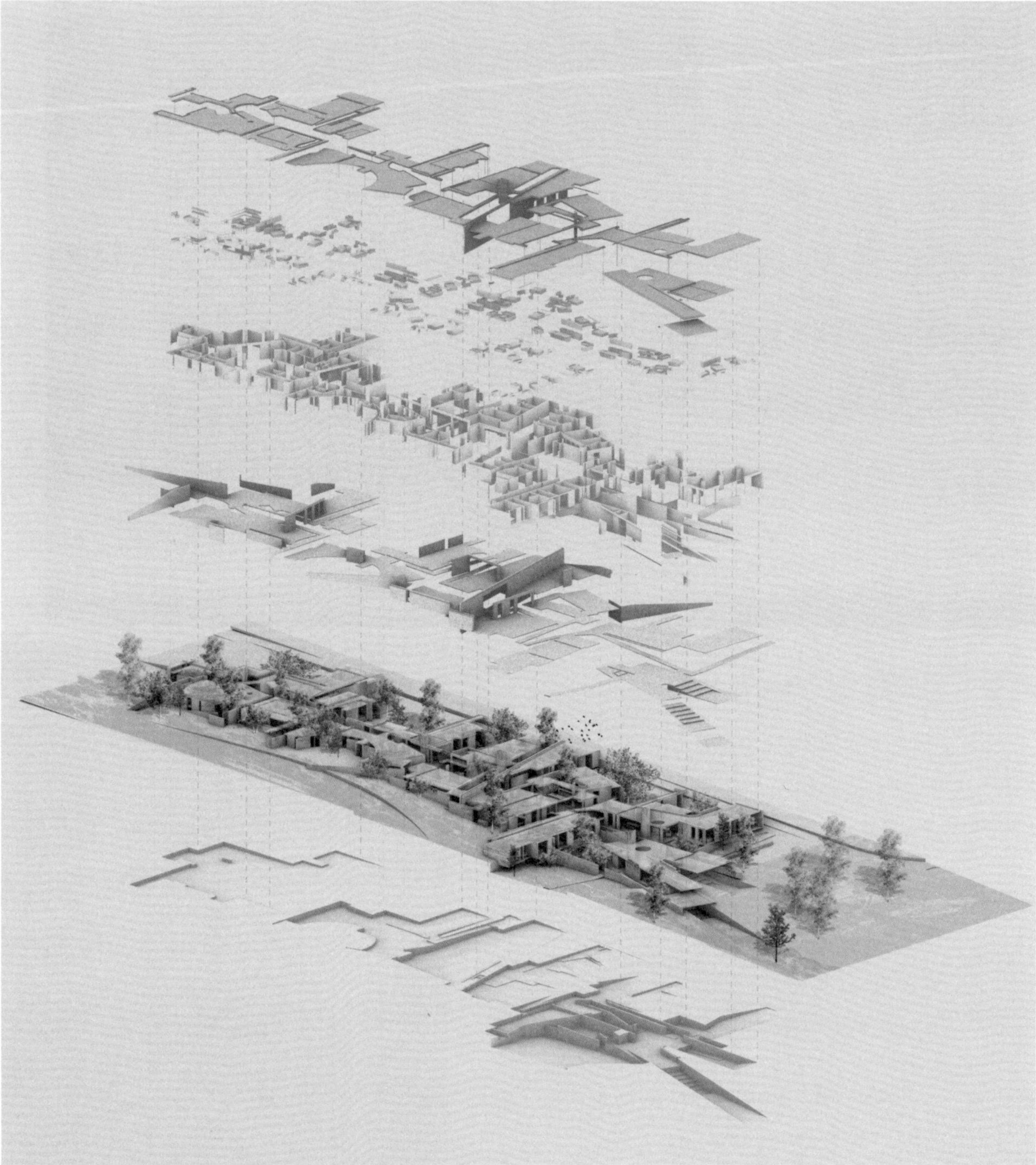

MAJOR PROJECT_SEM2_2021_ZAC BUNSTON_D1_EXPLODED SITE PLAN.png

For past generations, death was familiar; now it is out of sight and shrouded in mystery. This project supports those who desire to die at home. Integrating faith, ritual, palliative care, the civic and multigenerational living, this project reconsiders the family home and the procedures surrounding death.

What if a housing typology existed allowing for the event, the ritual and the civic in a dignified exit? Through an analysis of Australians' social perception of death, as influenced by education, religion and existing mechanisms, this proposition offers informed, integrated proposals.

A place where we could live and die together, across generations, faiths and backgrounds.

A place capable of a ceremony, while also being a family home.

With this project, our understanding of suburbia and entitlement is challenged. We are no longer connected across a picket fence, but instead a courtyard, a hallway or a verandah. We are reconnected across generations — the young gain access to history, the old gain access to care, and we remove isolation and exclusion.

Through an unfamiliar lens, the lens of death, a new living is unveiled.

STUDENT Zachary Bunston
PROJECT WAYOUT
SUPERVISOR Amy Muir
YEAR 2021

MAJOR PROJECT_SEM2_2021_ZAC BUNSTON_D8_VIEW_3.png

MAJOR PROJECT_SEM2_2021_ZAC BUNSTON_D9_VIEW_4.png

STUDENT Zachary Bunston
PROJECT WAYOUT
SUPERVISOR Amy Muir
YEAR 2021

MAJOR PROJECT_SEM2_2021_ZAC BUNSTON_D8_VIEW_1.png

MAJOR PROJECT_SEM2_2021_ZAC BUNSTON_D9_VIEW_2.png

STUDENT Zachary Bunston
PROJECT WAYOUT
SUPERVISOR Amy Muir
YEAR 2021

Australians want to die at home. And yet despite '70% of people expressing a desire to die at home, only 14% do.' Where for past generations death was familiar, now it is 'out of sight and shrouded in mystery.' This project takes Australia's current understanding of death as a 'problem' as both a hurdle to overcome and a potential driver of change.

The procedures surrounding death have historically been governed by religion. As a country, we are moving away from faith, but despite this shift we continue to gravitate towards the infrastructure of religion for important events. Integrating faith, ritual, palliative care, the civic and multigenerational living, this project reconsiders the family home and the procedures surrounding death. This project supports those who desire to die at home.

While I began this project by designing facilities, it soon became clear that the answer was in the home. And to assist dying at home, we must attend to ritual. Can rituals overlap? Can they educate? Can rituals designed by one culture be lived in by another? A range of rituals were interrogated, and accommodated. A table of metrics pragmatically illustrated different procedures alongside the significance of different rooms. What started to evolve was the concept of a multicultural, multi-generational village.

The nature of the site generates a long skinny space, like that of an alley, a small street, a narrow dog park or a verandah that runs across several houses. Rooms are arranged around a central courtyard. There is shared ownership of and responsibility for this space, between young and old. The dwellings that surround the courtyard are designed for the duration of a life. This is not a nursing home, which excludes the young; this is not a multi-residential estate, which excludes the elderly. This is a space where living and stories are passed across and between generations.

1/1

MAJOR PROJECT_SEM2_2021_ZAC BUNSTON_D10_VIEW_5.png

2022

Rebecca Boland, Lost Property

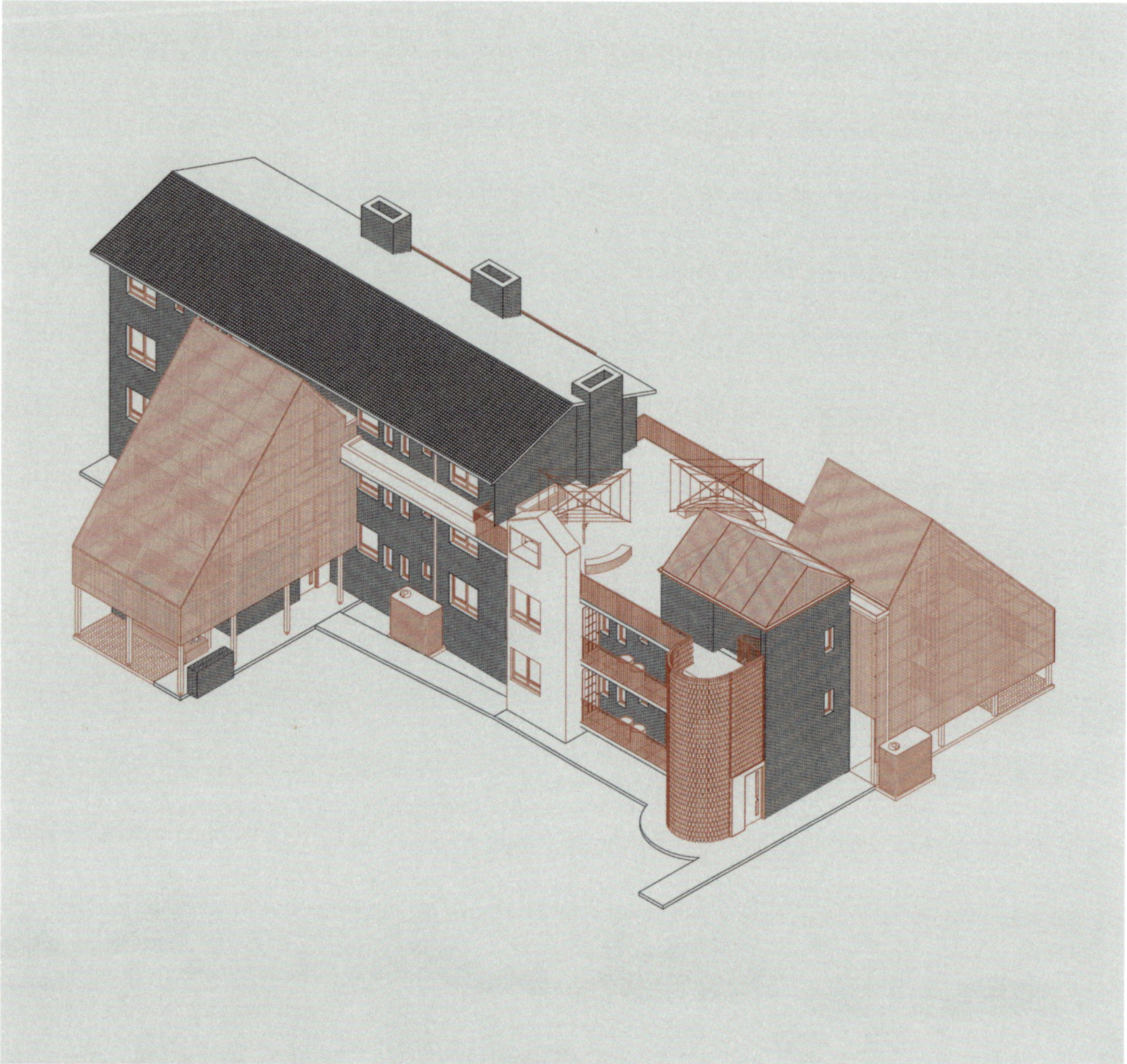

2022 REBECCA BOLAND Drawing 06_WOMEN'S WALK-UP FLATS_AXO FRONT.jpg

Lost Property is a project concerned with the privatisation of public housing. As a counterfactual 'what if?' project, it explores strategies to retain, restore and reuse existing buildings. In doing so, original site conditions are interrogated to address housing on previously government-owned land, which was home to an established community. Lost Property identifies women over the age of 45 as the fastest growing group at risk of homelessness and explores conditions of threshold, surveillance and security to seek outcomes that cater to the housing needs of these women.

Alongside this, the project seeks to underscore housing as a universal human right, rather than a commodity. The project asks: what is the purpose of a house? What makes a house a home? Can we rewrite the development model to resolve the current public housing crisis? How can we keep communities in their homes? Can we imagine ways to adapt and renew existing public housing with a view to rediscover, revitalise, reinvent or reuse?

With a community of women as its primary tenant, Lost Property seeks to reconceive public housing from a set of universal needs, prioritising its amenity as a basic human right.

STUDENT Rebecca Boland
PROJECT Lost Property
SUPERVISOR Anna Jankovic
YEAR 2022

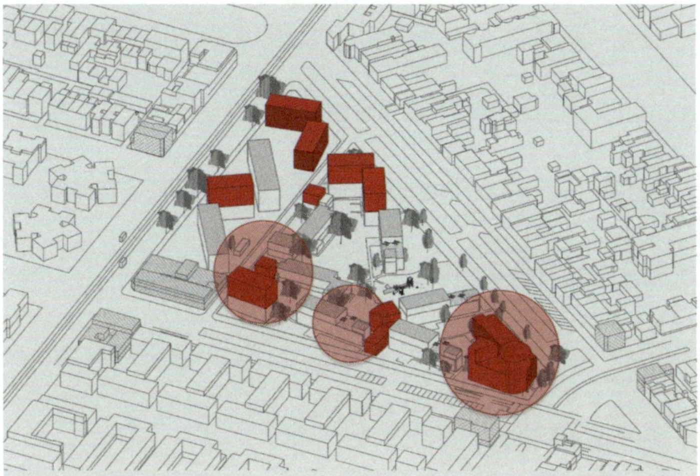

2022 REBECCA BOLAND Drawing 04_PROPOSED SITE_ADDITIONS AND ALTERATIONS.jpg

2022 Boland 03_BUILDING THRESHOLD_ INTERCOM ENTRANCE.png
2022 Boland 04_APARTMENT THRESHOLD_EXTERNAL.png
2022 Boland 05_APARTMENT THRESHOLD_INTERNAL.png

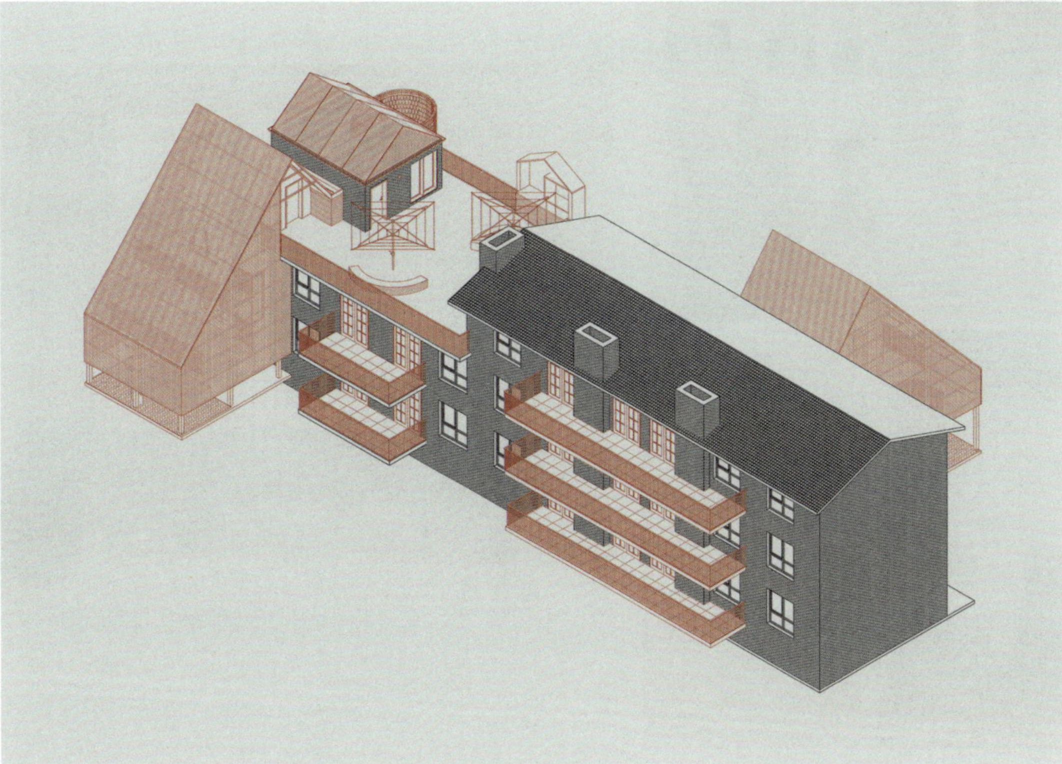

2022 REBECCA BOLAND Drawing 07_WOMEN'S WALK-UP FLATS_AXO BACK.jpg

STUDENT Rebecca Boland
PROJECT Lost Property
SUPERVISOR Anna Jankovic
YEAR 2022

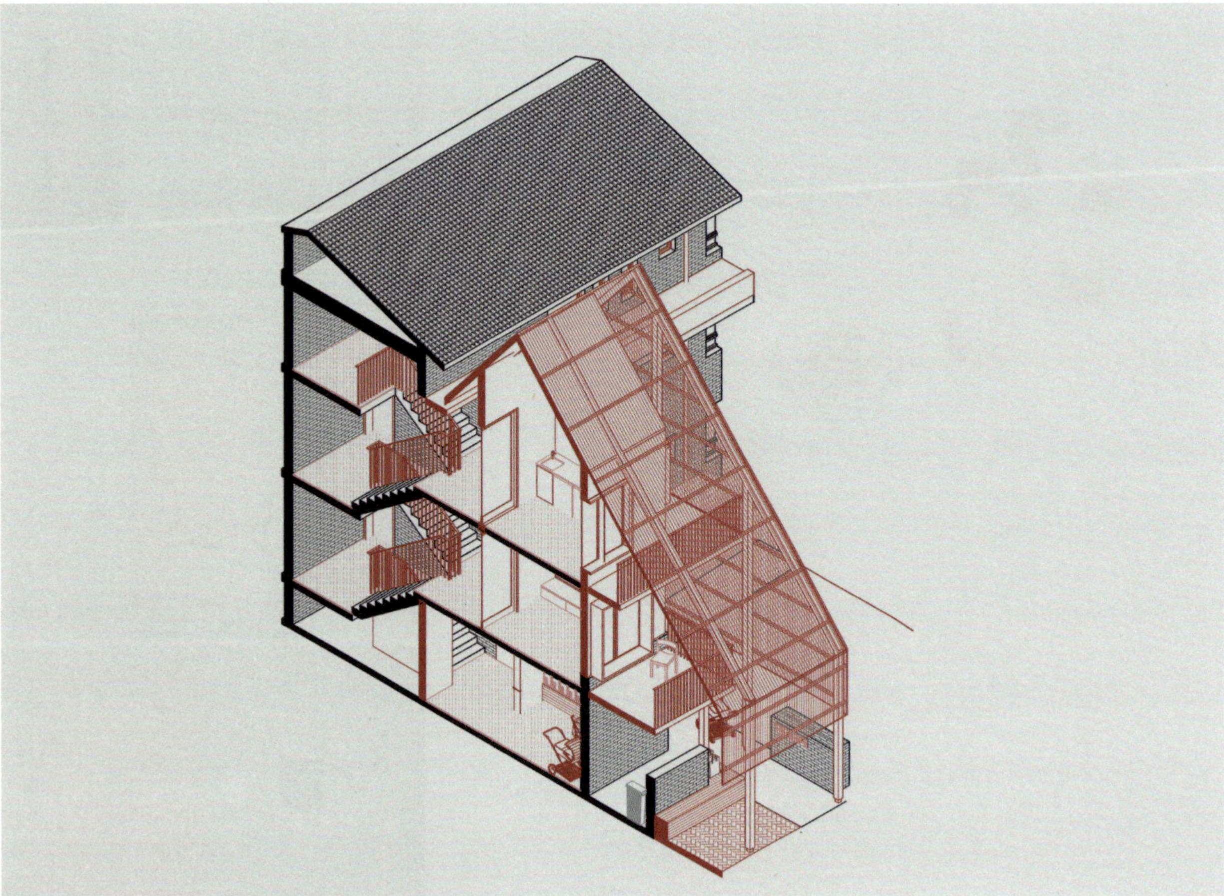

2022 REBECCA BOLAND Drawing 11_WOMEN'S WALK-UP FLATS ENTRANCE THRESHOLD_SECTIONAL AXO.jpg

2022 REBECCA BOLAND Image 02_STREET THRESHOLD_MAILBOX.png
2022 REBECCA BOLAND Image 06 MULTIPURPOSE SPACE_STORAGE&PRAMS.png

2022 REBECCA BOLAND Image 07_MULTIPURPOSE SPACE_OFFICE & PLAYROOM.png

STUDENT Rebecca Boland
PROJECT Lost Property
SUPERVISOR Anna Jankovic
YEAR 2022

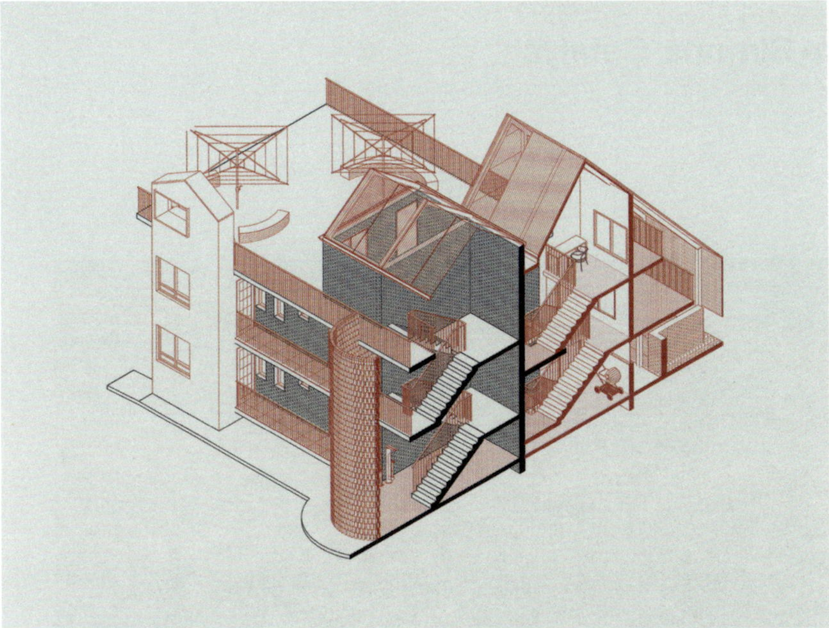

2022 REBECCA BOLAND Drawing 13_WOMEN'S WALK-UP FLATS ROOFTOP THRESHOLD_SECTIONAL AXO.jpg

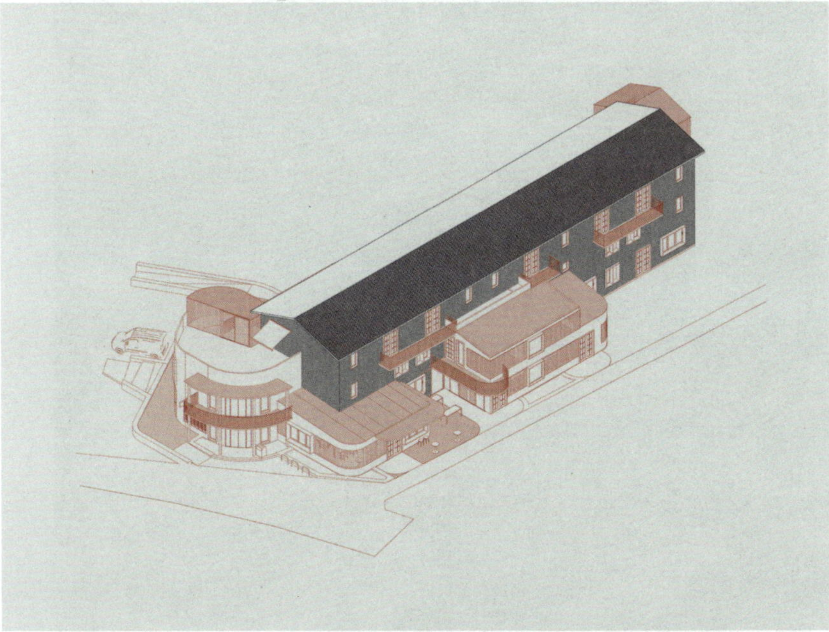

2022 REBECCA BOLAND Drawing 19_PUBLIC AMENITY BUILDING_AXO FRONT.jpg

2022 REBECCA BOLAND Image 10_MULTIPURPOSE SPACE_BIKE REPAIR STATION.png
2022 REBECCA BOLAND Image 11_MULTIPURPOSE SPACE_ROOFTOP.png

2022 REBECCA BOLAND Image 18_PUBLIC AMENITY_CAFE INDOORS.
2022 REBECCA BOLAND Image 19_PUBLIC AMENITY_CAFE OUTDOORS.png

2019

Jessica Simons, Catalyst

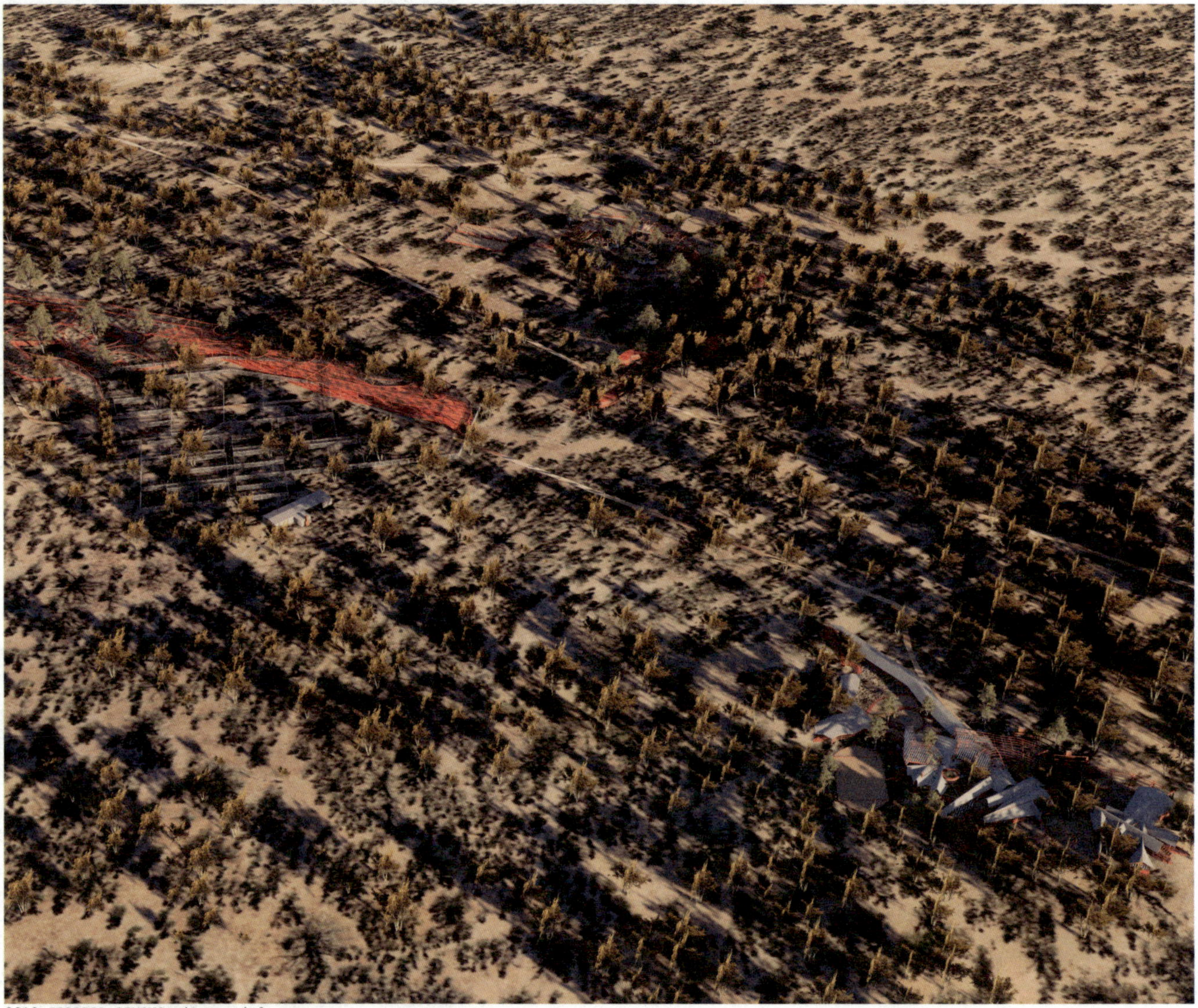

2019 JESSICA SIMONS site aerial.png

This project is concerned with the agency, or lack thereof, of architecture in regional towns, and their consequent ability to catalyse regional tourism or further architectural growth. More specifically, the proposal is a series of small, yet well connected, architectural interventions intended to embed themselves within the site, negotiate with the landscape and seed growth for attracting tourism to a region. It is a series of smaller gestures rather than a large ineffective one.

Regional towns are far too often simply a remnant of colonial settlement, a main street and a sprawl of ill-adapted suburbia. As such, I don't believe the fix lies in a new library or civic centre. The case study for the project is a town called Barmah on the Murray River. I have tested this proposal through a series of architectural interventions: a cultural visitor centre, a historical educational boardwalk and an all-seasons campsite. They are aligned in their attitude, their celebration of both the Indigenous and colonial histories that this site is so rich with, their negotiation with nature and their ability to seed growth that responds as needed, never without provocation.

STUDENT Jessica Simons
PROJECT Catalyst
SUPERVISOR Emma Jackson
YEAR 2019

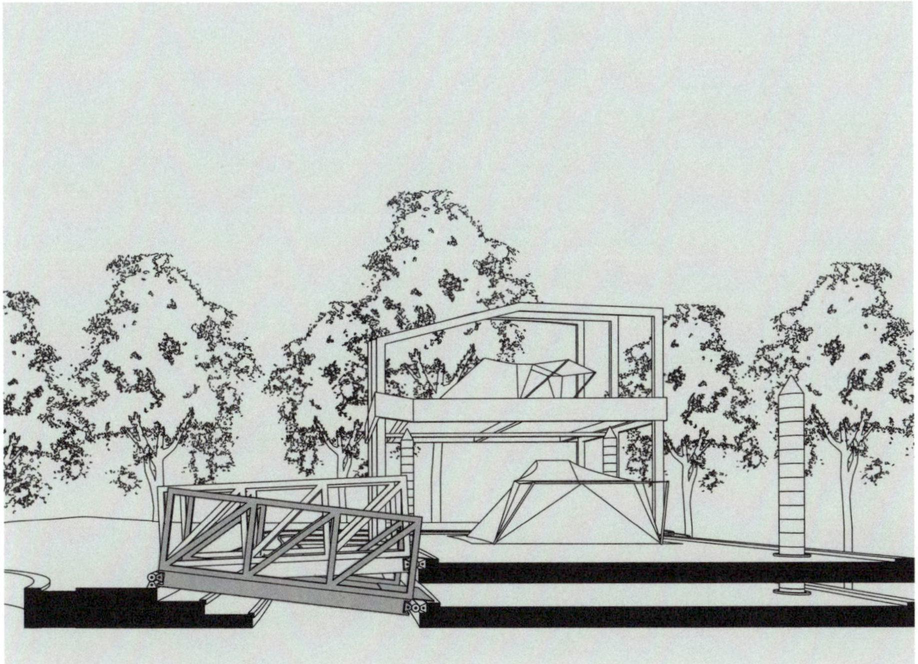

2019 JESSICA SIMONS PONTOON PERSPECTIVE SECTION.ai

2019 JESSICA SIMONS boardwalk 02.png
2019 JESSICA SIMONS boardwalk 03.png

2019 JESSICA SIMONS campsite 03.png

STUDENT Jessica Simons
PROJECT Catalyst
SUPERVISOR Emma Jackson
YEAR 2019

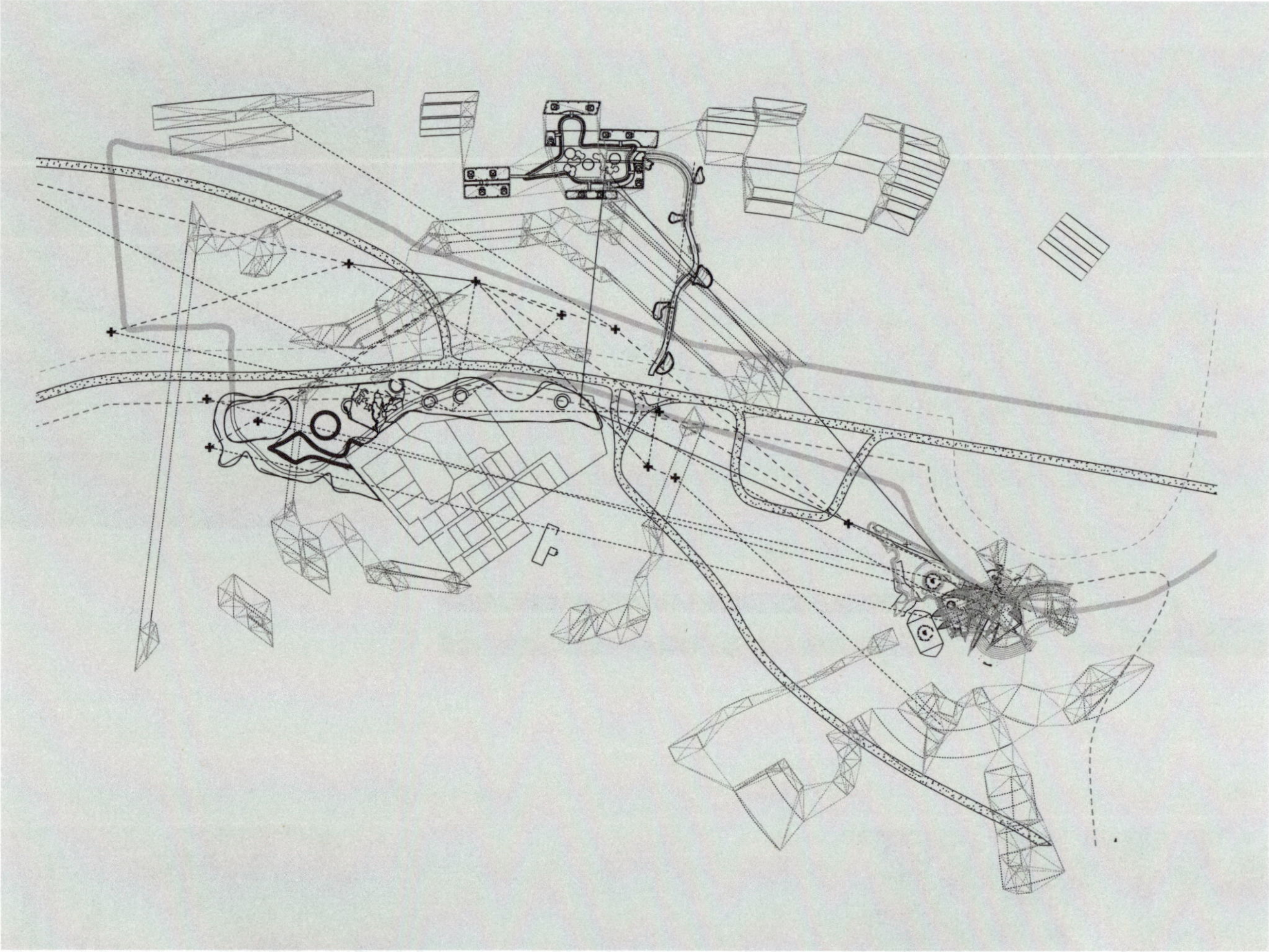

2019 JESSICA SIMONS planning diagram.ai

2019 JESSICA SIMONS cultural centre 02.png

STUDENT Jessica Simons
PROJECT Catalyst
SUPERVISOR Emma Jackson
YEAR 2019

2019 JESSICA SIMONS cultural centre 03.png
2019 JESSICA SIMONS campsite 02.png

2019 JESSICA SIMONS elevated path perspective SECTION.ai

STUDENT Alexandra Waldron-Clark
PROJECT Every-ware and Know-ware
SUPERVISOR Simon Drysdale
YEAR 2021

2021 Alexandra Waldron-Clark, Every-ware and Know-ware

2021 ALEXANDRA WALDRON-CLARK_ORBOST CARE SERVICE STATION, EXTERNAL VIEW.png

2021 ALEXANDRA WALDRON-CLARK_ORBOST CARE SERVICE STATION, VIEW FROM IRVINES ROAD.png

If time suddenly stopped, what would our model of care look like? Would we question our values as we watched people isolated in rooms, separated, alone, void of community and celebration? Care is not a one-size fits all solution. This is a proposal that tackles real issues within our current healthcare settings. It asks what we deem acceptable solutions for care typologies, and investigates how a new architecture typology can transform the way we view care.

Sited in East Gippsland — which, with almost 40 percent of the population being over 60 years old in 2020, has one of Victoria's highest per capita populations of ageing people — this project focuses on the town of Orbost, a timber town located off the Princes Highway on the Snowy River plains. The project's condition of service is introduced at the Golden Fleece Service Station, an icon on the road whose inviting glow offers a welcome to town. Combining age-friendly care services and emergency youth care in a drive-in drive-out typology, this is a future-present design. The location on the highway at the entrance to town embeds wellness and health into communities; rather than a new McDonalds, healthcare becomes a catalyst to bring together the community.

STUDENT Alexandra Waldron-Clark
PROJECT Every-ware and Know-ware
SUPERVISOR Simon Drysdale
YEAR 2021

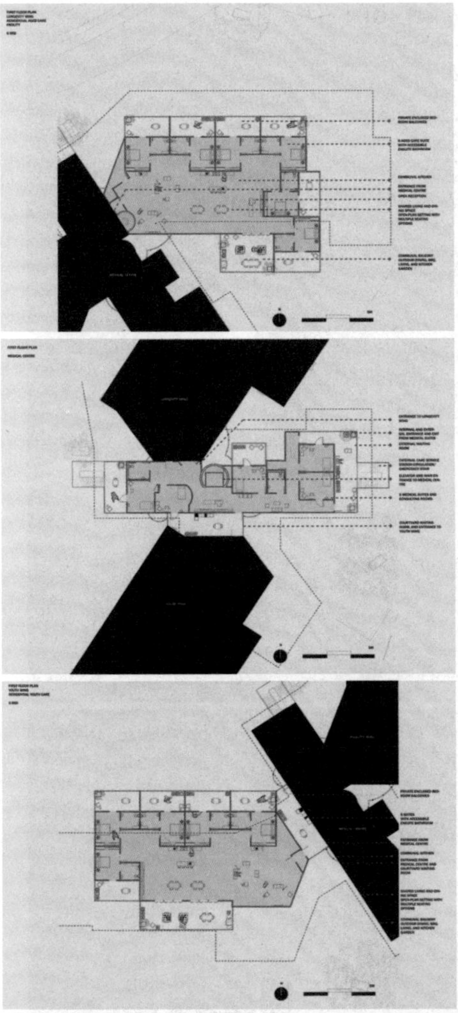

MEDIUM QUALITY YOUTH CENTRE.JPG

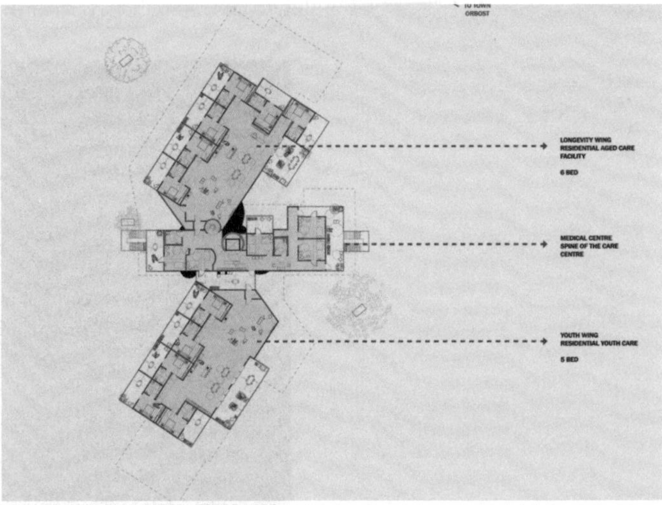

MEDIUM QUALITY FIRST FLOOR.JPG

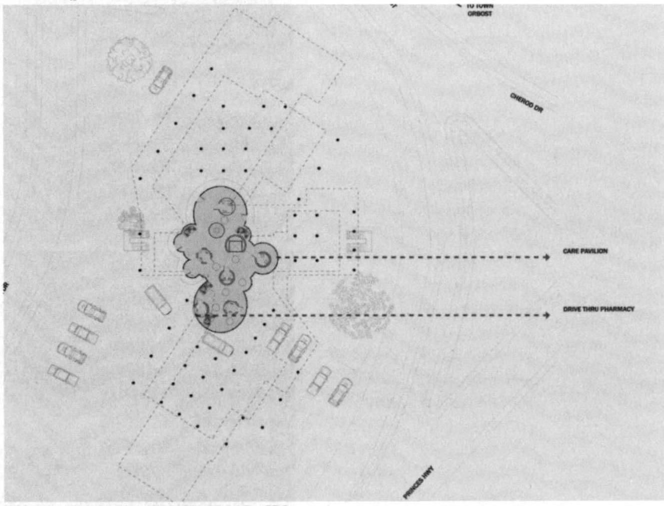

MEDIUM QUALITY GROUND FLOOR.JPG

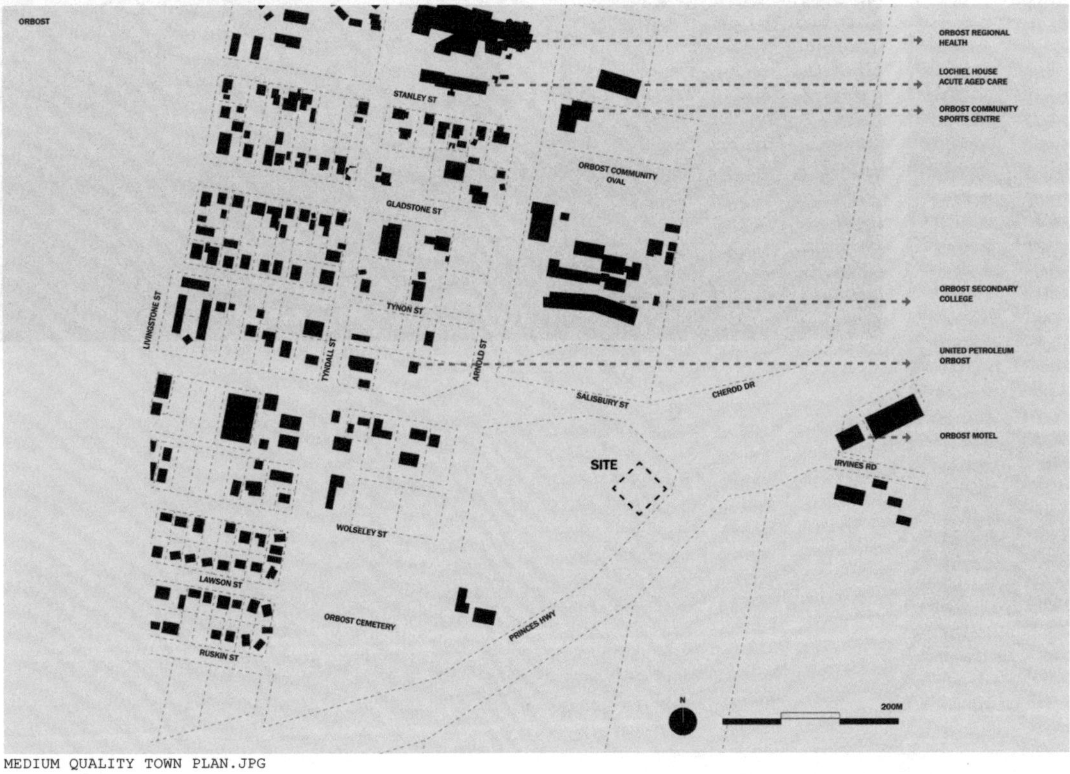

MEDIUM QUALITY TOWN PLAN.JPG

STUDENT Alexandra Waldron-Clark
PROJECT Every-ware and Know-ware
SUPERVISOR Simon Drysdale
YEAR 2021

2021 ALEXANDRA WALDRON-CLARK_ENTRANCE TO 'TOWN AS LIVING LAB' FROM PRINCES HWY.png
2021 ALEXANDRA WALDRON-CLARK_ENTRANCE VIA PORTE COCHERE.png

SHARED COMMUNAL BALCONY, LONGEVITY WING.png
SHARED INTERNAL SPACE, LONGEVITY WING.png
PRIVATE APARTMENT BALCONY, LONGEVITY WING.png

STUDENT Alexandra Waldron-Clark
PROJECT Every-ware and Know-ware
SUPERVISOR Simon Drysdale
YEAR 2021

2021 ALEXANDRA WALDRON-CLARK_DRIVE THU MEDICAL CENTRE AND CARE PAVILION.PNG

2021 ALEXANDRA WALDRON-CLARK_VIEW FROM SAILSBURY STREET OF ENTRANCE TO TOWN.PNG

STUDENT Christopher Buchhorn
PROJECT See you in the in between
SUPERVISOR Emma Jackson
YEAR 2021

2021 Christopher Buchhorn, See you in the in between

MAJOR PROJECT S1 2021 Chris Buchhorn Image 38.jpg

MAJOR PROJECT S1 2021 Chris Buchhorn Image 37.jpg

While the suburbs provide desirable qualities like privacy, space and individuality, they congruently present a sheltered, dewy-eyed view of the world. An isolated suburban sensibility fostered through common experience is developed through a ruthless attitude towards context and landscape, establishing borders of segregated territories that often feature a blurred mass of uniform buildings.

So, what if we challenge this accepted condition? What if architecture extended these narrow borderlines and was persuaded to loop into an articulated in-between realm?

This project questions what limitations we place on ourselves by adhering to a cartesian logic of absolute boundaries, and the agency afforded societal behaviours and our ability to change. It seeks to challenge established urban hierarchies by exploring the uncomfortable negotiations of urban thresholds and current framework models. It aims to walk the lines of boundary and enclosure, inside and outside, for an architecture that is not absolute but responsive to its contextual conditions — and where outcomes can be broken up to reveal unexpected opportunities, shifting from traditional modes of intervention towards decolonising a system that privileges the right angle above all else.

STUDENT Christopher Buchhorn
PROJECT See you in the in between
SUPERVISOR Emma Jackson
YEAR 2021

2021 CHRIS BUCHHORN Image 16.png
2021 CHRIS BUCHHORN Image 15.png

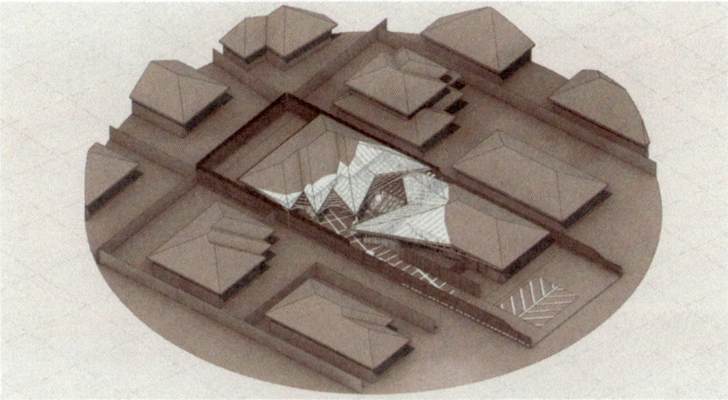
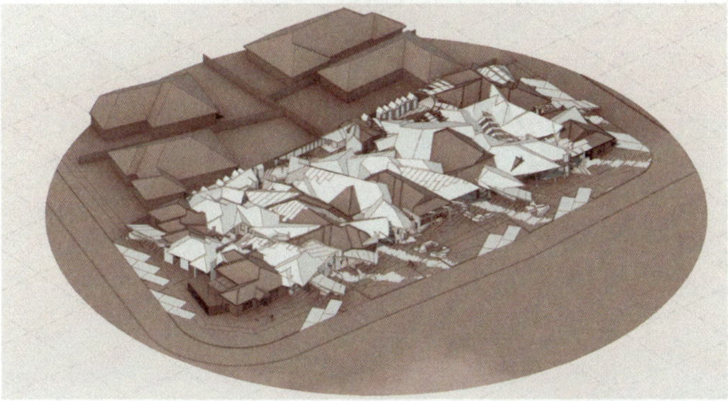

2021 CHRIS BUCHHORN Drawing 05.png
2021 CHRIS BUCHHORN Drawing 20.png

2021 CHRIS BUCHHORN Image 05.png
2021 CHRIS BUCHHORN Image 04.png

STUDENT Christopher Buchhorn
PROJECT See you in the in between
SUPERVISOR Emma Jackson
YEAR 2021

2021 CHRIS BUCHHORN Image 12.png
2021 CHRIS BUCHHORN Image 11.png

2021 CHRIS BUCHHORN Image 16.png
2021 CHRIS BUCHHORN Image 31.png
2021 CHRIS BUCHHORN Image 32.png

2021 CHRIS BUCHHORN Drawing 16.png

STUDENT Christopher Buchhorn
PROJECT See you in the in between
SUPERVISOR Emma Jackson
YEAR 2021

2021 CHRIS BUCHHORN Image 15.png
2021 CHRIS BUCHHORN Image 16.png
2021 CHRIS BUCHHORN Image 17.png

2021 CHRIS BUCHHORN Image 25.png
2021 CHRIS BUCHHORN Image 24.png

2021 CHRIS BUCHHORN Image 29.png
2021 CHRIS BUCHHORN Image 28.png

STUDENT Eilidh Ross
PROJECT Here
SUPERVISOR Emma Jackson
YEAR 2020

2020

Eilidh Ross, HERE

2020 EILIDH ROSS Drawing(5)_KITCHEN.jpg

Seventy percent of new Australian homes are built by volume builders. If we are to affect change in the way we live, we need to start with volume housing. HERE investigates how we can plausibly implement changes to housing structures to deliver a living situation that is more connected to Country.

The test site is an estate in Braybrook, in Melbourne's west. An audit is performed to reconcile the homogenous housing, and a set of rules is applied to the existing housing estate in order to shuffle current value systems and allow for new ways of occupying. The plausibility of the project lies in its pragmatism — only 10 percent of the estate needs to change in order for big shifts to happen. As there is more built form in volume housing than required, this project takes the unnecessary pieces and reassigns them to provide opportunities for communal living and a connection to the land down by the river.

HERE is the start of an ongoing discussion about how we begin to affect change where it is most needed.

STUDENT Eilidh Ross
PROJECT Here
SUPERVISOR Emma Jackson
YEAR 2020

MAJOR PROJECT (2) (2020) (Eilidh Ross) Drawing(18)_AXO 2.jpg

2020 EILIDH ROSS Drawing(2)_BATHROOM VIEW.jpg

2020 EILIDH ROSS Drawing(4)_RIVER.jpg

2020 EILIDH ROSS Drawing(10)_AMPHITHEATRE AXO.pdf
2020 EILIDH ROSS Drawing(11)_BATHROOM AXO.pdf

EILIDH ROSS Drawing(12)_ENTRANCE AXO.pdf

EILIDH ROSS Drawing(13)_FISHING AXO.pdf

EILIDH ROSS Drawing(14)_KITCHEN AXO.pdf

STUDENT Eilidh Ross
PROJECT Here
SUPERVISOR Emma Jackson
YEAR 2020

2020 EILIDH ROSS Drawing(7)_FISHING.jpg

2020 EILIDH ROSS Drawing(3)_KITCHEN.jpg

2020 EILIDH ROSS Drawing(8)_ENTRY.jpg

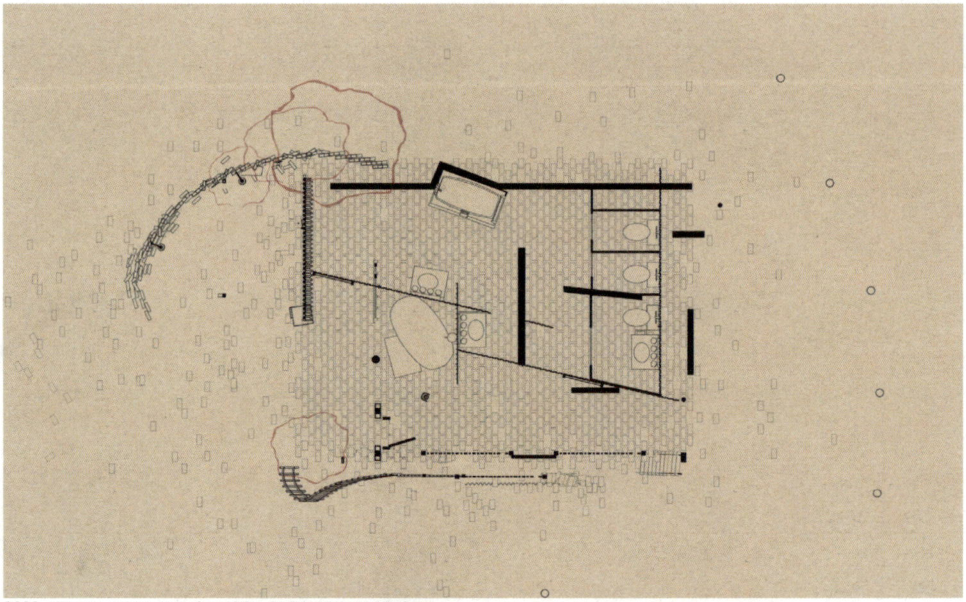
2020 EILIDH ROSS Drawing(14)_BATHROOM PLAN.jpg

2020 EILIDH ROSS Drawing(15)_PRE COLONISATION.jpg

2020 EILIDH ROSS Drawing(6)_SCHOOL.jpg

STUDENT Eilidh Ross
PROJECT Here
SUPERVISOR Emma Jackson
YEAR 2020

2020 EILIDH ROSS Drawing(1)_BATHROOM VIEW.jpg

2020 EILIDH ROSS Drawing(9)_AMPHITHEATRE.jpg

2021

Longge Zhang, DaShiLar Creepers

2021 LONGGE ZHANG Drawing 02_Communal Care Centre Axonometric.png

2021 LONGGE ZHANG Images 13_Corner Recreation_Street View.jpg

The Dashilar is a remnant of Beijing's old city, sitting adjacent to Tiananmen Square and the Forbidden City — physically close, yet materially distant from the centre of power. Here, the turmoil of China's recent history — still in living memory of its now mostly-elderly residents—is marked into the city's fabric.

Collectivisation, reform and the blurring of public and private has resulted in many contradictions between the residents and the government. To survive, residents have used abandoned or cheap materials to expand and adapt the Siheyuan house type. However, for safety reasons and to 'protect' the traditional hutong-style street, the Beijing Municipal Government has completely banned all additional structures. By also removing additions that occurred after 1949, the government aims to return the Dashilar to how it appeared at the end of the Qing Dynasty. If these marks are fully erased, the lived culture and experience of Beijing's old city life will disappear forever.

DaShiLar Creepers co-opts the bottom-up organic building that constitutes the unique hutong architectural form. Infrastructure to facilitate the continued occupation of the elderly is inserted into the gaps, extending and adapting the nature of the Dashilar. Further blurring the boundary between private and public space, it brings new vitality to the Dashilar area, balancing the contradictions between government policy and the lived experiences of the residents.

STUDENT Longge Zhang
PROJECT DaShiLar Creepers
SUPERVISOR Tim Pyke
YEAR 2021

2021 LONGGE ZHANG Drawing 05_Cultural Centre Axonometric.png

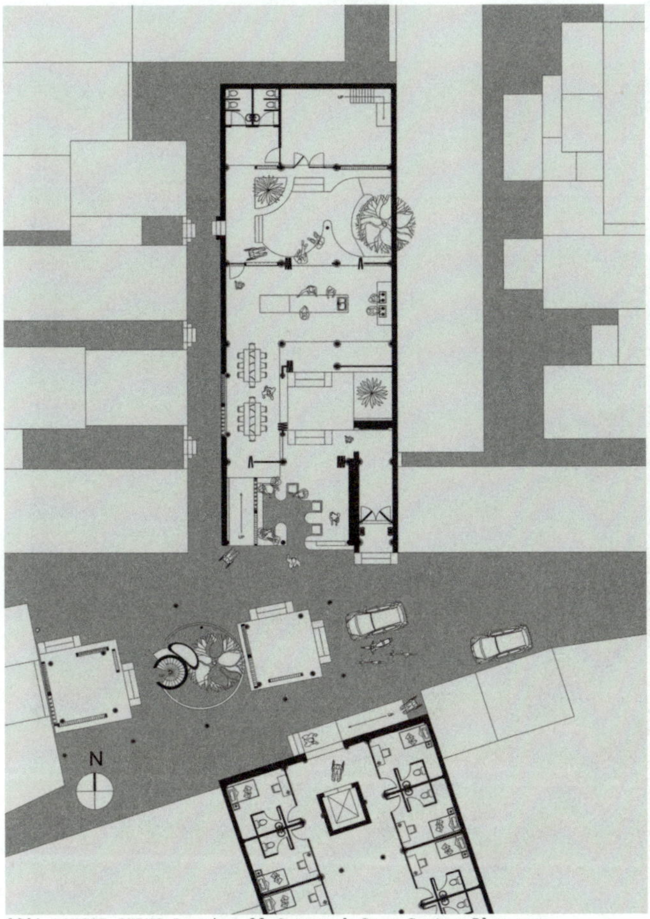

2021 LONGGE ZHANG Drawing 03_Communal Care Centre Plan.png

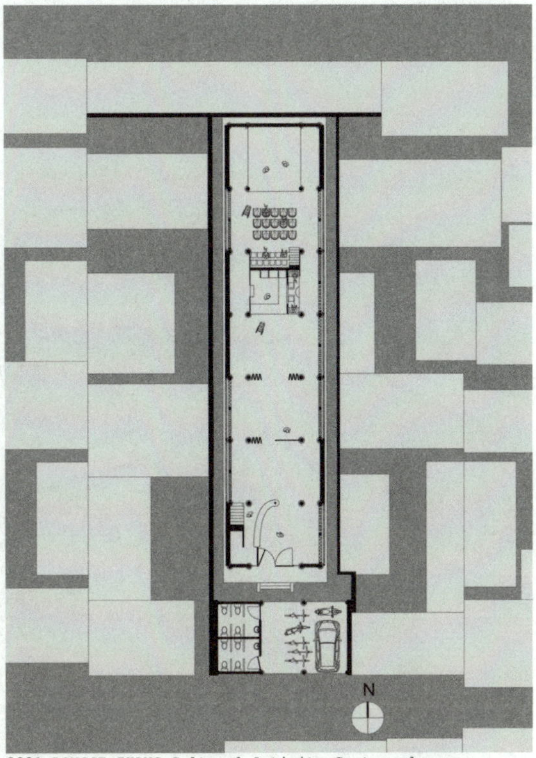

2021 LONGGE ZHANG Cultural Activity Centre plan.png

STUDENT Longge Zhang
PROJECT DaShiLar Creepers
SUPERVISOR Tim Pyke
YEAR 2021

2021 LONGGE ZHANG Images 05_Communal Care Centre_Aged Care Dormitory.png

2021 LONGGE ZHANG Images 02_Communal Care Centre_Dinning Room.png

2021 LONGGE ZHANG Images 04_Communal Care Centre_Second Layer Space.png

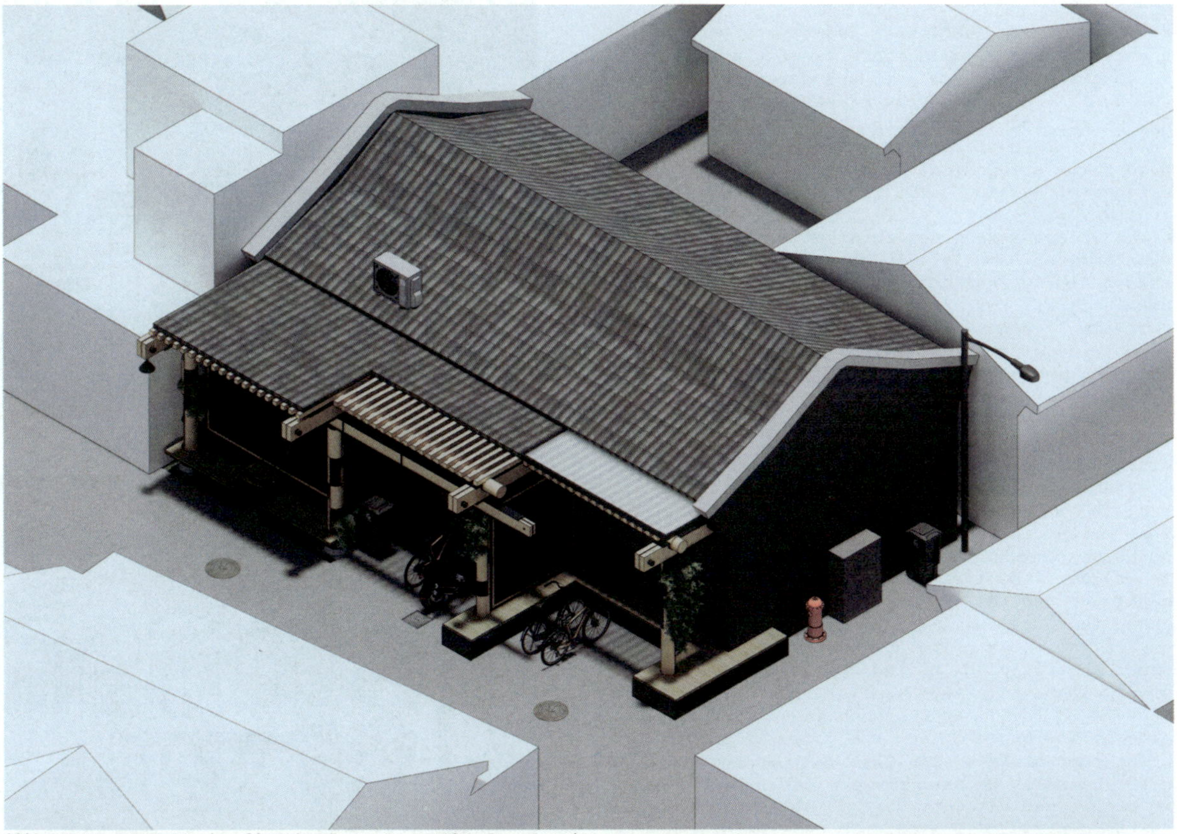

2021 LONGGE ZHANG Drawing 08_Under Eaves Recreation Axonometric.png

The Dashilar area is where my parents grew up and where I live now. It is a remnant of Beijing's old city, sitting adjacent to Tiananmen Square with the Forbidden City only a five-minute walk away – physically close, yet materially distant from the centre of power. Here, the turmoil of China's recent history is marked into the city's fabric. For the now mostly-elderly residents of the area, this turmoil is in living memory. They have lived through the founding of the People's Republic of China, collectivisation, the reform and the opening up period that has led to contemporary China's success and affluence. The elderly residents of the Dashilar area have experienced private ownership, complete collectivisation and now incomplete privatisation. The boundary between public and private has become blurred, resulting in many contradictions between the residents and the government.

The Dashilar hutongs – a traditional style of street – are like a history book. In the past, residents adapted their houses by adding additional structures. Through these built forms, and the different materials used, we can clearly see the development of Beijing across historical periods. However, for safety reasons and to 'protect' the traditional hutong-style street, the Beijing Municipal Government has completely banned all additional structures. By also removing additions that occurred after 1949, the government aims to return the Dashilar to how it appeared at the end of the Qing Dynasty. At the same time, for those siheyuans – a historical Chinese dwelling situated around a courtyard – with low historic value, the government repairs the exterior walls to make them look like traditional hutongs but leaves the interiors crowded and messy. This is beautification for the sake of tourists, with disregard for the residents.

1/2 continues on next page

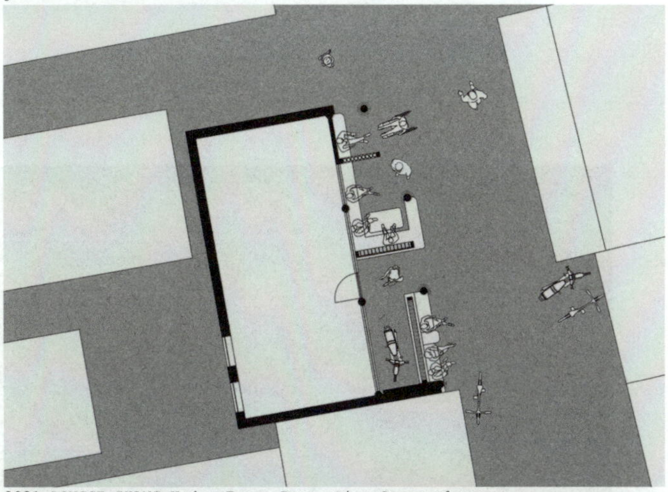

2021 LONGGE ZHANG Under Eaves Recreation Space plan.png

2021 LONGGE ZHANG Images 01_Communal Care Centre_Street View.png

STUDENT Longge Zhang
PROJECT DaShiLar Creepers
SUPERVISOR Tim Pyke
YEAR 2021

These unreasonable demolition and renovation policies entrench a contradiction between the lives of the residents and the goals of the government. The removal of additional structures erases the residents' lived experience, and the material history of 20th century Beijing. Even if most of the siheyuans are restored to their original appearance, the culture and experience of Beijing's old city atmosphere will disappear forever.

DaShiLar Creepers is a new intervention proposition for the Dashilar. It uses the bottom-up, organic building that constitutes the unique hutong architectural form as a kind of grassroots action, offering the government a way to approach infrastructure development on a local level.

The project proposes a network of interventions to support the Dashilar's elderly residents. To both celebrate the unique culture of the area and provide accommodation for the elderly, I distributed a community aged care centre throughout the Dashilar by using established models for building public infrastructure in leftover spaces. This includes a cultural activity centre, a communal care centre, a nursing home, communal toilets and a series of recreation spaces. The ideas in the project are explored through four design approaches: renovating an abandoned factory, formalising existing practices, extending existing structures and a new architecture that responds to the opportunistic nature of development in the Dashilar. In this way, infrastructure to facilitate the continued occupation of the elderly is inserted into the gaps, extending and adapting the nature of the Dashilar. Further blurring the boundary between private and public space, it brings new vitality to the Dashilar area, balancing the contradictions between government policy and the lived experiences of the residents. It also allows the Dashilar's elderly residents to live in the area for longer.

2/2

2021 LONGGE ZHANG Images 09_Cultural Centre_Auditorium and Observation.png

2021 LONGGE ZHANG Images 10_Cultural Centre_Drinking Bar.png

2021 LONGGE ZHANG Images 06_Communal Care Centre_Night View.jpg

STUDENT Longge Zhang
PROJECT DaShiLar Creepers
SUPERVISOR Tim Pyke
YEAR 2021

2021 LONGGE ZHANG Images 08_Cultural Centre_Night View.png

2021 LONGGE ZHANG Drawing 11_Corner Recreation Space Axonometric.png

2021 Guled Elyas, Formalisation of Nomadic Urbanism

2021 GULED ELYAS Image 07_.png

The Afar are nomadic pastoralists of Ethiopia who trade their prized livestock and salt in Dire Dawa city during the dry season. They informally settle and trade on the Dechatu riverbed, which fills up during the rainy season, washing away memories of the transient Afar.

This project seeks to formalise this informal settlement using memory of the geography and settled groups such as the Harar and Oromo peoples. The first of the three proposals is new housing on the riverbed, which offers the Afar a hub for their seasonal visits. By allowing the river to flow through the site during the rainy season, the urbanised population are reminded of Afar's seasonal occupation. The second proposal is short-term housing along the river's edge, with some scattered in the urban fabric to further strengthen connection between the nomadic and urban populations. This housing can also accommodate those who wish to stay for longer periods of time. The third proposal is the development of housing and shop fronts along the river wall, which is the city's solution to mitigate flooding. This will enable the Afar to have a long-term base in Dire Dawa, increasing the frequency and volume of trading.

STUDENT Guled Elyas
PROJECT Formalisation of Nomadic Urbanism
SUPERVISOR Helen Duong and Tim Pyke
YEAR 2021

2021 GULED ELYAS Image 08_.png

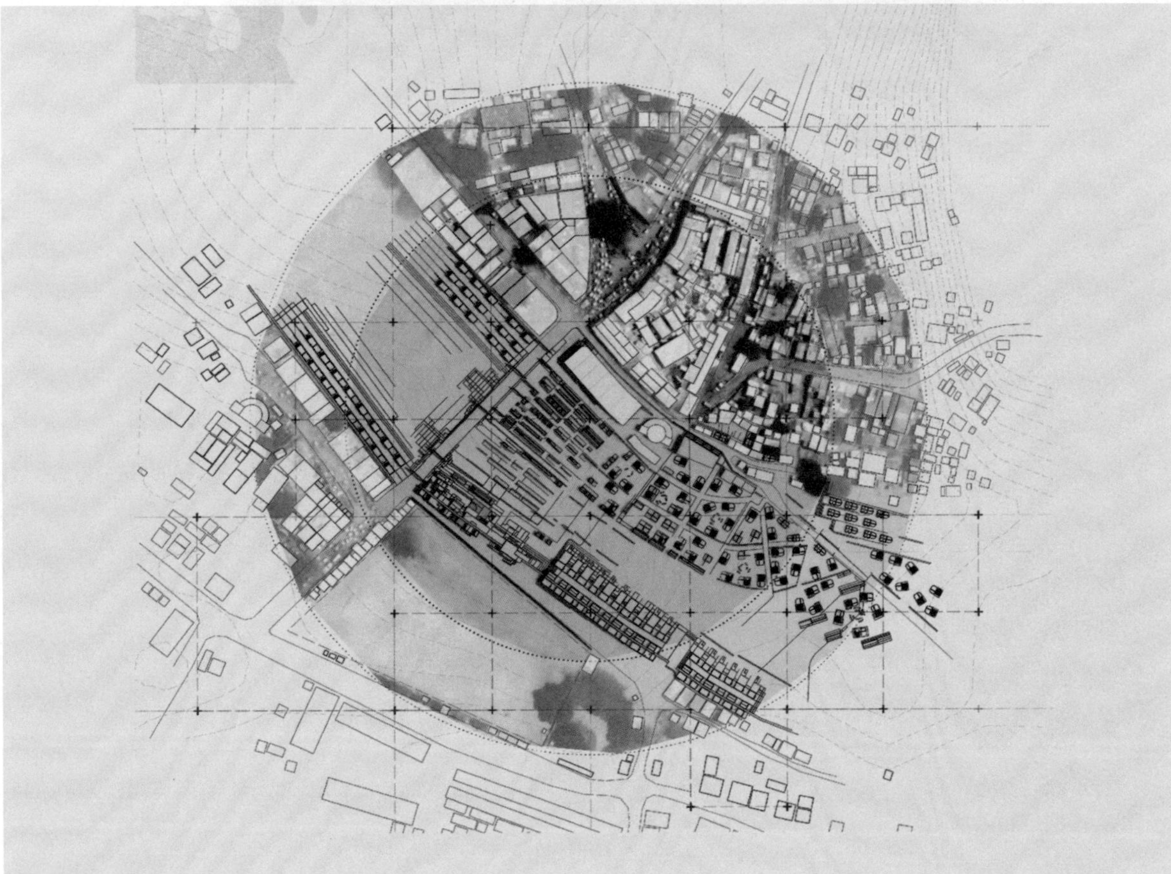

2021 GULED ELYAS Drawing 05_Site Plan.png

STUDENT Guled Elyas
PROJECT Formalisation of Nomadic Urbanism
SUPERVISOR Helen Duong and Tim Pyke
YEAR 2021

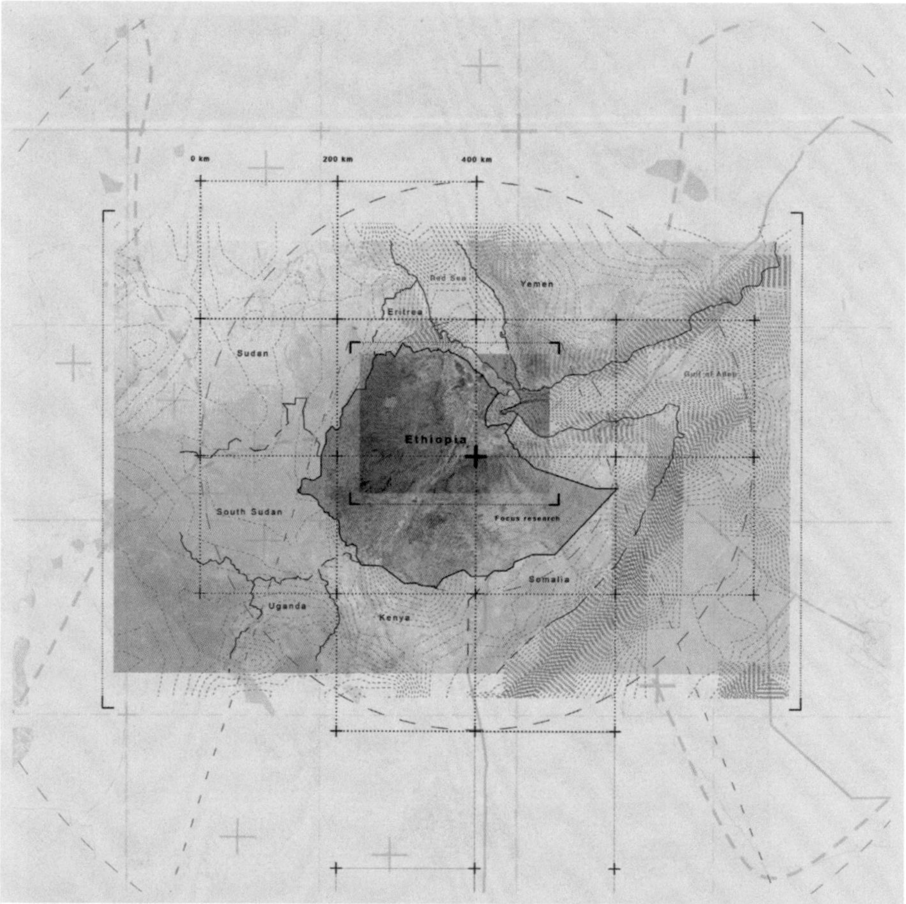

2021 GULED ELYAS Drawing 01_Location Plan 01.png

2021 GULED ELYAS Image 01_.png

STUDENT Guled Elyas
PROJECT Formalisation of Nomadic Urbanism
SUPERVISOR Helen Duong and Tim Pyke
YEAR 2021

2021 GULED ELYAS Presentation.pdf:58

2021 GULED ELYAS Presentation.pdf:63

2021 GULED ELYAS Image 10_.png

2021 GULED ELYAS Image 13_.png

STUDENT Gavrila Mandy Kahuni
PROJECT Revitalisasi Kampong Dolly
SUPERVISOR Helen Duong and Tim Pyke
YEAR 2020

2020 Gavrila Mandy Kahuni, Revitalisasi Kampong Dolly: Community, Cultural Identity and Dignity

2020 GAVRILA MANDY_ Image 01_North Entrance Gate.png

This project explores the future relationship between the urban *kampung* and the city. It evaluates government policy and planning that affects urban socio-economic conditions. It aims to revitalise Kampung Dolly, and set an example for other *kampungs* by intensifying the urban grain and street quality as well as adding new functions to prepare for future expansion.

The new image presented of Kampung Dolly is like a living museum, showcasing the area's history and daily life as experienced by both locals and tourists.

Responding to different issues, each intervention creates varied types, sizes and scales. Sites include: food towers, community halls, super-kiosks and government offices, as well as civic space and laneway shelters. The project explores different design approaches, from additions to the street edge, rooftop and laneway, to insertions into existing buildings.

This project challenges the design of a public space that is inviting but also restrictive, using architecture to bridge social gaps as well as physical boundaries. By integrating the iconic vernacular architecture of the *joglo* (Javanese house), it is designed to attract visitors while maintaining a strong cultural identity for the local community.

STUDENT Gavrila Mandy Kanuni
PROJECT Revitalisasi Kampong Dolly
SUPERVISOR Helen Duong and Tim Pyke
YEAR 2020

2020 GAVRILA MANDY_ Image 04_South Entrance Gate.png

2020 GAVRILA MANDY_ Image 03_North Entrance Food Tower Night View.png
2020 GAVRILA MANDY_ Image 03_North Entrance Food Tower.png

STUDENT Gavrila Mandy Kahuni
PROJECT Revitalisasi Kampong Dolly
SUPERVISOR Helen Duong and Tim Pyke
YEAR 2020

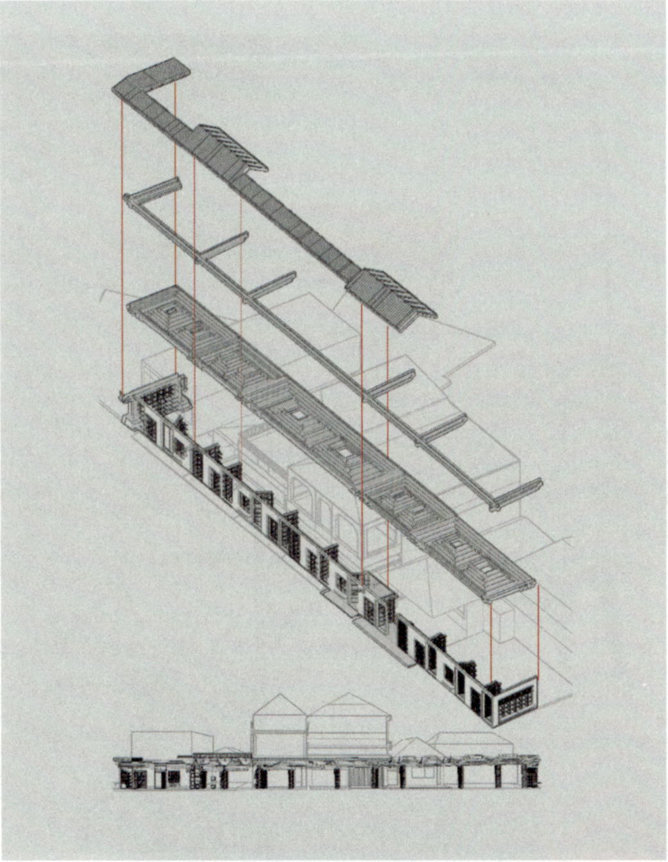

2020 GAVRILA MANDY_ Drawing 02_Diagram 5b.png

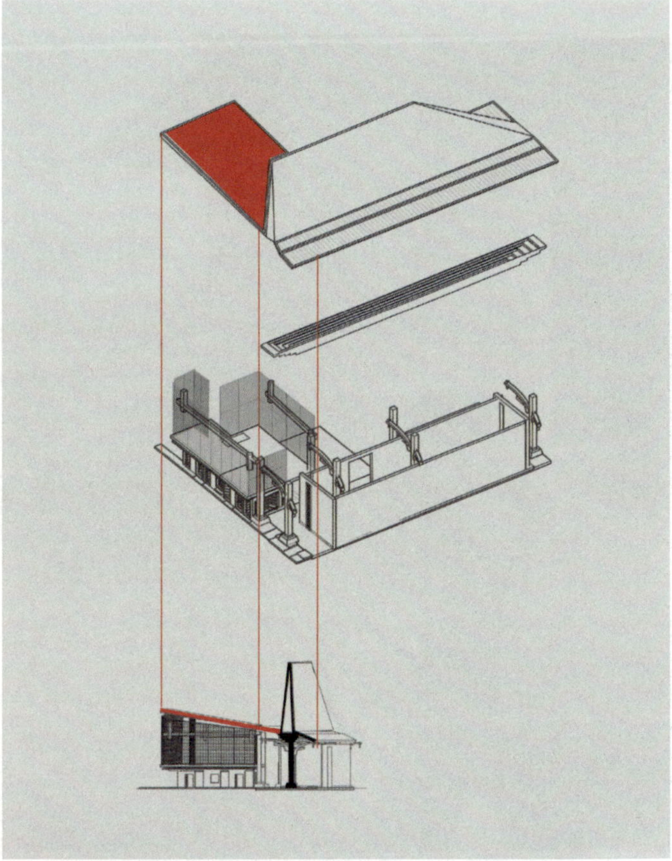

2020 GAVRILA MANDY_ Drawing 02_Diagram 2.png

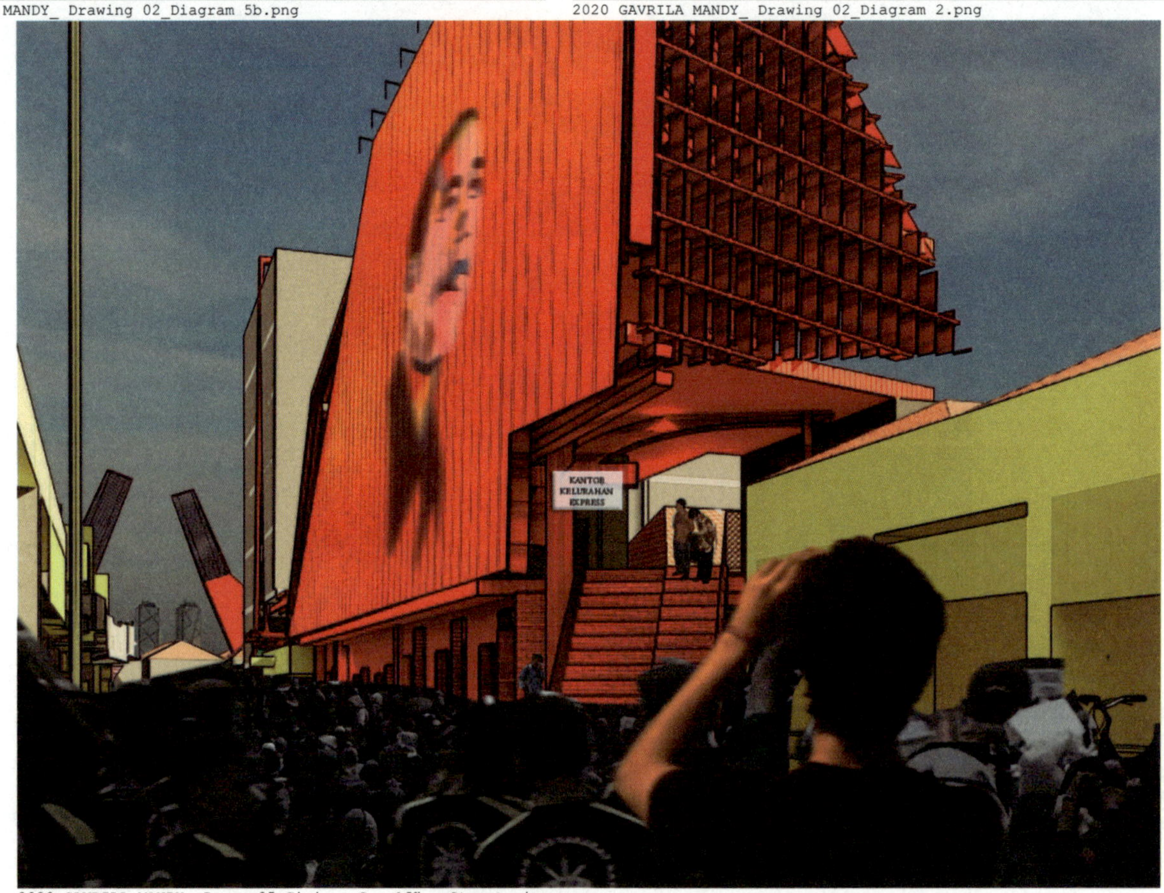

2020 GAVRILA MANDY_ Image 05_Civic & Gov Office Street view.png

STUDENT Gavrila Mandy Kahuni
PROJECT Revitalisasi Kampong Dolly
SUPERVISOR Helen Duong and Tim Pyke
YEAR 2020

2020 GAVRILA MANDY_ Image 07_Street view.png

2020 GAVRILA MANDY_ Drawing 01_Site Plan 1.1500 @A1.png

STUDENT Justin Chong
PROJECT Recipe for Redemption
SUPERVISOR Anna Johnson
YEAR 2021

2021

Justin Chong, Recipe for Redemption

2021_JUSTIN CHONG_Image 10_Biased Atrium.jpg

Recipe for Redemption is a gesture towards the rejuvenation of Chinatown, also known as Petaling Street, in the city of Kuala Lumpur, Malaysia. Through the lens of an architectural performance, the project gives back to place. Its significant history as the catalyst for the introduction of the Chinese community into Malaysia is acknowledged by reinterpreting the entire site as an opera stage.

This project involves iconic food vendors within the street at different scales, translating their unique recipes into architecture. By converting these standalone stalls into mixed-use extensions of the existing built fabric, they become part food stall and part street performance theatre, with strong heritage influences from Cantonese opera. At the same time, the extensions facilitate the provision of aid to those not as fortunate, repurposing redundant and abandoned buildings within the site for shelter, rehabilitation and food distribution.

The goal is for Petaling Street to never have a curtain call. The project proposes a utilitarian counterpart to the existing cultural heritage, inspiring a new design language that can revitalise and showcase Malaysia's multiculturalism.

STUDENT Justin Chong
PROJECT Recipe for Redemption
SUPERVISOR Anna Johnson
YEAR 2021

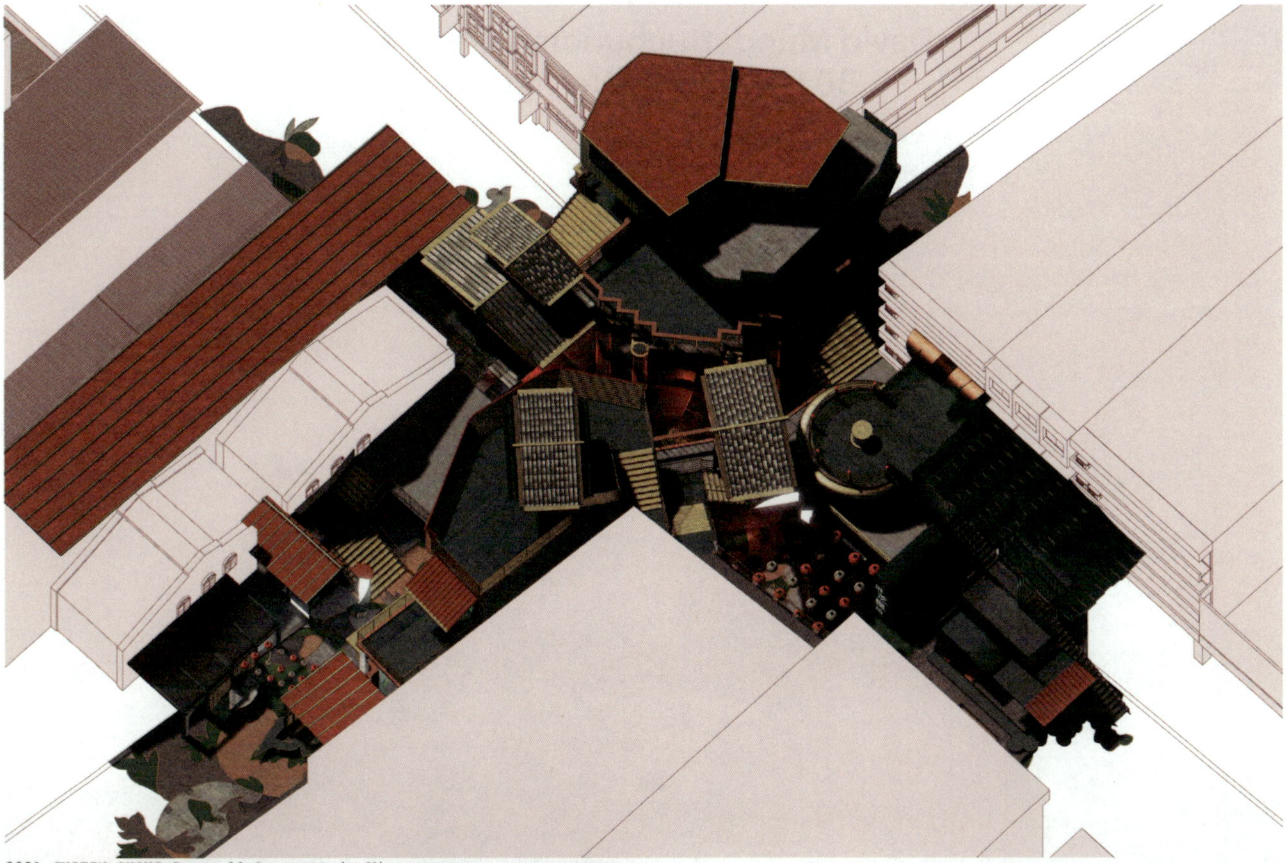

2021_JUSTIN CHONG_Image 11_Axonometric View.png

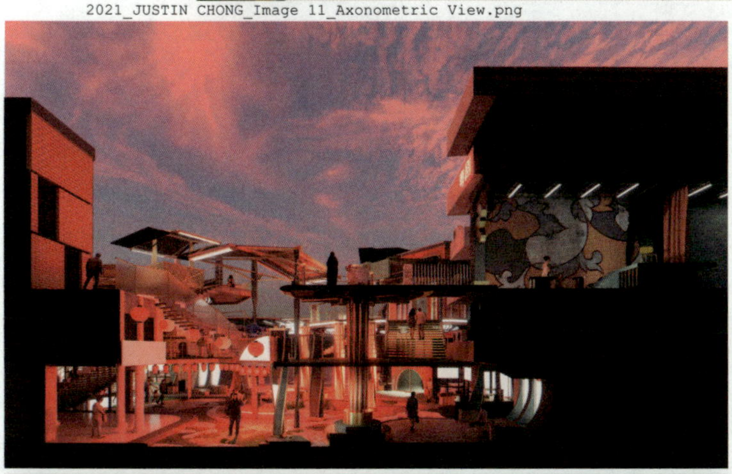

2021_JUSTIN CHONG_Drawing 03_Section.png
2021_JUSTIN CHONG_Image 02_The Roasted Duck Stall.jpg

2021_JUSTIN CHONG_Image 01_Porous Laneway.jpg
2021_JUSTIN CHONG_I...03_The Muachi Stall.jpg
2021_J...04_The Outdoor Performance Stage.jpg

STUDENT David Mundattuchundayil Thomas
PROJECT 30 x 40 Digital Vernacular
SUPERVISOR John Doyle
YEAR 2019

2019

David Mundattuchundayil Thomas, 30 × 40 Digital Vernacular

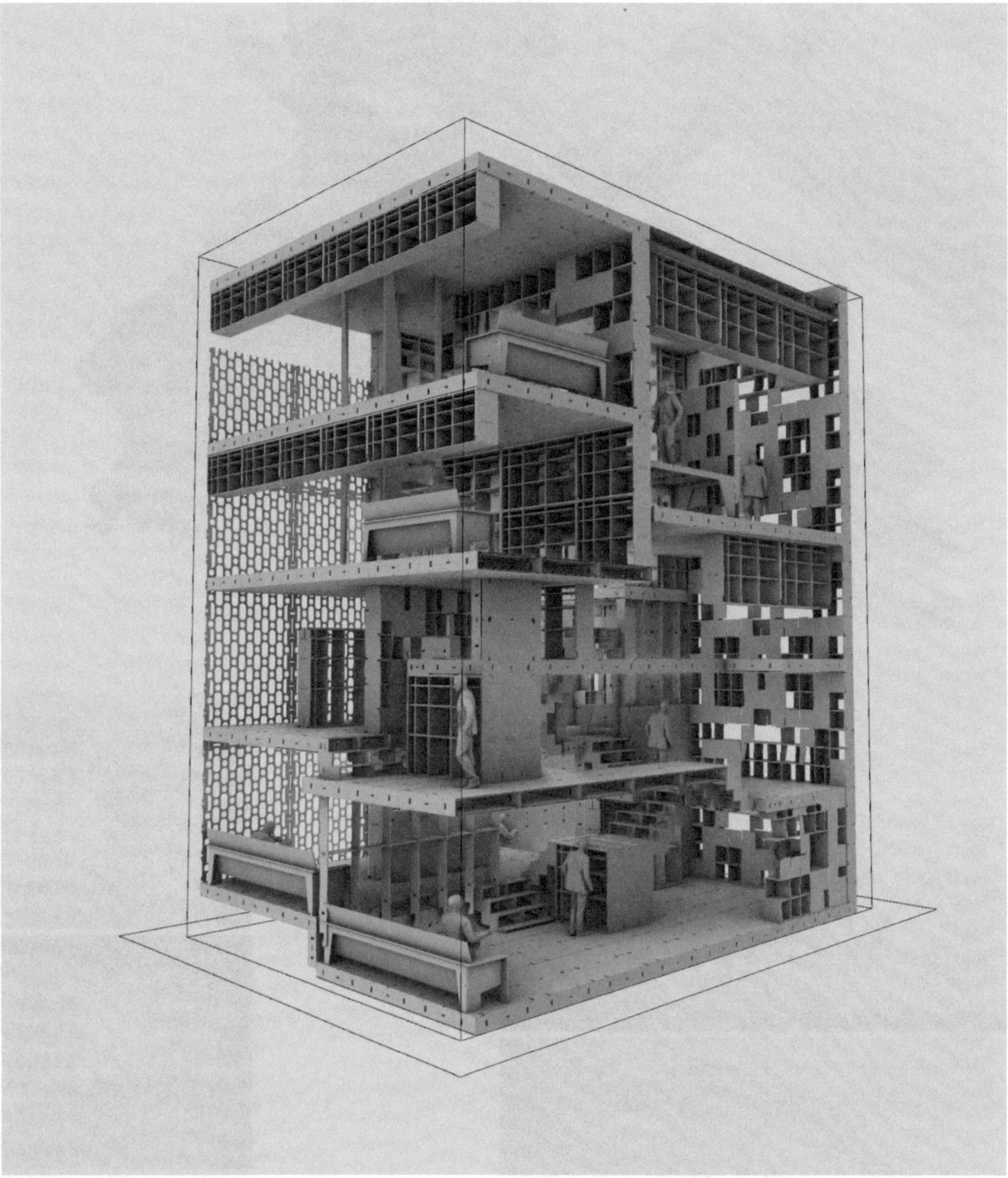

2019 DAVID THOMAS Image_01_Commercial.pdf

A strange and compelling contradiction exists in architecture today. Digital communication and digital tools make everyone and everything in the world more accessible and more alike, and yet there remains a powerful desire to express qualities of difference, unique to each regional community, each specific place and each individual designer. At the same time, global digital unification fosters a desire to express new ideas in architecture built around common ideas rather than specific places. This project is an attempt to respond to this paradox of wanting to be the same and different simultaneously.

Digital Vernacular is an idea that combines vernacular design principles of the past and digital technologies of the present with goals of accessibility and innovation in a contemporary context. The design approach looks at the construction process as a system of discrete building parts with a logic and amenity encoded into their form. From there, the project looks at how these parts could be replicated and adapted to a constant flux of change, all the while being informed by the surrounding built environment and vernacular context.

STUDENT David Mundattuchundayil Thomas
PROJECT 30 x 40 Digital Vernacular
SUPERVISOR John Doyle
YEAR 2019

2019 DAVID THOMAS Image_01_Commercial.pdf

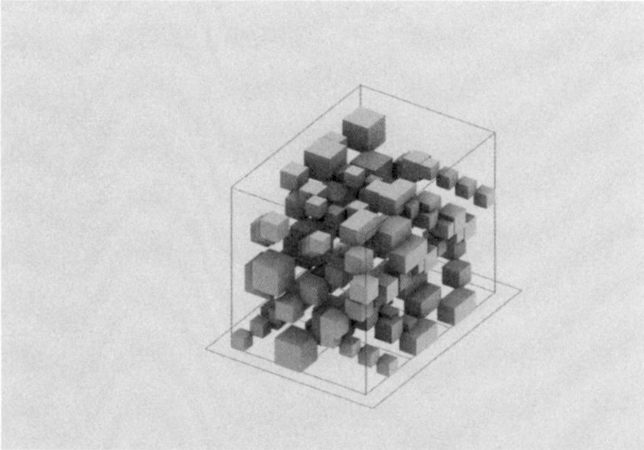

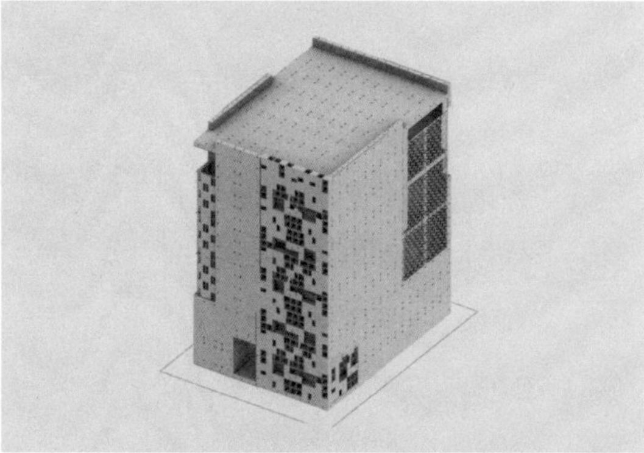

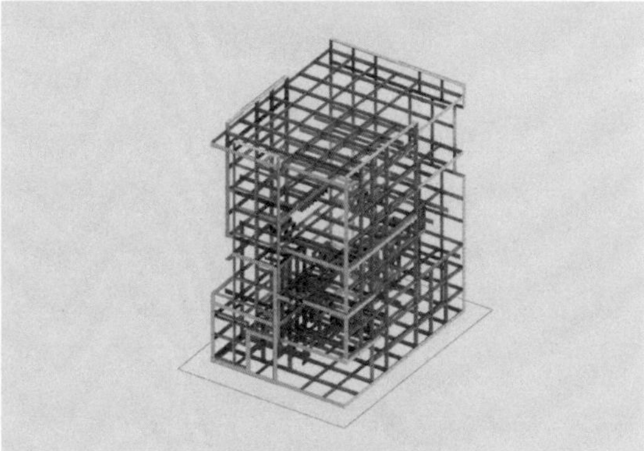

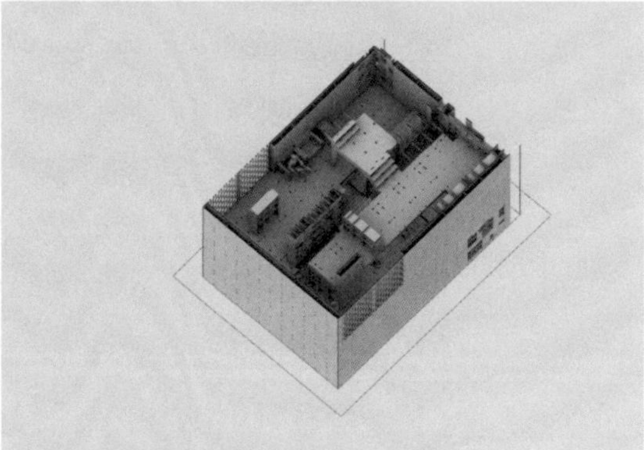

2019 DAVID THOMAS Image_01_Commercial.pdf
2019 DAVID THOMAS Image_01_Commercial.pdf
2019 DAVID THOMAS Image_01_Commercial.pdf
2019 DAVID THOMAS Image_01_Commercial.pdf

STUDENT David Mundattuchundayil Thomas
PROJECT 30 x 40 Digital Vernacular
SUPERVISOR John Doyle
YEAR 2019

2019 DAVID THOMAS Image_02_Residential.pdf

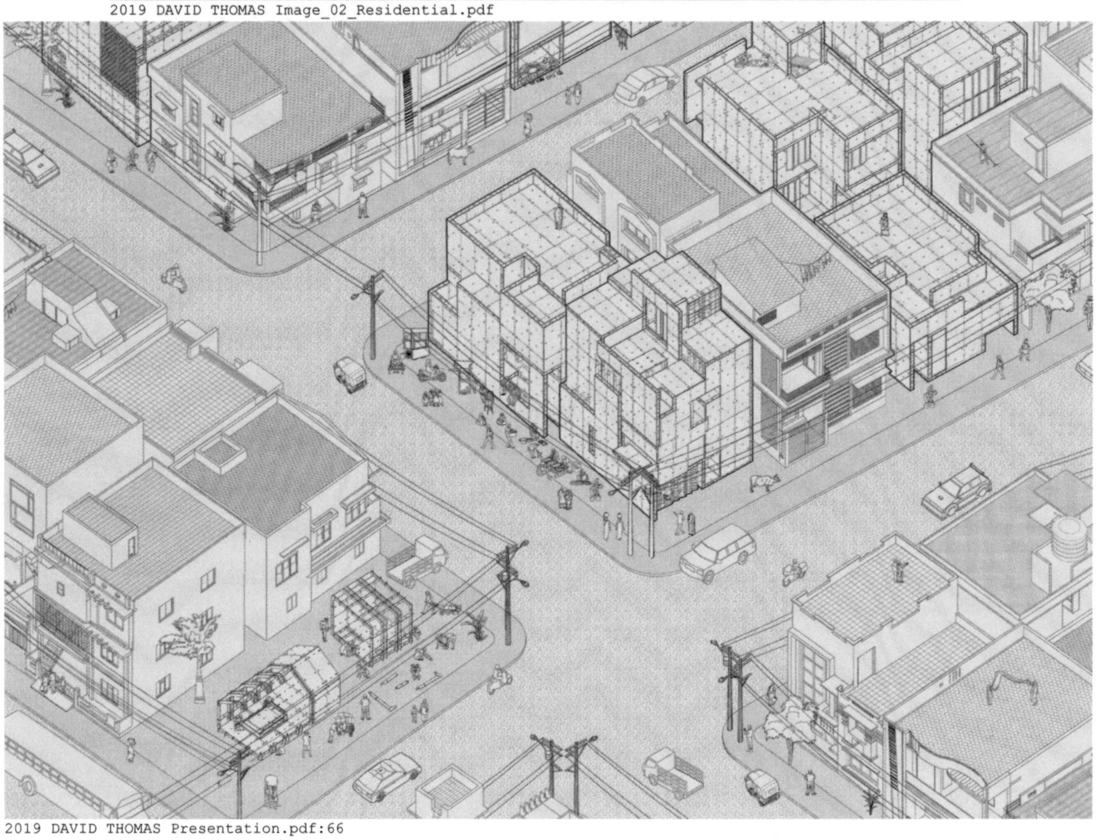

2019 DAVID THOMAS Presentation.pdf:66

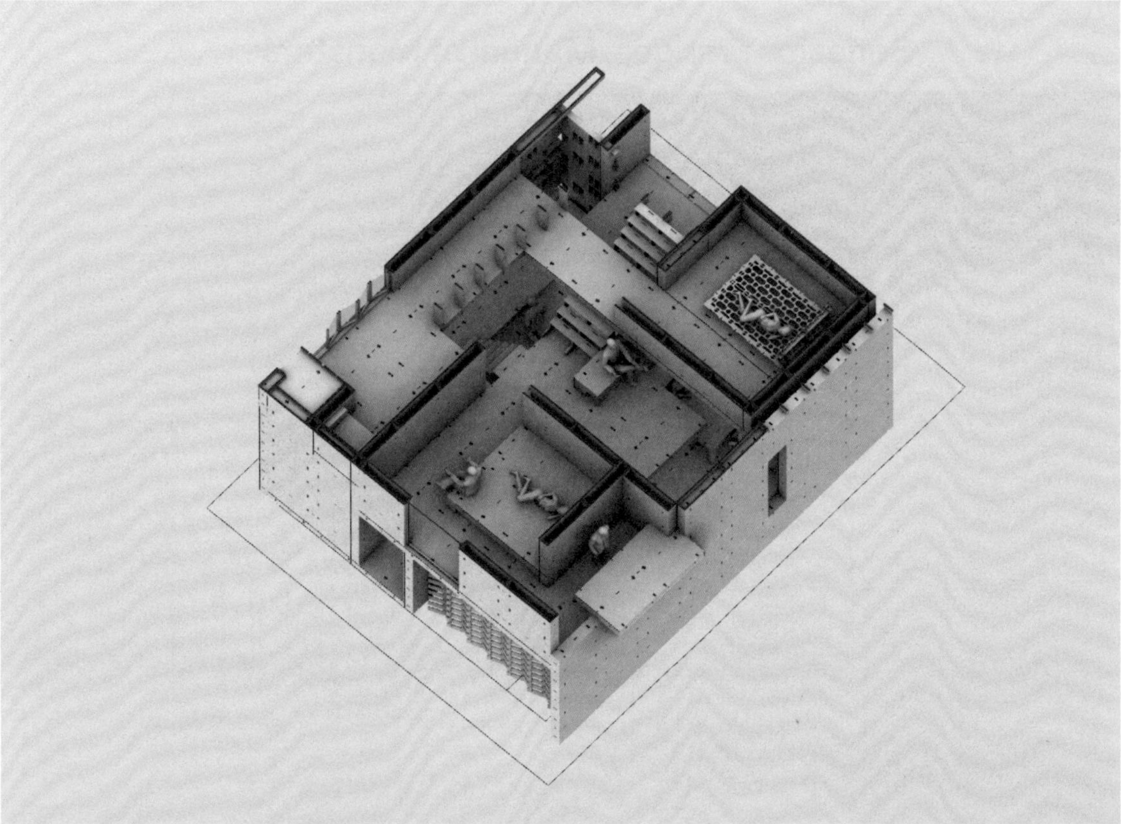

2019 DAVID THOMAS Image_02_Residential.pdf

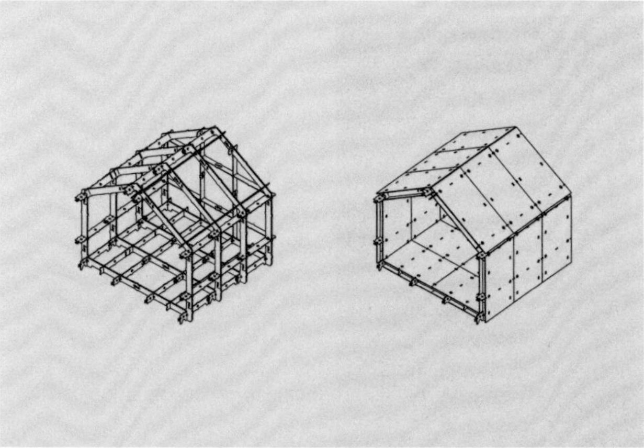

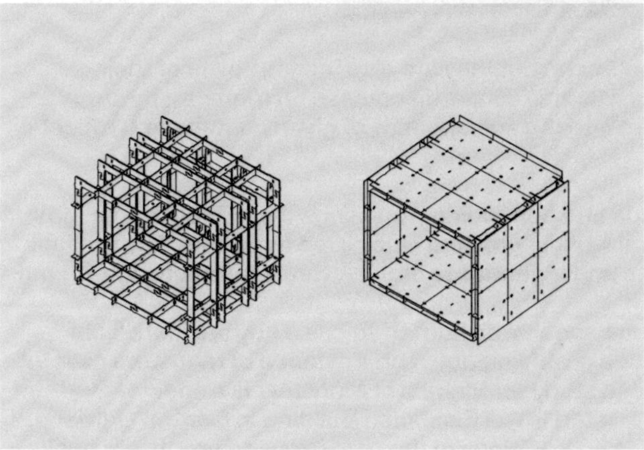

2019 DAVID THOMAS Presentation.pdf:33
2019 DAVID THOMAS Presentation.pdf:34

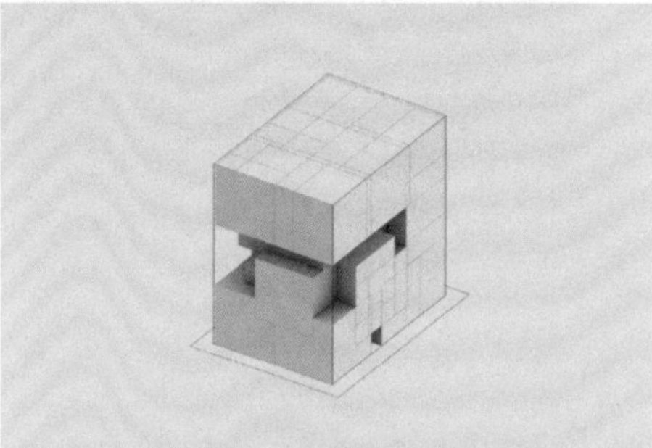

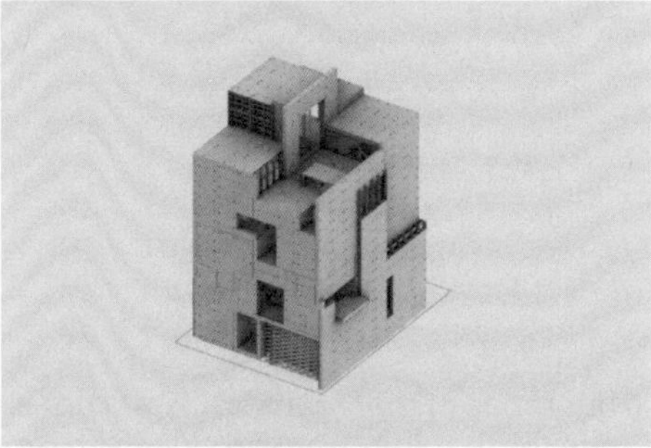

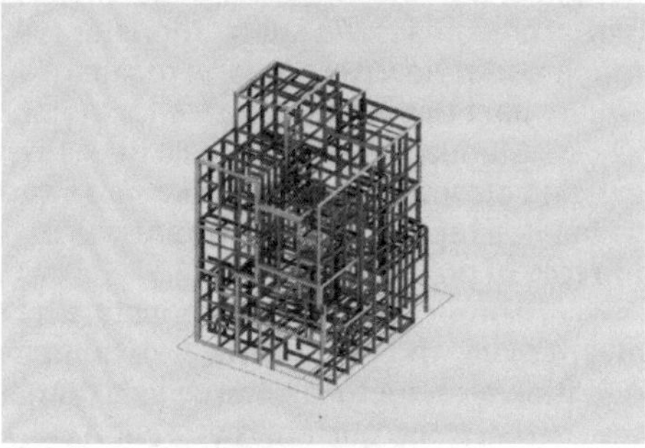

2019 DAVID THOMAS Image_02_Residential.pdf
2019 DAVID THOMAS Image_02_Residential.pdf
2019 DAVID THOMAS Image_02_Residential.pdf

STUDENT Senesios Frangos
PROJECT Manual of Monsters
SUPERVISOR Neil Masterton and Ian McDougall
YEAR 2019

2019 Senesios Frangos, Manual of Monsters

2019 SENESIOS FRANGOS Image 02_Rathdowne Street.jpg

2019 SENESIOS FRANGOS Image 03_Rathdowne Street Aerial.jpg

'[R]hetorics of the "monstrous" are not simply "constructed by their social contexts" but they are also "constructive of their contexts: that they both *produce* and *reproduce* social discourse and practice. In this sense, discourses on monstrosity serve as global currencies. As such, "monster talk" may function as a means to inquire into the sociopolitics of given cultures and reflect much about how porous, and resistant, its boundaries are.'

Isn't this what we strive for in public architecture?

Manual of Monsters is a how-to guide for designing annexes, addenda and appendices, buildings that rework and augment existing structures — and which are increasingly a part of public architectural work in growing cities like Melbourne. The manual translates techniques and strategies of the monstrous, as found in film, myth and legend, into architectural operations to reframe the role of public buildings.

Throughout history, monsters have been like the animals in a fable who speak with human voices. They are incredibly aware of us, and yet the image of humanity reflected through their eyes is not a gratifying one. The existence of monsters calls into question architecture's status as a domain of cultural representation. The case study for Manual of Monsters is a speculative brief that extends the current restoration works being done at the World Heritage-listed Royal Exhibition Building in Carlton Gardens, and designs an annex to the adjacent Melbourne Museum. The project draws on traditions of the monstrous to propose a public architecture of critical reflection rather than imposition.

STUDENT Senesios Frangos
PROJECT Manual of Monsters
SUPERVISOR Neil Masterton and Ian McDougall
YEAR 2019

Manual of Monsters is presented as a print-based publication, a 'manual' highlighting a methodology for the design of public architecture that could be applied to any context but will return different results based purely on place. It is a reaction to a homogenising world, where the ability for architecture to belong to a place is being left behind. At this crossroads resides the monster — a body of pure culture, a manifestation that exists in all global civilisations yet is intrinsically connected to specific places. Using this base idea as the point of departure, the thesis develops a series of architectural techniques and operations to be used like a utilitarian handbook, a universal design theory that satisfies contemporary culture's short attention span and obsession with mass production, while at the same time being grassroots and local, responsive to a specific time, place and culture.

The project is conceived as a contemporary bestiary inspired by the mediaeval tradition of illustrated books, which were true compendiums of fantastic beasts drawn from a collective imagination and thus impossible to 'spot' in the real world. Monsters mark the boundaries of cultural values, and as self-defined outcasts from our constructed systems they fascinate and frighten. Film and art philosopher Noel Carroll's 'Taxonomy of Monsters' theorises that all monsters of myth, legend, film and literature can be grouped into five categories: fusion, fission, magnification, massification and horrific metonymy. This idea is used as a lens to restage examples of built architecture, boiling them down to the monstrous techniques with which they operate.

1/2 continues on next page

2019 SENESIOS FRANGOS Image 05_Nicholson Street Aerial.jpg

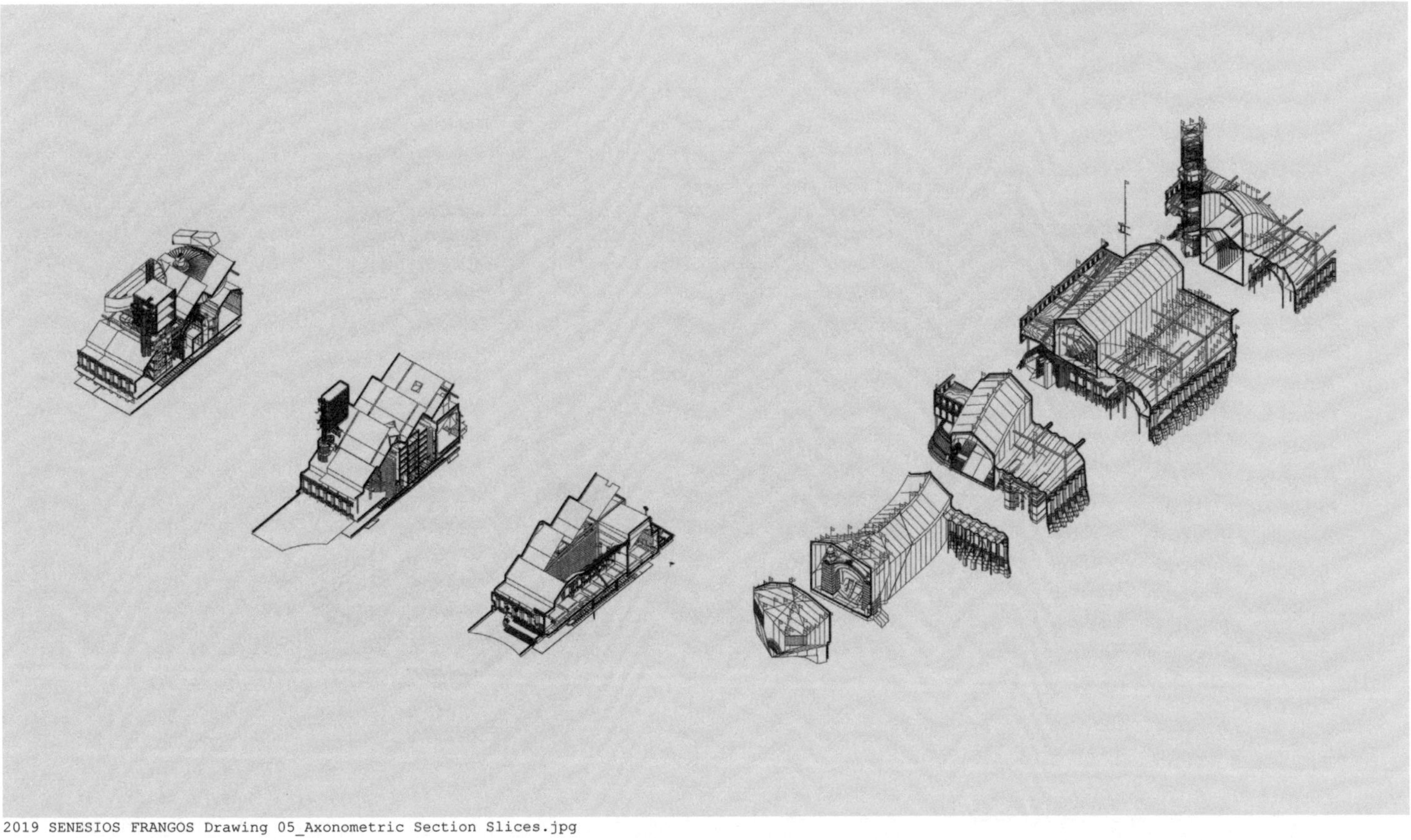

2019 SENESIOS FRANGOS Drawing 05_Axonometric Section Slices.jpg

STUDENT Senesios Frangos
PROJECT Manual of Monsters
SUPERVISOR Neil Masterton and Ian McDougall
YEAR 2019

2019 SENESIOS FRANGOS Image 01_Northern Aerial.jpg

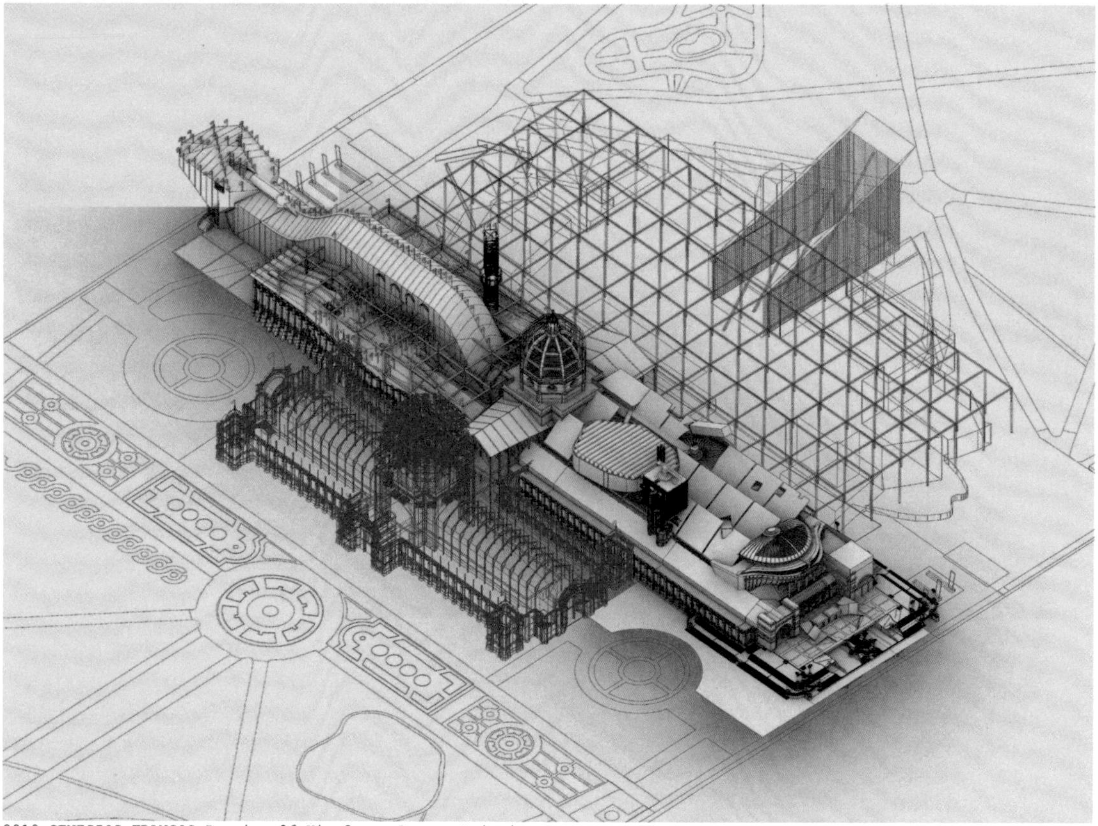

2019 SENESIOS FRANGOS Drawing 06_Wireframe Axonometric.jpg

STUDENT Senesios Frangos
PROJECT Manual of Monsters
SUPERVISOR Neil Masterton and Ian McDougall
YEAR 2019

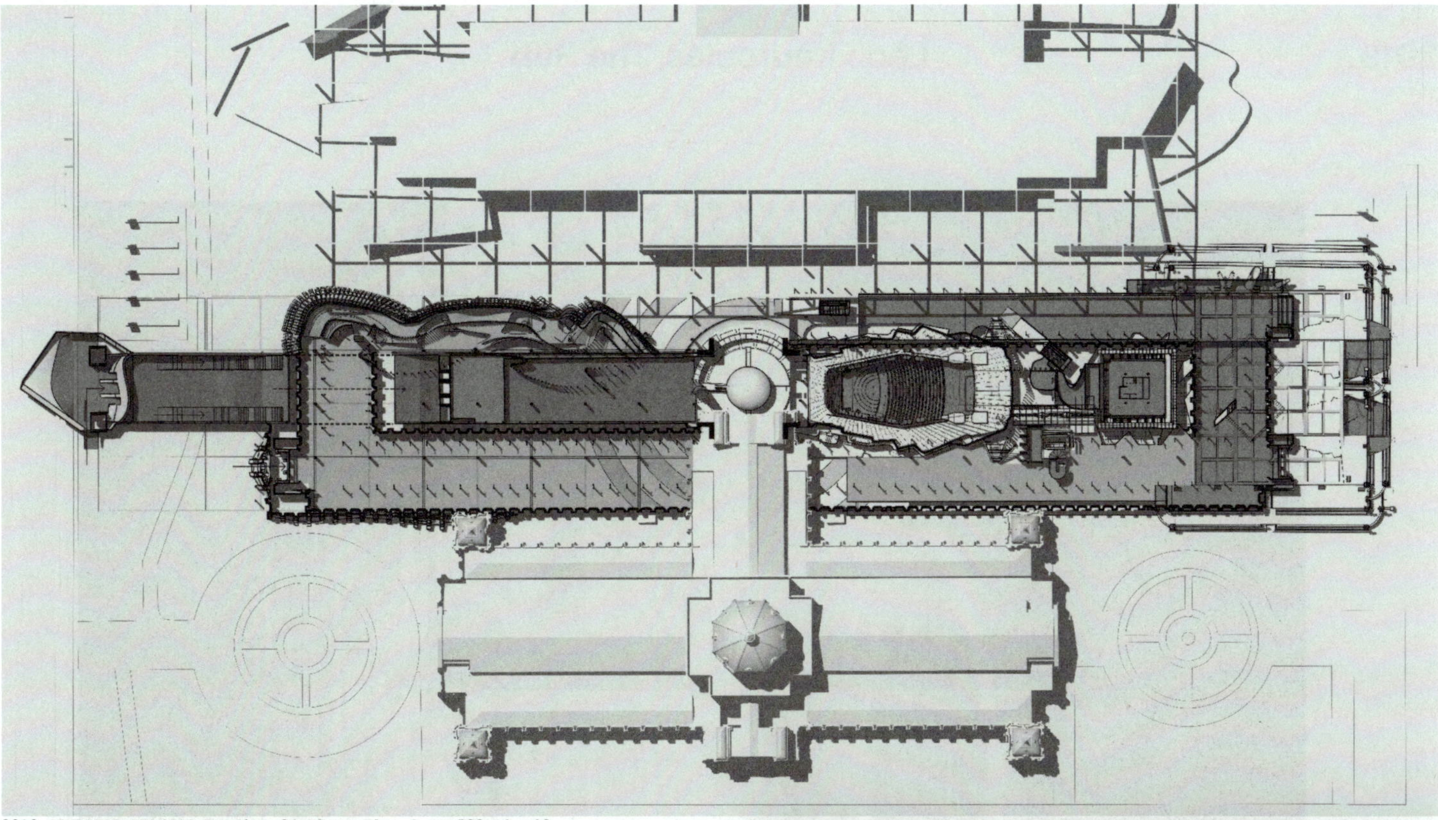

2019 SENESIOS FRANGOS Drawing 04_Floor Plan_1 to 500_A1.pdf

2019 SENESIOS FRANGOS 190617_LONG SECTION.jpg

Drawing on concepts from outside of the architectural discipline, the themes of the taxonomy operate to construct the monster as an operative informant. Beginning with a normal or host, an incision is made or deviation point located, which is then either replaced or grafted onto, transforming the 'informatint' into a reflection of its former self but with an embedded critique. The embedded critique, or the part that defines the monster, works as an expository tool, however it needs to know what it is exposing. The monster homes in on its terrain of exposition by treating context as content, exorcising references, histories, lost stories, traumas, triumphs, hopes and dreams from a place. This content is then plugged into the techniques developed and highlighted in the manual (informed by the taxonomy) to manifest a language of built form that is in direct dialogue with a physical site set within a certain civilisation and time period.

The project adopts the monster's most effective paradigm, an elegant and respectful extension building designed as a host. This takes the form of an extension built in the space between the Royal Exhibition Building and the Melbourne Museum. Through a series of deliberate incisions, operations and loaded interventions, the monster physically constructs an architecture that references the narrative context of its place, challenging public architecture´s role in the affirmation of dominant ideologies and public architecture's legacy of imposing culture upon others. The project imagines a future of public work that embraces the idea that the utopian *tabula rasa* is dead and the future of the city is reimagination and revision.

STUDENT Leon Koutoulas
PROJECT The Rub
SUPERVISOR Michael Spooner
YEAR 2019

2019

Leon Koutoulas, The Rub

2019 LEON KOUTOULAS Image 3_Corner Tall .jpg

In *Hamlet: Poem Unlimited* (2003), Harold Bloom writes about Shakespeare's own environmental experiences at the time of writing *Hamlet* as having given rise to the character of the same name.

John Hejduk speculates, as an extension of this thinking, that one of those experiences was witnessing the Globe Theatre deconstructed, transported across the River Thames and reconstructed as an exact copy. He goes further to surmise that it was this particular action, where the playwright was able to witness the architectural artifice deconstructed and reconstructed, that enabled Shakespeare to conceive of *Hamlet* — the dramatic construct who constantly deconstructs and reconstructs himself, the play in which he exists and the world beyond the confines of the play.

Out of architecture is born a self-perpetuating crisis: a character anxious to preserve themself, while just as anxious to move forward with decisive action. This project is concerned with embedding the same productive critical energy into the architectural systems of an institution. Procured through a series of 16 architectural operations, it seeks to repeat the 'crossing of the Thames' and interrogate the productive capacity of architecture when 'time present and time past are perhaps present in time future.' In search of *Hamlet*, the Design Hub is plunged into a state of crisis, with hopes that perhaps something more could emerge — perhaps something of a dream?

STUDENT Leon Koutoulas
PROJECT The Rub
SUPERVISOR Michael Spooner
YEAR 2019

2019 LEON KOUTOULAS Image 8_Wall View .jpg

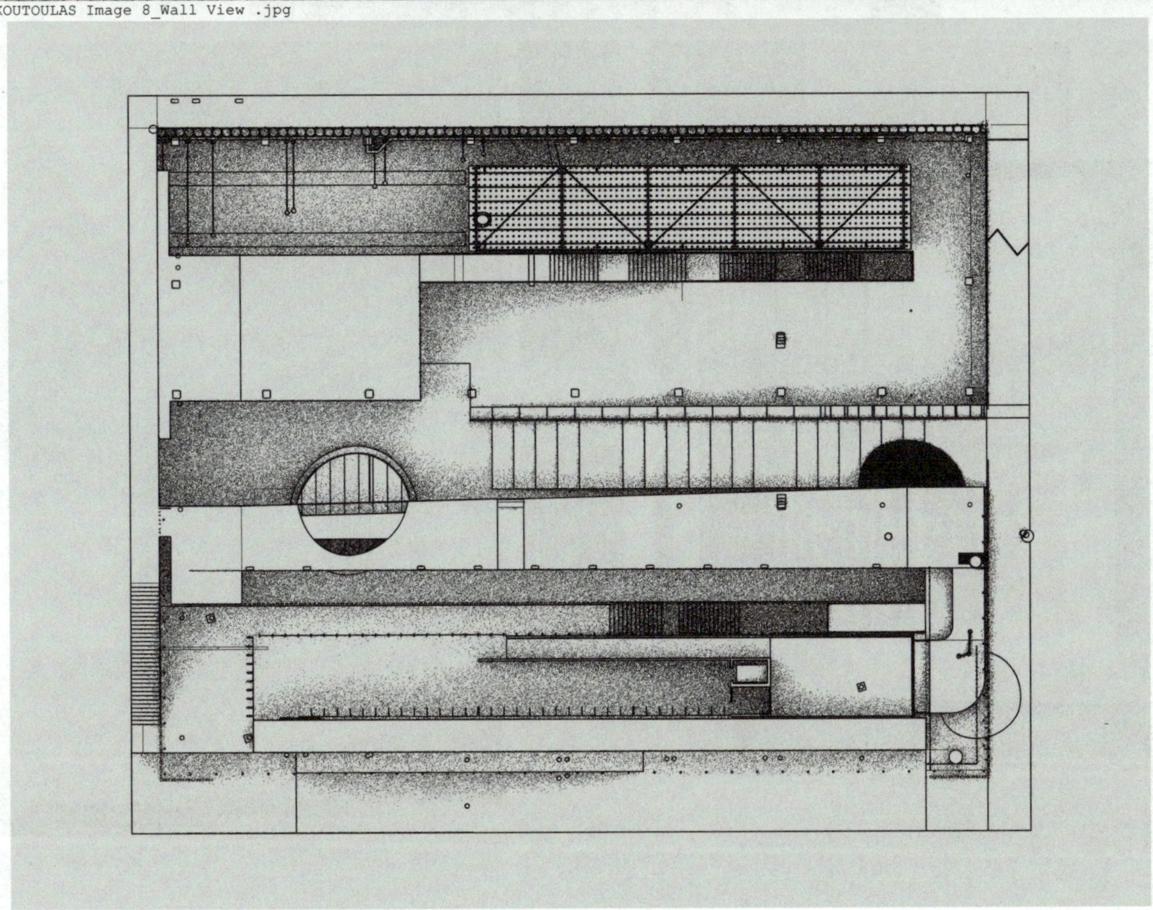

2019 LEON KOUTOULAS Drawing 1_Ground Floor Plan .pdf

STUDENT Leon Koutoulas
PROJECT The Rub
SUPERVISOR Michael Spooner
YEAR 2019

2019 LEON KOUTOULAS Image 10_Laurentian Library .jpg

2019 LEON KOUTOULAS Image 2_Archive View .jpg

STUDENT Leon Koutoulas
PROJECT The Rub
SUPERVISOR Michael Spooner
YEAR 2019

2019 LEON KOUTOULAS Image 1_Classroom View .jpg

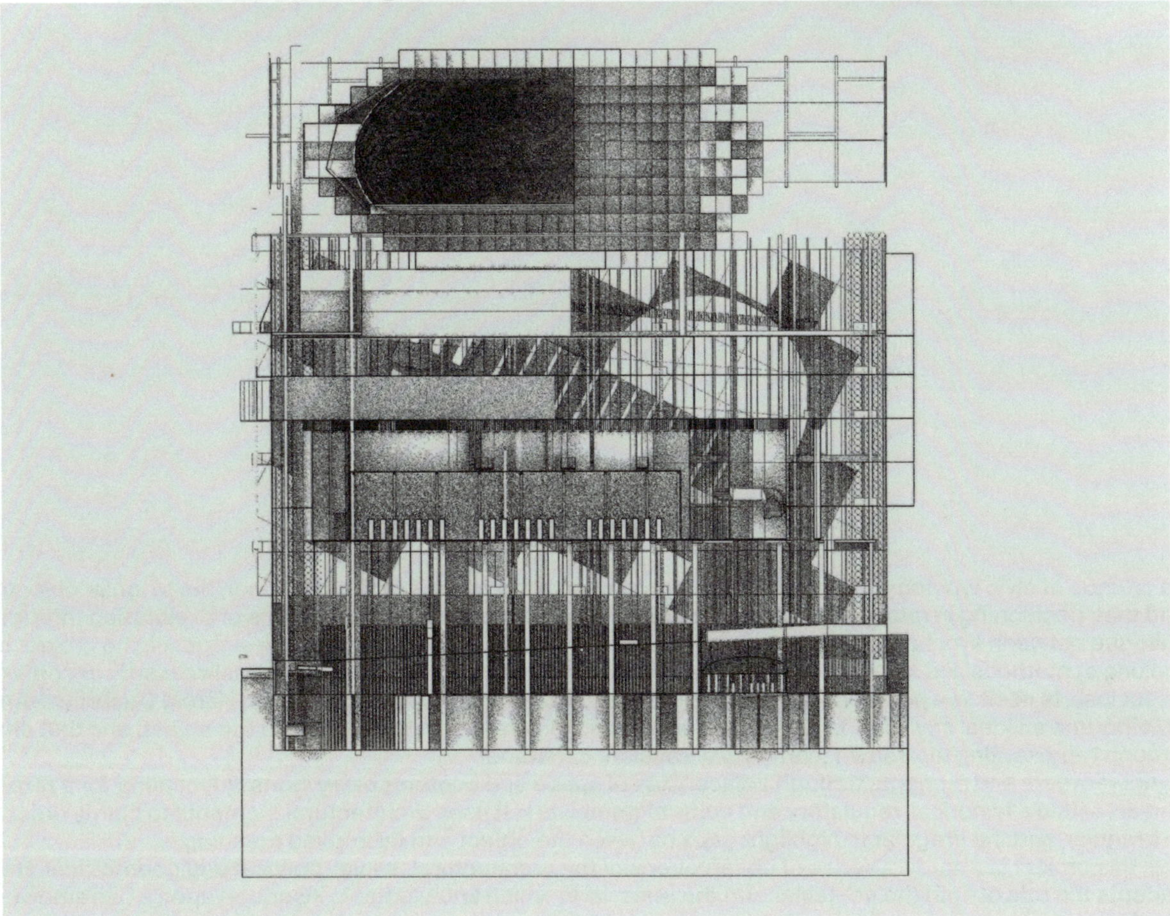

2019 LEON KOUTOULAS Drawing 6_Section 1 .pdf

STUDENT Temitope Adesina
PROJECT Fiction-ism
SUPERVISOR Anna Jankovic and Andre Bonnice
YEAR 2020

2020

Temitope Adesina, Fiction-ism

2020 TEMITOPE ADESINA axo 02_2.png

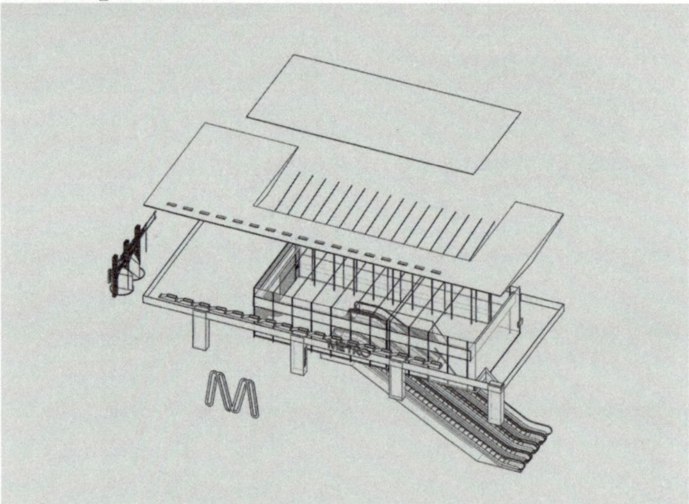

2020 TEMITOPE ADESINA Drawing 12_Metro Axon 03.png

Fiction-ism is a critique of civic typology. This project is concerned with the politics of the container, the singular objects of architecture and their positioning in relation to art and the archive. It employs a museum as a lens of exploration through which to develop a dialogue between synchrony and change in linguistic systems over time. As the title suggests, the project is interested in looking at methods and systems that are open to interpretation as tools to recontextualise clarify or confer validity.

The project inserts itself as a presence on Swanston Street, Melbourne in accordance with Harold Desbrowe-Annear's 'How to make Melbourne an ideal city' plan. In doing so, it advocates for a return of the archive to the object, one that challenges the 'idealist' through representing the known to the city's transient consumer.

The project reorders and reorients through adjacencies of space and contemporary icons, advocating for a rereading of architecture and art within a historical, regulatory and cultural framework. It uses architectural elements to clarify order and to emphasise the irregular, and the irregular to highlight gaps between the object and its implied meaning.

Above all, this project is a study, a series of observations of the architectural, social, political and geometrical. Here, the built form adopts the role of both the container and the material in which knowledge is inscribed upon — a framework of microcosmic truths.

STUDENT Temitope Adesina
PROJECT Fiction-ism
SUPERVISOR Anna Jankovic and Andre Bonnice
YEAR 2020

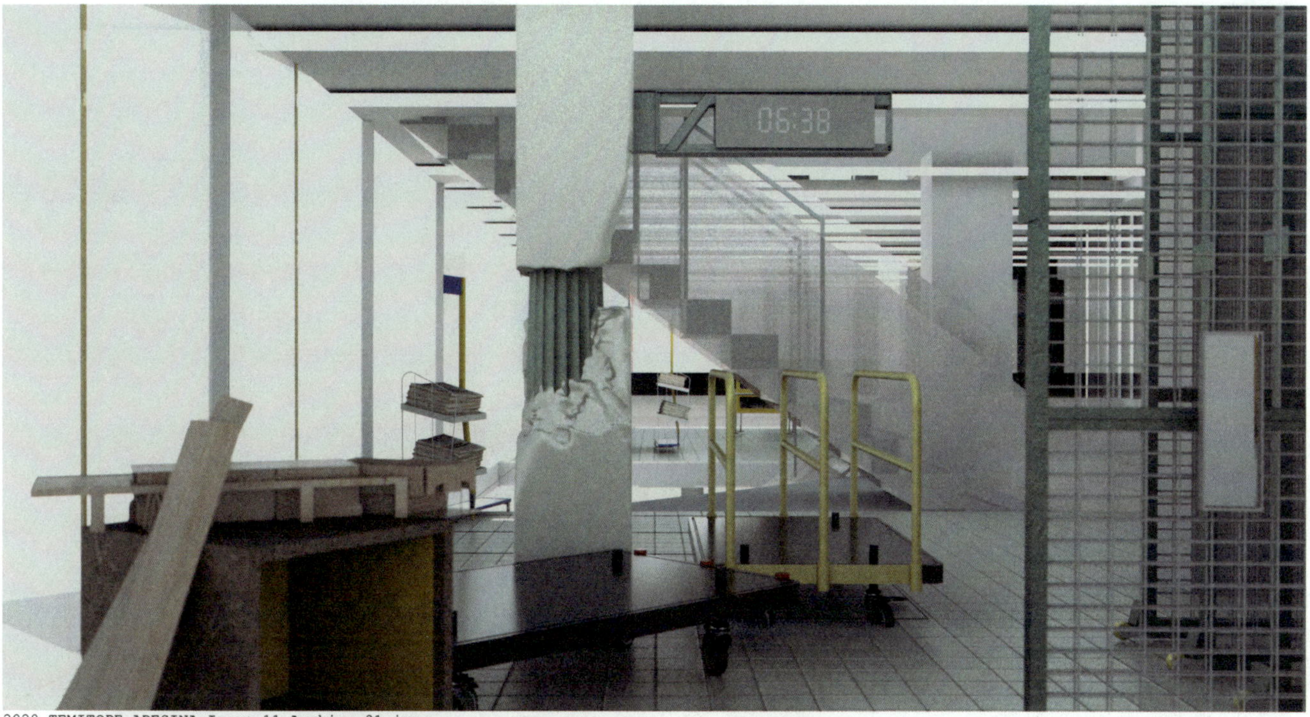

2020 TEMITOPE ADESINA Image 11_Archive 01.jpg

2020 TEMITOPE ADESINA hub 03.png

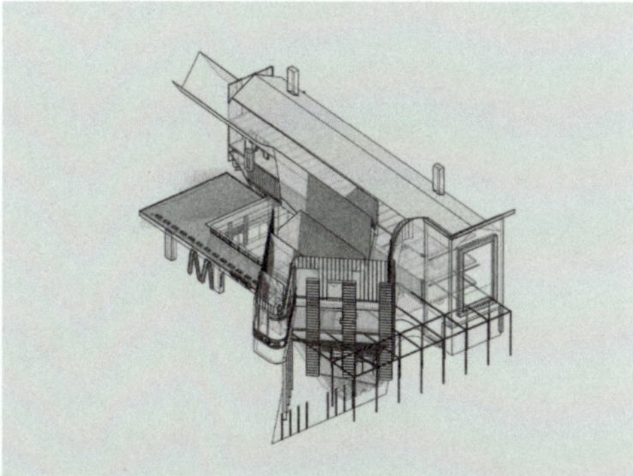

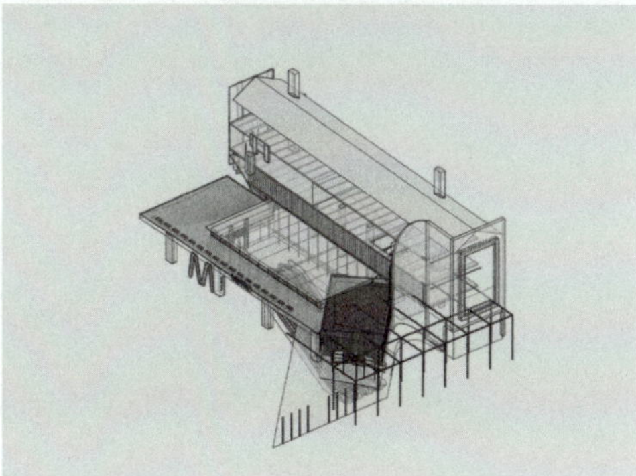

2020 TEMITOPE ADESINA Mass 01png.291.png
2020 TEMITOPE ADESINA Drawing 01_Axonometric.png

STUDENT Temitope Adesina
PROJECT Fiction-ism
SUPERVISOR Anna Jankovic and Andre Bonnice
YEAR 2020

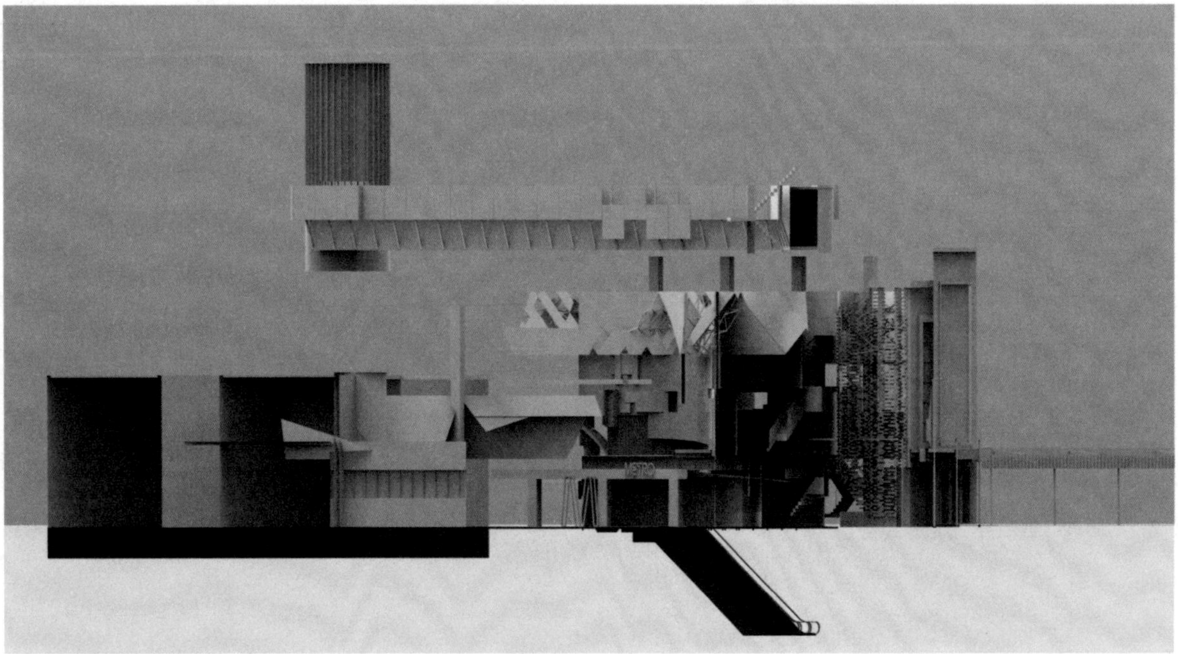

2020 TEMITOPE ADESINA DRAWING 05_GEOMETRY INTERSECTION.PDF

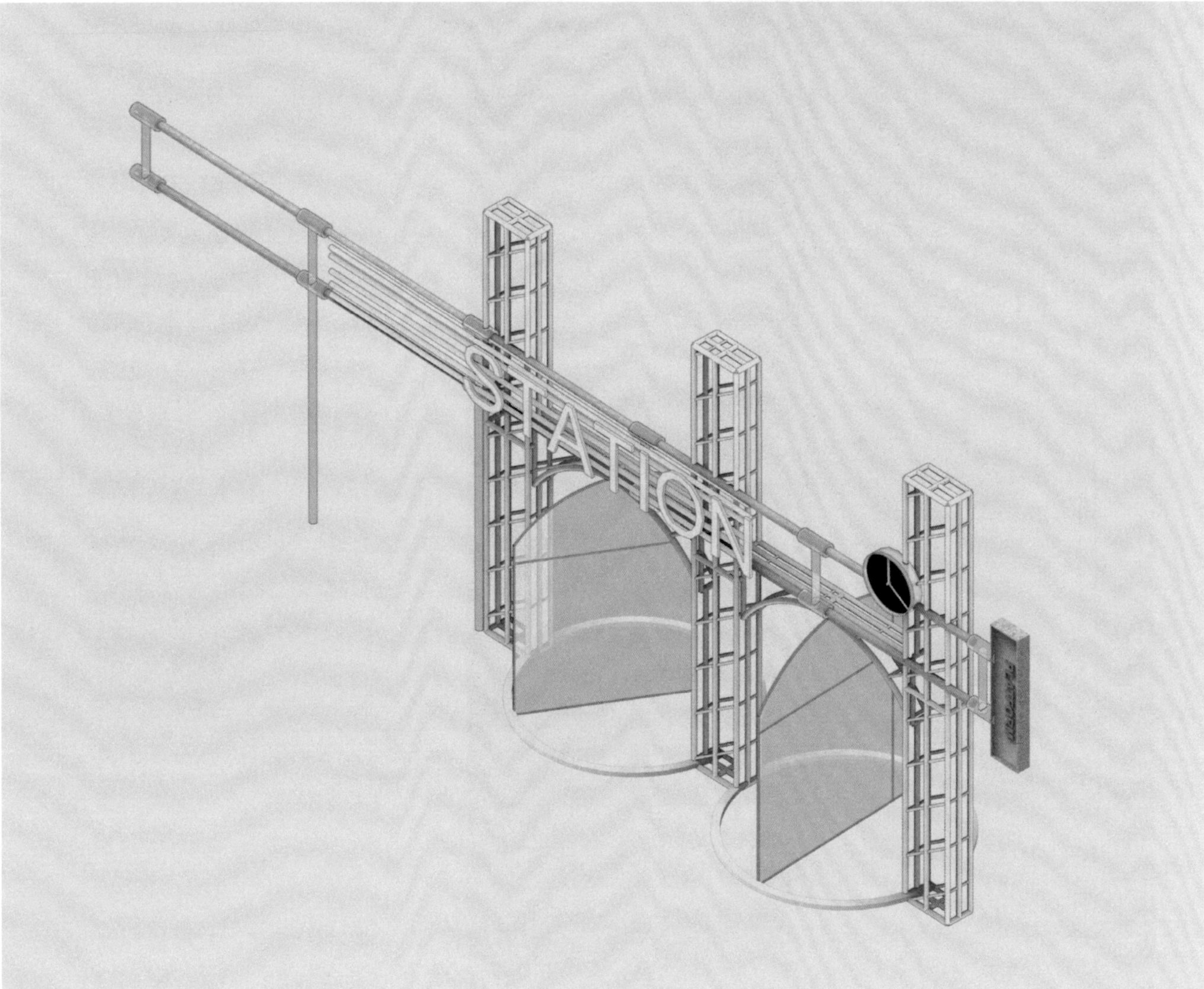

2020 TEMITOPE ADESINA Drawing 02_Station Entry Detailed Axonometric.png

STUDENT Temitope Adesina
PROJECT Fiction-ism
SUPERVISOR Anna Jankovic and Andre Bonnice
YEAR 2020

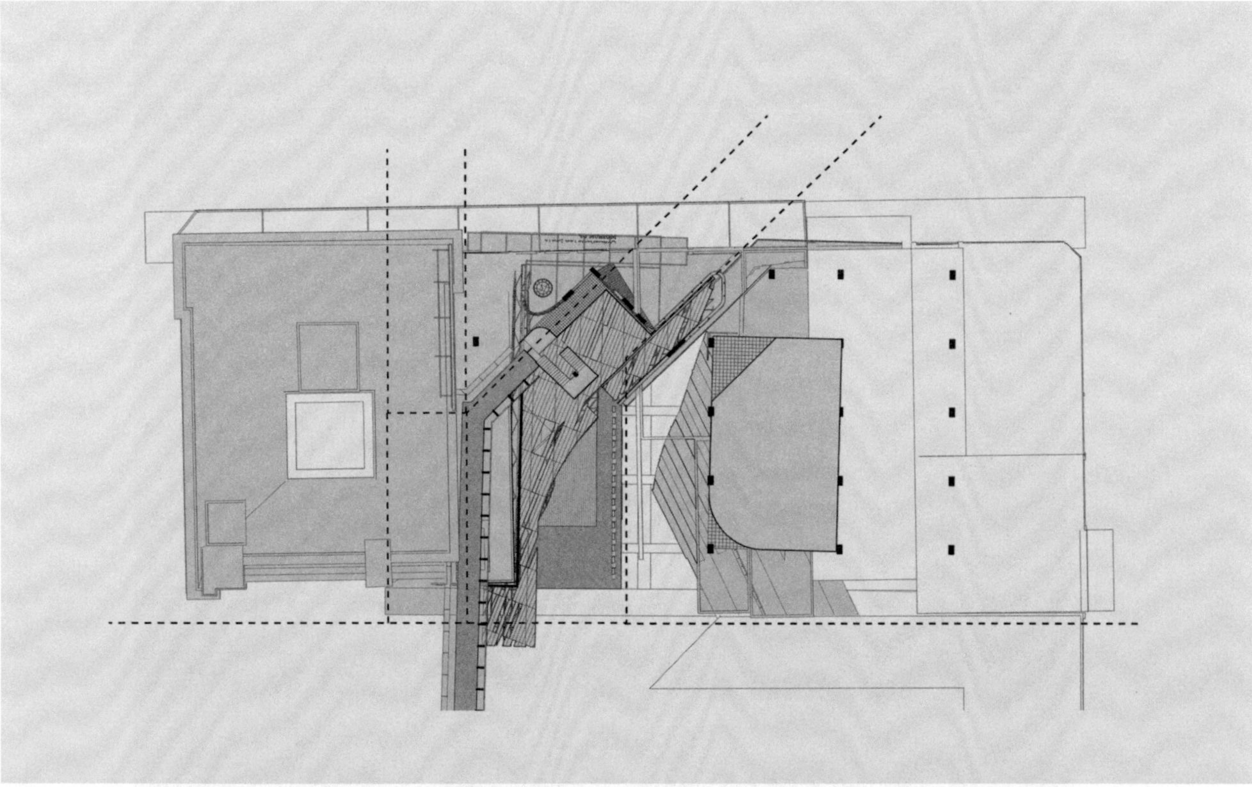

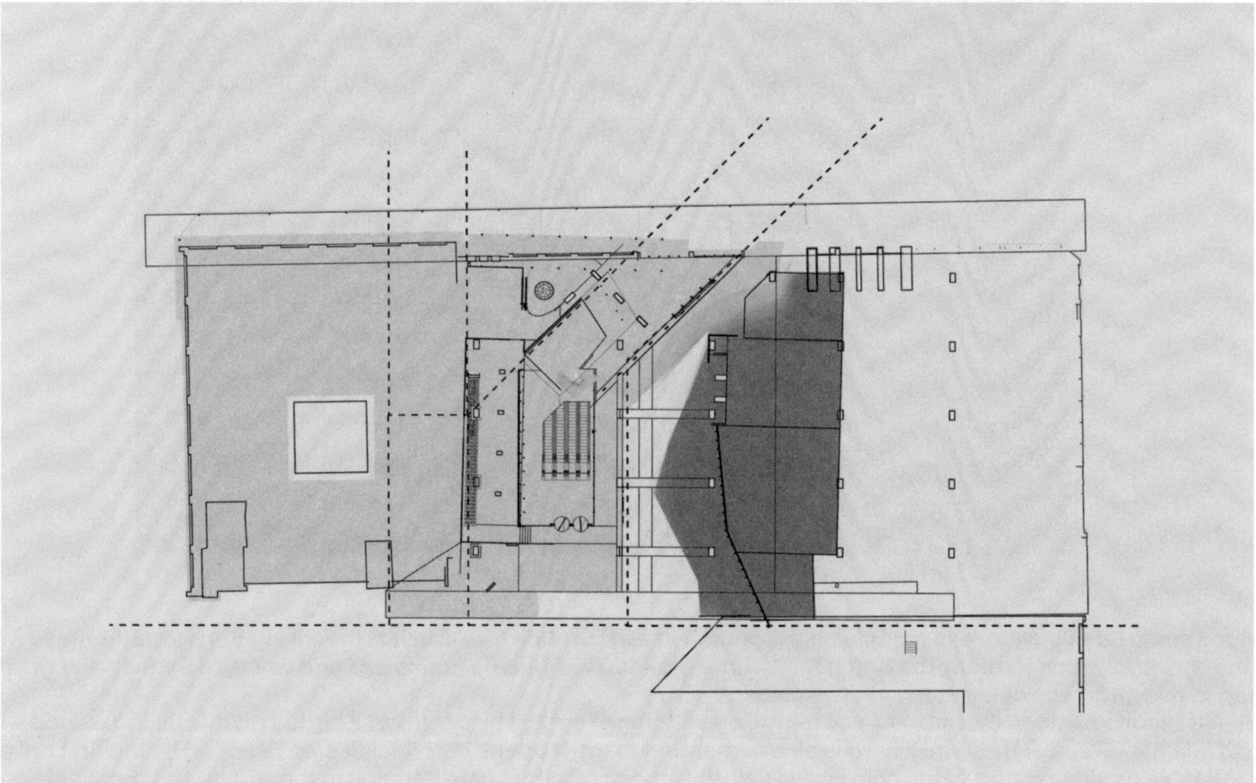

2020 TEMITOPE ADESINA DRAWING 11_AXIS PLAN 01.PDF
2020 TEMITOPE ADESINA DRAWING 11_AXIS PLAN 02.PDF

2019

Emma Ka Wing Li, In the Blood

SEM2_2019_EMMALI_20_CARLTON BAR.png

In the Blood could be mistaken for a magpie on the branch of a Jacaranda tree. But it is the Rising Sun Hotel, home to Melbourne fans of the Sydney Swans, formerly the South Melbourne Swans. This swan is both black and white, of Sydney and of Melbourne, belonging to one club yet existing between two cities.

In the Blood imagines the pub as a site for the dissolution of concrete identities, a partial myth-making exercise that makes explicit the fallacy of these truths while also cementing them. It opens potentialities, as revealed by the first roll of the dice on the table or the first toss of the coin on the field. It is the details that cause tumult in the whole, and the acute incisions and inflections that explain how things grow, disappear, die and yet endlessly find themselves again. The fact that they resemble other things while remaining as they are is a matter of conjuncture.

In the Blood is a crisis of place, the affirmation of identity and the burden of happiness. It is only in the incremental discernment of difference where we may find our true likeness.

STUDENT	Emma Ka Wing Li
PROJECT	In the Blood
SUPERVISOR	Michael Spooner
YEAR	2019

SEM2_2019_EMMALI_02_RISING SUN HOTEL DOUBLE DOOR.jpg

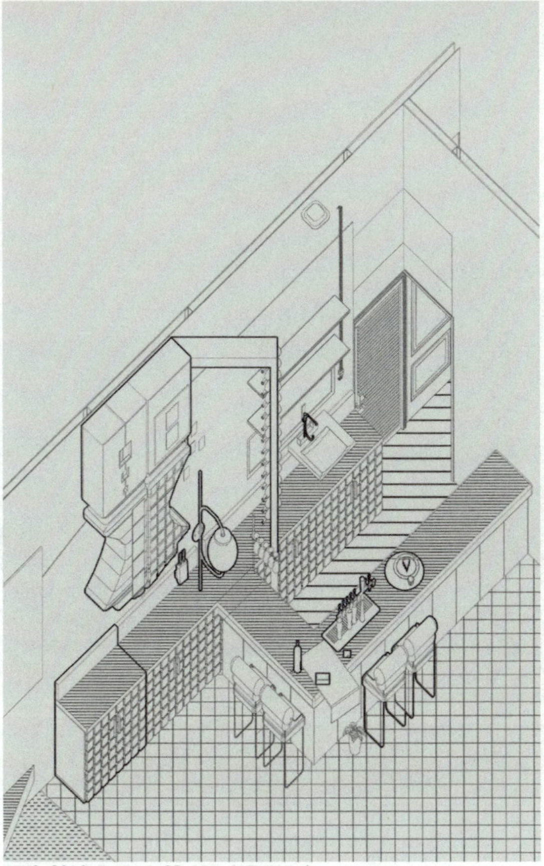

SEM2_2019_EMMALI_05_BAR CARLTON.jpg

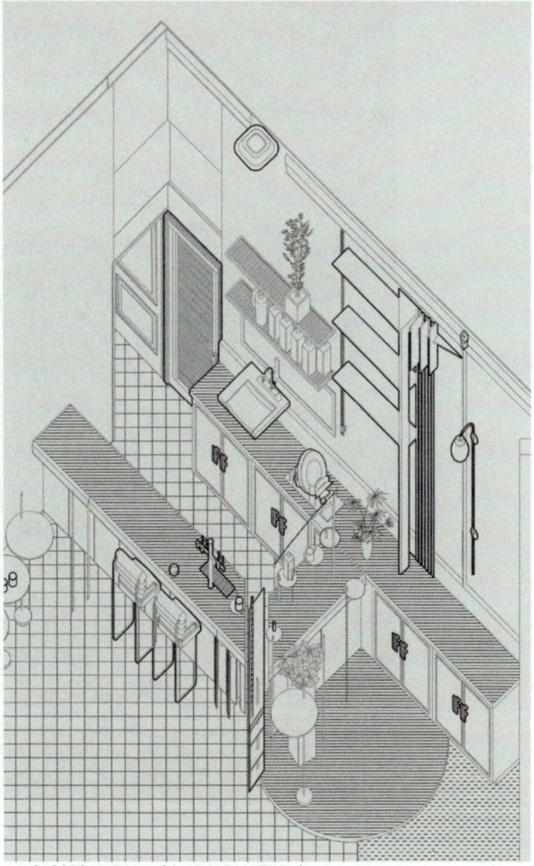

SEM2_2019_EMMALI_04_AXO TOOHEYS.jpg

STUDENT Emma Ka Wing Li
PROJECT In the Blood
SUPERVISOR Michael Spooner
YEAR 2019

SEM2_2019_EMMALI_21_TOOHEYS BAR.jpg

STUDENT Emma Ka Wing Li
PROJECT In the Blood
SUPERVISOR Michael Spooner
YEAR 2019

SEM2_2019_EMMALI_15_MELBOURNES HALFTIME CLUB.png

SEM2_2019_EMMALI_29_DELIVEROO.png

SEM2_2019_EMMALI_07_RIGHT ELEVATION.jpg

STUDENT Michelle Zhang
PROJECT Over Dressed, Over Coloured
SUPERVISOR Graham Crist
YEAR 2022

2022 Michelle Zhang, Over Dressed, Over Coloured

2022 MICHELLE ZHANG Drawing 01_New Hotel.png

Over Dressed, Over Coloured is an extension to Carlton's Rydges Hotel, which was recently used as an asylum seeker detention centre. The redevelopment of the building will allocate half of the rooms to emergency accommodation, while the hotel's public functions double as community facilities for displaced arrivals. Its form aims to ignite the grey box and its history.

The over-dressed design consumes the host building as well as cultures, religions and personal identities to spit out a building that intensifies cultural diversity. The project layers identities over one another, creating a messy, overworked collage of identities. Nothing of the past is erased but several iterations are added until they form a blurry image, dissolving familiar architectural features from different cultures and religions. Its expression aims to be both all of these identities and none of them.

This project calls to everyone here. It is for those recently arrived, for those wishing to reconnect with their histories and for those who are simply curious. Through a kaleidoscope of patterns, it celebrates a multifaceted environment as more identities pass through and imprint themselves upon the architecture. Over Dressed, Over Coloured is calling you.

STUDENT Michelle Zhang
PROJECT Over Dressed, Over Coloured
SUPERVISOR Graham Crist
YEAR 2022

2022 MICHELLE ZHANG Drawing 05_Bath House.png

2022 MICHELLE ZHANG Drawing 04_Hotel Entrance.png

2022 MICHELLE ZHANG Drawing 02_Hotel Facade.png

STUDENT Michelle Zhang
PROJECT Over Dressed, Over Coloured
SUPERVISOR Graham Crist
YEAR 2022

2022 MICHELLE ZHANG Drawing 03_Hotel Facade.png

STUDENT Michelle Zhang
PROJECT Over Dressed, Over Coloured
SUPERVISOR Graham Crist
YEAR 2022

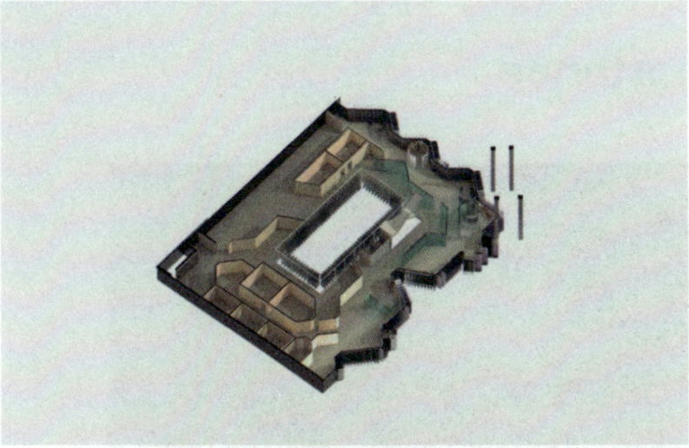

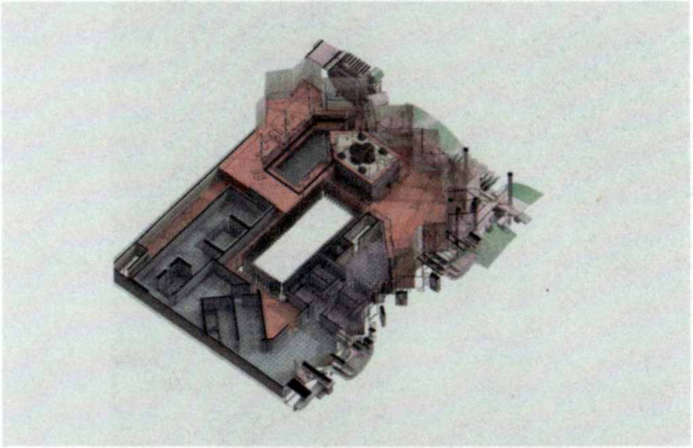

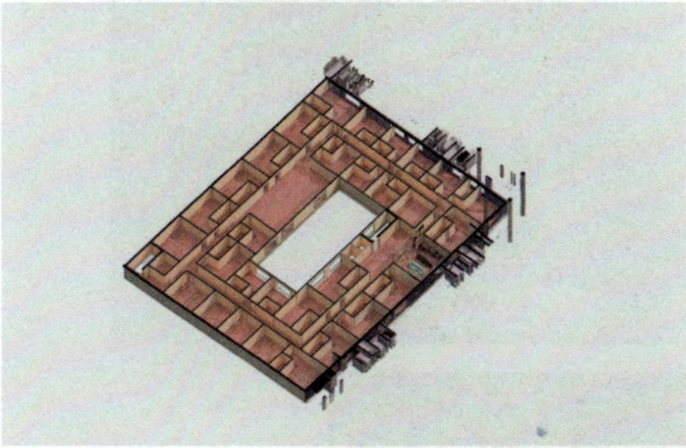

2022 MICHELLE ZHANG 03_10th FloorAccommodation.png
2022 MICHELLE ZHANG 02_5th Floor Bath House.png
2022 MICHELLE ZHANG 01_1st Floor Accommodation.png

2022 MICHELLE ZHANG Drawing 00_Collage.jpg

2022 MICHELLE ZHANG Drawing 06_Hall.png

STUDENT Tidus Lok Tin Shing
PROJECT Library of Importance
SUPERVISOR Vicky Lam
YEAR 2019

2019 Tidus Lok Tin Shing, Library of Importance

2019 TIDUS SHING Image 08_Theatre Exterior.jpg

2019 TIDUS SHING Image 04_House of Origin.jpg

Library of Importance is a mnemonic device for survival, the first act of resistance against erasure.

Cities rarely end. I think Hong Kong, once known as the City of Victoria, is now close to its second extinction. This project digs deep into the hidden layer of the city and explores — through archaeology — methods of retrieving buried ideas with faint traces. Hong Kong's cultural identity is embedded into the architecture, which in turn inscribes and codes its languages, symbols and urban experiences. The Library of Importance is a magnified stone boundary of the original city, mute from afar but within which architects and citizens are invited to connect with origin, borrow from the lost and celebrate their language.

The project is a path towards Hong Kong's survival, establishing a new language of hope for architects working in a surveillance society. Through recognition, naming and decoding, values embedded in the city by architects are resurrected as immutable ideas.

Each time a patron borrows from the library, it is an act of preservation, resisting erasure. This is how a city can survive — and how we could possibly survive in the worst of times.

STUDENT Tidus Lok Tin Shing
PROJECT Library of Importance
SUPERVISOR Vicky Lam
YEAR 2019

2019 TIDUS SHING Image 05_Recognition Hall.jpg

STUDENT Tidus Lok Tin Shing
PROJECT Library of Importance
SUPERVISOR Vicky Lam
YEAR 2019

2019 TIDUS SHING Drawing 05_Section.jpg

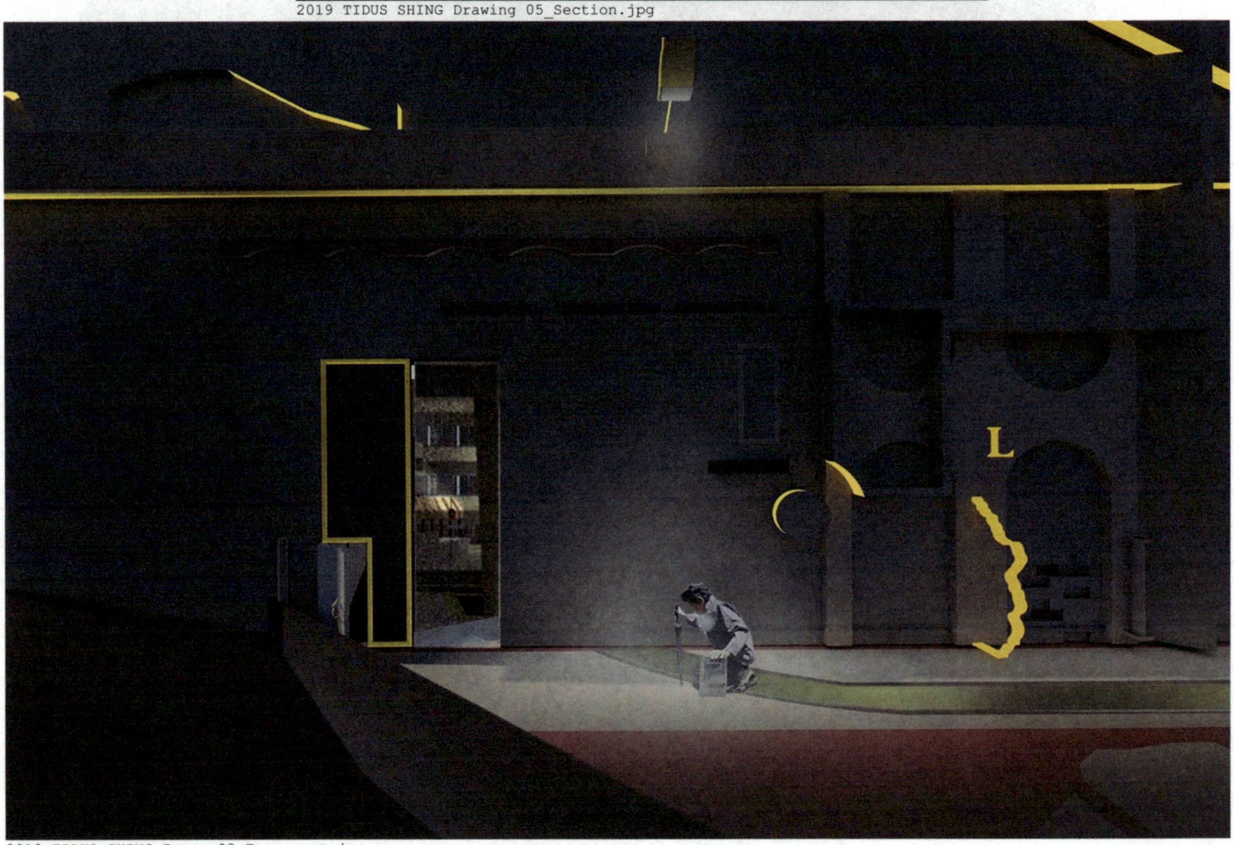

2019 TIDUS SHING Image 02_Forecourt.jpg

2019 TIDUS SHING Image 03_Chamber of Memory.jpg

2019 TIDUS SHING Image 01_Exterior.jpg

The *library of Importance* is designed for people who have lost their souls, and for architects who did not surrender. It is a pilgrimage, a journey of resurrection. It is an alienated object landed on the mountain like a lost boundary stone. It is not easy to reach.

Climbing up the well-lit path carved along the original boundary of the Lost City, you are attracted to the source. When you come close, you realise there are traces embedded in the surface of the façade; they remain difficult to understand, but the glowing parts seem to be of particular importance.

The library is organised into four sections: Chamber of Memory, House of Origin, Recognition Hall and Garden of Remembrance. It is a process of cognition, from unknown to known. From patterns that you never cared about to those that you will never forget.

The black stones mark the boundary and lead you in. The visitor's guide holder looks familiar, it seems to represent something, but you have no clue as to what. These are the methods that embed values into architecture, even after your building permit has been approved. These are the coded languages which, when placed together, create an image that you cannot yet fully comprehend.

Starting at the entrance, you step into the Chamber of Memory. It is a coded version of the original. It is probably something you have previously seen in the city without understanding it. Architecture as container of information, of historical traces. There are things abstracted into colour, pattern and codes. Some can only be read from a specific angle. Some appear in plans. Some are only sensed. The Chamber of Memory contains references to what has been lost — it reveals the existence of the hidden city, the City of Victoria, the erased part of Hong Kong.

1/2 continues on p. 295.

STUDENT Tidus Lok Tin Shing
PROJECT Library of Importance
SUPERVISOR Vicky Lam
YEAR 2019

2019 TIDUS SHING Image 06_Music Library.jpg

STUDENT Tidus Lok Tin Shing
PROJECT Library of Importance
SUPERVISOR Vicky Lam
YEAR 2019

The House of Origin is an archive of physical items of importance. Taking form as the exterior of an important independent publishing house and artist space that will likely be gone soon, it displays the original, or a copy of the original. It reflects the lost fabric of Kowloon Walled City and its narrow laneways. It glorifies the things we should treasure, a dedicated room for each one signifying their importance. It revives the objects, histories and modes of living that have been erased. The shape of the visitor's guide holder that made you wonder flows into the middle of the central court. You realise that it is a mountain, the Lion Rock, which holds the spirit of the people of this city.

Through the erased clock of Star Ferry Pier, you look back at the Hong Kong that is no longer there. You see the fragment of the architect's resistance. The remaining pieces of the struggle become your favourite places in the city.

2/2

2019 TIDUS SHING Image 07_Theatre.jpg

2019 TIDUS SHING Image 09_Garden of Rememberance.jpg

2020 Natalie Angus, Grounded

2020 NATALIE ANGUS Drawing 05_DJEEMBANA.tif

How can architecture allow for multiple histories to be shared and celebrated, while also providing an unrestricted platform for First Nations people to engage with and contribute to from the outset?

Grounded is a project that responds to this question by asking the profession how we might reconsider the persistent architectural trends of exclusivity and permanency that are endemic in our cities. It does this by inverting these modern-day implications to become more inclusive of the unceded lands in which they are sited.

The project invites non-Indigenous designers to take accountability and unite with Indigenous knowledge holders, with the intention of forging connections that stimulate a process of continual evolvement and expansion. It presents itself as a framework allowing for Traditional Owners to leave their mark and tell their story, prioritising architecture as a facilitator rather than a monument. This will not only generate an inclusive urban agenda, it will also establish a lasting outcome — a work in progress with the potential to facilitate a re-grounding of sorts, not just of the landscape but of the people too.

STUDENT Natalie Angus
PROJECT Grounded
SUPERVISOR Christine Phillips
YEAR 2020

2020 NATALIE ANGUS Drawing 07_DERRIMUT GROUNDS (02).tif

2020 NATALIE ANGUS Drawing 02_BUNDJIL ARCADE.tif

STUDENT Natalie Angus
PROJECT Grounded
SUPERVISOR Christine Phillips
YEAR 2020

2020 NATALIE ANGUS Drawing 03_NATIONAL GALLERY OF INDIGENOUS ART (NGIA).tif

2020 NATALIE ANGUS Drawing 06_LOVETT SQUARE.tif

STUDENT Natalie Angus
PROJECT Grounded
SUPERVISOR Christine Phillips
YEAR 2020

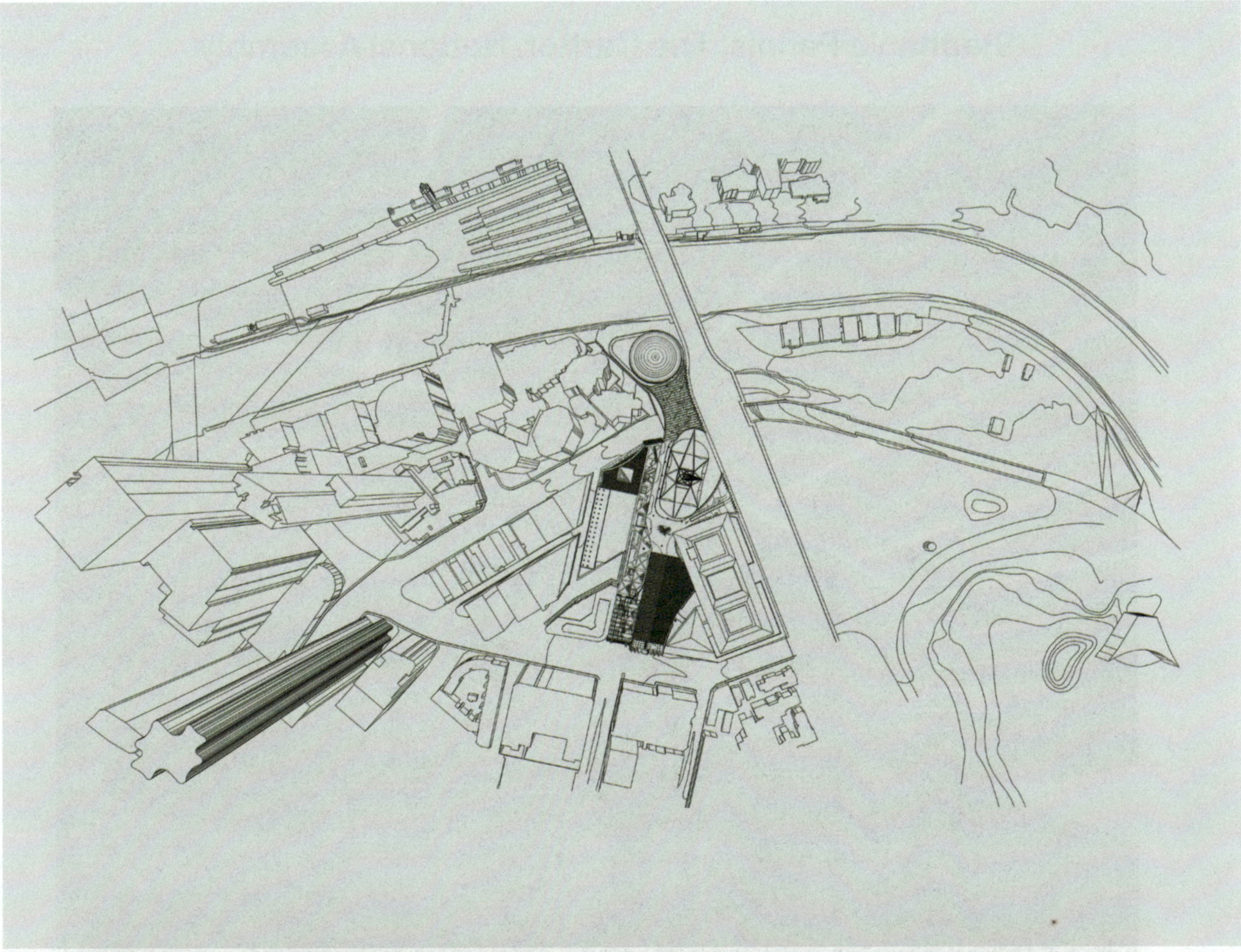

2020 NATALIE ANGUS Drawing 08_SITE PLAN.tif

2020 NATALIE ANGUS Drawing 08_CHARLES AMPHITHEATRE.tif

STUDENT Stephanie Pahnis
PROJECT The Carlton National Assembly
SUPERVISOR Michael Spooner
YEAR 2019

2019 Stephanie Pahnis, The Carlton National Assembly

2019 STEPHANIE PAHNIS Chamber View 2.jpg

As a reaction to the Uluru Statement from the Heart (2017) and the recent establishment of the Victorian Treaty Advancement Committee, this project speculates on the infrastructure required to facilitate the uncertain process of negotiating a treaty between the First Peoples' Assembly of Victoria and the Victorian Parliament in a modern context.

The project is explored through time, in parallel with the process of negotating treaty and the workings of democracy. It is a manifestation of the ongoing negotiation of the law in the event of establishing treaty: there is no foreseeable conclusion. The outcome is a speculation on the constant fossilisation, erasure, amendment and extension of the architecture at different points in time throughout its constant occupation and re-occupation.

It affirms architecture's profound role in embodying and distributing power.

The project challenges static architectural expressions of parliament while maintaining adjacency to them, giving substance to the sovereignty of Victoria's First Peoples. It is staged as a series of infrastructures that arrive immediately at a solution. There is no negotiation; the negotiation happens after. The conclusions we make at each stage are re-evaluated, amended and adapted. Each stage is a recognition of our fallibility, our obligation to keep trying and the responsibility of architecture to commit to the community it harbours.

STUDENT Stephanie Pahnis
PROJECT The Carlton National Assembly
SUPERVISOR Michael Spooner
YEAR 2019

2019 STEPHANIE PAHNIS Chamber View 1.jpg

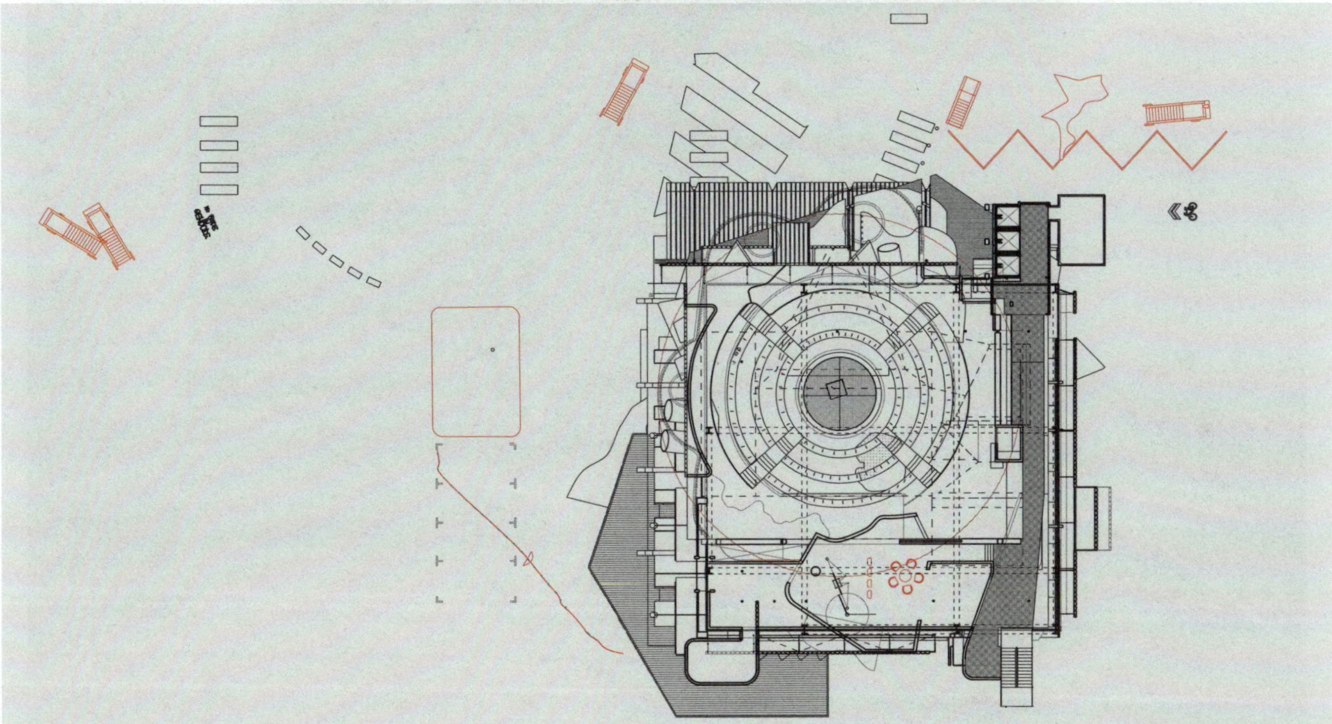

MAJOR PROJECT S1 2019 Stephanie Pahnis Archaeological Chamber Plan.ai

STUDENT Stephanie Pahnis
PROJECT The Carlton National Assembly
SUPERVISOR Michael Spooner
YEAR 2019

2019 STEPHANIE PAHNIS Exterior View 1.jpg

2019 STEPHANIE PAHNIS Exterior View 2.jpg

STUDENT Stephanie Pahnis
PROJECT The Carlton National Assembly
SUPERVISOR Michael Spooner
YEAR 2019

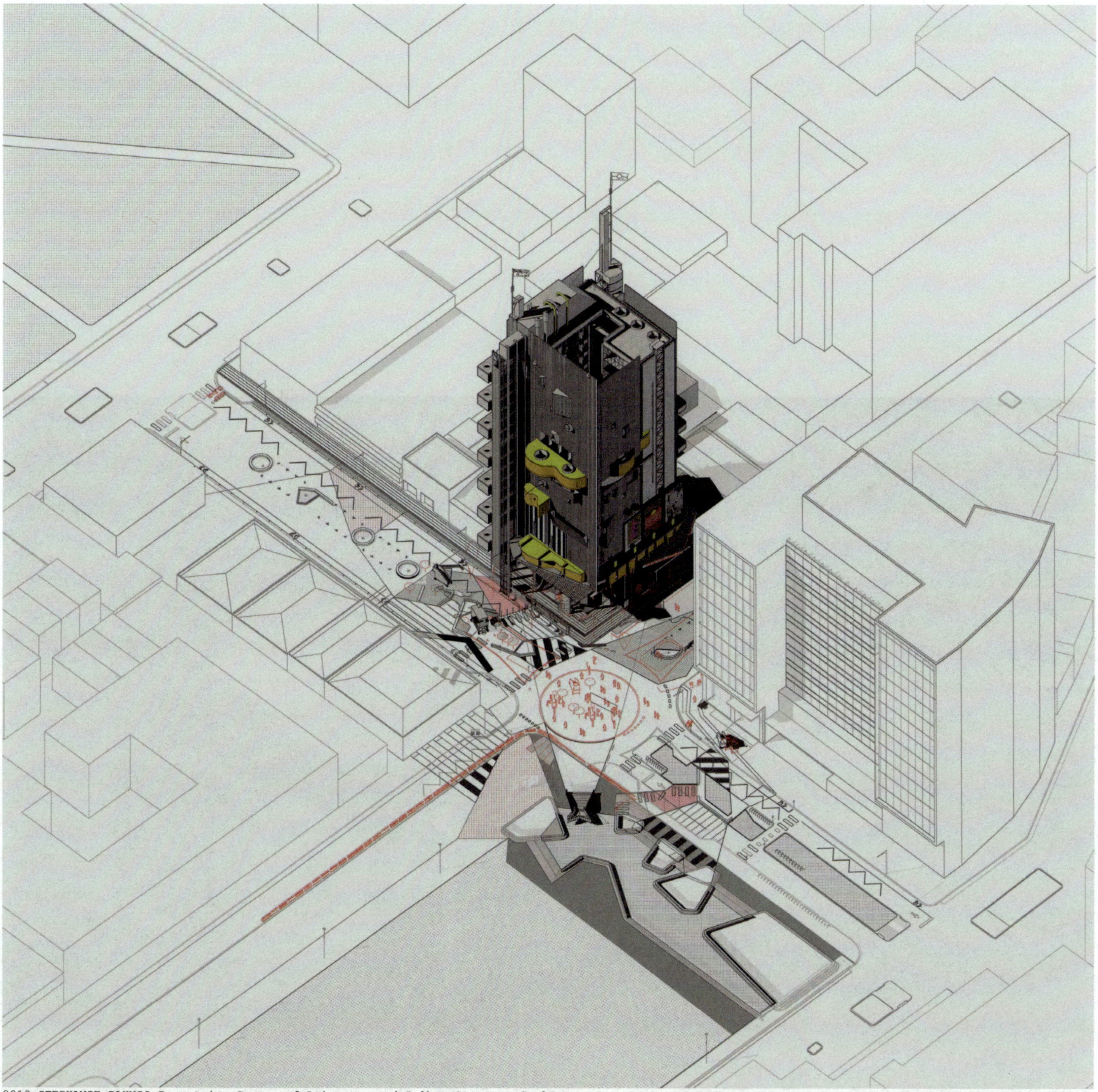

2019 STEPHANIE PAHNIS Isometric, Corner of Leicester and Pelham Streets, Carlton
Built on top of the ruins of The Corkman.jpg

STUDENT	Stephanie Pahnis
PROJECT	The Carlton National Assembly
SUPERVISOR	Michael Spooner
YEAR	2019

2019 STEPHANIE PAHNIS Plenery View 1.jpg

STUDENT Stephanie Pahnis
PROJECT The Carlton National Assembly
SUPERVISOR Michael Spooner
YEAR 2019

2019 STEPHANIE PAHNIS Library View 1.jpg

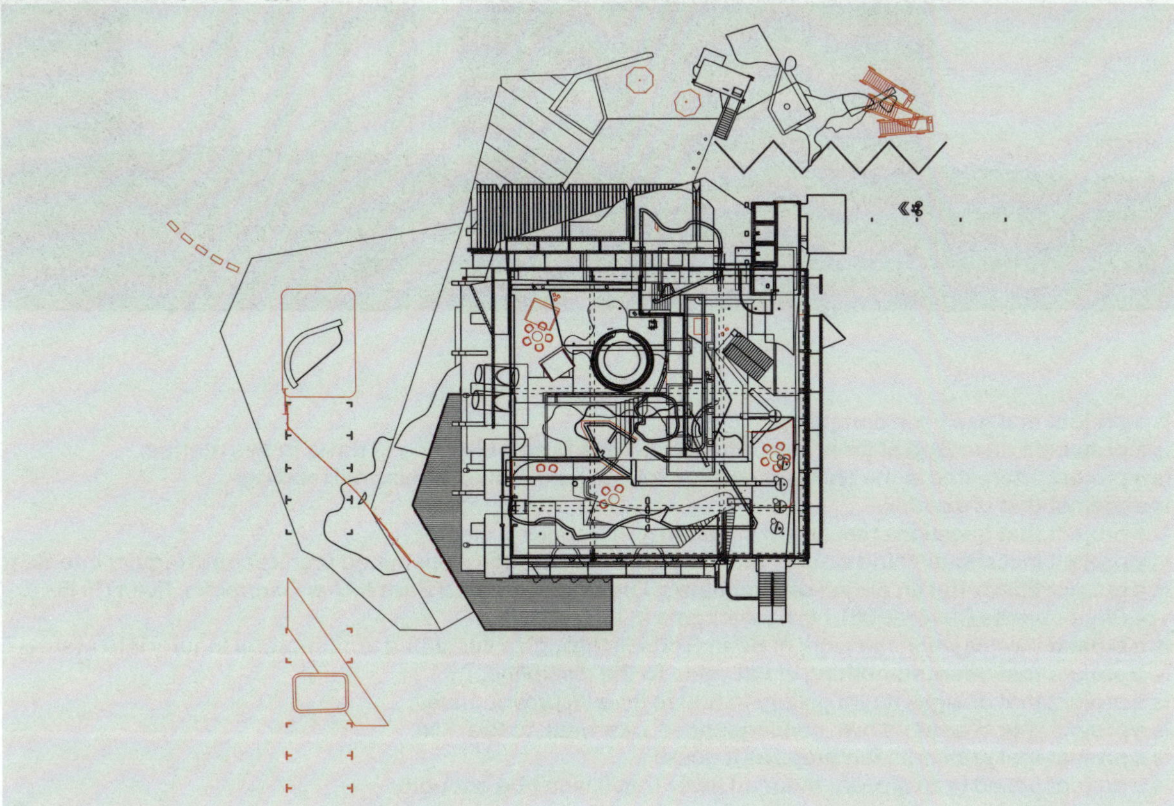

2019 STEPHANIE PAHNIS Archaeological Library Plan.pdf

STUDENT Jack Murray
PROJECT Given, Even
SUPERVISOR Michael Spooner
YEAR 2021

2021 Jack Murray, Given, Even

2021 JACK MURRAY Image 042.png

Given, Even is a project that has been completed.
Given, Even is a project to be looked at for at least fifteen minutes from a distance of three to five metres.
Given, Even is a project interested in the ability of architecture to hold multiple personal readings.
Given, Even is a project that is a codex.
Given, Even is a project that questions the idea of singularity in a major project.
Given, Even is a project investigating the work of Marcel Duchamp through a sustained architectural inquiry into Sean Godsell.
Given, Even is a project titled after an elision of Duchamp's *The Bride Stripped Bare by her Bachelors,* Even (1915–1923) and Given or *Étant donnés* (1946–1966), his final enigma in Philadelphia.
Given, Even is a project investigating the work of Sean Godsell through a sustained architectural inquiry into Marcel Duchamp.
Given, Even is a project that offers something of fiat value to the discipline.
Given, Even is a project that designs an art gallery to house its own provenance.
Given, Even is a project that chases its own consequences, one week to the next.
Given, Even is a project that erases its footsteps as it goes.
Given, Even is a project based in an anxiety-induced fever that it won't be enough.
Given, Even is a project that has not been completed.

STUDENT Jack Murray
PROJECT Given, Even
SUPERVISOR Michael Spooner
YEAR 2021

At week 10 of the 15-week semester, I threatened to delete my project once again, to start over as I had again and again every single week leading up to that critique. I thought about getting to week 15 and dropping out, an appropriate end to the narrative of the project's conception. But it's not a nihilistic project — it's anxious, but also joyful. It is the excess of architecture.

Despite protestations from the critics, I decided that as the project was still five weeks from completion it was time to take a red pen to it. I set up a site office from the Bachelor Machine God Cell and began the process of editing and curation.

I deleted my project. I reconstructed it. I propped it up as if in the middle of being built, or perhaps the middle of being excavated. Funny little remainders swept across the site. Strangely, this project seems to me to have got closest to Duchamp's *Large Glass* (1915–1923). Each element carries with it a provenance, a genealogy stretching back all 10 weeks to the odd little tortoise that occupied a corner of Collingwood.

I had a sense that the project wasn't a half-finished construction site, occupied like the ruins of the Parthenon, nor was it a shed, no matter how highly designed. I sensed one last project, one that would take up the final week and a half and collapse the ideas together — maybe not perfectly, but in a way that might produce an experimental result of creative, or at least fiat, value.

1/2 continues on next page

2021 JACK MURRAY Image 024.png

2021 JACK MURRAY Image 041.png

STUDENT Jack Murray
PROJECT Given, Even
SUPERVISOR Michael Spooner
YEAR 2021

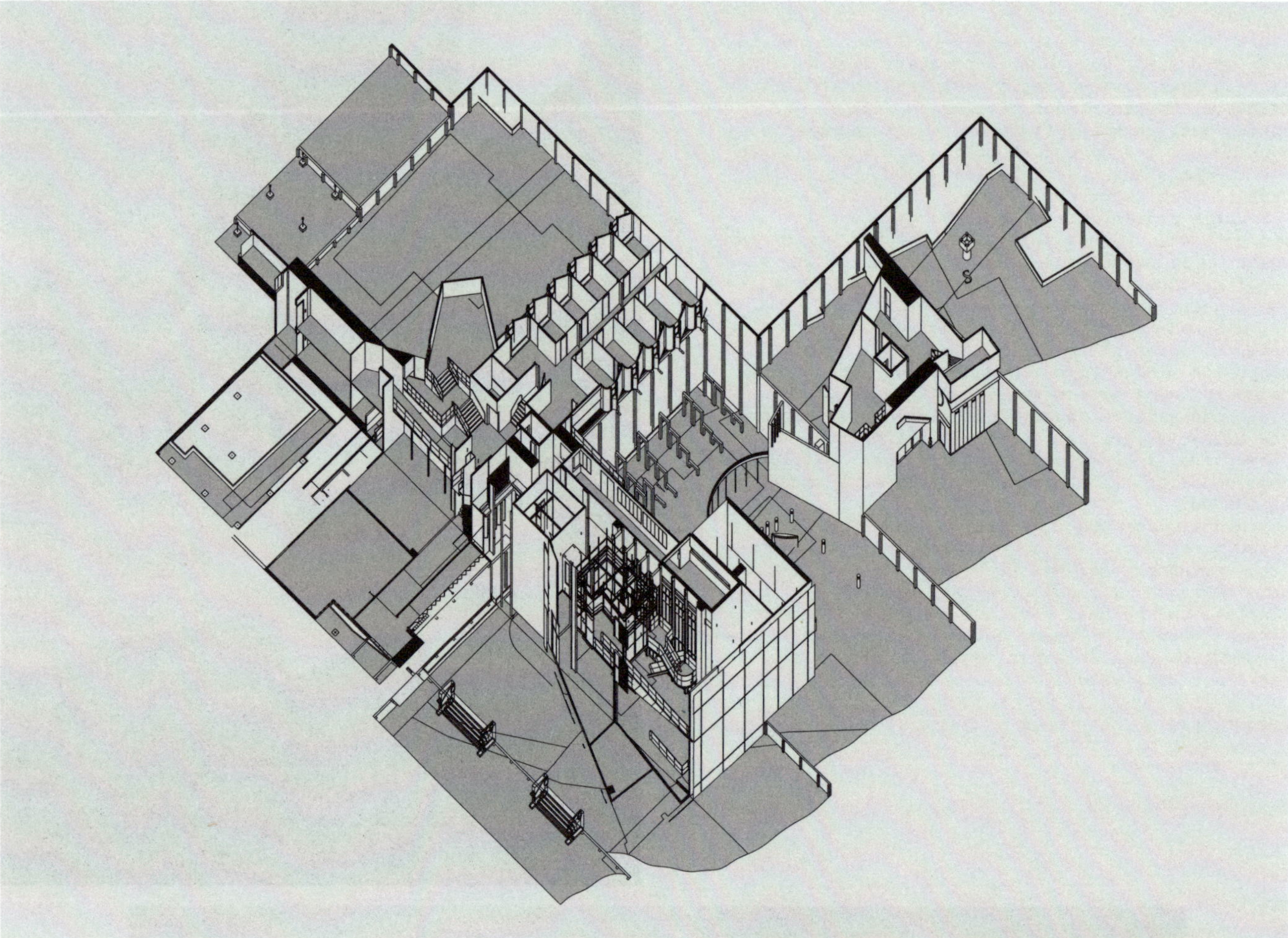

2021 JACK MURRAY Drawing 001.pdf

I took all the characterful remainders.
And drew a line around them.
I took all the characterful remainders.
And put a box around them.
The boxes were removed from the line.
Leaving me with space.
Spaces that would fit the remainders perfectly.
A gallery that exhibited its own provenance.

A gallery of dissemination, after Kipnis. Not monosemy, not polysemy, but dissemination — a critique of architecture's comparatively 'weak' discourse, an open-ended engendering of reference or association, the poetic excess of the symbolists. After Derrida, dissemination is a word that means both production and distribution, as well as the confoundment and interruption of meaning.

There are repeats in this project. There are hesitations. There is the overwhelming sense that I have swallowed the world and that this is a project that is valuable only to me at this stage. But I don't think so. Every question is major to someone, even if that someone must be me. I want to share the joy of this project with you, in all its *strangenesses*. Pick the bit you enjoy, and we'll talk about that.

Given, Even is many things, all at the same time, and I refuse to choose. After a semester of discernment, curation, editing and reformatting, and after a semester of choice, I now choose everything and write 17 lessons for whoever follows. I hope it's me.

2021 JACK MURRAY Image 032.png

STUDENT Jack Murray
PROJECT Given, Even
SUPERVISOR Michael Spooner
YEAR 2021

2021 JACK MURRAY Image 017.png

2021 JACK MURRAY Image 031.png

2021 JACK MURRAY Image 021.png

2021 JACK MURRAY Image 023.png

2021 JACK MURRAY Image 027.png

STUDENT Jack Murray
PROJECT Given, Even
SUPERVISOR Michael Spooner
YEAR 2021

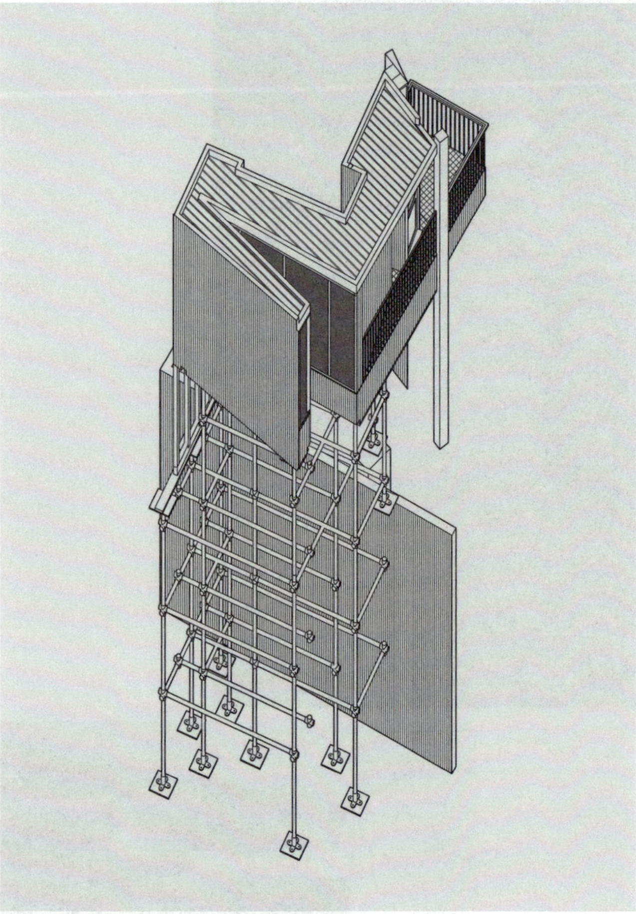

2021 JACK MURRAY Image 013.pdf

2021 JACK MURRAY Image 020.png

2021 JACK MURRAY Image 018.png

STUDENT Jack Murray
PROJECT Given, Even
SUPERVISOR Michael Spooner
YEAR 2021

2021 JACK MURRAY Image 028.png
2021 JACK MURRAY Image 034.png

2021 JACK MURRAY Image 033.png

2021 JACK MURRAY Image 026.png

STUDENT Laura Szyman
PROJECT project/project
SUPERVISOR Peter Brew
YEAR 2019

2019 Laura Szyman, project/project

LauraSzyman_03_Academia_Tunnel.jpg

The model of this project describes the way in which utopian precedents, and the fragments they leave behind, have their meaning subsumed and consumed by the forms that follow and are inspired by them. Each discussion and form of the precedent becomes the precedent for the discussion and form that follows. The model describes the model, the project describes the project, and my presentation describes my presentation, a presentation of the performance of the project.

It began as a pedagogical proposition, one that would allow practitioners and academics greater control over the teaching of these precedents, and morphed into an ontological discussion of the current architectural paradigm and the position of both the object and the practitioner within the discourse.

The project concluded by highlighting its own subjectivities and anxieties and using those to escape from the model. Ultimately, these anxious subjectivities are an acknowledgement that my discussion of utopia, and my conclusions, are imperfect. All models develop cracks, and what is utopia but a model for life given form by architects, as architecture is the mechanism by which we act upon the world.

With all my post-Masters idealism, I believe this could help me create an architecture of uncertainty, but with confidence. The confidence of believing that my utopian vision will last hundreds of years, but the wisdom of knowing it won't.

STUDENT Laura Szyman
PROJECT project/project
SUPERVISOR Peter Brew
YEAR 2019

LauraSzyman_01_Modernist_ManholeCover.jpg

LauraSzyman_04_Urbanist_Stairs.jpg

LauraSzyman_06_Secessionist_Apartment.jpg

LauraSzyman_00_Tableaux.jpg

STUDENT Laura Szyman
PROJECT project/project
SUPERVISOR Peter Brew
YEAR 2019

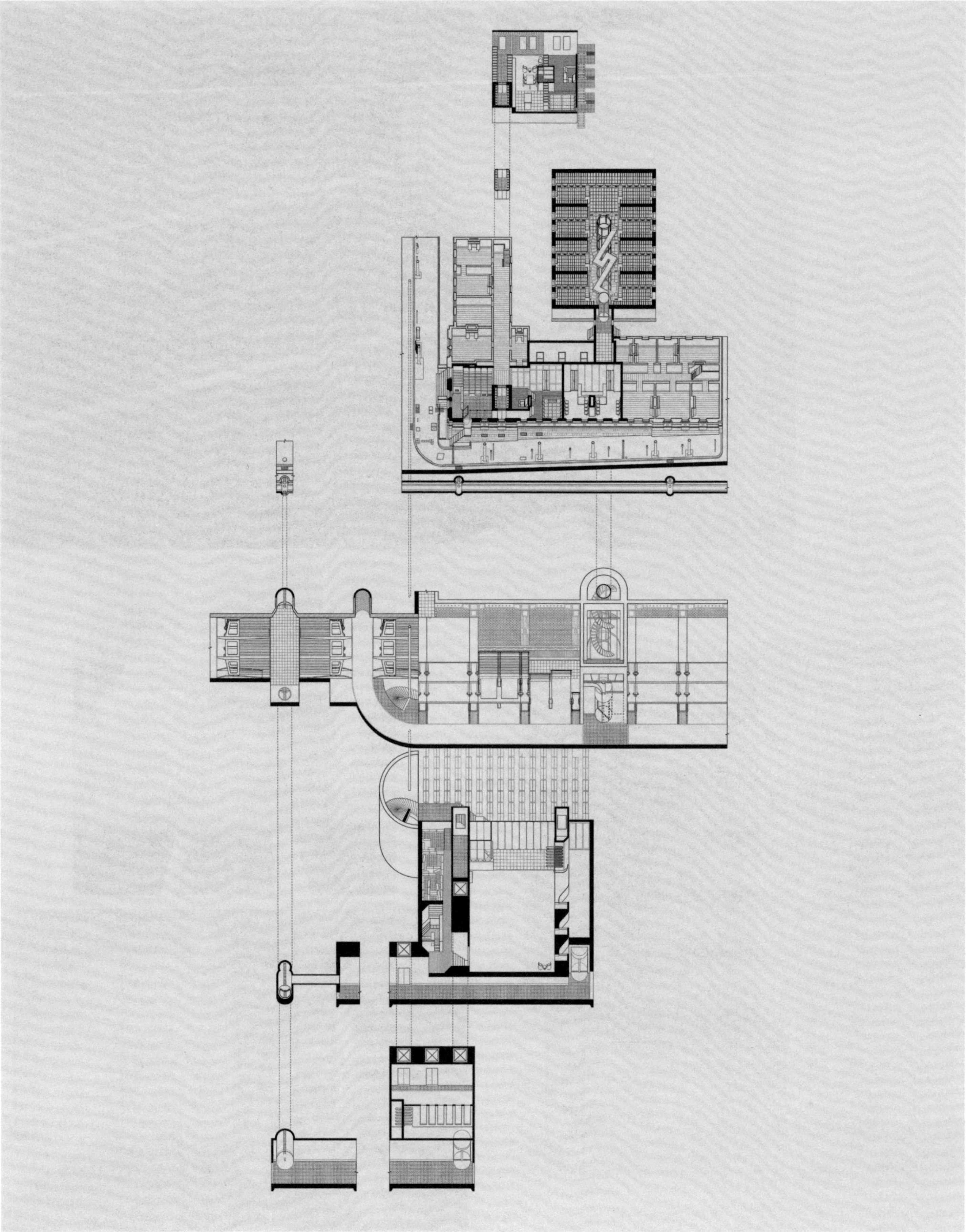

20191105_MythopoeticDrawing.tif

STUDENT Laura Szyman
PROJECT project/project
SUPERVISOR Peter Brew
YEAR 2019

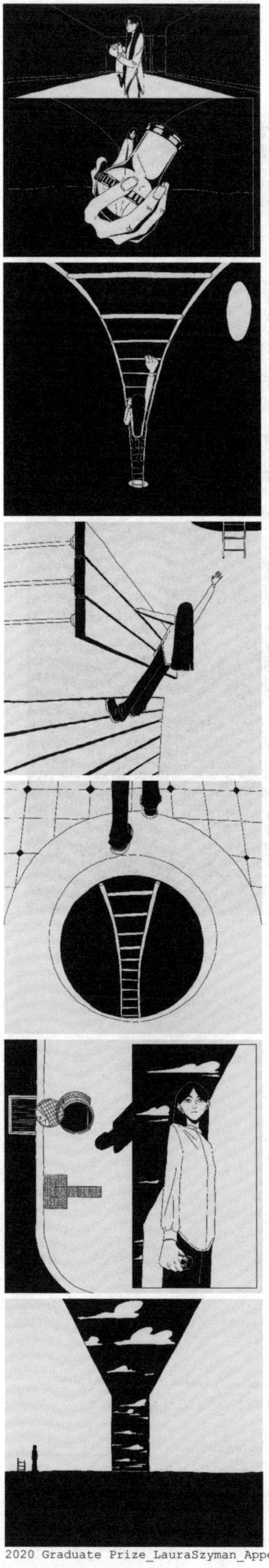

2020 Graduate Prize_LauraSzyman_AppendixB_Comic.pdf

STUDENT Dylan Findlay
PROJECT Obscure Knowledge
SUPERVISOR Christine Phillips
YEAR 2019

2019 Dylan Findlay, Obscure Knowledge

MAJOR PROJECT SEM 1 2019 DYLAN FINDLAY IMAGE 12.tif

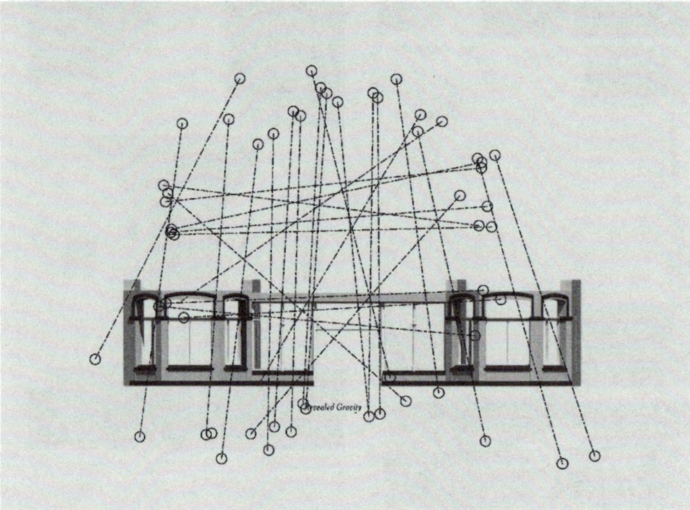

MAJOR PROJECT SEM 1 2019 DYLAN FINDLAY OBSCURE ELEVATION.pdf

Obscure Knowledge proposes alternative perspectives to the existing architecture of Wilcannia, a town in New South Wales. It is a provocation, exploring alternative knowledge frameworks as a medium through which to skew and distort existing understandings of the present.

This project does not result in an explicit building. Instead, I invite you to read it through the imaginative potential of place as an unknown force. I question and challenge normative architectural frameworks, dislodging understanding to make way for new design approaches. Through Indigenous knowledge holders, photographic documentation and personal experience, I question the stability of the existing, and its fidelity to the logics of construction and accepted knowledge.

STUDENT Dylan Findlay
PROJECT Obscure Knowledge
SUPERVISOR Christine Phillips
YEAR 2019

MAJOR PROJECT SEM 1 2019 DYLAN FINDLAY PERIPHERAL VIEW A.pdf

MAJOR PROJECT SEM 1 2019 DYLAN FINDLAY PERIPHERAL VIEW B.pdf

MAJOR PROJECT SEM 1 2019 DYLAN FINDLAY ELEMENT REALIGNED TO OBSCURITY.pdf

BIOGRAPHIES

EDITORIAL TEAM

PROFESSOR VIVIAN MITSOGIANNI (Architect ARBV) is Dean of the School of Architecture & Urban Design, RMIT University, Melbourne. Vivian was the Associate Dean and Head of RMIT Architecture (2013-2022) and is a partner in M@ STUDIO Architects.

TOM MURATORE (Architect ARBV) an Associate Lecturer at RMIT Architecture in the School of Architecture & Urban Design, RMIT University, Melbourne.

DR JOHN DOYLE (Architect ARBV) is Associate Dean and Head of RMIT Architecture in the School of Architecture & Urban Design, RMIT University, Melbourne. John was the Master of Architecture Program Manager (2013-2022). John is a partner at Common.

AMY MUIR (Architect ARBV) is a Lecturer and the Master of Architecture Major Project Coordinator (2019 -) at RMIT Architecture in the School of Architecture & Urban Design, RMIT University, Melbourne. Amy is director of MUIR Architecture.

LIAM OXLADE completed the RMIT Master of Architecture Major Project in Semester 2, 2020.

MIETTA MULLALY completed the RMIT Master of Architecture Major Project in Semester 1, 2021.

ESSAY CONTRIBUTORS

PROFESSOR ALISA ANDRASEK is Professor of Architecture in the School of Architecture & Urban Design, RMIT University, Melbourne.

DR PETER BREW (Architect ARBV) is a Lecturer at RMIT Architecture in the School of Architecture & Urban Design, RMIT University, Melbourne and a Director of Architect Brew Koch.

HELEN DUONG (Architect ARBV) is an Associate Lecturer at RMIT Architecture in the School of Architecture & Urban Design, RMIT University, Melbourne and a Director of Pyke and Duong Architecture.

DR EMMA JACKSON (Architect ARBV) is the Director of Emma Jackson Studio and an industry sessional staff member at RMIT Architecture. Emma was a Lecturer at RMIT Architecture (2015-2023), and was the Bachelor of Architectural Design Program Manager (2019-2021) in the School of Architecture & Urban Design, RMIT University, Melbourne.

SIMONE KOCH (Architect ARBV) is a Director of Architect Brew Koch and an industry sessional staff member at RMIT Architecture, in the School of Architecture & Urban Design, RMIT University, Melbourne.

VICKY LAM is an Associate Lecturer at RMIT Architecture in the School of Architecture & Urban Design, RMIT University, Melbourne.

TIM PYKE (Architect ARBV) is an Associate at Baldasso Cortese and an industry sessional staff member at RMIT Architecture, in the School of Architecture & Urban Design, RMIT University, Melbourne. Tim is a Director of Pyke and Duong Architecture.

PROFESSOR ROLAND SNOOKS is Professor of Architecture in the School of Architecture & Urban Design, RMIT University, Melbourne where he directs the RMIT Architecture | Tectonic Formation Lab. Roland is the Director of Snooks + Harper.

DR MICHAEL SPOONER is a Lecturer at RMIT Architecture in the School of Architecture & Urban Design, RMIT University, Melbourne.

MAJOR PROJECT CONTRIBUTORS

TEMITOPE ADESINA completed the RMIT Master of Architecture Major Project in Semester 1, 2020.

NATALIE ANGUS completed the RMIT Master of Architecture Major Project in Semester 2, 2020.

HARRY BARDOEL completed the RMIT Master of Architecture Major Project in Semester 2, 2019.

BROOKE BARKER completed the RMIT Master of Architecture Major Project in Semester 2, 2021.

REBECCA BOLAND completed the RMIT Master of Architecture Major Project in Semester 1, 2022.

MEAGAN BROOKS completed the RMIT Master of Architecture Major Project in Semester 1, 2022.

CHRISTOPHER BUCHHORN completed the RMIT Master of Architecture Major Project in Semester 1, 2021.

ZACHARY BUNSTON completed the RMIT Master of Architecture Major Project in Semester 2, 2021.

JENNIFER CHEN completed the RMIT Master of Architecture Major Project in Semester 2, 2022.

JUSTIN CHONG completed the RMIT Master of Architecture Major Project in Semester 2, 2021.

NICOLA CORTESE completed the RMIT Master of Architecture Major Project in Semester 1, 2019.

FLYNN EADY-JENNINGS completed the RMIT Master of Architecture Major Project in Semester 1, 2021.

GULED ELYAS completed the RMIT Master of Architecture Major Project in Semester 2, 2021.

BRIONY EWING completed the RMIT Master of Architecture Major Project in Semester 1, 2020.

DYLAN FINDLAY completed the RMIT Master of Architecture Major Project in Semester 1, 2019.

SENESIOS FRANGOS completed the RMIT Master of Architecture Major Project in Semester 1, 2019.

AIMEE HOWARD completed the RMIT Master of Architecture Major Project in Semester 1, 2021.

YOUJIA HUANG completed the RMIT Master of Architecture Major Project in Semester 2, 2021.

WANG JINGYUAN completed the RMIT Master of Architecture Major Project in Semester 2, 2020.

GAVRILA MANDY KAHUNI completed the RMIT Master of Architecture Major Project in Semester 2, 2020.

ALAN HO KYEONG KIM completed the RMIT Master of Architecture Major Project in Semester 2, 2021.

NICOLE KIRBY completed the RMIT Master of Architecture Major Project in Semester 2, 2019.

LEON KOUTOULAS completed the RMIT Master of Architecture Major Project in Semester 2, 2019.

RUBY LANG completed the RMIT Master of Architecture Major Project in Semester 2, 2021.

CALEB KA LOK LEE completed the RMIT Master of Architecture Major Project in Semester 1, 2022.

EMMA KA WING LI completed the RMIT Master of Architecture Major Project in Semester 2, 2019.

MATTHEW LOCHERT completed the RMIT Master of Architecture Major Project in Semester 1, 2019.

JAMES MCLENNAN completed the RMIT Master of Architecture Major Project in Semester 2, 2021.

ANDREA MILOVANOVIC completed the RMIT Master of Architecture Major Project in Semester 1, 2020.

NIC MORGANTE completed the RMIT Master of Architecture Major Project in Semester 2, 2020.

JACK MURRAY completed the RMIT Master of Architecture Major Project in Semester 1, 2021.

STEPHANIE PAHNIS completed the RMIT Master of Architecture Major Project in Semester 1, 2019.

RILEY PELHAM-THORMAN completed the RMIT Master of Architecture Major Project in Semester 2, 2021.

EILIDH ROSS completed the RMIT Master of Architecture Major Project in Semester 2, 2020.

JITESH SAPRA completed the RMIT Master of Architecture Major Project in Semester 1, 2021.

TIDUS LOK TIN SHING completed the RMIT Master of Architecture Major Project in Semester 2, 2019.

JESSICA SIMONS completed the RMIT Master of Architecture Major Project in Semester 2, 2019.

BENJAMIN STRONG completed the RMIT Master of Architecture Major Project in Semester 1, 2020.

LAURA SZYMAN completed the RMIT Master of Architecture Major Project in Semester 2, 2019.

JACQUELINE TANG completed the RMIT Master of Architecture Major Project in Semester 2, 2019.

SHUAI TANG completed the RMIT Master of Architecture Major Project in Semester 2, 2021.

XU TANG completed the RMIT Master of Architecture Major Project in Semester 2, 2021.

DAVID MUNDATTUCHUNDAYIL THOMAS completed the RMIT Master of Architecture Major Project in Semester 1, 2019.

MATTHEW TIBBALLS completed the RMIT Master of Architecture Major Project in Semester 1, 2021.

AKASH VAZIRANI completed the RMIT Master of Architecture Major Project in Semester 1, 2021.

DARCIE VELLA completed the RMIT Master of Architecture Major Project in Semester 2, 2021.

LACHLAN WILES completed the RMIT Master of Architecture Major Project in Semester 2, 2020.

MICHELLE ZHANG completed the RMIT Master of Architecture Major Project in Semester 1, 2022.

LONGGE ZHANG completed the RMIT Master of Architecture Major Project in Semester 1, 2021.

MAJOR PROJECT SUPERVISORS

LOREN ADAMS is an industry sessional staff member at RMIT Architecture in the school of Architecture & Urban Design, RMIT University, Melbourne.

PROFESSOR ALISA ANDRASEK is Professor of Architecture in the School of Architecture & Urban Design, RMIT University, Melbourne.

DR MAURO BARACCO, formerly a full-time staff member and Associate Professor at RMIT Architecture (1996-2020), is currently a RMIT University Fellow and industry sessional staff member. Mauro is a director of Baracco+Wright Architects.

ANDRE BONNICE (Architect ARBV) is an industry sessional staff member at RMIT Architecture in the School of Architecture & Urban Design, RMIT University, Melbourne. Andre is a Director of SIMULAA.

DEAN BOOTHROYD is an an industry sessional staff member at RMIT Architecture, in the School of Architecture & Urban Design, Melbourne Australia and a Director of M@ STUDIO Architects.

DR PETER BREW (Architect ARBV) is a Lecturer at RMIT Architecture in the School of Architecture & Urban Design, RMIT University, Melbourne and a Director of Architect Brew Koch.

DR GRAHAM CRIST (Architect ARBV) is an Associate Professor at RMIT Architecture in the School of Architecture & Urban Design, RMIT University, Melbourne and a Director of Antarctica Architects.

DR JOHN DOYLE (Architect ARBV) is Associate Dean and Head of RMIT Architecture in the School of Architecture & Urban Design, RMIT University, Melbourne (2023-). John was the Master of Architecture Program Manager (2013-2022). John is a partner at Common.

SIMON DRYSDALE (Architect ARBV) is an industry sessional staff member at RMIT Architecture in the School of Architecture & Urban Design, RMIT University, Melbourne. Simon is the founder of Care3d.

HELEN DUONG (Architect ARBV) is an Associate Lecturer at RMIT Architecture in the School of Architecture & Urban Design, RMIT University, Melbourne and a director of Pyke and Duong Architecture.

DR EMMA JACKSON (Architect ARBV) is the director of Emma Jackson Studio and an industry sessional staff member at RMIT Architecture. Emma was a Lecturer at RMIT Architecture (2015-2023), the Bachelor of Architectural Design Program Manager (2019-2021) in the School of Architecture & Urban Design, RMIT University, Melbourne.

PROFESSOR MARK JACQUES (Landscape Architect AILA) is Professor of Architecture (Urbanism) in the School of Architecture & Urban Design, RMIT University, Melbourne. Mark is the founder of OPENWORK Pty Ltd.

ANNA JANKOVIC (Architect ARBV) is an Associate Lecturer at RMIT Architecture in the School of Architecture & Urban Design, RMIT University, Melbourne. Anna is a Director of SIMULAA.

DR ANNA JOHNSON is a Senior Lecturer at RMIT Architecture in the School of Architecture & Urban Design, RMIT University, Melbourne.

SIMONE KOCH (Architect ARBV) is a Director of Architect Brew Koch and an industry sessional staff member at RMIT Architecture in the School of Architecture & Urban Design, RMIT University, Melbourne.

PROFESSOR TOM KOVAC is Professor of Architecture in the School of Architecture & Urban Design, RMIT University, Melbourne.

VICKY LAM is an Associate Lecturer at RMIT Architecture in the School of Architecture & Urban Design, RMIT University, Melbourne.

PATRICK MACASAET is a Lecturer at RMIT Architecture in the School of Architecture & Urban Design, RMIT University, Melbourne and the Co-Director of SUPERSCALE.

NEIL MASTERTON (Architect ARBV) is an industry sessional staff member at RMIT Architecture in the School of Architecture & Urban Design, RMIT University, Melbourne. Neil is a Design Director at ARM Architecture.

PROFESSOR IAN MCDOUGALL (Architect ARBV) is an Adjunct Professor at RMIT Architecture in the School of Architecture & Urban Design, RMIT University, Melbourne. Ian is a Founding Director of ARM Architecture.

AMY MUIR (Architect ARBV) is a Lecturer and the Master of Architecture Major Project Coordinator (2019-) at RMIT Architecture in the School of Architecture & Urban Design, RMIT University, Melbourne. Amy is Director of MUIR Architecture.

IAN NAZARETH (Architect COA, India) is a Lecturer at RMIT Architecture in the School of Architecture & Urban Design, RMIT University, Melbourne. Ian is the Director of TRAFFIC.

LIAM OXLADE completed the RMIT Master of Architecture Major Project in Semester 2, 2020. Liam is an industry sessional staff member at RMIT Architecture in the School of Architecture & Urban Design, RMIT University, Melbourne. Liam is an Associate at NH Architecture.

DR CHRISTINE PHILLIPS (Architect ARBV) is a Senior Lecturer at RMIT Architecture in the School of Architecture & Urban Design, RMIT University, Melbourne, where she is co-director of the Yulendj Weelam Lab.

TIM PYKE (Architect ARBV) is an Associate at Baldasso Cortese and an industry sessional staff member at RMIT Architecture, in the School of Architecture & Urban Design, RMIT University, Melbourne. Tim is a director of Pyke and Duong Architecture.

PROFESSOR ROLAND SNOOKS is Professor of Architecture in the School of Architecture & Urban Design, RMIT University, Melbourne where he directs the RMIT Architecture | Tectonic Formation Lab. Roland is the Director of Snooks + Harper.

JEAN-MARIE SPENCER (Architect ARBV) is an industry sessional staff member at RMIT Architecture in the school of Architecture & Urban Design, RMIT University, Melbourne. Jean-Marie is the Co-Director of SSdH.

DR MICHAEL SPOONER is a Lecturer at RMIT Architecture in the School of Architecture & Urban Design, RMIT University, Melbourne.

ACKNOWLEDGEMENTS AND THANKS

The editors would like to acknowledge and thank the students and staff of RMIT Architecture as well as the RMIT School of Architecture & Urban Design, the RMIT College of Design & Social Context and RMIT University for their support of this publication.

DEAN, SCHOOL OF ARCHITECTURE & URBAN DESIGN
Professor Vivian Mitsogianni (2023-)
Professor Martyn Hook, (2017-2022)

ASSOCIATE DEAN AND ARCHITECTURE DISCIPLINE LEADER
Dr John Doyle (2023-)
Professor Vivian Mitsogianni (2013-2022)

MASTER OF ARCHITECTURE PROGRAM MANAGER
Dr Ben Milbourne (2023-)
Dr John Doyle (2013-2022)

MASTER OF ARCHITECTURE MAJOR PROJECT COORDINATOR
Amy Muir (2019-)

Ian Nazareth (Major Project Exhibition and Catalogue Coordinator)
Patrick Macasaet (Architecture Culture & Capture Project)
Marc Gibson (Architecture Culture & Capture Project)

Thank you to all the contributors to this publication: Professor Vivian Mitsogianni, Amy Muir, Dr John Doyle, Dr Emma Jackson, Helen Duong, Tim Pyke, Professor Roland Snooks, Professor Alisa Andrasek, Simone Koch, Dr Peter Brew, Vicky Lam, Dr Michael Spooner, Liam Oxlade, Mietta Mullaly, Caleb Ka Lok Lee, Flynn Eady-Jennings, Nicole Kirby, Riley Pelham-Thorman, Brooke Barker, Matthew Tibballs, Lachlan Wiles, Youjia Huang, Wang Jingyuan, Meagan Brooks, Benjamin Strong, Jacqueline Tang, Akash Vazirani, Shuai Tang, Xu Tang, Jitesh Sapra, Alan Ho Kyeong Kim, Aimee Howard, Nic Morgante, Nicola Cortese, Darcie Vella, Jennifer Chen, Briony Ewing, Ruby Lang, Matthew Lochert, Harry Bardoel, James McLennan, Andrea Milovanovic, Zachary Bunston, Rebecca Boland, Alexandra Waldron-Clark, Jessica Simons, Christopher Buchhorn, Eilidh Ross, Longge Zhang, Gavrila Mandy Kahuni, Guled Elyas, Justin Chong, David Mundattuchundayil Thomas, Senesios Frangos, Leon Koutoulas, Temitope Adesina, Emma Ka Wing Li, Michelle Zhang, Tidus Lok Tin Shing, Natalie Angus, Stephanie Pahnis, Jack Murray, Laura Szyman, Dylan Findlay.

The projects captured in this publication were selected using responses to a survey the editors sent to RMIT Architecture graduates and supervisors. The editors would like to thank the following contributors for their responses to the survey:

RMIT ARCHITECTURE GRADUATES
Christian Lionis, Paarija Saxena, Liam Oxlade, James McLennan, Senesios Frangos, Tidus Lok Tin Shing, Longge Zhang, Kari Vitalich, Bryn Murrell, Hannah Zhu, Ruby Lang, Carrie Lu, Laura Szyman, Jack Murray, Mietta Mullaly, Jack Heatley, Nicola Cortese

RMIT ARCHITECTURE MAJOR PROJECT SUPERVISORS
Dr Peter Brew, Simone Koch, Dr John Doyle, Liam Oxlade, Dr Anna Johnson, Professor Vivian Mitsogianni, Dean Boothroyd, Dr Leanne Zilka, Patrick Macasaet, Dr Christine Phillips, Tim Pyke, Professor Roland Snooks, Vicky Lam, Helen Duong, Professor Alisa Andrasek, Associate Professor Graham Crist, Anna Jankovic, Professor Mark Jacques

COLOPHON

Major: RMIT Architecture Graduating Projects 2019-2022

First published in 2024

PUBLISHED BY
Actar D, Inc. New York, Barcelona.
www.actar.com

EDITORS
Vivian Mitsogianni, Tom Muratore, John Doyle, Amy Muir, Mietta Mullaly and Liam Oxlade
PUBLICATION DESIGN
Stuart Geddes, Žiga Testen and Kim Mumm Hansen
COPY EDITING
Sarah Gory
PRINTING
Musumeci, Italy

DISTRIBUTION
Actar D, Inc. New York, Barcelona.

New York
440 Park Avenue South, 17th Floor
New York, NY 10016, USA
T +1 2129662207
salesnewyork@actar-d.com

Barcelona
Roca I Batlle 2-4
08023 Barcelona, Spain
T +34 933 282 183
eurosales@actar-d.comPublication date 2023

EDITION
Actar Publishers
TEXTS
Authors
DESIGN, DRAWINGS, ILLUSTRATIONS AND PHOTOGRAPHS
Authors

ISBN
978-1-63840-128-5

Library of Congress Control Number: 2023950944